WORDSWORTH
OF WORLD LI

General Editor: Tom Griffith

FOUR PLAYS

HENRIK IBSEN

Four Plays

Peer Gynt   A Doll's House
Hedda Gabler
The Master Builder

Translated by William Archer

with an Introduction by
Ellen Rees

WORDSWORTH CLASSICS
OF WORLD LITERATURE

Readers who are interested in other titles from
Wordsworth Editions are invited to visit our
website at www.wordsworth-editions.com

For our latest list and a full mail order service contact
Bibliophile Books, Unit 5 Datapoint,
South Crescent, London E16 4TL
Tel: +44 (0) 20 74 74 24 74
Fax: +44 (0) 20 74 74 85 89
orders@bibliophilebooks.com
www.bibliophilebooks.com

This edition published 2014 by Wordsworth Editions Limited
8B East Street, Ware, Hertfordshire SG12 9HJ

ISBN 978 1 84022 727 7

This edition © Wordsworth Editions Limited 2014
Introduction © Ellen Rees 2014

Wordsworth® is a registered trademark of
Wordsworth Editions Limited

Wordsworth Editions is
the company founded in 1987 by
MICHAEL TRAYLER

Typeset in Great Britain by Roperford Editorial
Printed and bound by Clays Ltd, St Ives plc

CONTENTS

INTRODUCTION

Henrik Ibsen: provincial, yet world-renowned; ideologically radical, yet something of a fuddy-duddy; viewed alternately as either a Nordic obscurantist or an incisive social critic; a merciless realist, yet also a master of lyrical fantasy – the character of this nineteenth-century Norwegian writer, who continues to capture the imagination of millions of readers and theater-goers around the globe, is hard to pin down. Henrik Johan Ibsen was born on 20 March 1828 in Skien, a small but booming trade center on the southern coast of Norway. Decades of economic growth turned to bust by the middle of the 1830s, and Ibsen's family, along with most of the ruling patrician class to which they belonged, experienced a severe economic decline.[1] With no opportunity to make his fortune in shipping as his forefathers had, the young Ibsen became instead an apothecary's apprentice soon after being confirmed in the Lutheran faith in 1843. Essays that he wrote in the late 1840s indicate that he already had profound doubts about Christianity, and he remained something of a skeptic throughout his adult life. Ibsen spent his late adolescence in the coastal town of Grimstad, learning the apothecary's trade and reading, writing, and painting as much as he could. In 1846 he fathered a child out of wedlock, yet despite the extra financial burden this entailed, he continued to educate himself, and by 1850 he was able to leave Grimstad for the capital city, Christiania (also known as Kristiania, and since 1925 renamed Oslo), and take the entrance exam for the university there.

1850 was a banner year for Ibsen in a number of ways: he was able to publish his first drama, *Catiline*, with the help of friends; he began writing criticism and commentary for the student newspaper, even though he failed to matriculate at the university; and he witnessed the first staging of a play he himself had written, *The Burial Mound*. Ibsen joined a circle of ambitious

and creative young men including the writer A. O. Vinje and the
critic Paul Botten Hansen; together with these two Ibsen founded
an unnamed weekly publication where he was able to hone his
critical skills in theater reviews and publish some of his first poetry.
Ibsen quickly made a name for himself in Norway's small capital as
a new critical voice. By the fall of the following year he was on his
way to Bergen, hand picked by the violin virtuoso and international celebrity, Ole Bull, to serve as artistic director of The
Norwegian Theater there. He was twenty-three years old and had
no previous experience as a theater practitioner. Ibsen remained
in Bergen until 1857, and these years were crucial for his development as a dramatist.[2] He learned the technical and aesthetic
potentials and limitations of theater practice; he had an arena
where he could develop and stage his own work, and he had a
platform from which to refine his theater criticism. He had one
popular success there, in 1856, the light-hearted national romantic
play The Feast at Solhoug. While in Bergen he also met Suzannah
Daae Thoresen, the woman whom he would marry in 1858 and –
according to Ibsen himself – his most important supporter. Ibsen
called her 'the eagle' and she functioned as a sounding board, a
critical reader, and a motivator. The Ibsens had one child, a boy
named Sigurd born in 1859. He later went on to an illustrious
career as a diplomat, serving as the head of Norway's foreign
ministry and also as the Minister for Norway, both of these while
Norway was still in the union with Sweden.

In 1857, Ibsen relocated from Bergen to Christiania, where
he took up the position of artistic director at the Kristiania Norwegian Theater. While there had always been an active private
amateur theater culture in the capital city, conditions for professional theater were not particularly good, in part because Danish
actors and theater culture dominated the professional stage; this
was a legacy from previous centuries of Danish political and
cultural domination over Norway.[3] The Danish-language Christiania Theater had opened its doors as early as 1827, and indeed
this is where The Burial Mound had its première. A growing
movement sought to make the theatrical culture of Christiania
more Norwegian; The Kristiania Norwegian Theater was established in 1852 in this nationalist spirit, but was never successful
economically. Ibsen was forced to leave when the theater went

bankrupt in 1862, and the Ibsens faced a period of economic hardship and uncertainty. Ibsen received a travel stipend to collect folk tales in rural areas, worked as an artistic consultant at the Danish-dominated Christiania Theater, and continued to write mostly historical dramas. Desperate for a change, Ibsen applied for a government travel grant, and in 1864 he was able to move with his wife and young son to Rome, where they lived for four years. This was the beginning of Ibsen's self-imposed exile, and he was not to settle in Norway again for another twenty-seven years.

Ibsen went through something of a transformation in Italy, personally, aesthetically, and not least economically. He became involved in the close-knit group of Scandinavian artists and writers in Rome, and acquaintances during his time there commented on how the unkempt and impoverished dramatist, now in his mid-thirties, began to cultivate a more dignified and elegant appearance, as he had in fact done earlier, while in Bergen, where he was something of a dandy. Aesthetically, Ibsen met with his first undisputed literary success with the verse drama *Brand*, published in 1866. *Brand*, a closet drama intended for the book market rather than for stage performance, depicts a minister willing to sacrifice everything, even his own child, for his calling. The play met with widespread critical acclaim, and established Ibsen as an important literary figure on the Danish-Norwegian literary market. Ibsen followed up the unrelenting *Brand* with its polar opposite, *Peer Gynt*. Where Brand is unwavering in his calling, Peer avoids commitment; where Brand never doubts the truth of his convictions, Peer prevaricates and lies without qualm. Both verse plays are deeply philosophical, and both present profound ethical challenges.

While in Italy, Ibsen began corresponding with the influential Danish literary critic Georg Brandes. Brandes eventually became one of the most important critical voices in Scandinavia calling for a new, more ethically engaged literature that could function as a forum for debating social problems. Ibsen was also moving in this direction, and by 1877 he had abandoned verse drama for good, and was beginning to develop the dramatic strategies that made his plays more realistic and socially relevant. He presented the world of the middle class on the stage – the spoken language, the interiors, the physical appearance of the actors, and the social norms represented were all immediately recognizable and received as more true to life than the historical dramas and melodramas that had previously dominated nineteenth-century drama. Ibsen ingeniously employed a retrospective logic in his plays, where past actions revealed through dialog motivate and justify the actions of the characters in the present of the play.

The Ibsens moved from Italy to Germany in 1868, first living in Dresden for seven years, then in Munich for three years, before returning to Rome in 1878, where they lived on and off for another seven years. The early 1870s was a time of transition for Ibsen; he collected and published his poetry from previous decades in a single volume in 1871, and in 1873 produced his remarkable 'double' drama in ten acts, *Emperor and Galilean*. He also began revising a number of his earlier historical dramas during this period, including *Lady Inger of Østeraad / Lady Inger of Østråt* (1855; revised 1874), *Catiline* (1850; revised 1875), and *The Feast at Solhaug* (1856; revised 1883). While Ibsen's early historical and national romantic dramas are little known outside of Norway, the thematic connections between them and his later works are clear, and make them important subjects of study for understanding his development as a dramatist.

In 1879, Ibsen published what remains his most famous and most widely performed work, *A Doll's House*. The play has become a touchstone in the struggle for the emancipation of oppressed groups around the world, in particular women struggling under patriarchal oppression. Ibsen's Nora provides a clarion call for the modern individual when she realizes her first duty is to herself, and that she must first become a whole person before she can be a wife and mother.

Starting in the late 1870s, Ibsen established a pattern of publishing a new play roughly every other year. A series of his most widely recognized works followed *A Doll's House* in rapid succession: *Ghosts* (1881), *An Enemy of the People* (1882), *The Wild Duck* (1884), *Rosmersholm* (1886), *The Lady from the Sea* (1888), *Hedda Gabler* (1890), *The Master Builder* (1892), *Little Eyolf* (1894), *John Gabriel Borkman* (1896), and finally his last published work, *When We Dead Awaken* in 1899. Ibsen exerted surprising control over his public persona and exerted great effort in order to maintain the

rights to and profit from his works, this in a time where modern
international copyright laws were not yet fully established. Recent
scholarship has also revealed how deliberately Ibsen cultivated a
'sphinx-like', uncompromising, and stern image through professional photographs.[4] Because of these widely circulated visual
images, generations of readers have regarded him as a humorless and
uncompromising author. In fact, quite the opposite is true; there is
much wry and understated humor in Ibsen's writing.[5]

The writing continued even after the Ibsens returned to Norway,
where they settled in a luxurious apartment near the royal palace in
Kristiania in 1895. In 1900, Ibsen suffered the first of a series of
strokes, and he died on 23 May 1906 at the age of 78. Norway had
only the year before become an independent nation for the first
time since the fourteenth century, having extracted itself through
diplomatic rather than military means from the union with Sweden.
Ibsen's legacy is impressive; he has had a lasting influence on world
theater and literature, and many twentieth-century writers from
around the globe acknowledge his influence. His works have been
translated into every language imaginable, and have been staged and
adapted in myriad cultural contexts and on every continent.

The plays gathered together in this volume represent four important, but quite different aspects of Ibsen's dramatic production.

Peer Gynt (1867)

While plays such as *A Doll's House*, *Hedda Gabler*, and *An Enemy
of the People* are much more well-known in the rest of the world,
Peer Gynt is by far the most popular and important Ibsen text in
Norway today. It is a tour-de-force of fantasy and imagination,
and Ibsen's use of language and verse virtually sparkles in the
Norwegian original. Not initially intended for stage production,
this dramatic poem tells the story of a ne'er-do-well who travels
the globe to avoid responsibility and commitment, only to return
home at the end in a remarkably ambiguous scene of what may or
may not be salvation.

The protagonist, Peer Gynt, is a liar and a layabout who rejects
his solid agrarian roots. The first three acts of the drama take place
in the Gudbrandsdalen region in Norway; Gudbrandsdalen is a
broad, fertile river valley that cuts north-south through wild,

expansive mountain ranges on either side. This is the area where Ibsen had in the summer of 1862 spent some weeks collecting folk tales, and it is to this day an area that maintains a strong folk cultural identity. The landscape and folkways are reflected in accurate detail in the first three acts of *Peer Gynt*. Peer's actions are all the more shocking because of his relatively high status in the rural community; he comes from a once-rich farm and stands to inherit it all, yet he squanders every opportunity and shows no respect for accepted social practice and tradition. Ibsen likewise breaks with any reliance upon dramatic unity of time, place, or action in *Peer Gynt*, for the fourth act of the play commences decades later, is set rather improbably in Morocco and Egypt, and – other than the much older Peer himself – features an entirely different set of characters. In the fifth and final act a now elderly Peer returns home to Gudbrandsdalen. There he meets a number of characters who figured in the first three acts; like Peer they have changed significantly, and these meetings are melancholy, disturbing, and at times comical.

In *Peer Gynt* Ibsen freely mixes realistic (human) and fantastical (non-human or semi-human) characters in a wild epic that can be understood on a deeper level as an existential inquiry into the nature of the self. The plot roughly follows the development of a romantic attachment between Peer and the younger and more naive Solveig, who pledges her love to Peer and willingly waits for him alone throughout a long life. Yet the romantic relationship is by most accounts secondary to the play's philosophical inquiry into the nature of the self. In one of its most famous scenes, Peer peels a wild onion, looking for its core and comparing the lack of a solid center in the onion to his own fluid and un-fixed identity. At the time when Ibsen wrote *Peer Gynt*, in which idealist philosophy and Hegelian notions of progress dominated, this is a surprisingly radical message about the nature of the self.

Peer Gynt also needs to be understood in the context of Norwegian national identity construction. Norway was under Danish rule from 1385 to 1814. In the midst of the Napoleonic War, Denmark was forced to forfeit the territory of Norway as punishment for opposing the British. Norwegian patriots saw a window of opportunity and wrote a constitution and elected a king, only to have their hopes of independence dashed; at the Treaty of Kiel

Norway was handed summarily over to Sweden, and became part
of a new union under the Swedish king. The work of the so-
called 'men of 1814' was not forgotten, however, and a new
national consciousness developed. This was expressed through
art and literature, and most especially through the collection of
folk tales. This movement is known in Norway as National
Romanticism, though it has little or nothing to do with the high
literary Romanticism that developed in Germany and England in
the late eighteenth and early nineteenth centuries. Inspired by
philosophers like Herder and Fichte, who argued for the unique
qualities of each '*volk*' or nation, and by the tale collecting of
the Brothers Grimm, educated Norwegians of the social elite
turned toward their own folk culture and toward the Viking Age
and the Old Norse Sagas for inspiration and for clues about what
made them culturally unique as a nation, and thus worthy of
political independence.

Early in his career, Ibsen participated actively in this movement.
His plays from the 1850s utilize historical or folkloric themes, and
he staged a number of national romantic plays by other dramatists
while active in the theater. Moreover, he wrote critical essays
about national romantic dramas that demonstrate his commitment
to the larger nationalistic project throughout the decade. His 1852
play *St John's Eve*, however, indicates that he viewed the movement with a certain critical irony, and by the 1860s he had fully
rejected the nationalist project. He himself attributes this to his loss
of faith in the ideal of pan-Scandinavianism; Norway, Sweden,
and Denmark share a common cultural and linguistic heritage, and
Ibsen supported activists who wanted to bring the three nations
closer together politically while recognizing and cultivating their
cultural uniqueness. When Danish territory was invaded by Prussia
in 1864, there were calls for the union of Sweden-Norway to aid
Denmark militarily, but the government refused to do so. Ibsen
found this unconscionable, and became an outright critic of both
nationalist and pan-Scandinavian idealism.

The many folkloric elements in *Peer Gynt* are thus quite complex, and there are a number of known satirical jabs at certain
historical figures, particularly in the scene set in a madhouse in
Cairo in the fourth act. More generally though, Ibsen appears to
have written *Peer Gynt* in something of a parodic relationship to

earlier national romantic dramas; that is to say, he activates many of
the same motifs, but he does so with an underlying irony. There is
an even greater irony in the play's later reception in Norway,
where it has become a national icon. References to the play
abound in both high and low culture, its language has entered
everyday speech (a hindrance or problem is often called a 'boyg',
for example), it is read and re-read by generations, adapted
to every imaginable medium, and staged in every context from
the National Theater to the open landscape of Gudbrandsdalen,
from experimental to community theater groups, to primary and
secondary schools throughout the land.

Ibsen himself adapted this closet drama for the stage in 1876,
commissioning composer Edvard Grieg to write incidental music
for the performance. Grieg's music has taken on a life of its own,
and is almost as well known as the text itself. This stage adaptation
marked the beginning of a long and complex performance history
of *Peer Gynt* in Norway, where the radical existential message
of the text has often been drowned out by national romantic
pageantry and spectacle. The text remains the wildest, most
philosophically radical, and most imaginative of Ibsen's twenty-
five completed plays.

A Doll's House (1879)

If *Peer Gynt* is Ibsen's most philosophically radical text, *A Doll's
House* is surely one of if not the most politically radical of his
works. Using perfectly honed realist dramatic techniques, the play
conveys a simple but explosive social message: a woman is first
and foremost a human being and only secondarily a wife, mother,
daughter, etc. Ibsen is not the first writer to make this claim, but
he is the first writer with enough prestige and market acumen to
bring the message to a large international audience, where it
could no longer be ignored or marginalized. In *A Doll's House*
the reader is first introduced to the seemingly perfect family life of
Nora and Torvald Helmer and their three children. As the action
unfolds, however, we soon become aware of cracks in the façade,
and we realize that there are very high ethical and emotional
stakes at play. Nora has secretly broken the law to save her
husband, who had been very ill; she views this as a necessary

sacrifice and as proof of her devotion, while he views it in a purely legalistic light, and is thus shocked and appalled at the actions his wife has taken in the past.

The play's title functions on a number of levels. On the one hand Nora feels trapped in her marriage, manipulated by her husband as though she were a doll rather than a living human being. The Helmer home is at the outset as isolated from harsh reality as a child's dollhouse. On the other hand the title also may refer meta-theatrically to the artifice of theater itself. In the famous 'Tarantella' scene of the second act, Nora practices a frenetic Italian dance in front of her husband; she also performs the dance later at a party that takes place off stage during act two. Nora dances wildly while Torvald attempts to correct her performance, which highlights the artificial nature of ostensibly 'natural' and 'realistic' performances such as the play *A Doll's House* itself.

Although the main plot line is deceptively simple – it can be reduced in its simplest form to the idea of the main character coming to the realization that her marriage is a sham and deciding to leave her husband – it is made richer by complex secondary characters such as Dr Rank, a close friend of both Nora and Torvald. Dr Rank is perhaps the most sympathetic of Ibsen's many 'husvenn' (friend of the household) characters; his love for Nora becomes obvious through the course of the action. The arrival of Nora's old friend Mrs Kristine Linde is crucial in a number of ways; it gives Ibsen a believable context in which Nora can relate on stage what has happened in the past, and her story demonstrates the dangers of sacrificing oneself entirely for others. Finally, Nils Krogstad, who is one of Torvald's employees at the bank, introduces intrigue into the plot through his threats of blackmail and, along with Kristine Linde, a certain degree of class anxiety. The Helmers are socially ambitious and live in constant fear of falling economically and socially back down to the level of their respective friend and employee.

The character of Nora is one of the truly great roles available to female actors. It demands a subtle transformation throughout the course of the play. It is crucial to remember that the character Nora is herself play-acting through much of the course of the play; she 'performs' constantly for Torvald, and in a way she deludes herself, convincing herself that she is happier than she really is.

Torvald cannot see the changes that take place in her, and is thus shocked by her radical decision at the end, but the reader or audience member can follow the subtle signs of her growing discomfort with playing the role of a little doll in Torvald's house.

The action of the play takes place at Christmas time, which gives Ibsen rich symbolic material that allows him to intensify the themes of the play. Anticipation of something wonderful permeates the first act; in addition to the eagerly awaited joy of sharing Christmas gifts with the children, Nora and Torvald hope they will soon be freed of financial worry. But just as in real life, the pressure to be (or at least appear) happy at Christmas time can be hard to bear, and the façade starts to crack. In the second act, the Christmas tree has been stripped, and the mood of anticipation has shifted subtly to one of anxiety, as the reality of the larger world outside the Helmer 'dollhouse' creeps in, relayed through the experiences of Kristine, Krogstad, and Rank. Torvald exerts his patriarchal power over Nora, dismissing her wishes and making it obvious that she is merely a sexual object for him. Torvald's shock at the revelation of Krogstad's blackmailing letter turns the Helmer world upside down, and it reveals to Nora who the man she married really is; the wonderful future she hoped for fails to materialize, leaving her with – in her eyes – only one choice, namely to leave her sham of a marriage. This ending has caused great controversy, both historically and today, and in performances in various places around the world it is still adapted to fit more conservative cultural norms about the role of women.

Hedda Gabler (1890)

Despite the many differences in details, it can be tempting to think of *Hedda Gabler* as the story of what might have happened to Nora had she stayed with Torvald. *Hedda Gabler* is a dark play, dealing with themes of suicide and despair. Again the title provides important information to the reader: the main character, Hedda, has recently married the boringly studious George Tesman (George is called Jørgen in Ibsen's original), so one would assume the play should be called 'Hedda Tesman'. But Hedda married out of boredom or desperation, and still identifies intensely with her late father, General Gabler. The General haunts the play; his portrait is prominently displayed in the bourgeois parlor that makes up the setting, and the two pistols that Hedda inherited from him are central to a number of points in the plot.

Like Nora, Hedda is a woman without a true calling in life, but where Nora earnestly and bravely seeks to find meaning in her life and become a whole human being, Hedda is disillusioned, and furthermore immobilized by her fear of public opinion. The action and crisis of the play are initiated by a number of factors: Hedda and George have just returned to a new home after an extensive honeymoon abroad; Hedda has become aware that she is pregnant against her wishes; she believes herself to be under the stifling control of her immediate circle, which includes George's aunts and the domineering and somewhat lecherous family friend, Judge Brack; finally, Hedda's old flame and George's rival for academic honors, Eilert Løvborg has recently returned to town. Eilert is a complex character. Ibsen portrays him as a brilliantly creative but self-destructive scholar who was on the brink of burning out completely until the angelic figure of Thea Elvsted motivated him and gave him the structure and stability to write an exceptional new book manuscript.

Lacking a calling of her own, Hedda reacts with spite and jealousy to the passion that those around her show for their various projects. She commits a kind of symbolic murder when she burns Eilert's book manuscript, a manuscript he earlier referred to as a 'child' he created together with Thea. Clearly the play is at least an indirect criticism of the lack of meaningful roles for women outside the family. Hedda is the third in a line of destructive, complex, and compelling female characters, starting with Furia in his debut play, *Catiline*, continuing with Hjørdis in *The Vikings at Helgeland* (1857) and Hedda herself, and on to Irene in Ibsen's last play, *When We Dead Awaken*. While hardly sympathetic characters, their self-destructive and amoral impulses, driven by revenge or boredom or despair, are entirely believable, and many readers forgive them their cruelty and madness because of the obvious injustices carried out against them within their personal relationships and within society at large.

Many of Ibsen's character take – or at least appear to take – their own lives, but none does so more dramatically than Hedda. Seeing that even her cruel behavior toward Eilert Løvborg can be smoothed over, and that there is no escaping the ministrations of Judge Brack, she sees no alternative but to end her own life. The play remains surprisingly modern, and in recent years it has been staged more and more in the West.

The Master Builder (1892)

With *The Master Builder*, Ibsen entered the final phase of his dramatic production. It was the first play written after the playwright's return from exile, and it introduced a new mode in which, as the novelist James Joyce noted, the characters break out of the stifling bourgeois parlors that characterize plays like *A Doll's House* and *Hedda Gabler* and enter the outdoors. In this sense, toward the end of his career Ibsen returned to the open landscape he created in *Peer Gynt*, although the mode is realistic rather than fantastical, and the mood melancholy and dark rather than energetic and parodic.

Although Ibsen is probably best known for his complex female characters, in *The Master Builder* he creates an unforgettable male protagonist, the architect Halvard Solness, who is desperately afraid that the younger generation is about to overtake him, while at the same time deeply attracted to the youthfulness and energy of the young woman who enters his life at the beginning of the play, Hilda Wangel. There is a certain autobiographical resonance in the relationship between Solness and Hilda; Ibsen had a number of well-documented infatuations with much younger women during the later years of his life, the most famous of which was a brief flirtation with a young Austrian woman, Emilie Bardach, during the summer of 1889.

As with most of Ibsen's social realist dramas, the backstory for the current action of the play is all-important, and is revealed retrospectively through dialog. In *The Master Builder*, two events in the past have a particularly strong influence on the present. Solness and his wife Aline suffered a terrible tragedy when a fire in their home took the lives of their children; Solness knew of a defect in a chimney that led directly to the fire, and thus neither Aline nor he himself can fully forgive him for these deaths. The other past event is a memory that Solness has apparently repressed at the start of the play; when Hilda arrives she reminds him of how he once climbed to the top of the steeple on a church he had designed for her village. Hilda as a child was overwhelmed by his perceived bravery and insists that he vowed to come and get her and build a castle in the air just for her. Seduced by the architect's attention, Hilda runs away from home to find him and claim what he had promised her. That Solness is in actuality terrified of heights is one of the play's great ironies; he is torn between his desire to satisfy Hilda's demands and his overpowering fear of what she asks him to do.

All of the events in the play and in its past action can be interpreted metaphorically, yet they all maintain a certain ambiguity that makes it impossible to reduce the meaning of the play to a simple formula. As in so many other Ibsen plays, the vertical axis of the landscape mirrors the psychological development of the main character; the notion of a 'tragic fall' is represented quite literally in *The Master Builder* through the motif of the climb up the steeple.

Taken as a whole, these four plays demonstrate both the sweeping breadth and the interconnectedness of Ibsen's dramatic oeuvre. Ibsen famously claimed that he didn't read any literature other than newspapers, but it is clear that each of his own works developed in intertextual dialog with the rest of his production, revising and rethinking problems that preoccupied the dramatist throughout his career from constantly shifting perspectives.

William Archer

This collection of Ibsen plays returns to the acclaimed translations of William Archer (1856–1924), who through these renditions played a major role in promoting Ibsen's reputation outside of Norway. Scottish by birth, Archer together with actress Elizabeth Robbins and dramatist George Bernard Shaw was central in the modernization of English theatre through his work as a critic. In what remains the only major critical study of Archer's so-called 'Ibsen Campaign' in Britain, Thomas Postlewait explains that 'From 1889, when the production of *A Doll's House* began the Ibsen campaign in earnest, until 1914, when *Ghosts* was finally allowed a public performance with the lifting of the censorship on it, the history of Ibsen in England is predominantly the history of Archer's translations on the stage.' (1986, 139) Moreover, given the status of English as an international language, initially 'Archer's Ibsen' influenced the way Ibsen was perceived through so-called 'serial translation', in which Archer's English rendering was used as the source for translations into various other languages, rather than direct translations from the original Dano-Norwegian. Understanding Archer's role in the development of Ibsen's international reputation is thus doubly important.

Translation is never a neutral process, no matter how literally accurate or 'close to the spirit' of the original it may be. It is thus useful for readers approaching Ibsen's texts through translation to have some knowledge of the context for the particular translations in hand.

Archer's grandfather had been the British consul in Norway for some years, which gave the young Archer the opportunity to learn the Norwegian language. His translations show an extreme respect for the original, and are in many cases much more literal than more modern translations, which often prioritize 'readability', or 'cultural translations' that seek to 'domesticate' the original for a new cultural context; or, alternatively, translations that seek deliberately to emphasize the culturally unfamiliar and 'foreignize' a given text for a new audience. Archer's more literal approach may make for a slightly less smooth reading experience, but this is outweighed by the fact that the translations were carried out in Ibsen's lifetime, and thus are the product of a shared experience of history and culture that has been in part lost today.

Ellen Rees
Centre for Ibsen Studies
University of Oslo

A NOTE ON SOURCES

This introduction draws heavily on recent research on Ibsen's life and works carried out by scholars in Norway. Starting with the 2010 project, 'Den biografiske Ibsen' ('The Biographical Ibsen'), a number of scholars have identified and corrected numerous errors and misrepresentations regarding Ibsen's life through painstaking archival research. Unfortunately, very little of this new material has been published in English. The notes that follow include the most significant sources of new information, with English translations of the titles where necessary.

1 In *Af stort est du kommen: Henrik Ibsen og Skien* (Of Greatness Have You Come: Henrik Ibsen and Skien; Centre for Ibsen Studies, 2013), Jon Nygaard argues that Ibsen's family was of much higher social status than has previously been presumed, and that the bankruptcy of his father was not a particular failing on his part individually, but rather part of a much larger socio-economic shift that affected the patrician class to which the Ibsens belonged particularly severely.

2 In *Creating a Theatrical Space: A Study of Henrik Ibsen's Production Books* (University of Bergen, 2010), Ellen Karoline Gjervan gives the first thorough analysis of Ibsen's work as a theater director during his time in Bergen.

3 In *Deus ex machina? Henrik Ibsen og teatret i norsk offentlighet 1780–1864* (Deus ex Machina? Henrik Ibsen and the Theater in the Norwegian Public Sphere 1780–1864; University of Oslo, 2010), Anette Storli Andersen gives quantitative and qualitative evidence for revising the view that Norwegian theater culture was especially primitive, and that Ibsen single-handedly revolutionized the theater in Norway; Andersen argues that the role of amateur theater has been much undervalued by scholars, and that Ibsen entered an already active and sophisticated theater culture when he started his career in the 1850s. According to both Andersen and Nygaard, theater as an art form as a whole began to decline in the 1850s and 1860s, prompting the ambitious Ibsen to leave the theater and concentrate on the book market instead.

Ann Schmiesing's 2006 book, *Norway's Christiania Theater, 1827–1867* (Fairleigh Dickinson University Press) gives a thorough overview of the particular issues faced by the two competing theaters in the capital city of Christiania.

4 In *Ibsen og fotografene: 1800-tallets visuelle kultur* (Ibsen and the Photographers: Nineteenth-Century Visual Culture; Universitetsforlaget, 2013) Peter Larsen analyzes Ibsen's deliberate use of the portrait photograph and other new forms of visual media to promote his image as a literary genius throughout Europe.

5 In *Den smilende Ibsen: Henrik Ibsens forfatterskap – stykkevis og delt* (The Smiling Ibsen: Henrik Ibsen's Oeuvre – in Bits and Pieces; Centre for Ibsen Studies, 2013), Ståle Dingstad attempts to rescue the wonderfully humorous aspects of Ibsen's works from obscurity; Dingstad argues that Ibsen was not the dry, humorless moralist that he is often assumed to be, and points out the many ways that Ibsen used humor to delight his audiences.

FURTHER READING

Scandinavian literature

Hans Christian Andersen. *Fairy Tales* (1835 and 1837)

Bjørnstjerne Bjørnson. *A Gauntlet* (1883); *Synnøve Solbakken* (1857)

Camilla Collett. *The District Governor's Daughters* (1854–55)

Jon Fosse. *Someone Is Going to Come* (1996)

Knut Hamsun. *Hunger* (1890) or *Pan* (1894)

Ludvig Holberg. *Erasmus Montanus* (1723) or *Jeppe of the Hill* (1722)

Søren Kierkegaard. *The Seducer's Diary* (1843)

Amalie Skram. *Constance Ring* (1855) or *Lucie* (1888)

August Strindberg. *Miss Julie* (1888) or *A Dream Play* (1901)

World literature

Anton Chekhov. *The Seagull* (1896), *Three Sisters* (1901) or *The Cherry Orchard* (1904)

Johann Wolfgang von Goethe. *Faust Part One* (1808) and *Faust Part Two* (1832)

Elizabeth Robbins. *Votes for Women!* (1907)

George Bernard Shaw. *Major Barbara* (1905) or *Pygmalion* (1912–13)

Rabindranath Tagore. Selected short stories (written between 1877 and 1941)

Tracie Chima Utoh. *Nneora: An African Doll's House* (2005)

PEER GYNT

Characters

ÅSE, *a peasant's widow*
PEER GYNT, *her son*
TWO OLD WOMEN *with corn-sacks*
ASLAK, *a smith*
WEDDING-GUESTS
A MASTER-COOK, A FIDDLER, *etc.*
A MAN *and* WIFE, *newcomers to the district*
SOLVEIG *and* LITTLE HELGA, *their daughters*
THE FARMER AT HEGSTAD
INGRID, *his daughter*
THE BRIDEGROOM *and* HIS PARENTS
THREE SAETER-GIRLS
A GREEN-CLAD WOMAN
THE OLD MAN OF THE DOVRË
A TROLL-COURTIER
SEVERAL OTHERS
TROLL-MAIDENS *and* TROLL-URCHINS
A COUPLE OF WITCHES
BROWNIES, NIXIES, GNOMES, *etc.*
AN UGLY BRAT
A VOICE IN THE DARKNESS
BIRD-CRIES
KARI, *a cottar's wife*
MASTER COTTON
MONSIEUR BALLON
HERREN VON EBERKOPF *and* TRUMPETERSTRALE,
    gentlemen on their travels
A THIEF *and* A RECEIVER
ANITRA, *daughter of a Bedouin chief*

ARABS, FEMALE SLAVES, DANCING-GIRLS, *etc.*

THE MEMNON-STATUE (*singing*)

THE SPHINX AT GIZEH (*muta persona*)

PROFESSOR BEGRIFFENFELDT, *Dr. Phil., Director of the madhouse at Cairo*

HUHU, *a language-reformer from the coast of Malabar*

HUSSEIN, *an eastern Minister*

A FELLAH, *with a royal mummy*

SEVERAL MADMEN, *with their keepers*

A NORWEGIAN SKIPPER *and* HIS CREW

A STRANGE PASSENGER

A PASTOR

A FUNERAL-PARTY

A PARISH-OFFICER

A BUTTON-MOULDER

A LEAN PERSON

* * * * *

The action, which opens in the beginning of the nineteenth century, and ends around the 1860's, takes place partly in Gudbrandsdalen, and on the mountains around it, partly on the coast of Morocco, in the desert of Sahara, in a madhouse at Cairo, at sea, etc.

ACT FIRST

SCENE FIRST

A wooded hillside near Åse's farm. A river rushes down the slope.
On the further side of it an old mill shed. It is a hot day in
summer.

    PEER GYNT, *a strongly-built youth of twenty, comes down the*
pathway. His mother, ÅSE, *a small, slightly built woman, follows*
him, scolding angrily.

ÅSE   Peer, you're lying!
PEER [*without stopping*]   No, I am not!
ÅSE   Well then, swear that it is true!
PEER   Swear? Why should I?
ÅSE   See, you dare not!
        It's a lie from first to last.
PEER [*stopping*] It is true – each blessed word!
ÅSE [*confronting him*] Don't you blush before your mother?
        First you skulk among the mountains
        Monthlong in the busiest season,
        Stalking reindeer in the snows;
        Home you come then, torn and tattered,
        Gun amissing, likewise game –
        And at last, with open eyes,
        Think to get me to believe
        All the wildest hunters' lies! –
        Well, where did you find the buck, then?
PEER   West near Gendin.
ÅSE [*laughing scornfully*]   Ah! Indeed!
PEER   Keen the blast towards me swept;
        Hidden by an alder-clump,

He was scraping in the snow-crust
After lichen –

ÅSE [*as before*]   Doubtless, yes!

PEER   Breathlessly I stood and listened,
Heard the crunching of his hoof,
Saw the branches of one antler.
Softly then among the boulders
I crept forward on my belly.
Crouched in the moraine I peered up –
Such a buck, so sleek and fat,
You, I'm sure, have ne'er set eyes on.

ÅSE   No, of course not!

PEER   Bang! I fired!
Clean he dropped upon the hillside.
But the instant that he fell,
I sat firm astride his back,
Gripped him by the left ear tightly,
And had almost sunk my knife-blade
In his neck, behind his skull –
When, behold! the brute screamed wildly,
Sprang upon his feet like lightning,
With a back-cast of his head
From my fist made knife and sheath fly,
Pinned me tightly by the thigh,
Jammed his horns against my legs,
Clenched me like a pair of tongs –
Then forthwith away he flew
Right along the Gendin-Edge!

ÅSE [*involuntarily*] Jesus save us – !

PEER   Have you ever
Chanced to see the Gendin-Edge?
Nigh on four miles long it stretches
Sharp before you like a scythe.
Down o'er glaciers, landslips, scaurs,
Down the toppling grey moraines,
You can see, both right and left,
Straight into the tarns that slumber,
Black and sluggish, more than seven
Hundred fathoms deep below you.

Right along the Edge we two
Clove our passage through the air.
Never rode I such a colt!
Straight before us as we rushed
'Twas as though there glittered suns.
Brown-backed eagles that were sailing
In the wide and dizzy void
Half-way 'twixt us and the tarns,
Dropped behind, like motes in air.
Ice-floes on the shores broke crashing,
But no murmur reached my ears.
Only sprites of dizziness sprang,
Dancing, round – they sang, they swung,
Circle-wise, past sight and hearing!

ÅSE [*dizzy*] Oh, God save me!

PEER   All at once,
At a desperate, break-neck spot,
Rose a great cock-ptarmigan,
Flapping, cackling, terrified,
From the crack where he lay hidden
At the buck's feet on the Edge.
Then the buck shied half around,
Leapt sky-high, and down we plunged
Both of us into the depths!

ÅSE [*totters, and catches at the trunk of a tree*]

PEER GYNT [*continues*] Mountain walls behind us, black,
And below a void unfathomed!
First we clove through banks of mist,
Then we clove a flock of sea-gulls,
So that they, in mid-air startled,
Flew in all directions, screaming.
Downward rushed we, ever downward.
But beneath us something shimmered,
Whitish, like a reindeer's belly. –
Mother, 'twas our own reflection
In the glass-smooth mountain tarn,
Shooting up towards the surface
With the same wild rush of speed
Wherewith we were shooting downwards.

ÅSE [*gasping for breath*] Peer! God help me – ! Quickly, tell – !

PEER   Buck from over, buck from under,
     In a moment clashed together,
     Scattering foam-flecks all around.
     There we lay then, floating, plashing –
     But at last we made our way
     Somehow to the northern shore;
     Buck, he swam, I clung behind him –
     I ran homewards –

ÅSE   But the buck, dear?

PEER   He's there still, for aught I know –
    [*snaps his fingers, turns on his heel, and adds*]
     Catch him, and you're welcome to him!

ÅSE   And your neck you haven't broken?
     Haven't broken both your thighs?
     And your backbone, too, is whole?
     Oh, dear Lord – what thanks, what praise,
     Should be thine who helped my boy!
     There's a rent, though, in your breeches;
     But it's scarce worth talking of
     When one thinks what dreadful things
     Might have come of such a leap – !
    [*stops suddenly, looks at him open-mouthed and wide-eyed;
    cannot find words for some time, but at last bursts out*]
     Oh, you devil's story-teller,
     Cross of Christ, how you can lie!
     All this screed you foist upon me,
     I remember now, I knew it
     When I was a girl of twenty.
     Gudbrand Glesne it befell,
     Never you, you –

PEER   Me as well.
     Such a thing can happen twice.

ÅSE [*exasperated*] Yes, a lie, turned topsy-turvy,
     Can be prinked and tinselled out,
     Decked in plumage new and fine,
     Till none knows its lean old carcass.
     That is just what you've been doing,
     Vamping up things, wild and grand,

Garnishing with eagles' backs
And with all the other horrors,
Lying right and lying left,
Filling me with speechless dread,
Till at last I recognised not
What of old I'd heard and known!

PEER   If another talked like that
I'd half kill him for his pains.

ÅSE [*weeping*] Oh, would God I lay a corpse;
Would the black earth held me sleeping!
Prayers and tears don't bite upon him. –
Peer, you're lost, and ever will be!

PEER   Darling, pretty little mother,
You are right in every word –
Don't be cross, be happy –

ÅSE   Silence!
Could I, if I would, be happy,
With a pig like you for son?
Think how bitter I must find it,
I, a poor defenceless widow,
Ever to be put to shame!

[*weeping again*] How much have we now remaining
From your grandsire's days of glory?
Where are now the sacks of coin
Left behind by Rasmus Gynt?
Ah, your father lent them wings –
Lavished them abroad like sand,
Buying land in every parish,
Driving round in gilded chariots.
Where is all the wealth he wasted
At the famous winter-banquet,
When each guest sent glass and bottle
Shivering 'gainst the wall behind him?

PEER   Where's the snow of yesteryear?

ÅSE   Silence, boy, before your mother!
See the farmhouse! Every second
Window-pane is stopped with clouts.
Hedges, fences, all are down,
Beasts exposed to wind and weather,

	Fields and meadows lying fallow,
	Every month a new distraint –
PEER	Come now, stop this old-wife's talk!
	Many a time has luck seemed dropping,
	And sprung up as high as ever!
ÅSE	Salt-strewn is the soil it grew from.

Lord, but you're a rare one, you –
Just as pert and jaunty still,
Just as bold as when the pastor,
Newly come from Copenhagen,
Bade you tell your Christian name,
And declared that such a headpiece
Many a prince down there might envy;
Till the cob your father gave him,
With a sledge to boot, in thanks
For his pleasant, friendly talk. –
Ah, but things went bravely then!
Provost, captain, all the rest,
Dropped in daily, ate and drank,
Swilling, till they well-nigh burst.
But 'tis need that tests one's neighbour.
Lonely here it grew, and silent
From the day that 'Gold-bag Jon'
Started with his pack, a pedlar.

[*dries her eyes with her apron*]

Ah, you're big and strong enough,
You should be a staff and pillar
For your mother's frail old age –
You should keep the farm-work going,
Guard the remnants of your gear –

[*crying again*] oh, God help me, small's the profit
You have been to me, you scamp!
Lounging by the hearth at home,
Grubbing in the charcoal embers;
Or, round all the country, frightening
Girls away from merry-makings –
Shaming me in all directions,
Fighting with the worst rapscallions –

PEER [*turning away from her*] Let me be.

ÅSE [*following him*]   Can you deny
              That you were the foremost brawler
              In the mighty battle royal
              Fought the other day at Lunde,
              When you raged like mongrels mad?
              Who was it but you that broke
              Blacksmith Aslak's arm for him –
              Or at any rate that wrenched
              One of his fingers out of joint?
PEER   Who has filled you with such prate?
ÅSE [*hotly*]   Cottar Kari heard the yells!
PEER [*rubbing his elbow*] Maybe, but 'twas I that howled.
ÅSE   You?
PEER   Yes, mother – *I* got beaten.
ÅSE   What d'you say?
PEER   He's limber, he is.
ÅSE   Who?
PEER   Why Aslak, to be sure.
ÅSE   Shame – and shame; I spit upon you!
              Such a worthless sot as that,
              Such a brawler, such a sodden
              Dram-sponge to have beaten you!
        [*weeping again*] Many a shame and slight I've suffered;
              But that this should come to pass
              Is the worst disgrace of all.
              What if he be ne'er so limber,
              Need you therefore be a weakling?
PEER   Though I hammer or am hammered –
              Still we must have lamentations.
        [*laughing*] Cheer up, mother –
ÅSE   What? You're lying
              Now again?
PEER   Yes, just this once.
              Come now, wipe your tears away –
        [*clenching his left hand*] See – with this same pair of tongs,
              Thus I held the smith bent double,
              While my sledge-hammer right fist –
ÅSE   Oh, you brawler! You will bring me
              With your doings to the grave!

PEER   No, you're worth a better fate;
                Better twenty thousand times!
                Little, ugly, dear old mother,
                You may safely trust my word –
                All the parish shall exalt you;
                Only wait till I have done
                Something – something really grand!

ÅSE [*contemptuously*] You!

PEER   Who knows what may befall one!

ÅSE   Would you'd get so far in sense
                One day as to do the darning
                Of your breeches for yourself!

PEER [*hotly*]   I will be a king, a kaiser!

ÅSE   Oh, God comfort me, he's losing
                All the wits that he had left!

PEER   Yes, I will! just give me time!

ÅSE   Give you time, you'll be a prince,
                So the saying goes, I think!

PEER   You shall see!

ÅSE   Oh, hold your tongue!
                You're as mad as mad can be. –
                Ah, and yet it's true enough –
                Something might have come of you,
                Had you not been steeped for ever
                In your lies and trash and moonshine.
                Hegstad's girl was fond of you.
                Easily you could have won her
                Had you wooed her with a will –

PEER   Could I?

ÅSE   The old man's too feeble
                Not to give his child her way.
                He is stiff-necked in a fashion
                But at last 'tis Ingrid rules;
                And where she leads, step by step,
                Stumps the gaffer, grumbling, after.

                [*begins to cry again*] Ah, my Peer! – a golden girl –
                Land entailed on her! just think,
                Had you set your mind upon it,
                You'd be now a bridegroom brave –

                     You that stand here grimed and tattered!
PEER [*briskly*] Come, we'll go a-wooing, then!
ÅSE   Where?
PEER   At Hegstad!
ÅSE   Ah, poor boy;
                     Hegstad way is barred to wooers!
PEER   How is that?
ÅSE   Ah, I must sigh!
                     Lost the moment, lost the luck –
PEER   Speak!
ÅSE [*sobbing*]   While in the Wester-hills
                     You in air were riding reindeer,
                     Here Mads Moen's won the girl!
PEER   What! That women's-bugbear! He – !
ÅSE   Ay, she's taking him for husband.
PEER   Wait you here till I have harnessed
                     Horse and waggon – [*going*]
ÅSE   Spare your pains.
                     They are to be wed tomorrow –
PEER   Pooh; this evening I'll be there!
ÅSE   Fie now! Would you crown our miseries
                     With a load of all men's scorn?
PEER   Never fear; 'twill all go well.
         [*shouting and laughing at the same time*]
                     Mother, jump! We'll spare the waggon;
                     'Twould take time to fetch the mare up –
         [*lifts her up in his arms*]
ÅSE   Put me down!
PEER   No, in my arms
                     I will bear you to the wedding!
         [*wades out into the stream*]
ÅSE   Help! The Lord have mercy on us!
                     Peer! We're drowning –
PEER   I was born
                     For a braver death –
ÅSE   Ay, true;
                     Sure enough you'll hang at last!
         [*tugging at his hair*] Oh, you brute!
PEER   Keep quiet now;

Here the bottom's slippery-slimy.

ÅSE   Ass!

PEER   That's right, don't spare your tongue;
               That does no one any harm.
               Now it's shelving up again –

ÅSE   Don't you drop me!

PEER   Heisan! Hop!
               Now we'll play at Peer and reindeer –
           [*curvetting*] I'm the reindeer, you are Peer!

ÅSE   Oh, I'm going clean distraught!

PEER   There see; now we've reached the shallows –
           [*wades ashore*] come, a kiss now, for the reindeer;
               Just to thank him for the ride –

ÅSE [*boxing his ears*] This is how I thank him!

PEER   Ow! That's a miserable fare!

ÅSE   Put me down!

PEER   First to the wedding.
               Be my spokesman. You're so clever;
               Talk to him, the old curmudgeon;
               Say Mads Moen's good for nothing –

ÅSE   Put me down!

PEER   And tell him then
               What a rare lad is Peer Gynt.

ÅSE   Truly, you may swear to that!
               Fine's the character I'll give you.
               Through and through I'll show you up;
               All about your devil's pranks
               I will tell them straight and plain –

PEER   Will you?

ÅSE [*kicking with rage*]   I won't stay my tongue
               Till the old man sets his dog
               At you, as you were a tramp!

PEER   H'm; then I must go alone.

ÅSE   Ay, but I'll come after you!

PEER   Mother dear, you haven't strength –

ÅSE   Strength? When I'm in such a rage,
               I could crush the rocks to powder!
               Hu! I'd make a meal of flints!
               Put me down!

PEER   You'll promise then –
ÅSE   Nothing! I'll to Hegstad with you!
           They shall know you, what you are!
PEER   Then you'll even have to stay here.
ÅSE   Never! To the feast I'm coming!
PEER   That you shan't.
ÅSE   What will you do?
PEER   Perch you on the mill-house roof.
     [*he puts her up on the roof. Åse screams*]
ÅSE   Lift me down!
PEER   Yes, if you'll listen –
ÅSE   Rubbish!
PEER   Dearest mother, pray – !
ÅSE [*throwing a sod of grass at him*]
           Lift me down this moment, Peer!
PEER   If I dared, be sure I would.
     [*coming nearer*] Now remember, sit quite still.
           Do not sprawl and kick about;
           Do not tug and tear the shingles –
           Else 'twill be the worse for you;
           You might topple down.
ÅSE   You beast!
PEER   Do not kick!
ÅSE   I'd have you blown,
           Like a changeling, into space!
PEER   Mother, fie!
ÅSE   Bah!
PEER   Rather give your
           Blessing on my undertaking.
           Will you? Eh?
ÅSE   I'll thrash you soundly,
           Hulking fellow though you be!
PEER   Well, goodbye then, mother dear!
           Patience; I'll be back ere long.
     [*is going, but turns, holds up his finger warningly, and says*]
           Careful now, don't kick and sprawl!   [*goes*]
ÅSE   Peer! – God help me, now he's off;
           Reindeer-rider! Liar! Hei!
           Will you listen! – No, he's striding

     O'er the meadow – ! [*shrieks*] Help! I'm dizzy!

  TWO OLD WOMEN, *with sacks on their backs, come down the*
  path to the mill.

FIRST WOMAN Christ, who's screaming?
ÅSE   It is I!
SECOND WOMAN Åse! Well, you are exalted!
ÅSE   This won't be the end of it –
    Soon, God help me, I'll be heaven-high!
FIRST WOMAN Bless your passing!
ÅSE   Fetch a ladder;
    I must be down! That devil Peer –
SECOND WOMAN Peer! Your son?
ÅSE   Now you can say
    You have seen how he behaves.
FIRST WOMAN We'll bear witness.
ÅSE   Only help me;
    Straight to Hegstad I will hasten –
SECOND WOMAN Is he there?
FIRST WOMAN   You'll be revenged, then;
    Aslak Smith will be there too.
ÅSE [*wringing her hands*] Oh, God help me with my boy;
    They will kill him ere they're done!
FIRST WOMAN Oh, that lot has oft been talked of;
    Comfort you: what must be must be!
SECOND WOMAN She is utterly demented.
    [*calls up the hill*] Eivind, Anders! Hei! Come here!
A MAN'S VOICE What's amiss?
SECOND WOMAN   Peer Gynt has perched
    His mother on the mill-house roof!

SCENE SECOND

A hillock, covered with bushes and heather. The high road runs behind it; a fence between.

   PEER GYNT *comes along a footpath, goes quickly up to the fence, stops, and looks out over the stretch of country below.*

PEER   There it lies, Hegstad. Soon I'll have reached it.
   [*puts one leg over the fence; then hesitates*]
      Wonder if Ingrid's alone in the house now?
   [*shades his eyes with his hand, and looks out*]
      No; to the farm guests are swarming like gnats. –
      Hm, to turn back now perhaps would be wisest.
   [*draws back his leg*] Still they must titter behind your back,
      And whisper so that it burns right through you.
   [*moves a few steps away from the fence, and begins absently plucking leaves*]
      Ah, if I'd only a good strong dram now.
      Or if I could pass to and fro unseen. –
      Or were I unknown. – Something proper and strong
      Were the best thing of all, for the laughter don't
                                             bite then.

Looks around suddenly as though afraid; then hides among the bushes. Some WEDDING-GUESTS *pass by, going downwards towards the farm.*

A MAN [*in conversation as they pass*]
      His father was drunken, his mother is weak.
A WOMAN Ay, then it's no wonder the lad's good for nought.

      They pass on. Presently PEER GYNT *comes forward, his face flushed with shame. He peers after them.*

PEER [*softly*] Was it me they were talking of?
                     [*with a forced shrug*] Oh, let them chatter!
      After all, they can't sneer the life out of my body.
   [*casts himself down upon the heathery slope; lies for some time flat on his back with his hands under his head, gazing up into the sky*]

What a strange sort of cloud! It is just like a horse.
There's a man on it too – and saddle – and bridle. –
And after it comes an old crone on a broomstick.
[*laughs quietly to himself*]
　　　It is mother. She's scolding and screaming: You beast!
　　　Hei you, Peer Gynt – [*his eyes gradually close*]
　　　　　　　　　　　　　Ay, now she is frightened. –
Peer Gynt he rides first, and there follow him many. –
His steed it is gold-shod and crested with silver.
Himself he has gauntlets and sabre and scabbard.
His cloak it is long, and its lining is silken.
Full brave is the company riding behind him.
None of them, though, sits his charger so stoutly.
None of them glitters like him in the sunshine. –
Down by the fence stand the people in clusters,
Lifting their hats, and agape gazing upwards.
Women are curtseying. All the world knows him,
Kaiser Peer Gynt, and his thousands of henchmen.
Sixpenny pieces and glittering shillings
Over the roadway he scatters like pebbles.
Rich as a lord grows each man in the parish.
High o'er the ocean Peer Gynt goes a-riding.
Engelland's Prince on the seashore awaits him;
There too await him all Engelland's maidens.
Engelland's nobles and Engelland's Kaiser,
See him come riding and rise from their banquet.
Raising his crown, hear the Kaiser address him –

ASLAK THE SMITH [*to some other young men, passing along the road*]
　　　Just look at Peer Gynt there, the drunken swine – !
PEER [*starting half up*] What, Kaiser – !
THE SMITH [*leaning against the fence and grinning*]
　　　　　　　　　　　　　Up with you, Peer, my lad!
PEER　　What the devil? The smith? What do you want here?
THE SMITH [*to the others*] He hasn't got over the Lunde-
　　　　　　　　　　　　　　　　　　　spree yet.
PEER [*jumping up*] You'd better be off!
THE SMITH　　　　　　　　　　　I am going, yes.
　　　But tell us, where have you dropped from, man?
　　　You've been gone six weeks. Were you troll-taken, eh?

PEER   I have been doing strange deeds, Aslak Smith!

THE SMITH [*winking to the others*] Let us hear them, Peer!

PEER   They are nought to you.

THE SMITH [*after a pause*] You're going to Hegstad?

PEER   No.

THE SMITH   Time was
    They said that the girl there was fond of you.

PEER   You grimy crow – !

THE SMITH [*falling back a little*] Keep your temper, Peer!
    Though Ingrid has jilted you, others are left –
    Think – son of Jon Gynt! Come on to the feast;
    You'll find there both lambkins and widows well on –

PEER   To hell – !

THE SMITH   You will surely find one that will have you. –
    Good evening! I'll give your respects to the bride. –
               [*they go off, laughing and whispering*]

PEER [*looks after them a while, then makes a defiant motion and turns
    half round*] For my part, may Ingrid of Hegstad go marry
    Whoever she pleases. It's all one to me.
    [*looks down at his clothes*]
    My breeches are torn. I am ragged and grim. –
    If only I had something new to put on now.
    [*stamps on the ground*]
    If only I could, with a butcher-grip,
    Tear out the scorn from their very vitals!
    [*looks round suddenly*]
    What was that? Who was it that tittered behind there?
    Hm, I certainly thought – No no, it was no one. –
    I'll go home to mother.

[*begins to go upwards, but stops again and listens towards Hegstad*]
                  They're playing a dance!

[*gazes and listens; moves downwards step by step,
his eyes glisten; he rubs his hands down his thighs*]
    How the lasses do swarm! Six or eight to a man!
    Oh, galloping death – I must join in the frolic! –
    But how about mother, perched up on the mill-house –

[*his eyes are drawn downwards again; he leaps and laughs*]
    Hei, how the Halling flies over the green!
    Ay, Guttorm, he can make his fiddle speak out!

It gurgles and booms like a foss o'er a scaur.
And then all that glittering bevy of girls! –
Yes, galloping death, I must join in the frolic!

[*leaps over the fence and goes down the road*]

SCENE THIRD

The farm-place at Hegstad. In the background, the dwelling-house. A THRONG OF GUESTS. *A lively dance in progress on the green.* THE FIDDLER *sits on a table.* THE MASTER COOK *is standing in the doorway.* COOKMAIDS *are going to and fro between the different buildings. Groups of* ELDERLY PEOPLE *sit here and there, talking.*

A WOMAN [*joins a group that is seated on some logs of wood*]
    The bride? Oh yes, she is crying a bit;
    But that, you know, isn't worth heeding.
THE MASTER COOK [*in another group*]
    Now then, good folk, you must empty the barrel.
A MAN Thanks to you, friend; but you fill up too quick.
A LAD [*to the Fiddler as he flies past, holding a Girl by the hand*]
    To it now, Guttorm, and don't spare the fiddlestrings!
THE GIRL Scrape till it echoes out over the meadows!
OTHER GIRLS [*standing in a ring round a lad who is dancing*]
    That's a rare fling!
A GIRL   He has legs that can lift him!
THE LAD [*dancing*] The roof here is high, and the walls wide
                               asunder!
THE BRIDEGROOM [*comes whimpering up to his Father, who is standing talking with some other men, and twitches his jacket*]
    Father, she will not; she is so proud!
HIS FATHER What won't she do?
THE BRIDEGROOM   She has locked herself in.
HIS FATHER Well, you must manage to find the key.
THE BRIDEGROOM I don't know how.
HIS FATHER   You're a nincompoop!

[*turns away to the others. The Bridegroom drifts across the yard*]

A LAD [*comes from behind the house*]

Wait a bit, girls! Things'll soon be lively!

Here comes Peer Gynt.

THE SMITH [*who has just come up*] Who invited him?

THE MASTER COOK   No one.

[*goes towards the house*]

THE SMITH [*to the girls*] If he should speak to you, never

take notice!

GIRL [*to the others*] No, we'll pretend that we don't even see him.

PEER GYNT [*comes in heated and full of animation, stops right in
front of the group, and claps his hands*]

Which is the liveliest girl of the lot of you?

GIRL [*as he approaches her*] I am not.

ANOTHER [*similarly*]   I am not.

A THIRD   No; nor I either.

PEER [*to a fourth*] You come along, then, for want of a better.

THE GIRL Haven't got time.

PEER [*to a fifth*]   Well then, you!

THE GIRL [*going*]   I'm for home.

PEER Tonight? are you utterly out of your senses?

THE SMITH [*after a moment, in a low voice*]

See, Peer, she's taken a greybeard for partner.

PEER [*turns sharply to an elderly man*]

Where are the unbespoke girls?

THE MAN   Find them out. [*goes away from him*]

[*Peer Gynt has suddenly become subdued. He glances shyly and
furtively at the group. All look at him, but no one speaks. He
approaches other groups. Wherever he goes there is silence; when
he moves away, they look after him and smile.*]

PEER [*to himself*]

Mocking looks; needle-keen whispers and smiles.

They grate like a sawblade under the file!

[*he slinks along close to the fence*]

SOLVEIG, *leading little* HELGA *by the hand, comes into the yard,
along with her* PARENTS.

A MAN [*to another, close to Peer Gynt*]

Look, here are the new folk.

THE OTHER.   The ones from the west?
THE FIRST MAN Ay, the people from Hedal.
THE OTHER.   Ah yes, so they are.
PEER [*places himself in the path of the newcomers, points to Solveig,*
      and asks the Father] May I dance with your daughter?
THE FATHER [*quietly*]   You may so; but first
      We must go to the farm-house and greet the good people.
                                              [*they go in*]

THE MASTER COOK [*to Peer Gynt, offering him drink*]
      Since you are here, you'd best take a pull at the liquor.
PEER [*looking fixedly after the new-comers*]
      Thanks; I'm for dancing; I am not athirst.
                              [*the Master-Cook goes away from him*]
    [*Peer Gynt gazes towards the house and laughs*]
      How fair! Did ever you see the like?
      Looked down at her shoes and her snow-white apron – !
      And then she held on to her mother's skirt-folds,
      And carried a psalm-book wrapped up in a kerchief – !
      I must look at that girl. [*going into the house*]
A LAD [*coming out of the house, with several others*]
                                  Are you off so soon, Peer,
      From the dance?
PEER   No, no.
THE LAD   Then you're heading amiss!
    [*takes hold of his shoulder to turn him round*]
PEER Let me pass!
THE LAD   I believe you're afraid of the smith.
PEER I afraid!
THE LAD   You remember what happened at Lunde?
                              [*they go off, laughing, to the dancing-green*]
SOLVEIG [*in the doorway of the house*]
      Are you not the lad that was wanting to dance?
PEER Of course it was me; don't you know me again?
    [*takes her hand*] Come, then!
SOLVEIG   We mustn't go far, mother said.
PEER Mother said! Mother said! Were you born yesterday?
SOLVEIG Now you're laughing – !
PEER   Why sure, you are almost a child.
      Are you grown up?

SOLVEIG   I read with the pastor last spring.
PEER   Tell me your name, lass, and then we'll talk easier.
SOLVEIG My name is Solveig. And what are you called?
PEER   Peer Gynt.
SOLVEIG [*withdrawing her hand*] Oh heaven!
PEER   Why, what is it now?
SOLVEIG My garter is loose; I must tie it up tighter.
                                        [*goes away from him*]
THE BRIDEGROOM [*pulling at his Mother's gown*]
        Mother, she will not – !
HIS MOTHER   She will not? What?
THE BRIDEGROOM She won't, mother –
HIS MOTHER   What?
THE BRIDEGROOM   Unlock the door.
HIS FATHER [*angrily, below his breath*]
        Oh, you're only fit to be tied in a stall!
A MOTHER Don't scold him. Poor dear, he'll be all right yet.
                                        [*they move away*]
A LAD [*coming with a whole crowd of others from the dancing-green*]
        Peer, have some brandy?
PEER   No.
THE LAD   Only a dram?
PEER [*looking darkly at him*] Got any?
THE LAD   Well, I won't say but I have.
    [*pulls out a pocket-flask and drinks*]
        Ah! How it stings your throat! – Well?
PEER [*drinks*]   Let me try it.
ANOTHER LAD Now you must try mine as well, you know.
PEER   No!
THE LAD   Oh, nonsense; now don't be a fool.
        Take a pull, Peer!
PEER   Well then, give me a drop. [*drinks again*]
A GIRL [*half aloud*] Come, let's be going.
PEER   Afraid of me, wench?
A THIRD LAD Who isn't afraid of you?
A FOURTH   At Lunde
        You showed us clearly what tricks you could play.
PEER   I can do more than that, when once I get started!
THE FIRST LAD [*whispering*] Now he's getting into swing!

SEVERAL OTHERS. [*forming a circle around him*]

                                    Tell away! Tell away!

    What can you – ?

PEER   Tomorrow – !

OTHERS.   No, now, tonight!

A GIRL Can you conjure, Peer?

PEER   I can call up the devil!

A MAN My grandam could do that before I was born!

PEER   Liar! What I can do, that no one else can.

    I one day conjured him into a nut.

    It was worm-bored, you see!

SEVERAL [*laughing*]   Ay, that's easily guessed!

PEER   He cursed, and he wept, and he wanted to bribe me

    With all sorts of things –

ONE OF THE CROWD   But he had to go in?

PEER   Of course. I stopped up the hole with a peg.

    Hei! If you'd heard him rumbling and grumbling!

A GIRL Only think!

PEER   It was just like a humble-bee buzzing.

THE GIRL Have you got him still in the nut?

PEER   Why, no;

    By this time that devil has flown on his way.

    The grudge the smith bears me is all his doing.

A LAD Indeed?

PEER   I went to the smithy, and begged

    That he would crack that same nutshell for me.

    He promised he would! – laid it down on his anvil;

    But Aslak, you know, is so heavy of hand –

    For ever swinging that great sledge-hammer –

A VOICE FROM THE CROWD Did he kill the foul fiend?

PEER   He laid on like a man.

    But the devil showed fight, and tore off in a flame

    Through the roof, and shattered the wall asunder.

SEVERAL VOICES And the smith – ?

PEER   Stood there with his hands all scorched.

    And from that day onwards, we've never been friends.

   [*general laughter*]

SOME OF THE CROWD That yarn is a good one.

OTHERS.   About his best.

PEER Do you think I am making it up?

A MAN   Oh no,
    That you're certainly not; for I've heard the most on't
    From my grandfather –

PEER   Liar! It happened to me!

THE MAN Yes, like everything else.

PEER [*with a fling*]   I can ride, I can,
    Clean through the air, on the bravest of steeds!
    Oh, many's the thing I can do, I tell you!
  [*another roar of laughter*]

ONE OF THE GROUP Peer, ride through the air a bit!

MANY.   Do, dear Peer Gynt – !

PEER You may spare you the trouble of begging so hard.
    I will ride like a hurricane over you all!
    Every man in the parish shall fall at my feet!

AN ELDERLY MAN Now he is clean off his head.

ANOTHER   The dolt!

A THIRD Braggart!

A FOURTH   Liar!

PEER [*threatening them*]   Ay, wait till you see!

A MAN [*half drunk*] Ay, wait; you'll soon get your jacket dusted!

OTHERS Your back beaten tender! Your eyes painted blue!

            [*The crowd disperses, the elder men angry,
                  the younger laughing and jeering*]

THE BRIDEGROOM [*close to Peer Gynt*]
    Peer, is it true you can ride through the air?

PEER [*shortly*] It's all true, Mads! You must know I'm a rare one!

THE BRIDEGROOM Then have you got the Invisible Cloak too?

PEER The Invisible Hat, do you mean? Yes, I have.
  [*turns away from him*]

      SOLVEIG *crosses the yard, leading little* HELGA

PEER [*goes towards them; his face lights up*]
    Solveig! Oh, it is well you have come!
    [*takes hold of her wrist*]
    Now will I swing you round fast and fine!

SOLVEIG Loose me!

PEER   Wherefore?

SOLVEIG   You are so wild.

PEER   The reindeer is wild, too, when summer is dawning.
        Come then, lass; do not be wayward now!
SOLVEIG [*withdrawing her arm*] Dare not.
PEER   Wherefore?
SOLVEIG   No, you've been drinking.
                                [*moves off with Helga*]
PEER   Oh, if I had but my knife-blade driven
        Clean through the heart of them – one and all!
THE BRIDEGROOM [*nudging him with his elbow*]
        Peer, can't you help me to get at the bride?
PEER [*absently*] The bride? Where is she?
THE BRIDEGROOM   In the store-house.
PEER   Ah.
THE BRIDEGROOM Oh, dear Peer Gynt, you must try at least!
PEER   No, you must get on without my help.
        [*a thought strikes him; he says softly but sharply*]
        Ingrid! The store-house!
        [*goes up to Solveig*]   Have you thought better on't?
        [*Solveig tries to go; he blocks her path*]
        You're ashamed to, because I've the look of a tramp.
SOLVEIG [*hastily*] No, that you haven't; that's not true at all!
PEER   Yes! And I've taken a drop as well;
        But that was to spite you, because you had hurt me.
        Come then!
SOLVEIG   Even if I would now, I daren't.
PEER   Who are you frightened of?
SOLVEIG   Father, most.
PEER   Father? Ay, ay; he is one of the quiet ones!
        One of the godly, eh? – Answer, come!
SOLVEIG What shall I say?
PEER   Is your father a psalm-singer?
        And you and your mother as well, no doubt?
        Come, will you speak?
SOLVEIG   Let me go in peace.
PEER   No! [*in a low but sharp and threatening tone*] I can turn
                                        myself into a troll!
        I'll come to your bedside at midnight tonight.
        If you should hear someone hissing and spitting,
        You mustn't imagine it's only the cat.

It's me, lass! I'll drain out your blood in a cup,
And your little sister, I'll eat her up;
Ay, you must know I'm a werewolf at night –
I'll bite you all over the loins and the back –
[*suddenly changes his tone, and entreats, as if in dread*]
Dance with me, Solveig!
SOLVEIG [*looking darkly at him*] Then you were grim.

[*goes into the house*]
THE BRIDEGROOM [*comes sidling up again*]
I'll give you an ox if you'll help me!
PEER   Then come!
[*they go out behind the house*]

*At the same moment a crowd of men come up from the dancing-
green; most of them are drunk. Noise and hubbub.* SOLVEIG,
HELGA, *and their* PARENTS *appear among a number of elderly
people in the doorway.*

THE MASTER COOK [*to the Smith, who is the foremost of the crowd*]
Keep peace now!
THE SMITH [*pulling off his jacket*] No, we must fight it out here.
Peer Gynt or I must be taught a lesson.
SOME VOICES Ay, let them fight for it!
OTHERS   No, only wrangle!
THE SMITH Fists must decide; for the case is past words.
SOLVEIG'S FATHER Control yourself, man!
HELGA   Will they beat him, mother?
A LAD Let us rather tease him with all his lies!
ANOTHER Kick him out of the company!
A THIRD.   Spit in his eyes!
A FOURTH [*to the Smith*] You're not backing out, smith?
THE SMITH [*flinging away his jacket*] The jade shall be slaughtered!
SOLVEIG'S MOTHER [*to Solveig*]
There, you can see how that windbag is thought of.
ÅSE [*coming up with a stick in her hand*]
Is that son of mine here? Now he's in for a drubbing!
Oh! how heartily I will dang him!
THE SMITH [*rolling up his shirt-sleeves*]
That switch is too light for a carcass like his.
The smith will dang him!

OTHERS.   Bang him!

THE SMITH [*spits on his hands and nods to Åse*] Hang him!

ÅSE   What? Hang my Peer? Ay, just try if you dare –
       Åse and I, we have teeth and claws! –
       Where is he? [*calls across the yard*] Peer!

THE BRIDEGROOM [*comes running up*] Oh, God's death on the
                                                    Cross!
       Come father, come mother, and – !

HIS FATHER   What is the matter?

THE BRIDEGROOM Just fancy, Peer Gynt – !

ÅSE [*screams*]   Have they taken his life?

THE BRIDEGROOM No, but Peer Gynt – ! Look, there on the
                                          hillside – !

THE CROWD. With the bride!

ÅSE [*lets her stick sink*]   Oh, the beast!

THE SMITH [*as if thunderstruck*]   Where the slope rises sheerest
       He's clambering upwards, by God, like a goat!

THE BRIDEGROOM [*crying*] He's shouldered her, mother, as I
                                          might a pig!

ÅSE [*shaking her fist up at him*]
       Would God you might fall, and – !
                [*screams out in terror*] Take care of your footing!

THE HEGSTAD FARMER [*comes in, bare-headed and white with rage*]
       I'll have his life for this bride-rape yet!

ÅSE   Oh no, God punish me if I let you!

ACT SECOND

SCENE FIRST

A narrow path, high up in the mountains. Early morning. PEER
GYNT *comes hastily and sullenly along the path.* INGRID, *still
wearing some of her bridal ornaments, is trying to hold him back.*

PEER	Get you from me!
INGRID [*weeping*]	After this, Peer?
	Whither?
PEER	Where you will for me.
INGRID [*wringing her hands*] Oh, what falsehood!
PEER	Useless railing.
	Each alone must go his way.
INGRID	Sin – and sin again unites us!
PEER	Devil take all recollections!
	Devil take the tribe of women –
	All but one – !
INGRID	Who is that one, pray?
PEER	'Tis not you.
INGRID	Who is it then?
PEER	Go! Go thither whence you came!
	Off! To your father!
INGRID	Dearest, sweetest –
PEER	Peace!
INGRID	You cannot mean it, surely,
	What you're saying?
PEER	Can and do.
INGRID	First to lure – and then forsake me!
PEER	And what terms have you to offer?
INGRID	Hegstad Farm, and more besides.
PEER	Is your psalm-book in your kerchief?

	Where's the gold-mane on your shoulders?
	Do you glance adown your apron?
	Do you hold your mother's skirt-fold?
	Speak!
INGRID	No, but –
PEER	Went you to the pastor
	This last spring-tide?
INGRID	No, but Peer –
PEER	Is there shyness in your glances?
	When I beg, can you deny?
INGRID	Heaven! I think his wits are going!
PEER	Does your presence sanctify?
	Speak!
INGRID	No, but –
PEER	What's all the rest then? [*going*]
INGRID	[*blocking his way*] Know you it will cost your neck
	should you fail me.
PEER	What do I care?
INGRID	You may win both wealth and honour
	If you take me –
PEER	Can't afford.
INGRID	[*bursting into tears*] Oh, you lured me – !
PEER	You were willing.
INGRID	I was desperate!
PEER	Frantic I.
INGRID	[*threatening*] Dearly shall you pay for this!
PEER	Dearest payment cheap I'll reckon.
INGRID	Is your purpose set?
PEER	Like flint.
INGRID	Good! we'll see, then, who's the winner!
	[*goes downwards*]
PEER	[*stands silent a moment, then cries*]
	Devil take all recollections!
	Devil take the tribe of women!
INGRID	[*turning her head, and calling mockingly upwards*]
	All but one!
PEER	Yes, all but one.
	[*they go their several ways*]

SCENE SECOND

Near a mountain tarn; the ground is soft and marshy round about.
A storm is gathering.

    ÅSE *enters, calling and gazing around her despairingly, in every*
direction. SOLVEIG *has difficulty in keeping up with her.* SOLVEIG'S
FATHER *and* MOTHER, *with* HELGA, *are some way behind.*

ÅSE [*tossing about her arms, and tearing her hair*]
       All things are against me with wrathful might!
       Heaven, and the waters, and the grisly mountains!
       Fog-scuds from heaven roll down to bewilder him!
       The treacherous waters are lurking to murder him!
       The mountains would crush him with landslip and rift! –
       And the people too! They're out after his life!
       God knows they shan't have it! I can't bear to lose him!
       Oh, the oaf! to think that the fiend should tempt him!
       [*turning to Solveig*]
       Now isn't it clean unbelievable this?
       He, that did nought but romance and tell lies –
       He, whose sole strength was the strength of his jaw;
       He, that did never a stroke of true work –
       He – ! Oh, a body could both cry and laugh! –
       Oh, we clung closely in sorrow and need.
       Ay, you must know that my husband, he drank,
       Loafed round the parish to roister and prate,
       Wasted and trampled our gear under foot.
       And meanwhile at home there sat Peerkin and I –
       The best we could do was to try to forget;
       For ever I've found it so hard to bear up.
       It's a terrible thing to look fate in the eyes;
       And of course one is glad to be quit of one's cares,
       And try all one can to keep thought far away.
       Some take to brandy, and others to lies;
       And we – why we took to fairy-tales
       Of princes and trolls and of all sorts of beasts;

And of bride-rapes as well. Ah, but who could have
                                                    dreamt
That those devil's yarns would have stuck in his head?
[*in a fresh access of terror*]
  Hu! What a scream! It's the nixie or droug!
  Peer! Peer! – Up there on that hillock – !
[*she runs to the top of a little rise, and looks out over the tarn.
Solveig's Father and Mother come up.*]

ÅSE   Not a sign to be seen!
THE FATHER [*quietly*]   It is worst for him!
ÅSE [*weeping*] Oh, my Peer! Oh, my own lost lamb!
THE FATHER [*nods mildly*] You may well say lost.
ÅSE   Oh no, don't talk like that!
  He is so clever. There's no one like him.
THE FATHER You foolish woman!
ÅSE   Oh ay; oh ay;
  Foolish I am, but the boy's all right!
THE FATHER [*still softly and with mild eyes*]
  His heart is hardened, his soul is lost.
ÅSE [*in terror*] No, no, he can't be so hard, our Lord!
THE FATHER Do you think he can sigh for his debt of sin?
ÅSE [*eagerly*] No, but he can ride through the air on a buck,
                                                    though!
THE MOTHER Christ, are you mad?
THE FATHER   Why, what do you mean?
ÅSE   Never a deed is too great for him.
  You shall see, if only he lives so long –
THE FATHER Best if you saw him on the gallows hanging.
ÅSE [*shrieks*] Oh, cross of Christ!
THE FATHER   In the hangman's hands,
  It may be his heart would be turned to repentance.
ÅSE [*bewildered*] Oh, you'll soon talk me out of my senses!
  We must find him!
THE FATHER   To rescue his soul.
ÅSE   And his body!
  If he's stuck in the swamp, we must drag him out;
  If he's taken by trolls, we must ring the bells for him.
THE FATHER Hm! – Here's a sheep-path –
ÅSE   The Lord will repay you

Your guidance and help!
THE FATHER   It's a Christian's duty.
ÅSE   Then the others, fie! they are heathens all;
       There wasn't one that would go with us –
THE FATHER They knew him too well.
ÅSE   He was too good for them!
    [*wrings her hands*] And to think – and to think that
                                        his life is at stake!
THE FATHER Here are tracks of a man.
ÅSE   Then it's here we must search!
THE FATHER We'll scatter around on this side of our saeter.
    [*he and his wife go on ahead*]
SOLVEIG [*to Åse*] Say on; tell me more.
ÅSE [*drying her eyes*]   Of my son, you mean?
SOLVEIG   Yes –
       Tell everything!
ÅSE [*smiles and tosses her head*] Everything? – Soon you'd be tired!
SOLVEIG Sooner by far will you tire of the telling
       Than I of the hearing.

SCENE THIRD

*Low, treeless heights, close under the mountain moorlands; peaks
in the distance. The shadows are long; it is late in the day.*
    PEER GYNT *comes running at full speed, and stops short on the
hillside.*

PEER   The parish is all at my heels in a pack!
       Every man of them armed or with gun or with club.
       Foremost I hear the old Hegstad–churl howling. –
       Now it's noised far and wide that Peer Gynt is abroad!
       It is different, this, from a bout with a smith!
       This is life! Every limb grows as strong as a bear's.
    [*strikes out with his arms and leaps in the air*]
       To crush, overturn, stem the rush of the foss!
       To strike! Wrench the fir-tree right up by the root!

This is life! This both hardens and lifts one high!

To hell then with all of the savourless lies!

THREE SAETER GIRLS [*rush across the hillside, screaming and singing*]

To crush! Trond of the Valfjeld! Bård and Kårë!

Troll-pack! Tonight would you sleep in our arms?

PEER To whom are you calling?

THE GIRLS To the trolls! to the trolls!

FIRST GIRL Trond, come with kindness!

SECOND GIRL Bård, come with force!

THIRD GIRL The cots in the saeter are all standing empty!

FIRST GIRL Force is kindness!

SECOND GIRL And kindness is force!

THIRD GIRL If lads are a-wanting, one plays with the trolls!

PEER Why, where are the lads, then?

ALL THREE [*with a horse-laugh*] They cannot come hither!

FIRST GIRL Mine called me his sweetheart and called me his
darling.

Now he has married a grey-headed widow.

SECOND GIRL Mine met a gipsy-wench north on the upland.

Now they are tramping the country together.

THIRD GIRL Mine put an end to our bastard brat.

Now his head's grinning aloft on a stake.

ALL THREE Trond of the Valfjeld! Bård and Kårë!

Troll-pack! Tonight would you sleep in our arms?

PEER [*stands, with a sudden leap, in the midst of them*]

I'm a three-headed troll, and the boy for three girls!

THE GIRLS Are you such a lad, eh?

PEER You shall judge for yourselves!

FIRST GIRL To the hut! To the hut!

SECOND GIRL We have mead!

PEER Let it flow!

THIRD GIRL No cot shall stand empty this Saturday night!

SECOND GIRL [*kissing him*]

He sparkles and glisters like white-heated iron.

THIRD GIRL [*doing likewise*]

Like a baby's eyes from the blackest tarn.

PEER [*dancing in the midst of them*]

Heavy of heart and wanton of mind.

The eyes full of laughter, the throat of tears!

THE GIRLS [*making mocking gestures towards the mountain-tops,
        screaming and singing*] Trond of the Valfjeld! Bård
                                                and Kårë!
        Troll-pack! – Tonight will you sleep in our arms?
                                [*they dance away over the heights,
                                        with Peer Gynt in their midst*]

SCENE FOURTH

*Among the Rondë mountains. Sunset. Shining snowpeaks all
around.* PEER GYNT *enters, dizzy and bewildered.*

PEER   Tower over tower arises!
                Hei, what a glittering gate!
                Stand! Will you stand! It's drifting
                Further and further away!
                High on the vane the cock stands
                Lifting his wings for flight –
                Blue spread the rifts and bluer,
                Locked is the fell and barred. –
                What are those trunks and tree-roots,
                That grow from the ridge's clefts?
                They are warriors heron-footed!
                Now they, too, are fading away.
                    A shimmering like rainbow-streamers
                Goes shooting through eyes and brain.
                What is it, that far-off chiming?
                What's weighing my eyebrows down?
                Hu, how my forehead's throbbing –
                A tightening red-hot ring – !
                I cannot think who the devil
                Has bound it around my head! [*sinks down*]
                    Flight o'er the Edge of Gendin –
                Stuff and accursed lies!
                Up o'er the steepest hill-wall
                With the bride – and a whole day drunk;
                Hunted by hawks and falcons,
                Threatened by trolls and such,

Sporting with crazy wenches –
Lies and accursed stuff!
[*gazes long upwards*] Yonder sail two brown eagles.
Southward the wild geese fly.
And here I must splash and stumble
In quagmire and filth knee-deep! [*springs up*]
    I'll fly too! I will wash myself clean in
The bath of the keenest winds!
I'll fly high! I will plunge myself fair in
The glorious christening-font!
I will soar far over the saeter;
I will ride myself pure of soul;
I will forth o'er the salt sea waters,
And high over Engelland's prince!
Ay, gaze as ye may, young maidens;
My ride is for none of you;
You're wasting your time in waiting – !
Yet maybe I'll swoop down, too. –
What has come of the two brown eagles – ?
They've vanished, the devil knows where! –
There's the peak of a gable rising;
It's soaring on every hand:
It's growing from out the ruins –
See, the gateway is standing wide!
Ha-ha, yonder house, I know it;
It's grandfather's new-built farm!
Gone are the clouts from the windows;
The crazy old fence is gone.
The lights gleam from every casement;
There's a feast in the hall tonight.
There, that was the provost clinking
The back of his knife on his glass –
There's the captain flinging his bottle,
And shivering the mirror to bits. –
Let them waste; let it all be squandered!
Peace, mother; what need we care!
'Tis the rich Jon Gynt gives the banquet;
Hurrah for the race of Gynt!
What's all this bustle and hubbub?

Why do they shout and bawl?
The captain is calling the son in –
Oh, the provost would drink my health.
In then, Peer Gynt, to the judgment;
It rings forth in song and shout:
Peer Gynt, thou art come of great things,
And great things shall come of thee!
[*leaps forward, but runs his head against a rock, falls, and
remains stretched on the ground*]

SCENE FIFTH

*A hillside, wooded with great soughing trees. Stars are gleaming
through the leaves; birds are singing in the tree-tops.*

    A GREEN-CLAD WOMAN *is crossing the hillside;* PEER GYNT
follows her, with all sorts of lover-like antics.

GREEN-CLAD ONE [*stops and turns round*] Is it true?
PEER [*drawing his finger across his throat*]
                                As true as my name is Peer –
    As true as that you are a lovely woman!
    Will you have me? You'll see what a fine man I'll be;
    You shall neither tread the loom nor turn the spindle.
    You shall eat all you want, till you're ready to burst.
    I never will drag you about by the hair –
GREEN-CLAD ONE Nor beat me?
PEER   No, can you think I would?
    We kings' sons never beat women and such.
GREEN-CLAD ONE You're a king's son?
PEER   Yes.
GREEN-CLAD ONE   I'm the Dovrë-King's daughter.
PEER   Are you? See there, now, how well that fits in!
GREEN-CLAD ONE Deep in the Rondë has father his palace.
PEER   My mother's is bigger, or much I'm mistaken.
GREEN-CLAD ONE Do you know my father? His name is
                                            King Brose.

PEER   Do you know my mother? Her name is Queen Åse.

GREEN-CLAD ONE When my father is angry the mountains
                                          are riven.

PEER   They reel when my mother by chance falls a-scolding.

GREEN-CLAD ONE My father can kick e'en the loftiest roof-tree.

PEER   My mother can ride through the rapidest river.

GREEN-CLAD ONE Have you other garments besides those rags?

PEER   Ho, you should just see my Sunday clothes!

GREEN-CLAD ONE My week-day gown is of gold and silk.

PEER   It looks to me liker tow and straws.

GREEN-CLAD ONE Ay, there is one thing you must remember –
         This is the Rondë-folk's use and wont:
         All our possessions have twofold form.
         When you shall come to my father's hall,
         It well may chance that you're on the point
         Of thinking you stand in a dismal moraine.

PEER   Well now, with us it's precisely the same.
         Our gold will seem to you litter and trash!
         And you'll think, mayhap, every glittering pane
         Is nought but a bunch of old stockings and clouts.

GREEN-CLAD ONE Black it seems white, and ugly seems fair.

PEER   Big it seems little, and dirty seems clean.

GREEN-CLAD ONE [falling on his neck]
         Ay, Peer, now I see that we fit, you and I!

PEER   Like the leg and the trouser, the hair and the comb.

GREEN-CLAD ONE [calls away over the hillside]
         Bridal-steed! Bridal-steed! Bridal-steed mine!
    [a gigantic pig comes running in with a rope's end for a bridle and an
    old sack for a saddle. Peer Gynt vaults on its back, and seats the
    Green-Clad One in front of him.]

PEER   Hark-away! Through the Rondë-gate gallop we in!
         Gee-up, gee-up, my courser fine!

GREEN-CLAD ONE [tenderly]
         Ah, but lately I wandered and moped and pined – .
         One never can tell what may happen to one!

PEER   [thrashing the pig and trotting off]
         You may know the great by their riding-gear!

SCENE SIXTH

The Royal Hall of the King of the Dovrë-Trolls. A great assembly of TROLL-COURTIERS, GNOMES, *and* BROWNIES. THE OLD MAN OF THE DOVRË *sits on the throne, crowned, and with his sceptre in his hand. His* CHILDREN *and* NEAREST RELATIONS *are ranged on both sides.* PEER GYNT *stands before him. Violent commotion in the hall.*

TROLL-COURTIERS Slay him! A Christian-man's son has deluded
 The Dovrë-King's loveliest maid!
A TROLL-IMP May I hack him on the fingers?
ANOTHER May I tug him by the hair?
A TROLL-MAIDEN Hu, hei, let me bite him in the haunches!
A TROLL-WITCH [*with a ladle*]
 Shall he be boiled into broth and bree?
ANOTHER TROLL-WITCH [*with a chopper*]
 Shall he roast on a spit or be browned in a stewpan?
OLD MAN OF THE DOVRË Ice to your blood, friends!
 [*beckons his counsellors nearer around him*] Don't let us talk big.
  We've been drifting astern in these latter years;
  We can't tell what's going to stand or to fall,
  And there's no sense in turning recruits away.
  Besides the lad's body has scarce a blemish,
  And he's strongly-built too, if I see aright.
  It's true, he has only a single head; but my daughter, too,
  Has no more than one. Three-headed trolls
  Are going clean out of fashion;
  One hardly sees even a two-header now,
  And even those heads are but so-so ones.
 [*to Peer Gynt*] It's my daughter, then, you demand of me?
PEER Your daughter and the realm to her dowry, yes.
THE OLD MAN You shall have the half while I'm still alive,
 And the other half when I come to die.
PEER I'm content with that.

THE OLD MAN   Ay, but stop, my lad –
    You also have some undertakings to give.
    If you break even one, the whole pact's at an end,
    And you'll never get away from here living.
    First of all you must swear that you'll never give heed
    To aught that lies outside Rondë-hills' bounds;
    Day you must shun, and deeds, and each sunlit spot.
PEER   Only call me king, and that's easy to keep.
THE OLD MAN And next – now for putting your wits to the test.
   [*draws himself up in his seat*]
OLDEST TROLL-COURTIER [*to Peer Gynt*]
    Let us see if you have a wisdom-tooth
    That can crack the Dovrë-King's riddle-nut!
THE OLD MAN What difference is there 'twixt trolls and men?
PEER   No difference at all, as it seems to me.
    Big trolls would roast you and small trolls would
                              claw you –
    With us it were likewise, if only they dared.
THE OLD MAN True enough; in that and in more we're alike.
    Yet morning is morning, and even is even,
    And there is a difference all the same. –
    Now let me tell you wherein it lies:
    Out yonder, under the shining vault,
    Among men the saying goes: 'Man, be thyself!'
    At home here with us, 'mid the tribe of the trolls,
    The saying goes: 'Troll, to thyself be – enough!'
TROLL-COURTIER [*to Peer Gynt*] Can you fathom the depth?
PEER   It strikes me as misty.
THE OLD MAN My son, that 'Enough', that most potent and
                                  sundering
    Word, must be graven upon your escutcheon.
PEER [*scratching his head*] Well, but –
THE OLD MAN   It must, if you here would be master!
PEER   Oh well, let it pass; after all, it's no worse –
THE OLD MAN And next you must learn to appreciate
    Our homely, everyday way of life.
   [*he beckons; two Trolls with pigs'-heads, white night-caps,*
   and so forth, bring in food and drink]
    The cow gives cakes and the bullock mead;

         Ask not if its taste be sour or sweet;
         The main matter is, and you mustn't forget it,
         It's all of it home-brewed.
PEER [*pushing the things away from him*]
         The devil fly off with your home-brewed drinks!
         I'll never get used to the ways of this land.
THE OLD MAN The bowl's given in, and it's fashioned of gold.
         Whoso owns the gold bowl, him my daughter holds dear.
PEER [*pondering*] It is written: Thou shalt bridle the natural man –
         And I dare say the drink may in time seem less sour.
         So be it! [*complies*]
THE OLD MAN   Ay, that was sagaciously said.
         You spit?
PEER   One must trust to the force of habit.
THE OLD MAN And next you must throw off your Christian-
                                                    man's garb;
         For this you must know to our Dovrë's renown:
         Here all things are mountain-made, nought's from
                                                    the dale,
         Except the silk bow at the end of your tail.
PEER [*indignant*] I haven't a tail!
THE OLD MAN   Then of course you must get one.
         See my Sunday-tail, Chamberlain, fastened to him.
PEER   I'll be hanged if you do! Would you make me a fool!
THE OLD MAN None comes courting my child with no tail
                                                    at his rear.
PEER   Make a beast of a man!
THE OLD MAN   Nay, my son, you mistake;
         I make you a mannerly wooer, no more.
         A bright orange bow we'll allow you to wear,
         And that passes here for the highest of honours.
PEER [*reflectively*] It's true, as the saying goes: Man's but a mote.
         And it's wisest to follow the fashion a bit.
         Tie away!
THE OLD MAN   You're a tractable fellow, I see.
THE COURTIER Just try with what grace you can waggle and
                                                    whisk it!
PEER [*peevishly*] Ha, would you force me to go still further?
         Do you ask me to give up my Christian faith?

THE OLD MAN No, that you are welcome to keep in peace.
        Doctrine goes free; upon that there's no duty;
        It's the outward cut one must tell a troll by.
        If we're only at one in our manners and dress,
        You may hold as your faith what to us is a horror.
PEER   Why, in spite of your many conditions, you are
        A more reasonable chap than one might have expected.
THE OLD MAN We troll-folk, my son, are less black than we're
                                       painted;
        That's another distinction between you and us. –
        But the serious part of the meeting is over;
        Now let us gladden our ears and our eyes.
        Music-maid, forth! Set the Dovrë-harp sounding!
        Dancing-maid, forth! Tread the Dovrë-hall's floor!
                [*music and a dance*]
THE COURTIER How like you it?
PEER   Like it? Hm –
THE OLD MAN   Speak without fear!
        What see you?
PEER   Why, something unspeakably grim:
        A bell-cow with her hoof on a gut-harp strumming,
        A sow in socklets a-trip to the tune.
THE COURTIERS Eat him!
THE OLD MAN   His sense is but human, remember!
TROLL-MAIDENS Hu, tear away both his ears and his eyes!
GREEN-CLAD ONE [*weeping*]
        Hu-hu! And this we must hear and put up with,
        When I and my sister make music and dance.
PEER   Oho, was it you? Well, a joke at the feast,
        You must know, is never unkindly meant.
GREEN-CLAD ONE Can you swear it was so?
PEER   Both the dance and the music
        Were utterly charming, the cat claw me else.
THE OLD MAN This same human nature's a singular thing;
        It sticks to people so strangely long.
        If it gets a gash in the fight with us,
        It heals up at once, though a scar may remain.
        My son-in-law, now, is as pliant as any;
        He's willingly thrown off his Christian-man's garb,

He's willingly drunk from our chalice of mead,
He's willingly tied on the tail to his back –
So willing, in short, did we find him in all things,
I thought to myself the old Adam, for certain,
Had for good and all been kicked out of doors;
But lo! in two shakes he's atop again!
Ay ay, my son, we must treat you, I see,
To cure this pestilent human nature.

PEER   What will you do?

THE OLD MAN In your left eye, first,
I'll scratch you a bit, till you see awry;
But all that you see will seem fine and brave.
And then I'll just cut your right window-pane out –

PEER   Are you drunk?

THE OLD MAN [lays a number of sharp instruments on the table]
                    See, here are the glazier's tools.
Blinkers you'll wear, like a raging bull.
Then you'll recognise that your bride is lovely –
And ne'er will your vision be troubled, as now,
With bell-cows harping and sows that dance.

PEER   This is madman's talk!

THE OLDEST COURTIER   It's the Dovrë-King speaking;
It's he that is wise, and it's you that are crazy!

THE OLD MAN Just think how much worry and mortification
You'll thus escape from, year out, year in.
You must remember, your eyes are the fountain
Of the bitter and searing lye of tears.

PEER   That's true; and it says in our sermon-book:
If thine eye offend thee, then pluck it out.
But tell me, when will my sight heal up
Into human sight?

THE OLD MAN   Nevermore, my friend.

PEER   Indeed! In that case, I'll take my leave.

THE OLD MAN What would you without?

PEER   I would go my way.

THE OLD MAN No, stop! It's easy to slip in here,
But the Dovrë-King's gate doesn't open outwards.

PEER   You wouldn't detain me by force, I hope?

THE OLD MAN Come now, just listen to reason, Prince Peer!

      You have gifts for trolldom. He acts, does he not,
      Even now in a passably troll-like fashion?
      And you'd fain be a troll?

PEER   Yes, I would, sure enough.
      For a bride and a well-managed kingdom to boot,
      I can put up with losing a good many things.
      But there is a limit to all things on earth.
      The tail I've accepted, it's perfectly true;
      But no doubt I can loose what the Chamberlain tied.
      My breeches I've dropped; they were old and patched;
      But no doubt I can button them on again.
      And lightly enough I can slip my cable
      From these your Dovrëfied ways of life.
      I am willing to swear that a cow is a maid;
      An oath one can always eat up again –
      But to know that one never can free oneself,
      That one can't even die like a decent soul;
      To live as a hill-troll for all one's days –
      To feel that one never can beat a retreat –
      As the book has it, that's what your heart is set on;
      But that is a thing I can never agree to.

THE OLD MAN Now, sure as I live, I shall soon lose my temper;
      And then I am not to be trifled with.
      You pasty-faced loon! Do you know who I am?
      First with my daughter you make too free –

PEER   There you lie in your throat!

THE OLD MAN   You must marry her.

PEER   Do you dare to accuse me – ?

THE OLD MAN   What? Can you deny
      That you lusted for her in heart and eye?

PEER [*with a snort of contempt*]
      No more! Who the deuce cares a straw for that?

THE OLD MAN It's ever the same with this humankind.
      The spirit you're ready to own with your lips,
      But in fact nothing counts that your fists cannot handle.
      So you really think, then, that lust matters nought?
      Wait; you shall soon have ocular proof of it –

PEER   You don't catch me with a bait of lies!

GREEN-CLAD ONE My Peer, ere the year's out, you'll be a father.

PEER   Open doors! let me go!
THE OLD MAN   In a he-goat's skin,
        You shall have the brat after you.
PEER [*mopping the sweat off his brow*]   Would I could waken!
THE OLD MAN Shall we send him to the palace?
PEER   You can send him to the parish!
THE OLD MAN Well well, Prince Peer; that's your own lookout.
        But one thing's certain, what's done is done;
        And your offspring, too, will be sure to grow;
        Such mongrels shoot up amazingly fast –
PEER   Old man, don't act like a headstrong ox!
        Hear reason, maiden! Let's come to terms.
        You must know I'm neither a prince nor rich –
        And whether you measure or whether you weigh me,
        Be sure you won't gain much by making me yours.
GREEN-CLAD ONE [*is taken ill, and is carried out by Troll-Maids*]
THE OLD MAN [*looks at him for a while in high disdain; then says*]
        Dash him to shards on the rock-walls, children!
TROLL-IMPS Oh dad, mayn't we play owl-and-eagle first!
        The wolf-game! Grey-mouse and glow-eyed cat!
THE OLD MAN Yes, but quick. I am worried and sleepy.
                                Good-night! [*he goes*]
PEER [*hunted by the Troll-Imps*] Let me be, devil's imps!
    [*tries to escape up the chimney*]
THE IMPS   Come brownies! Come nixies!
        Bite him behind!
PEER   Ow! [*tries to slip down the cellar trap-door*]
THE IMPS   Shut up all the crannies!
TROLL-COURTIER Now the small-fry are happy!
PEER [*struggling with a little imp that has bit himself fast to his ear*]
        Let go, will you, beast!
THE COURTIER [*hitting him across the fingers*]
        Gently, you scamp, with a scion of royalty!
PEER   A rat-hole – ! [*runs to it*]
THE IMPS   Be quick, Brother Nixie, and block it!
PEER   The old one was bad, but the youngsters are worse!
THE IMPS Slash him!
PEER   Oh, would I were small as a mouse! [*rushing around*]
THE IMPS [*swarming round him*] Close the ring! Close the ring!

PEER [*weeping*]　　　　　Would that I were a louse! [*he falls*]

THE IMPS Now into his eyes!

PEER [*buried in a heap of imps*]　Mother, help me, I die!

　[*church-bells sound far away*]

THE IMPS Bells in the mountain! The Black-Frock's cows!

　　　　　[*the Trolls take to flight, amid a confused uproar of yells and shrieks. The palace collapses; everything disappears.*]

SCENE SEVENTH

Pitch darkness. PEER GYNT is heard beating and slashing about him with a large bough.

PEER　Answer! Who are you?

A VOICE IN THE DARKNESS　　Myself.

PEER　　　　　　　　　　Clear the way!

THE VOICE Go roundabout, Peer! The hill's roomy enough.

PEER [*tries to force a passage at another place, but strikes against something*] Who are you?

THE VOICE　　　　　　Myself. Can you say the same?

PEER　I can say what I will; and my sword can smite!

　　Mind yourself! Hu, hei, now the blow falls crushing!

　　King Saul slew hundreds; Peer Gynt slew thousands!

　[*cutting and slashing*] Who are you?

THE VOICE　　　　　　Myself.

PEER　　　　　　　　　　That stupid reply

　　You may spare; it doesn't clear up the matter.

　　What are you?

THE VOICE　　　The great Boyg.

PEER　　　　　　　　　　Ah, indeed!

　　The riddle was black; now I'd call it grey.

　　Clear the way then, Boyg!

THE VOICE　　　　　　Go roundabout, Peer!

PEER　No, through! [*cuts and slashes*] There he fell!

　[*tries to advance, but strikes against something*]

　　　　　　　　　　Ho ho, are there more here?

THE VOICE The Boyg, Peer Gynt! the one only one.
      It's the Boyg that's unwounded, and the Boyg that
                                                    was hurt,
      It's the Boyg that is dead, and the Boyg that's alive.
PEER [*throws away the branch*]
      The weapon is troll-smeared; but I have my fists!
   [*fights his way forward*]
THE VOICE Ay, trust to your fists, lad, trust to your body.
      Hee-hee, Peer Gynt, so you'll reach the summit.
PEER [*falling back again*] Forward or back, and it's just as far –
      Out or in, and it's just as strait!
      He is there! And there! And he's round the bend!
      No sooner I'm out than I'm back in the ring. –
      Name who you are! Let me see you! What are you?
THE VOICE The Boyg.
PEER [*groping around*] Not dead, not living; all slimy; misty.
      Not so much as a shape! It's as bad as to battle
      In a cluster of snarling, half-wakened bears!
      [*screams*] Strike back at me, can't you!
THE VOICE   The Boyg isn't mad.
PEER   Strike!
THE VOICE   The Boyg strikes not.
PEER   Fight! You shall.
THE VOICE The great Boyg conquers, but does not fight.
PEER   Were there only a nixie here that could prick me!
      Were there only as much as a year-old troll!
      Only something to fight with. But here there is nothing –
      Now he's snoring! Boyg!
THE VOICE   What's your will?
PEER   Use force!
THE VOICE The great Boyg conquers in all things without it.
PEER [*biting his own arms and hands*]
      Claws and ravening teeth in my flesh!
      I must feel the drip of my own warm blood.
   [*a sound is heard like the wing-strokes of great birds*]
BIRD-CRIES Comes he now, Boyg?
THE VOICE   Ay, step by step.
BIRD-CRIES All our sisters far off! Gather here to the tryst!
PEER   If you'd save me now, lass, you must do it quick!

Gaze not adown so, lowly and bending. –
Your clasp-book! Hurl it straight into his eyes!
BIRD–CRIES He totters!
THE VOICE   We have him.
BIRD–CRIES   Sisters! Make haste!
PEER   Too dear the purchase one pays for life
In such a heart-wasting hour of strife. [*sinks down*]
BIRD–CRIES Boyg, there he's fallen! Seize him! Seize him!
[*a sound of bells and of psalm-singing is heard far away*]
THE BOYG [*shrinks up to nothing, and says in a gasp*]
He was too strong. There were women behind him.

SCENE EIGHTH

*Sunrise. The mountain-side in front of Åse's saeter. The door is
shut; all is silent and deserted.*
   PEER GYNT *is lying asleep by the wall of the saeter.*

PEER [*wakens, and looks about him with dull and heavy eyes. He spits*].
        What wouldn't I give for a pickled herring!
   [*spits again, and at the same moment catches sight of* HELGA,
   who appears carrying a basket of food]
        Ha, child, are you there? What is it you want?
HELGA It is Solveig –
PEER [*jumping up*]   Where is she?
HELGA   Behind the saeter.
SOLVEIG [*unseen*] If you come nearer, I'll run away!
PEER [*stopping short*] Perhaps you're afraid I might take you
                                    in my arms?
SOLVEIG For shame!
PEER   Do you know where I was last night? –
        Like a horse-fly the Dovrë-King's daughter is after me.
SOLVEIG Then it was well that the bells were set ringing.
        Peer Gynt's not the lad they can lure astray. –
        What do you say?
HELGA [*crying*]   Oh, she's running away! [*running after her*]
        Wait!

PEER [*catches her by the arm*] Look here, what I have in

                                     my pocket!

      A silver button, child! You shall have it –

      Only speak for me!

HELGA   Let me be; let me go!

PEER   There you have it.

HELGA   Let go; there's the basket of food.

PEER   God pity you if you don't – !

HELGA   Uf, how you scare me!

PEER [*gently; letting her go*]

      No, I only meant: beg her not to forget me!

                                     [*Helga runs off*]

ACT THIRD

SCENE FIRST

Deep in the pine-woods. Grey autumn weather. Snow is falling.
PEER GYNT *stands in his shirt-sleeves, felling timber.*

PEER [*hewing at a large fir-tree with twisted branches*]
      Oh ay, you are tough, you ancient churl;
      But it's all in vain, for you'll soon be down.
  [*hews at it again*]
      I see well enough you've a chain-mail shirt,
      But I'll hew it through, were it never so stout. –
      Ay, ay, you're shaking your twisted arms;
      You've reason enough for your spite and rage;
      But none the less you must bend the knee – !
  [*breaks off suddenly*]
      Lies! 'Tis an old tree, and nothing more.
      Lies! It was never a steel-clad churl;
      It's only a fir-tree with fissured bark. –
      It is heavy labour this hewing timber;
      But the devil and all when you hew and dream too. –
      I'll have done with it all – with this dwelling in mist,
      And, broad-awake, dreaming your senses away. –
      You're an outlaw, lad! You are banned to the woods.
  [*hews for a while rapidly*]
      Ay, an outlaw, ay. You've no mother now
      To spread your table and bring your food.
      If you'd eat, my lad, you must help yourself,
      Fetch your rations raw from the wood and stream,
      Split your own fir-roots and light your own fire,
      Bustle around, and arrange and prepare things.

Would you clothe yourself warmly, you must stalk
$\qquad\qquad\qquad$ your deer;
Would you found you a house, you must quarry
$\qquad\qquad\qquad$ the stones;
Would you build up its walls, you must fell the logs,
And shoulder them all to the building-place. –
[*his axe sinks down; he gazes straight in front of him*]
Brave shall the building be. Tower and vane
Shall rise from the roof-tree, high and fair.
And then I will carve, for the knob on the gable,
A mermaid, shaped like a fish from the navel.
Brass shall there be on the vane and the door-locks.
Glass I must see and get hold of too.
Strangers, passing, shall ask amazed
What that is glittering far on the hillside.
[*laughs angrily*] Devil's own lies! There they come again.
You're an outlaw, lad!
[*hewing vigorously*]$\qquad$ A bark-thatched hovel
Is shelter enough both in rain and frost.
[*looks up at the tree*]
Now he stands wavering. There; only a kick,
And he topples and measures his length on the ground –
The thick-swarming undergrowth shudders around him!
[*begins lopping the branches from the trunk; suddenly he listens,
and stands motionless with his axe in the air*]
There's someone after me! – Ay, are you that sort,
Old Hegstad-churl – would you play me false?
[*crouches behind the tree, and peeps over it*]
A lad! One only. He seems afraid.
He peers all round him. What's that he hides
'Neath his jacket? A sickle. He stops and looks around –
Now he lays his hand on a fence-rail flat.
What's this now? Why does he lean like that – ?
Ugh, ugh! Why, he's chopped his finger off!
A whole finger off! – He bleeds like an ox. –
Now he takes to his heels with his fist in a clout.
[*rises*] What a devil of a lad! An unmendable finger!
Right off! And with no one compelling him to it!
Ho, now I remember! It's only thus

You can 'scape from having to serve the King.
That's it. They wanted to send him soldiering,
And of course the lad didn't want to go. –
But to chop off – ? To sever for good and all – ?
Ay, think of it – wish it done – will it to boot –
But do it – ! No, that's past my understanding!
               [shakes his head a little; then goes on with his work]

SCENE SECOND

*A room in Åse's house. Everything in disorder; boxes standing
open; wearing apparel strewn around. A cat is lying on the bed.*

   ÅSE *and the* COTTAR'S WIFE *are hard at work packing things
together and putting them straight.*

ÅSE [*running to one side*] Kari, come here!
KARI   What now?
ÅSE [*on the other side*]   Come here – !
      Where is – ? Where shall I find – ? Tell me where – ?
      What am I seeking? I'm out of my wits!
      Where is the key of the chest?
KARI   In the key-hole.
ÅSE   What is that rumbling?
KARI   The last cart-load
      They're driving to Hegstad.
ÅSE [*weeping*]   How glad I'd be
      In the black chest myself to be driven away!
      Oh, what must a mortal abide and live through!
      God help me in mercy! The whole house is bare!
      What the Hegstad-churl left now the bailiff has taken.
      Not even the clothes on my back have they spared.
      Fie! Shame on them all that have judged so hardly!
      [*seats herself on the edge of the bed*]
      Both the land and the farm-place are lost to our line;
      The old man was hard, but the law was still harder –
      There was no one to help me, and none would show
                                                     mercy;

Peer was away; not a soul to give counsel.

KARI But here, in this house, you may dwell till you die.

ÅSE Ay, the cat and I live on charity.

KARI God help you, mother; your Peer's cost you dear.

ÅSE Peer? Why, you're out of your senses, sure!
      Ingrid came home none the worse in the end.
      The right thing had been to hold Satan to reckoning –
      He was the sinner, ay, he and none other;
      The ugly beast tempted my poor boy astray!

KARI Had I not better send word to the parson?
      Mayhap you're worse than you think you are.

ÅSE To the parson? Truly I almost think so.
   [starts up] But, oh God, I can't! I'm the boy's own mother;
      And help him I must; it's no more than my duty;
      I must do what I can when the rest forsake him.
      They've left him this coat; I must patch it up.
      I wish I dared snap up the fur-rug as well!
      What's come of the hose?

KARI   They are there, 'mid that rubbish.

ÅSE [rummaging about]
      Why, what have we here? I declare it's an old
      Casting-ladle, Kari! With this he would play
      Button-moulder, would melt, and then shape, and
                                        then stamp them.
      One day – there was company – in the boy came,
      And begged of his father a lump of tin.
      'No tin,' says Jon, 'but King Christian's coin;
      Silver; to show you're the son of Jon Gynt.'
      God pardon him, Jon; he was drunk, you see,
      And then he cared neither for tin nor for gold.
      Here are the hose. Oh, they're nothing but holes;
      They want darning, Kari!

KARI   Indeed but they do.

ÅSE When that is done, I must get to bed;
      I feel so broken, and frail, and ill –
   [joyfully] Two woollen-shirts, Kari – they've passed them by!

KARI So they have indeed.

ÅSE   It's a bit of luck.
      One of the two you may put aside;

Or rather, I think we'll e'en take them both –
The one he has on is so worn and thin.
KARI   But oh, Mother Åse, I fear it's a sin!
ÅSE   Maybe; but remember, the priest holds out
Pardon for this and our other sinnings.

SCENE THIRD

*In front of a settler's newly-built hut in the forest. A reindeer's
horns over the door. The snow is lying deep around. It is dusk.*
     PEER GYNT *is standing outside the door, fastening a large
wooden bar to it.*

PEER [*laughing betweenwhiles*]
Bars I must fix me; bars that can fasten
The door against troll-folk, and men, and women.
Bars I must fix me; bars that can shut out
All the cantankerous little hobgoblins. –
They come with the darkness, they knock and they rattle:
Open, Peer Gynt, we're as nimble as thoughts are!
'Neath the bedstead we bustle, we rake in the ashes,
Down the chimney we hustle like fiery-eyed dragons.
Hee-hee! Peer Gynt; think you staples and planks
Can shut out cantankerous hobgoblin-thoughts?

     SOLVEIG *comes on snow-shoes over the heath; she has a shawl
over her head, and a bundle in her hand*

SOLVEIG God prosper your labour. You must not reject me.
You sent for me hither, and so you must take me.
PEER Solveig! It cannot be – ! Ay, but it is!
And you're not afraid to come near to me!
SOLVEIG One message you sent me by little Helga;
Others came after in storm and in stillness.
All that your mother told bore me a message,
That brought forth others when dreams sank upon me.
Nights full of heaviness, blank, empty days,
Brought me the message that now I must come.

It seemed as though life had been quenched down there;
I could nor laugh nor weep from the depths of my heart.
I knew not for sure how you might be minded;
I knew but for sure what I should do and must do.

PEER But your father?

SOLVEIG In all of God's wide earth
I have none I can call either father or mother.
I have loosed me from all of them.

PEER Solveig, you fair one –
And to come to me?

SOLVEIG Ay, to you alone;
You must be all to me, friend and consoler.
[*in tears*] The worst was leaving my little sister –
But parting from father was worse, still worse;
And worst to leave her at whose breast I was borne –
Oh no, God forgive me, the worst I must call
The sorrow of leaving them all, ay all!

PEER And you know the doom that was passed in spring?
It forfeits my farm and my heritage.

SOLVEIG Think you for heritage, goods, and gear,
I forsook the paths all my dear ones tread?

PEER And know you the compact? Outside the forest
Whoever may meet me may seize me at will.

SOLVEIG I ran upon snow-shoes; I asked my way on;
They said 'Whither go you?' I answered, 'I go home.'

PEER Away, away then with nails and planks!
No need now for bars against hobgoblin-thoughts.
If you dare dwell with the hunter here,
I know the hut will be blessed from ill.
Solveig! Let me look at you! Not too near!
Only look at you! Oh, but you are bright and pure!
Let me lift you! Oh, but you are fine and light!
Let me carry you, Solveig, and I'll never be tired!
I will not soil you. With outstretched arms
I will hold you far out from me, lovely and warm one!
Oh, who would have thought I could draw you to me –
Ah, but I have longed for you, daylong and nightlong.
Here you may see I've been hewing and building –
It must down again, dear; it is ugly and mean –

SOLVEIG Be it mean or brave – here is all to my mind.
          One so lightly draws breath in the teeth of the wind.
          Down below it was airless; one felt as though choked;
          That was partly what drove me in fear from the dale.
          But here, with the fir-branches soughing o'erhead –
          What a stillness and song! – I am here in my home.
PEER   And know you that surely? For all your days?
SOLVEIG The path I have trodden leads back nevermore.
PEER   You are mine then! In! In the room let me see you!
          Go in! I must go to fetch fir-roots for fuel.
          Warm shall the fire be and bright shall it shine,
          You shall sit softly and never be a-cold.
    [*he opens the door; Solveig goes in. He stands still for a while,
    then laughs aloud with joy and leaps into the air*]
PEER   My king's daughter! Now I have found her and won her!
          Hei! Now the palace shall rise, deeply founded!
                                    [*he seizes his axe and moves away*]

    At the same moment an OLD-LOOKING WOMAN, *in a tattered
    green gown, comes out from the wood; an* UGLY BRAT, *with an
    ale-flagon in his hand, limps after, holding on to her skirt*

THE WOMAN Good evening, Peer Lightfoot!
PEER   What is it? Who's there?
THE WOMAN Old friends of yours, Peer Gynt! My home
                                                    is near by.
          We are neighbours.
PEER   Indeed? That is more than I know.
THE WOMAN Even as your hut was builded, mine built itself too.
PEER [*going*] I'm in haste –
THE WOMAN   Yes, that you are always, my lad;
          But I'll trudge behind you and catch you at last.
PEER You're mistaken, good woman!
THE WOMAN   I was so before;
          I was when you promised such mighty fine things.
PEER I promised – ? What devil's own nonsense is this?
THE WOMAN You've forgotten the night when you drank
                                                    with my sire?
          You've forgot – ?
PEER   I've forgot what I never have known.

What's this that you prate of? When last did we meet?
THE WOMAN When last we met was when first we met.
   [to the Brat] Give your father a drink; he is thirsty, I'm sure.
PEER   Father? You're drunk, woman! Do you call him – ?
THE WOMAN I should think you might well know the pig
                                             by its skin!
      Why, where are your eyes? Can't you see that he's lame
      In his shank, just as you too are lame in your soul?
PEER   Would you have me believe – ?
THE WOMAN   Would you wriggle away – ?
PEER   This long-legged urchin – !
THE WOMAN   He's shot up apace.
PEER   Dare you, you troll-snout, father on me – ?
THE WOMAN Come now, Peer Gynt, you're as rude as an ox!
   [weeping] Is it my fault if no longer I'm fair,
      As I was when you lured me on hillside and lea?
      Last fall, in my labour, the Fiend held my back,
      And so 'twas no wonder I came out a fright.
      But if you would see me as fair as before,
      You have only to turn yonder girl out of doors,
      Drive her clean out of your sight and your mind –
      Do but this, dear my love, and I'll soon lose my snout!
PEER   Begone from me, troll-witch!
THE WOMAN   Ay, see if I do!
PEER   I'll split your skull open – !
THE WOMAN   Just try if you dare!
      Ho-ho, Peer Gynt, I've no fear of blows!
      Be sure I'll return every day of the year.
      I'll set the door ajar and peep in at you both.
      When you're sitting with your girl on the fireside bench –
      When you're tender, Peer Gynt – when you'd pet
                                             and caress her –
      I'll seat myself by you, and ask for my share.
      She there and I – we will take you by turns.
      Farewell, dear my lad, you can marry tomorrow!
PEER   You nightmare of hell!
THE WOMAN   By-the-bye, I forgot!
      You must rear your own youngster, you light-footed
                                             scamp!

Little imp, will you go to your father?
THE BRAT. [*spits at him*]   Faugh!
        I'll chop you with my hatchet; only wait, only wait!
THE WOMAN [*kisses the Brat*]
        What a head he has got on his shoulders, the dear!
        You'll be father's living image when once you're a man!
PEER [*stamping*] Oh, would you were as far – !
THE WOMAN   As we now are near?
PEER [*clenching his hands*] And all this – !
THE WOMAN   For nothing but thoughts and desires!
        It is hard on you, Peer!
PEER   It is worst for another! –
        Solveig, my fairest, my purest gold!
THE WOMAN Oh ay, 'tis the guiltless must smart, said the devil;
        His mother boxed his ears when his father was drunk!
                          [*she trudges off into the thicket with the
                          Brat, who throws the flagon at Peer Gynt*]
PEER [*after a long silence*]
        The Boyg said, 'Go roundabout!' – so one must here. –
        There fell my fine palace, with crash and clatter!
        There's a wall around her whom I stood so near,
        Of a sudden all's ugly – my joy has grown old. –
        Roundabout, lad! There's no way to be found
        Right through all this from where you stand to her.
        Right through? Hm, surely there should be one.
        There's a text on repentance, unless I mistake.
        But what? What is it? I haven't the book,
        I've forgotten it mostly, and here there is none
        That can guide me aright in the pathless wood. –
            Repentance? And maybe 'twould take whole years,
        Ere I fought my way through. 'Twere a meagre life, that.
        To shatter what's radiant, and lovely, and pure,
        And clinch it together in fragments and shards?
        You can do it with a fiddle, but not with a bell.
        Where you'd have the sward green, you must mind
                                          not to trample.
        'Twas nought but a lie though, that witch-snout business!
        Now all that foulness is well out of sight. –
        Ay, out of sight maybe, not out of mind.

Thoughts will sneak stealthily in at my heel.
Ingrid! And the three, they that danced on the heights!
Will they too want to join us? With vixenish spite
Will they claim to be folded, like her, to my breast,
To be tenderly lifted on outstretched arms?
Roundabout, lad; though my arms were as long
As the root of the fir, or the pine-tree's stem –
I think even then I should hold her too near,
To set her down pure and untarnished again. –
I must roundabout here, then, as best I may,
And see that it bring me nor gain nor loss.
One must put such things from one, and try to forget. –
[*goes a few steps towards the hut, but stops again*]
Go in after this? So befouled and disgraced?
Go in with that troll-rabble after me still?
Speak, yet be silent; confess, yet conceal – ?
[*throws away his axe*]
It's holy-day evening. For me to keep tryst,
Such as now I am, would be sacrilege.
SOLVEIG [*in the doorway*] Are you coming?
PEER [*half aloud*]   Roundabout!
SOLVEIG   What?
PEER   You must wait.
It is dark, and I've got something heavy to fetch.
SOLVEIG Wait; I will help you; the burden we'll share.
PEER   No, stay where you are! I must bear it alone.
SOLVEIG But don't go too far, dear!
PEER   Be patient, my girl;
Be my way long or short – you must wait.
SOLVEIG [*nodding to him as he goes*]   Yes, I'll wait!
                    [*Peer Gynt goes down the wood-path*]
SOLVEIG [*remains standing in the open half-door*]

SCENE FOURTH

Åse's room. Evening. The room is lighted by a wood fire on the open hearth. A cat is lying on a chair at the foot of the bed.

ÅSE lies in the bed, fumbling about restlessly with her hands on the coverlet.

ÅSE   Oh, Lord my God, isn't he coming?
                   The time drags so drearily on.
             I have no one to send with a message;
                   And I've much, oh so much, to say.
             I haven't a moment to lose now!
                   So quickly! Who could have foreseen!
             Oh me, if I only were certain
                   I'd not been too strict with him!

PEER GYNT [*enters*] Good evening!

ÅSE   The Lord give you gladness!
                   You've come then, my boy, my dear!
             But how dare you show face in the valley?
                   You know your life's forfeit here.

PEER   Oh, life must e'en go as it may go;
                   I felt that I must look in.

ÅSE   Ay, now Kari is put to silence,
                   And I can depart in peace!

PEER   Depart? Why, what are you saying?
                   Where is it you think to go?

ÅSE   Alas, Peer, the end is nearing;
                   I have but a short time left.

PEER [*writhing, and walking towards the back of the room*]
                   See there now! I'm fleeing from trouble;
                       I thought at least here I'd be free – !
                   Are your hands and your feet a-cold, then?

ÅSE   Ay, Peer; all will soon be o'er. –
                   When you see that my eyes are glazing,
                       You must close them carefully.

And then you must see to my coffin;
    And be sure it's a fine one, dear.
Ah no, by-the-bye –

PEER   Be quiet!
    There's time yet to think of that.

ÅSE   Ay, ay. [*looks restlessly around the room*]
            Here you see the little
    They've left us! It's like them, just.

PEER [*with a writhe*]

        Again! [*harshly*] Well, I know it was my fault.
           What's the use of reminding me?

ÅSE   You! No, that accursed liquor,
          From that all the mischief came!
    Dear my boy, you know you'd been drinking;
         And then no one knows what he does;
    And besides, you'd been riding the reindeer;
         No wonder your head was turned!

PEER   Ay, ay; of that yarn enough now.
         Enough of the whole affair.
    All that's heavy we'll let stand over
        Till after – some other day.

   [*sits on the edge of the bed*]

        Now, mother, we'll chat together;
          But only of this and that –
    Forget what's awry and crooked,
         And all that is sharp and sore. –
    Why see now, the same old pussy;
         So she is alive then, still?

ÅSE   She makes such a noise o' nights now;
         You know what that bodes, my boy!

PEER [*changing the subject*] What news is there here in the parish?

ÅSE [*smiling*]   There's somewhere about, they say,
         A girl who would fain to the uplands –

PEER [*hastily*]   Mads Moen, is he content?

ÅSE   They say that she hears and heeds not
         The old people's prayers and tears.
    You ought to look in and see them –
         You, Peer, might perhaps bring help –

PEER   The smith, what's become of him now?

ÅSE   Don't talk of that filthy smith.
                Her name I would rather tell you,
                    The name of the girl, you know –

PEER   No, now we will chat together,
                    But only of this and that –
                Forget what's awry and crooked,
                    And all that is sharp and sore.
                Are you thirsty? I'll fetch you water.
                    Can you stretch you? The bed is short.
                Let me see – if I don't believe, now,
                    It's the bed that I had when a boy!
                Do you mind, dear, how oft in the evenings
                    You sat at my bedside here,
                And spread the fur-coverlet o'er me,
                    And sang many a lilt and lay?

ÅSE   Ay, mind you? And then we played sledges
                    When your father was far abroad.
                The coverlet served for sledge-apron,
                    And the floor for an ice-bound fiord.

PEER   Ah, but the best of all, though –
                    Mother, you mind that too? –
                The best was the fleet-foot horses –

ÅSE   Ay, think you that I've forgot? –
                It was Kari's cat that we borrowed;
                    It sat on the log-scooped chair –

PEER   To the castle west of the moon,
                    And the castle east of the sun,
                To Soria-Moria Castle
                    The road ran both high and low.
                A stick that we found in the closet,
                    For a whip-shaft you made it serve.

ÅSE   Right proudly I perked on the box-seat –

PEER   Ay, ay; you threw loose the reins,
                And kept turning round as we travelled,
                    And asked me if I was cold.
                God bless you, ugly old mother –
                    You were ever a kindly soul – !
                What's hurting you now?

ÅSE   My back aches,

	Because of the hard, bare boards.
PEER	Stretch yourself; I'll support you.
	There now, you're lying soft.
ÅSE *[uneasily]*	No, Peer, I'd be moving!
PEER	Moving?
ÅSE	Ay, moving; 'tis ever my wish.
PEER	Oh, nonsense! Spread o'er you the bed-fur.
	Let me sit at your bedside here.
	There; now we'll shorten the evening
	With many a lilt and lay.
ÅSE	Best bring from the closet the prayer-book:
	I feel so uneasy of soul.
PEER	In Soria-Moria Castle
	The King and the Prince give a feast.
	On the sledge-cushions lie and rest you;
	I'll drive you there over the heath —
ÅSE	But, Peer dear, am I invited?
PEER	Ay, that we are, both of us.

[he throws a string round the back of the chair on which the cat is lying, takes up a stick, and seats himself at the foot of the bed]

	Gee-up! Will you stir yourself, Black-boy?
	Mother, you're not a-cold?
	Ay, ay; by the pace one knows it,
	When Grane begins to go!
ÅSE	Why, Peer, what is it that's ringing — ?
PEER	The glittering sledge-bells, dear!
ÅSE	Oh, mercy, how hollow it's rumbling!
PEER	We're just driving over a fiord.
ÅSE	I'm afraid! What is that I hear rushing
	And sighing so strange and wild?
PEER	It's the sough of the pine-trees, mother,
	On the heath. Do you but sit still.
ÅSE	There's a sparkling and gleaming afar now;
	Whence comes all that blaze of light?
PEER	From the castle's windows and doorways.
	Don't you hear, they are dancing?
ÅSE	Yes.
PEER	Outside the door stands Saint Peter,
	And prays you to enter in.

ÅSE   Does he greet us?
PEER   He does, with honor,
           And pours out the sweetest wine.
ÅSE   Wine! Has he cakes as well, Peer?
PEER   Cakes? Ay, a heaped-up dish.
           And the dean's wife is getting ready
               Your coffee and your dessert.
ÅSE   Oh, Christ; shall we two come together?
PEER   As freely as ever you will.
ÅSE   Oh, deary, Peer, what a frolic
               You're driving me to, poor soul!
PEER [*cracking his whip*]
               Gee-up; will you stir yourself, Black-boy!
ÅSE   Peer, dear, you're driving right?
PEER [*cracking his whip again*] Ay, broad is the way.
ÅSE   This journey,
               It makes me so weak and tired.
PEER   There's the castle rising before us;
               The drive will be over soon.
ÅSE   I will lie back and close my eyes then,
               And trust me to you, my boy!
PEER   Come up with you, Grane, my trotter!
               In the castle the throng is great;
           They bustle and swarm to the gateway.
               Peer Gynt and his mother are here!
           What say you, Master Saint Peter?
               Shall mother not enter in?
           You may search a long time, I tell you,
               Ere you find such an honest old soul.
           Myself I don't want to speak of;
               I can turn at the castle gate.
           If you'll treat me, I'll take it kindly;
               If not, I'll go off just as pleased.
           I have made up as many flim-flams
               As the devil at the pulpit-desk,
           And called my old mother a hen, too,
               Because she would cackle and crow.
           But her you shall honour and reverence,
               And make her at home indeed;

There comes not a soul to beat her
    From the parishes nowadays. –
Ho-ho; here comes God the Father!
    Saint Peter! you're in for it now!
[*in a deep voice*]
    'Have done with these jack-in-office airs, sir;
    Mother Åse shall enter free!'
[*laughs loudly, and turns towards his mother*]
    Ay, didn't I know what would happen?
    Now they dance to another tune!
[*uneasily*] Why, what makes your eyes so glassy?
    Mother! Have you gone out of your wits – ?
[*goes to the head of the bed*]
    You mustn't lie there and stare so – !
    Speak, mother; it's I, your boy!
[*feels her forehead and hands cautiously; then throws the
string on the chair, and says softly*]
    Ay, ay! – You can rest yourself, Grane;
    For even now the journey's done.
[*closes her eyes, and bends over her*]
    For all of your days I thank you,
    For beatings and lullabies! –
    But see, you must thank me back, now –
[*presses his cheek against her mouth*]
    There; that was the driver's fare.

THE COTTAR'S WIFE [*entering*]
    What? Peer! Ah, then we are over
    The worst of the sorrow and need!
    Dear Lord, but she's sleeping soundly –
    Or can she be – ?

PEER   Hush; she is dead.
[*Kari weeps beside the body; Peer Gynt walks up and down
the room for some time; at last he stops beside the bed*]

PEER   See mother buried with honour.
    I must try to fare forth from here.

KARI   Are you faring afar?

PEER   To seaward.

KARI   So far!

PEER   Ay, and further still.
                                 [*he goes.*

ACT FOURTH

SCENE FIRST

On the south-west coast of Morocco. A palm-grove. Under an awning, on ground covered with matting, a table spread for dinner. Further back in the grove hammocks are slung. In the offing lies a steam-yacht, flying the Norwegian and American colours. A jolly-boat drawn up on the beach. It is towards sunset.

    PEER GYNT, *a handsome middle-aged gentleman, in an elegant travelling-dress, with a gold-rimmed double eyeglass hanging at his waistcoat, is doing the honours at the head of the table.* MR COTTON, MONSIEUR BALLON, HERR VON EBERKOPF, *and* HERR TRUMPETERSTRALE, *are seated at the table finishing dinner.*

PEER GYNT   Drink, gentlemen! If man is made
             For pleasure, let him take his fill then.
             You know 'tis written: Lost is lost,
             And gone is gone – . What may I hand you?

TRUMPETERSTRALE As host you're princely, Brother Gynt!

PEER   I share the honour with my cash,
             With cook and steward –

MR COTTON   Very well;
             Let's pledge a toast to all the four!

MONSIEUR BALLON Monsieur, you have a *goût*, a *ton*
             That nowadays is seldom met with
             Among men living *en garçon* –
             A certain – what's the word – ?

VON EBERKOPF   A dash,
             A tinge of free soul-contemplation,
             And cosmopolitanisation,
             An outlook through the cloudy rifts

                    By narrow prejudice unhemmed,
                    A stamp of high illumination,
                    An *Ur-Natur*, with lore of life,
                    To crown the trilogy, united.
                    Nicht wahr, Monsieur, 'twas that you meant?
MONSIEUR BALLON Yes, very possibly; not quite
                    So loftily it sounds in French.
VON EBERKOPF *Ei was*! That language is so stiff. –
                    But the phenomenon's final cause
                    If we would seek –
PEER   It's found already.
                    The reason is that I'm unmarried.
                    Yes, gentlemen, completely clear
                    The matter is. What should a man be?
                    Himself, is my concise reply.
                    He should regard himself and his.
                    But can he, as a sumpter-mule
                    For others' woe and others' weal?
VON EBERKOPF But this same in-and-for-yourself-ness,
                    I'll answer for't, has cost you strife –
PEER   Ay yes, indeed; in former days;
                    But always I came off with honour.
                    Yet one time I ran very near
                    To being trapped against my will.
                    I was a brisk and handsome lad,
                    And she to whom my heart was given,
                    She was of royal family –
MONSIEUR BALLON Of royal – ?
PEER [*carelessly*]   One of those old stocks,
                    You know the kind –
TRUMPETERSTRALE [*thumping the table*] Those noble-trolls!
PEER [*shrugging his shoulders*] Old fossil Highnesses who make it
                    Their pride to keep plebeian blots
                    Excluded from their line's escutcheon.
MR COTTON Then nothing came of the affair?
MONSIEUR BALLON The family opposed the marriage?
PEER   Far from it!
MONSIEUR BALLON   Ah!
PEER [*with forbearance*]   You understand

That certain circumstances made for
Their marrying us without delay.
But, truth to tell, the whole affair
Was, first to last, distasteful to me.
I'm finical in certain ways,
And like to stand on my own feet.
And when my father-in-law came out
With delicately veiled demands
That I should change my name and station,
And undergo ennoblement,
With much else that was most distasteful,
Not to say quite inacceptable –
Why then I gracefully withdrew,
Point-blank declined his ultimatum –
And so renounced my youthful bride.

[*drums on the table with a devout air*]

Yes, yes; there is a ruling Fate!
On that we mortals may rely;
And 'tis a comfortable knowledge.

MONSIEUR BALLON And so the matter ended, eh?

PEER   Oh no, far otherwise I found it;
For busy-bodies mixed themselves,
With furious outcries, in the business.
The juniors of the clan were worst;
With seven of them I fought a duel.
That time I never shall forget,
Though I came through it all in safety.
It cost me blood; but that same blood
Attests the value of my person,
And points encouragingly towards
The wise control of Fate aforesaid.

VON EBERKOPF Your outlook on the course of life
Exalts you to the rank of thinker.
Whilst the mere commonplace empiric
Sees separately the scattered scenes,
And to the last goes groping on,
You in one glance can focus all things.
One norm to all things you apply.
You point each random rule of life,

               Till one and all diverge like rays
               From one full-orbed philosophy. —
               And you have never been to college?
PEER   I am, as I've already said,
               Exclusively a self-taught man.
               Methodically naught I've learned;
               But I have thought and speculated,
               And done much desultory reading.
               I started somewhat late in life,
               And then, you know, it's rather hard
               To plough ahead through page on page,
               And take in all of everything.
               I've done my history piecemeal;
               I never have had time for more.
               And, as one needs in days of trial
               Some certainty to place one's trust in,
               I took religion intermittently.
               That way it goes more smoothly down.
               One should not read to swallow all,
               But rather see what one has use for.
MR COTTON Ay, that is practical!
PEER [lights a cigar]   Dear friends,
               Just think of my career in general.
               In what case came I to the West?
               A poor young fellow, empty-handed.
               I had to battle sore for bread;
               Trust me, I often found it hard.
               But life, my friends, ah, life is dear,
               And, as the phrase goes, death is bitter.
               Well! Luck, you see, was kind to me;
               Old Fate, too, was accommodating.
               I prospered; and, by versatility,
               I prospered better still and better.
               In ten years' time I bore the name
               Of Croesus 'mongst the Charleston shippers.
               My fame flew wide from port to port,
               And fortune sailed on board my vessels —
MR COTTON What did you trade in?
PEER   I did most

In Negro slaves for Carolina,
And idol-images for China.

MONSIEUR BALLON *Fi donc!*

TRUMPETERSTRALE   The devil, Uncle Gynt!

PEER   You think, no doubt, the business hovered
On the outer verge of the allowable?
Myself I felt the same thing keenly.
It struck me even as odious.
But, trust me, when you've once begun,
It's hard to break away again.
At any rate it's no light thing,
In such a vast trade-enterprise,
That keeps whole thousands in employ,
To break off wholly, once for all.
That 'once for all' I can't abide,
But own, upon the other side,
That I have always felt respect
For what are known as consequences;
And that to overstep the bounds
Has ever somewhat daunted me.
Besides, I had begun to age,
Was getting on towards the fifties –
My hair was slowly growing grizzled;
And, though my health was excellent,
Yet painfully the thought beset me:
Who knows how soon the hour may strike,
The jury-verdict be delivered
That parts the sheep and goats asunder?
What could I do? To stop the trade
With China was impossible.
A plan I hit on – opened straightway
A new trade with the self-same land.
I shipped off idols every spring,
Each autumn sent forth missionaries,
Supplying them with all they needed,
As stockings, Bibles, rum, and rice –

MR COTTON Yes, at a profit?

PEER   Why, of course.
It prospered. Dauntlessly they toiled.

For every idol that was sold
They got a coolie well baptised,
So that the effect was neutralised.
The mission-field lay never fallow,
For still the idol-propaganda
The missionaries held in check.
MR COTTON Well, but the African commodities?
PEER   There, too, my ethics won the day.
I saw the traffic was a wrong one
For people of a certain age.
One may drop off before one dreams of it.
And then there were the thousand pitfalls
Laid by the philanthropic camp;
Besides, of course, the hostile cruisers,
And all the wind-and-weather risks.
All this together won the day.
I thought: Now, Peter, reef your sails;
See to it you amend your faults!
So in the South I bought some land,
And kept the last meat-importation,
Which chanced to be a superfine one.
They throve so, grew so fat and sleek,
That 'twas a joy to me, and them too.
Yes, without boasting, I may say
I acted as a father to them –
And found my profit in so doing.
I built them schools, too, so that virtue
Might uniformly be maintained
At a certain general *niveau*,
And kept strict watch that never its
Thermometer should sink below it.
Now, furthermore, from all this business
I've beat a definite retreat –
I've sold the whole plantation, and its
Tale of live-stock, hide and hair.
At parting, too, I served around,
To big and little, gratis grog,
So men and women all got drunk,
And widows got their snuff as well.

So that is why I trust – provided
The saying is not idle breath:
Whoso does not do ill, does good –
My former errors are forgotten,
And I, much more than most, can hold
My misdeeds balanced by my virtues.

VON EBERKOPF [*clinking glasses with him*]

How strengthening it is to hear
A principle thus acted out,
Freed from the night of theory,
Unshaken by the outward ferment!

PEER [*who has been drinking freely during the preceding passages*]

We Northland men know how to carry
Our battle through! The key to the art
Of life's affairs is simply this:
To keep one's ear close shut against
The ingress of one dangerous viper.

MR COTTON   What sort of viper, pray, dear friend?

PEER   A little one that slyly wiles you
To tempt the irretrievable.

[*drinking again*] The essence of the art of daring,
The art of bravery in act,
Is this: to stand with choice-free foot
Amid the treacherous snares of life –
To know for sure that other days
Remain beyond the day of battle –
To know that ever in the rear
A bridge for your retreat stands open.
This theory has borne me on,
Has given my whole career its colour;
And this same theory I inherit,
A race-gift, from my childhood's home.

MONSIEUR BALLON You are Norwegian?

PEER   Yes, by birth;
But cosmopolitan in spirit.
For fortune such as I've enjoyed
I have to thank America.
My amply-furnished library
I owe to Germany's later schools.

From France, again, I get my waistcoats,
My manners, and my spice of wit –
From England an industrious hand,
And keen sense for my own advantage.
The Jew has taught me how to wait.
Some taste for *dolce far niente*
I have received from Italy –
And one time, in a perilous pass,
To eke the measure of my days,
I had recourse to Swedish steel.

TRUMPETERSTRALE [*lifting up his glass*]
    Ay, Swedish steel – ?

VON EBERKOPF   The weapon's wielder
    Demands our homage first of all!
   [*They clink glasses and drink with him. The wine begins
   to go to his head*]

MR COTTON All this is very good indeed –
    But, sir, I'm curious to know
    What with your gold you think of doing.

PEER [*smiling*] H'm, doing? Eh?

ALL FOUR [*coming closer*]   Yes, let us hear!

PEER   Well, first of all, I want to travel.
    You see, that's why I shipped you four,
    To keep me company, at Gibraltar.
    I needed such a dancing-choir
    Of friends around my gold-calf-altar –

VON EBERKOPF Most witty!

MR COTTON   Well, but no one hoists
    His sails for nothing but the sailing.
    Beyond all doubt, you have a goal;
    And that is – ?

PEER   To be Emperor.

ALL FOUR   What?

PEER [*nodding*]   Emperor!

THE FOUR.   Where?

PEER   O'er all the world.

MONSIEUR BALLON But how, friend – ?

PEER   By the might of gold!
    That plan is not at all a new one;

It's been the soul of my career.
Even as a boy, I swept in dreams
Far o'er the ocean on a cloud.
I soared with train and golden scabbard –
And flopped down on all-fours again.
But still my goal, my friends, stood fast. –
There is a text, or else a saying,
Somewhere, I don't remember where,
That if you gained the whole wide world,
But lost yourself, your gain were but
A garland on a cloven skull.
That is the text – or something like it;
And that remark is sober truth.

VON EBERKOPF But what then is the Gyntish Self?

PEER   The world behind my forehead's arch,
            In force of which I'm no one else
            Than I, no more than God's the Devil.

TRUMPETERSTRALE I understand now where you're aiming!

MONSIEUR BALLON Thinker sublime!

VON EBERKOPF   Exalted poet!

PEER [*more and more elevated*] The Gyntish Self – it is the host
            Of wishes, appetites, desires –
            The Gyntish Self, it is the sea
            Of fancies, exigencies, claims,
            All that, in short, makes my breast heave,
            And whereby I, as I, exist.
            But as our Lord requires the clay
            To constitute him God o' the world,
            So I, too, stand in need of gold,
            If I as Emperor would figure.

MONSIEUR BALLON You have the gold, though!

PEER   Not enough.
            Ay, maybe for a nine-days' flourish,
            As Emperor *à la* Lippe-Detmold.
            But I must be myself *en bloc*,
            Must be the Gynt of all the planet,
            Sir Gynt throughout, from top to toe!

MONSIEUR BALLON [*enraptured*]
            Possess the earth's most exquisite beauty!

VON EBERKOPF All century-old Johannisberger!

TRUMPETERSTRALE And all the blades of Charles the Twelfth!

MR COTTON But first a profitable opening
                      For business –

PEER   That's already found;
                      Our anchoring here supplied me with it.
                      Tonight we set off northward ho!
                      The papers I received on board
                      Have brought me tidings of importance – !
         [rises with uplifted glass]
                      It seems that Fortune ceaselessly
                      Aids him who has the pluck to seize it –

THE GUESTS Well? Tell us – !

PEER   Greece is in revolt.

ALL FOUR [springing up] What! Greece – ?

PEER   The Greeks have risen in Hellas.

THE FOUR   Hurrah!

PEER   And Turkey's in a fix! [empties his glass]

MONSIEUR BALLON To Hellas! Glory's gate stands open!
                      I'll help them with the sword of France!

VON EBERKOPF And I with war-whoops – from a distance!

MR COTTON And I as well – by taking contracts!

TRUMPETERSTRALE Lead on! I'll find again in Bender
                      The world-renowned spur-strap-buckles!

MONSIEUR BALLON [falling on Peer Gynt's neck]
                      Forgive me, friend, that I at first
                      Misjudged you quite!

VON EBERKOPF [pressing his hands]   I, stupid hound,
                      Took you for next door to a scoundrel!

MR COTTON Too strong that; only for a fool –

TRUMPETERSTRALE [trying to kiss him]
                      I, Uncle, for a specimen
                      Of Yankee riff-raff's meanest spawn – !
                      Forgive me – !

VON EBERKOPF   We've been in the dark –

PEER   What stuff is this?

VON EBERKOPF   We now see gathered
                      In glory all the Gyntish host
                      Of wishes, appetites, and desires – !

MONSIEUR BALLON [*admiringly*] So this is being Monsieur Gynt!

VON EBERKOPF [*in the same tone*]
                    This I call being Gynt with honour!

PEER   But tell me – ?

MONSIEUR BALLON   Don't you understand?

PEER   May I be hanged if I begin to!

MONSIEUR BALLON What? Are you not upon your way
                    To join the Greeks, with ship and money – ?

PEER [*contemptuously*] No, many thanks! I side with strength,
                    And lend my money to the Turks.

MONSIEUR BALLON Impossible!

VON EBERKOPF   Witty, but a jest!

PEER   [*after a short silence, leaning on a chair and assuming
            a dignified mien*] Come, gentlemen, I think it best
                    We part before the last remains
                    Of friendship melt away like smoke.
                    Who nothing owns will lightly risk it.
                    When in the world one scarce commands
                    The strip of earth one's shadow covers,
                    One's born to serve as food for powder.
                    But when a man stands safely landed,
                    As I do, then his stake is greater.
                    Go you to Hellas. I will put you
                    Ashore, and arm you gratis too.
                    The more you eke the flames of strife,
                    The better will it serve my purpose.
                    Strike home for freedom and for right!
                    Fight! Storm! Make hell hot for the Turks –
                    And gloriously end your days
                    Upon the Janissaries' lances. –
                    But I – excuse me – [*slaps his pocket*] I have cash,
                    And am myself, Sir Peter Gynt.
                            [*puts up his sunshade, and goes into the
                                grove,where the hammocks are partly visible*]

TRUMPETERSTRALE The swinish cur!

MONSIEUR BALLON   No taste for glory – !

MR COTTON Oh, glory's neither here nor there;
                    But think of the enormous profits
                    We'd reap if Greece should free herself.

MONSIEUR BALLON I saw myself a conqueror,
By lovely Grecian maids encircled.
TRUMPETERSTRALE Grasped in my Swedish hands, I saw
The great, heroic spur-strap-buckles!
VON EBERKOPF I my gigantic Fatherland's culture
Saw spread o'er earth and sea – !
MR COTTON The worst's the loss in solid cash.
God dam! I scarce can keep from weeping!
I saw me owner of Olympus.
If to its fame the mountain answers,
There must be veins of copper in it,
That could be opened up again.
And furthermore, that stream Castalia,
Which people talk so much about,
With fall on fall, at lowest reckoning,
Must mean a thousand horse-power good – !
TRUMPETERSTRALE Still I will go! My Swedish sword
Is worth far more than Yankee gold!
MR COTTON Perhaps; but, jammed into the ranks,
Amid the press we'd all be drowned;
And then where would the profit be?
MONSIEUR BALLON Accurst! So near to fortune's summit,
And now stopped short beside its grave!
MR COTTON [shakes his fist towards the yacht]
That long black chest holds coffered up
The nabob's golden nigger-sweat – !
VON EBERKOPF A royal notion! Quick! Away!
It's all up with his empire now!
Hurrah!
MONSIEUR BALLON   What would you?
VON EBERKOPF   Seize the power!
The crew can easily be bought.
On board then! I annex the yacht!
MR COTTON You – what – ?
VON EBERKOPF   I grab the whole concern!
                              [goes down to the jolly-boat]
MR COTTON Why then self-interest commands me
To grab my share.   [goes after him]
TRUMPETERSTRALE   What scoundrelism!

MONSIEUR BALLON A scurvy business – but – *enfin*!
                                        [*follows the others*]
TRUMPETERSTRALE I'll have to follow, I suppose –
              But I protest to all the world – !   [*follows*]

SCENE SECOND

*Another part of the coast. Moonlight with drifting clouds. The
yacht is seen far out, under full steam.*

    PEER GYNT *comes running along the beach; now pinching his
arms, now gazing out to sea.*

PEER   A nightmare! – Delusion! – I'll soon be awake!
        She's standing to sea! And at furious speed! –
        Mere delusion! I'm sleeping! I'm dizzy and drunk!
    [*clenches his hands*]
        It's not possible I should be going to die!
    [*tearing his hair*]
        A dream! I'm determined it shall be a dream!
        Oh, horror! It's only too real, worse luck!
        My brute-beasts of friends – ! Do but hear me, oh Lord!
        Since thou art so wise and so righteous – ! Oh judge – !
    [*with upstretched arms*]
        It is I, Peter Gynt! Oh, Lord, give but heed!
        Hold thy hand o'er me, Father; or else I must perish!
        Make them back the machine! Make them lower the gig!
        Stop the robbers! Make something go wrong with
                                        the rigging!
        Hear me! Let other folks' business lie over!
        The world can take care of itself for the time!
        I'm blessed if he hears me! He's deaf as his wont is!
        Here's a nice thing! A God that is bankrupt of help!
    [*beckons upwards*]
        Hist! I've abandoned the nigger-plantation!
        And missionaries I've exported to Asia!
        Surely one good turn should be worth another!
        Oh, help me on board – !

[*a jet of fire shoots into the air from the yacht, followed by thick
clouds of smoke; a hollow report is heard. Peer Gynt utters a
shriek, and sinks down on the sands. Gradually the smoke clears
away; the ship has disappeared.*]

PEER [*softly, with a pale face*] That's the sword of wrath!
    In a crack to the bottom, every soul, man and mouse!
    Oh, for ever blest be the lucky chance –
[*with emotion*] A chance? No, no, it was more than chance.
    I was to be rescued and they to perish.
    Oh, thanks and praise for that thou hast kept me,
    Hast cared for me, spite of all my sins! –
[*draws a deep breath*]
    What a marvellous feeling of safety and peace
    It gives one to know oneself specially shielded!
    But the desert! What about food and drink?
    Oh, something I'm sure to find. He'll see to that.
    There's no cause for alarm –
[*loud and insinuatingly*]   He would never allow
    A poor little sparrow like me to perish!
    Be but lowly of spirit. And give him time.
    Leave it all in the Lord's hands; and don't be cast down. –
[*with a start of terror*]
    Can that be a lion that growled in the reeds – ?
[*his teeth chattering*]
    No, it wasn't a lion.
[*mustering up courage*]   A lion, forsooth!
    Those beasts, they'll take care to keep out of the way.
    They know it's no joke to fall foul of their betters.
    They have instinct to guide them – they feel, what's a fact,
    That it's dangerous playing with elephants. –
    But all the same – I must find a tree.
    There's a grove of acacias and palms over there;
    If I once can climb up, I'll be sheltered and safe –
    Most of all if I knew but a psalm or two.
[*clambers up*] Morning and evening are not alike;
    That text has been oft enough weighed and pondered.
[*seats himself comfortably*]
    How blissful to feel so uplifted in spirit.
    To think nobly is more than to know oneself rich.

Only trust in Him. He knows well what share
Of the chalice of need I can bear to drain.
He takes fatherly thought for my personal weal –
[*casts a glance over the sea, and whispers with a sigh*]
But economical – no, that he isn't!

SCENE THIRD

*Night. An encampment of Moroccan troops on the edge of the
desert. Watchfires, with Soldiers resting by them.*

A SLAVE [*enters, tearing his hair*]
Gone is the Emperor's milk-white charger!
ANOTHER SLAVE [*enters, rending his garments*]
The Emperor's sacred robes are stolen!
AN OFFICER [*enters*] A hundred stripes upon the foot-soles
For all who fail to catch the robber!

[*the troopers mount their horses,
and gallop away in every direction*]

SCENE FOURTH

Daybreak. The grove of acacias and palms. PEER GYNT *in his tree
with a broken branch in his hand, trying to beat off a swarm of
monkeys.*

PEER   Confound it! A most disagreeable night.
[*laying about him*]
Are you there again? This is most accursed!
Now they're throwing fruit. No, it's something else.
A loathsome beast is your Barbary ape!
The Scripture says: Thou shalt watch and fight.
But I'm blest if I can; I am heavy and tired.
[*is again attacked*]

[*impatiently*] I must put a stopper upon this nuisance!
　　I must see and get hold of one of these scamps,
　　Get him hung and skinned, and then dress myself up,
　　As best I may, in his shaggy hide,
　　That the others may take me for one of themselves. –
　　What are we mortals? Motes, no more;
　　And it's wisest to follow the fashion a bit. –
　　Again a rabble! They throng and swarm.
　　Off with you! Shoo! They go on as though crazy.
　　If only I had a false tail to put on now –
　　Only something to make me a bit like a beast. –
　　What now? There's a pattering over my head – !
[*looks up*] It's the grandfather ape – with his fists full of filth – !
[*huddles together apprehensively, and keeps still for a while. The
ape makes a motion; Peer Gynt begins coaxing and wheedling him,
as he might a dog.*]
　　Ay – are you there, my good old Bus!
　　He's a good beast, he is! He will listen to reason!
　　He wouldn't throw – I should think not, indeed!
　　It is me! Pip-pip! We are first-rate friends!
　　Ai-ai! Don't you hear, I can talk your language?
　　Bus and I, we are kinsfolk, you see –
　　Bus shall have sugar tomorrow – ! The beast!
　　The whole cargo on top of me! Ugh, how disgusting! –
　　Or perhaps it was food? 'Twas in taste – indefinable;
　　And taste's for the most part a matter of habit.
　　What thinker is it who somewhere says:
　　You must spit and trust to the force of habit? –
　　Now here come the small-fry!
[*hits and slashes around him*]　　　　It's really too bad
　　That man, who by rights is the lord of creation,
　　Should find himself forced to – ! O murder! murder!
　　The old one was bad, but the youngsters are worse!

SCENE FIFTH

*Early morning. A stony region, with a view out over the desert.
On one side a cleft in the hill, and a cave.*

    A THIEF *and a* RECEIVER *hidden in the cleft, with the Emperor's
horse and robes. The horse, richly caparisoned, is tied to a stone.
Horsemen are seen afar off.*

THE THIEF   The tongues of the lances
                All flickering and flashing –
                See, see!

THE RECEIVER Already my head seems
                To roll on the sand-plain!
                Woe, woe!

THE THIEF [*folds his arms over his breast*] My father he thieved;
                So his son must be thieving.

THE RECEIVER. My father received;
                So his son keeps receiving.

THE THIEF   Thy lot shalt thou bear still;
                Thyself shalt thou be still.

THE RECEIVER [*listening*] Steps in the brushwood!
                Flee, flee! But where?

THE THIEF   The cavern is deep,
                And the Prophet great!
                       [*They make off, leaving the booty behind them.
                       The horsemen gradually disappear in the distance.*]

PEER [*enters, cutting a reed whistle*]
                What a delectable morning-tide! –
                The dung-beetle's rolling his ball in the dust;
                The snail creeps out of his dwelling-house.
                  The morning; ay, it has gold in its mouth –
                  It's a wonderful power, when you think of it,
                  That Nature has given to the light of day.
                  One feels so secure, and so much more courageous –
                  One would gladly, at need, take a bull by the horns –
                  What a stillness all round! Ah, the joys of Nature –

Strange enough I should never have prized them before.
Why go and imprison oneself in a city,
For no end but just to be bored by the mob. –
Just look how the lizards are whisking about,
Snapping, and thinking of nothing at all.
What innocence ev'n in the life of the beasts!
Each fulfils the Creator's behest unimpeachably,
Preserving its own special stamp undefaced;
Is itself, is itself, both in sport and in strife,
Itself, as it was at his primal: Be!
[*puts on his eye-glasses*] A toad. In the middle of a sandstone
                                                    block.

Petrifaction all round him. His head alone peering.
There he's sitting and gazing as though through a window
At the world, and is – to himself enough –
[*reflectively*] Enough? To himself – ? Where is it that's
                                                    written?

I've read it, in youth, in some so-called classic.
In the family prayer-book? Or Solomon's Proverbs?
Alas, I notice that, year by year,
My memory for dates and for places is fading.
[*seats himself in the shade*]

Here's a cool spot to rest and to stretch out one's feet.
Why, look, here are ferns growing – edible roots.
[*eats a little*] 'Twould be fitter food for an animal –
But the text says: Bridle the natural man!
Furthermore it is written: The proud shall be humbled,
And whoso abaseth himself, exalted.
[*uneasily*] Exalted? Yes, that's what will happen with me –
No other result can so much as be thought of.
Fate will assist me away from this place,
And arrange matters so that I get a fresh start.
This is only a trial; deliverance will follow –
If only the Lord lets me keep my health.
[*dismisses his misgivings, lights a cigar, stretches himself,
and gazes out over the desert*]

What an enormous, limitless waste! –
Far in the distance an ostrich is striding. –
What can one fancy was really God's meaning

In all of this voidness and deadness?
This desert, bereft of all sources of life;
This burnt-up cinder, that profits no one;
This patch of the world, that for ever lies fallow;
This corpse, that never, since earth's creation,
Has brought its Maker so much as thanks –
Why was it created? – How spendthrift is Nature! –
Is that sea in the east there, that dazzling expanse
All gleaming? It can't be; 'tis but a mirage.
The sea's to the west; it lies piled up behind me,
Dammed out from the desert by a sloping ridge.

[*a thought flashes through his mind*]

Dammed out? Then I could – ? The ridge is narrow.
Dammed out? It wants but a gap, a canal –
Like a flood of life would the waters rush
In through the channel, and fill the desert!
Soon would the whole of yon red-hot grave
Spread forth, a breezy and rippling sea.
The oases would rise in the midst, like islands;
Atlas would tower in green cliffs on the north;
Sailing-ships would, like stray birds on the wing,
Skim to the south, on the caravans' track.
Life-giving breezes would scatter the choking
Vapours, and dew would distil from the clouds.
People would build themselves town on town,
And grass would grow green round the swaying
                                          palm-trees.
The southland, behind the Sahara's wall,
Would make a new seaboard for civilisation.
Steam would set Timbuctoo's factories spinning;
Bornu would be colonised apace;
The naturalist would pass safely through Habes
In his railway-car to the Upper Nile.
In the midst of my sea, on a fat oasis,
I will replant the Norwegian race;
The Dalesman's blood is next door to royal;
Arabic crossing will do the rest.
Skirting a bay, on a shelving strand,
I'll build the chief city, Peeropolis.

The world is decrepit! Now comes the turn
Of Gyntiana, my virgin land!
[*springs up*] Had I but capital, soon 'twould be done. –
A gold key to open the gate of the sea!
A crusade against Death! The close-fisted old churl
Shall open the sack he lies brooding upon.
Men rave about freedom in every land –
Like the ass in the ark, I will send out a cry
O'er the world, and will baptise to liberty
The beautiful, thrall-bounden coasts that shall be.
I must on! To find capital, eastward or west!
My kingdom – well, half of it, say – for a horse!
[*the horse in the cleft neighs*]
A horse! Ay, and robes! – jewels too – and a sword!
[*goes closer*] It can't be! It is though – ! But how? I have read,
I don't quite know where, that the will can move
                                        mountains –
But how about moving a horse as well – ?
Pooh! Here stands the horse, that's a matter of fact;
For the rest, why, *ab esse ad posse, et cetera.*
[*puts on the dress and looks down at it*]
Sir Peter – a Turk, too, from top to toe!
Well, one never knows what may happen to one. –
Gee-up, now, Grane, my trusty steed! [*mounts the horse*]
Gold-slipper stirrups beneath my feet! –
You may know the great by their riding-gear!
                              [*gallops off into the desert*]

SCENE SIXTH

The tent of an Arab chief, standing alone on an oasis. PEER GYNT,
*in his Eastern dress, resting on cushions. He is drinking coffee, and
smoking a long pipe.* ANITRA, *and a* BEVY OF GIRLS, *dancing
and singing before him.*

CHORUS OF GIRLS The Prophet is come!
The Prophet, the Lord, the All-Knowing One,
To us, to us is he come,

O'er the sand-ocean riding!
The Prophet, the Lord, the Unerring One,
To us, to us is he come,
O'er the sand-ocean sailing!
Wake the flute and the drum!
The Prophet, the Prophet is come!

ANITRA His courser is white as the milk is
That streams in the rivers of Paradise.
Bend every knee! Bow every head!
His eyes are as bright-gleaming, mild-beaming stars.
Yet none earth-born endureth
The rays of those stars in their blinding splendour!
    Through the desert he came.
Gold and pearl-drops sprang forth on his breast.
Where he rode there was light.
Behind him was darkness;
Behind him raged drought and the simoom.
He, the glorious one, came!
Through the desert he came,
Like a mortal appareled.
Kaaba, Kaaba stands void –
He himself hath proclaimed it!

CHORUS OF GIRLS Wake the flute and the drum!
The Prophet, the Prophet is come!
    [*they continue the dance, to soft music*]

PEER   I have read it in print – and the saying is true –
That no one's a prophet in his native land. –
This position is very much more to my mind
Than my life over there 'mong the Charleston merchants.
There was something hollow in the whole affair,
Something foreign at the bottom,
Something dubious behind it –
I was never at home in their company,
Nor felt myself really one of the guild.
What tempted me into that galley at all?
To grub and grub in the bins of trade –
As I think it all over, I can't understand it –
It happened so; that's the whole affair. –
To be oneself on a basis of gold

Is no better than founding one's house on the sand.
For your watch, and your ring, and the rest of your
                                                    trappings
The good people fawn on you, grovelling to earth;
They lift their hats to your jewelled breast-pin;
But your ring and your breast-pin are not your person. –
A prophet; ay, that is a clearer position.
At least one knows on what footing one stands.
If you make a success, it's yourself that receives
The ovation, and not your pounds-sterling and shillings.
One is what one is, and no nonsense about it;
One owes nothing to chance or to accident,
And needs neither licence nor patent to lean on. –
A prophet; ay, that is the thing for me.
And I slipped so utterly unawares into it –
Just by coming galloping over the desert,
And meeting these children of nature *en route*.
The Prophet had come to them; so much was clear.
It was really not my intent to deceive –
There's a difference 'twixt lies and oracular answers;
And then I can always withdraw again.
I'm in no way bound; it's a simple matter – ;
The whole thing is private, so to speak;
I can go as I came; there's my horse ready saddled;
I am master, in short, of the situation.

ANITRA [*approaching from the tent-door*]
      Prophet and Master!
PEER   What would my slave?
ANITRA The sons of the desert await at thy tent-door;
      They pray for the light of thy countenance –
PEER   Stop!
      Say in the distance I'd have them assemble;
      Say from the distance I hear all their prayers.
      Add that I suffer no menfolk in here!
      Men, my child, are a worthless crew –
      Inveterate rascals you well may call them!
      Anitra, you can't think how shamelessly
      They have swind– I mean they have sinned, my child! –
      Well, enough now of that; you may dance for me,
                                              damsels!

The Prophet would banish the memories that gall him.

THE GIRLS [*dancing*]

> The Prophet is good! The Prophet is grieving
> For the ill that the sons of the dust have wrought!
> The Prophet is mild; to his mildness be praises;
> He opens to sinners his Paradise!

PEER [*his eyes following Anitra during the dance*]

> Legs as nimble as drumsticks flitting.
> She's a dainty morsel indeed, that wench!
> It's true she has somewhat extravagant contours –
> Not quite in accord with the norms of beauty.
> But what is beauty? A mere convention –
> A coin made current by time and place.
> And just the extravagant seems most attractive
> When one of the normal has drunk one's fill.
> In the law-bound one misses all intoxication.
> Either plump to excess or excessively lean;
> Either parlously young or portentously old –
> The medium is mawkish. –
> Her feet – they are not altogether clean;
> No more are her arms; in especial one of them.
> But that is at bottom no drawback at all.
> I should rather call it a qualification –
> Anitra, come listen!

ANITRA [*approaching*]Thy handmaiden hears!

PEER   You are tempting, my daughter! The Prophet is touched.
>   If you don't believe me, then hear the proof –
>   I'll make you a Houri in Paradise!

ANITRA Impossible, Lord!

PEER   What? You think I am jesting?
>   I'm in sober earnest, as true as I live!

ANITRA But I haven't a soul.

PEER   Then of course you must get one!

ANITRA How, Lord?

PEER   Just leave me alone for that –
>   I shall look after your education.
>   No soul? Why, truly you're not over bright,
>   As the saying goes. I've observed it with pain.
>   But pooh! for a soul you can always find room.

Come here! let me measure your brain-pan, child. –
There is room, there is room, I was sure there was.
It's true you never will penetrate
Very deep; to a large soul you'll scarcely attain –
But never you mind; it won't matter a bit –
You'll have plenty to carry you through with credit –
ANITRA The Prophet is gracious –
PEER   You hesitate? Speak!
ANITRA But I'd rather –
PEER   Say on; don't waste time about it!
ANITRA I don't care so much about having a soul –
Give me rather –
PEER   What, child?
ANITRA [*pointing to his turban*]   That lovely opal.
PEER [*enchanted, handing her the jewel*]
Anitra ! Anitra! True daughter of Eve!
I feel thee magnetic; for I am a man.
And, as a much-esteemed author has phrased it:
'*Das Ewig-Weibliche ziehet uns an!*'

SCENE SEVENTH

A moonlight night. The palm-grove outside Anitra's tent. PEER
GYNT *is sitting beneath a tree, with an Arabian lute in his hands.
His beard and hair are clipped; he looks considerably younger.*

PEER GYNT [*plays and sings*] I double-locked my Paradise,
                    And took its key with me.
                The north-wind bore me seaward ho!
                While lovely women all forlorn
                    Wept on the ocean strand.

                Still southward, southward clove my keel
                    The salt sea-currents through.
                Where palms were swaying proud and fair,
                A garland round the ocean-bight,
                    I set my ship afire.

I climbed aboard the desert ship,
    A ship on four stout legs.
It foamed beneath the lashing whip –
Oh, catch me; I'm a flitting bird –
    I'm twittering on a bough!

Anitra, thou'rt the palm-tree's must;
    That know I now full well!
Ay, even the Angora goat-milk cheese
Is scarcely half such dainty fare,
    Anitra, ah, as thou!

[*he hangs the lute over his shoulder, and comes forward*]
    Stillness! Is the fair one listening?
Has she heard my little song?
Peeps she from behind the curtain,
Veil and so forth cast aside? –
Hush! A sound as though a cork
From a bottle burst amain!
Now once more! And yet again!
Love-sighs can it be? Or songs? –
No, it is distinctly snoring. –
Dulcet strain! Anitra sleepeth!
Nightingale, thy warbling stay!
Every sort of woe betide thee,
If with gurgling trill thou darest –
But, as says the text: Let be!
Nightingale, thou art a singer;
Ah, even such an one am I.
He, like me, ensnares with music
Tender, shrinking little hearts.
Balmy night is made for music;
Music is our common sphere;
In the act of singing, we are
We, Peer Gynt and nightingale.
And the maiden's very sleeping
Is my passion's crowning bliss –
For the lips protruded o'er the
Beaker yet untasted quite –
But she's coming, I declare!

After all, it's best she should.

ANITRA [*from the tent*] Master, call'st thou in the night?

PEER Yes indeed, the Prophet calls.
  I was wakened by the cat
  With a furious hunting-hubbub –

ANITRA Ah, not hunting-noises, Master;
  It was something much, much worse.

PEER What, then, was't?

ANITRA   Oh, spare me!

PEER   Speak.

ANITRA Oh, I blush to –

PEER [*approaching*]   Was it, mayhap,
  That which filled me so completely
  When I let you have my opal?

ANITRA [*horrified*] Liken thee, O earth's great treasure,
  To a horrible old cat!

PEER Child, from passion's standpoint viewed,
  May a tom-cat and a prophet
  Come to very much the same.

ANITRA Master, jest like honey floweth
  From thy lips.

PEER   My little friend,
  You, like other maidens, judge
  Great men by their outsides only.
  I am full of jest at bottom,
  Most of all when we're alone.
  I am forced by my position
  To assume a solemn mask.
  Duties of the day constrain me;
  All the reckonings and worry
  That I have with one and all,
  Make me oft a cross-grained prophet;
  But it's only from the tongue out. –
  Fudge, avaunt! *En tête-à-tête*
  I'm Peer – well, the man I am.
  Hei, away now with the prophet;
  Me, myself, you have me here!
 [*seats himself under a tree, and draws her to him*]
  Come, Anitra, we will rest us

Underneath the palm's green fan-shade!
I'll lie whispering, you'll lie smiling;
Afterwards our roles exchange we;
Then shall your lips, fresh and balmy,
To my smiling, passion whisper!

ANITRA [*lies down at his feet*]

All thy words are sweet as singing,
Though I understand but little.
Master, tell me, can thy daughter
Catch a soul by listening?

PEER

Soul, and spirit's light and knowledge,
All in good time you shall have them.
When in east, on rosy streamers
Golden types print: Here is day –
Then, my child, I'll give you lessons;
You'll be well brought-up, no fear.
But, 'mid night's delicious stillness,
It were stupid if I should,
With a threadbare wisdom's remnants,
Play the part of pedagogue. –
And the soul, moreover, is not,
Looked at properly, the main thing.
It's the heart that really matters.

ANITRA

Speak, O Master! When thou speakest,
I see gleams, as though of opals!

PEER

Wisdom in extremes is folly;
Coward blossoms into tyrant;
Truth, when carried to excess,
Ends in wisdom written backwards.
Ay, my daughter, I'm forsworn
As a dog if there are not
Folk with o'erfed souls on earth
Who shall scarce attain to clearness.
Once I met with such a fellow,
Of the flock the very flower;
And even he mistook his goal,
Losing sense in blatant sound. –
See the waste round this oasis.
Were I but to swing my turban,

I could force the ocean-flood
To fill up the whole concern.
But I were a blockhead, truly,
Seas and lands to go creating.
Know you what it is to live?

ANITRA   Teach me!

PEER   It is to be wafted
Dry-shod down the stream of time,
Wholly, solely as oneself.
Only in full manhood can I
Be the man I am, dear child!
Aged eagle moults his plumage,
Aged fogey lags declining,
Aged dame has ne'er a tooth left,
Aged churl gets withered hands –
One and all get withered souls.
Youth! Ah, youth! I mean to reign,
As a sultan, whole and fiery –
Not on Gyntiana's shores,
Under trellised vines and palm-leaves –
But enthroned in the freshness
Of a woman's virgin thoughts. –
    See you now, my little maiden,
Why I've graciously bewitched you –
Why I have your heart selected,
And established, so to speak,
There my being's Caliphate?
All your longings shall be mine.
I'm an autocrat in passion!
You shall live for me alone.
I'll be he who shall enthral
You like gold and precious stones.
Should we part, then life is over –
That is, your life, *nota bene*!
Every inch and fibre of you,
Will-less, without yea or nay,
I must know filled full of me.
Midnight beauties of your tresses,
All that's lovely to be named,

Shall, like Babylonian gardens,
Tempt your Sultan to his tryst.
　　　After all, I don't complain, then,
Of your empty forehead-vault.
With a soul, one's oft absorbed in
Contemplation of oneself.
Listen, while we're on the subject –
If you like it, faith, you shall
Have a ring about your ankle –
'Twill be best for both of us.
I will be your soul by proxy;
Or the rest – why, status quo.

[*Anitra snores*]

What! She sleeps! Then has it glided
Bootless past her, all I've said? –
No; it marks my influence o'er her
That she floats away in dreams
On my love-talk as it flows.

[*rises, and lays trinkets in her lap*]

Here are jewels! Here are more!
Sleep, Anitra! Dream of Peer – .
Sleep! In sleeping, you the crown have
Placed upon your Emperor's brow!
Victory on his Person's basis
Has Peer Gynt this night achieved.

SCENE EIGHTH

A caravan route. The oasis is seen far off in the background. PEER
GYNT *comes galloping across the desert on his white horse, with*
ANITRA *before him on his saddle-bow.*

ANITRA Let be, or I'll bite you!
PEER   You little rogue!
ANITRA What would you?
PEER   What would I? Play hawk and dove!
　　　Run away with you! Frolic and frisk a bit!

ANITRA For shame! An old prophet like you – !

PEER Oh, stuff! The prophet's not old at all, you goose!
    Do you think all this is a sign of age?

ANITRA Let me go! I want to go home!

PEER   Coquette!
    What, home! To father-in-law! That would be fine!
    We madcap birds that have flown from the cage
    Must never come into his sight again.
    Besides, my child, in the self-same place
    It's wisest never to stay too long;
    For familiarity lessens respect –
    Most of all when one comes as a prophet or such.
    One should show oneself glimpse-wise, and pass like
                             a dream.
    Faith, 'twas time that the visit should come to an end.
    They're unstable of soul, are these sons of the desert –
    Both incense and prayers dwindled off towards the end.

ANITRA Yes, but are you a prophet?

PEER   Your Emperor I am! [*tries to kiss her*]
    Why just see now how coy the wee woodpecker is!

ANITRA Give me that ring that you have on your finger.

PEER Take, sweet Anitra, the whole of the trash!

ANITRA Thy words are as songs! Oh, how dulcet their sound!

PEER How blessed to know oneself loved to this pitch!
    I'll dismount! Like your slave, I will lead your palfrey!
    [*hands her his riding-whip, and dismounts*]
    There now, my rosebud, my exquisite flower!
    Here I'll go trudging my way through the sand,
    Till a sunstroke o'ertakes me and finishes me.
    I'm young, Anitra; bear that in mind!
    You mustn't be shocked at my escapades.
    Frolics and high-jinks are youth's sole criterion!
    And so, if your intellect weren't so dense,
    You would see at a glance, oh my fair oleander –
    Your lover is frolicsome – *ergo*, he's young!

ANITRA Yes, you are young. Have you any more rings?

PEER Am I not? There, grab! I can leap like a buck!
    Were there vine-leaves around, I would garland my brow.
    To be sure I am young! Hei, I'm going to dance!

[*dances and sings*] I am a blissful game-cock!
     Peck me, my little pullet!
     Hop-sa-sa! Let me trip it –
     I am a blissful game-cock!

ANITRA You are sweating, my prophet; I fear you will melt –
     Hand me that heavy bag hung at your belt.

PEER   Tender solicitude! Bear the purse ever –
     Hearts that can love are content without gold!

  [*dances and sings again*]
     Young Peer Gynt is the maddest wag –
     He knows not what foot he shall stand upon.
       Pooh, says Peer – pooh, never mind!
     Young Peer Gynt is the maddest wag!

ANITRA What joy when the Prophet steps forth in the dance!

PEER   Oh, bother the Prophet! – Suppose we change clothes!
     Heisa! Strip off!

ANITRA   Your caftan were too long,
     Your girdle too wide, and your stockings too tight –

PEER   *Eh bien!*
  [*kneels down*] But vouchsafe me a vehement sorrow –
     To a heart full of love, it is sweet to suffer!
     Listen; as soon as we're home at my castle –

ANITRA In your Paradise – have we far to ride?

PEER   Oh, a thousand miles or –

ANITRA   Too far!

PEER   Oh, listen –
     You shall have the soul that I promised you once –

ANITRA Oh, thank you; I'll get on without the soul.
     But you asked for a sorrow –

PEER [*rising*]   Ay, curse me, I did!
     A keen one, but short – to last two or three days!

ANITRA Anitra obeyeth the Prophet! – Farewell!
          [*gives him a smart cut across the fingers, and dashes
            off, at a tearing gallop, back across the desert*]

PEER [*stands for a long time thunderstruck*]
     Well now, may I be – !

SCENE NINTH

The same place, an hour later. PEER GYNT *is stripping off his Turkish costume; soberly and thoughtfully, bit by bit. Last of all, he takes his little travelling-cap out of his coat-pocket, puts it on, and stands once more in European dress.*

PEER GYNT [*throwing the turban far away from him*]
    There lies the Turk, then, and here stand I! –
    These heathenish doings are no sort of good.
    It's lucky 'twas only a matter of clothes,
    And not, as the saying goes, bred in the bone. –
    What tempted me into that galley at all?
    It's best, in the long run, to live as a Christian,
    To put away peacock-like ostentation,
    To base all one's dealings on law and morality,
    To be ever oneself, and to earn at the last
    Speech at one's grave-side, and wreaths on one's coffin.
[*walks a few steps*] The hussy – she was on the very verge
    Of turning my head clean topsy-turvy.
    May I be a troll if I understand
    What it was that dazed and bemused me so.
    Well; it's well that's done: had the joke been carried
    But one step on, I'd have looked absurd. –
    I have erred – but at least it's a consolation
    That my error was due to the false situation.
    It wasn't my personal self that fell.
    'Twas in fact this prophetical way of life,
    So utterly lacking the salt of activity,
    That took its revenge in these qualms of bad taste.
    It's a sorry business this prophetising!
    One's office compels one to walk in a mist;
    In playing the prophet, you throw up the game
    The moment you act like a rational being.
    In so far I've done what the occasion demanded,
    In the mere fact of paying my court to that goose.

But, nevertheless –
[*bursts out laughing*]   Hm, to think of it now!
To try to make time stop by jigging and dancing,
And to cope with the current by capering and prancing!
To thrum on the lute-strings, to fondle and sigh,
And end, like a rooster – by getting well plucked!
Such conduct is truly prophetic frenzy. –
Yes, plucked! – Phew! I'm plucked clean enough indeed.
Well, well, I've a trifle still left in reserve;
I've a little in America, a little in my pocket;
So I won't be quite driven to beg my bread. –
And at bottom this middle condition is best.
I'm no longer a slave to my coachman and horses;
I haven't to fret about postchaise or baggage;
I am master, in short, of the situation. –
What path should I choose? Many paths lie before me;
And a wise man is known from a fool by his choice.
My business life is a finished chapter;
My love-sports, too, are a cast-off garment.
I feel no desire to live back like a crab.
'Forward or back, and it's just as far;
Out or in, and it's just as strait,' –
So I seem to have read in some luminous work. –
I'll try something new, then; ennoble my course;
Find a goal worth the labour and money it costs.
Shall I write my life without dissimulation –
A book for guidance and imitation?
Or stay – ! I have plenty of time at command –
What if, as a travelling scientist,
I should study past ages and time's voracity?
Ay, sure enough; that is the thing for me!
Legends I read e'en in childhood's days,
And since then I've kept up that branch of learning. –
I will follow the path of the human race!
Like a feather I'll float on the stream of history,
Make it all live again, as in a dream –
See the heroes battling for truth and right,
As an onlooker only, in safety ensconced –
See thinkers perish and martyrs bleed,

See empires founded and vanish away —
See world-epochs grow from their trifling seeds;
In short, I will skim off the cream of history. —
I must try to get hold of a volume of Becker,
And travel as far as I can by chronology. —
It's true — my grounding's by no means thorough,
And history's wheels within wheels are deceptive —
But pooh; the wilder the starting-point,
The result will oft be the more original. —
How exalting it is, now, to choose a goal,
And drive straight for it, like flint and steel!
[*with quiet emotion*] To break off all round one, on every side,
The bonds that bind one to home and friends —
To blow into atoms one's hoarded wealth —
To bid one's love and its joys good-night —
All simply to find the arcana of truth —
[*wiping a tear from his eye*]
That is the test of the true man of science! —
I feel myself happy beyond all measure.
Now I have fathomed my destiny's riddle.
Now 'tis but persevering through thick and thin!
It's excusable, sure, if I hold up my head,
And feel my worth, as the man, Peer Gynt,
Also called Human-life's Emperor. —
I will own the sum-total of bygone days;
I'll nevermore tread in the paths of the living.
The present is not worth so much as a shoe-sole;
All faithless and marrowless the doings of men;
Their soul has no wings and their deeds no weight;
[*shrugs his shoulders*]
And women — ah, they are a worthless crew!

                                        [*goes off*]

SCENE TENTH

A summer day. Far up in the North. A hut in the forest. The door, with a large wooden bar, stands open. Reindeer-horns over it. A flock of goats by the wall of the hut.

A MIDDLE-AGED WOMAN, *fair-haired and comely, sits spinning outside in the sunshine.*

THE WOMAN [*glances down the path, and sings*]
    Maybe both the winter and spring will pass by,
    And the next summer too, and the whole of the year –
    But thou wilt come one day, that know I full well;
    And I will await thee, as I promised of old.
    [*calls the goats, and sings again*]
    God strengthen thee, whereso thou goest in the world!
    God gladden thee, if at his footstool thou stand!
    Here will I await thee till thou comest again;
    And if thou wait up yonder, then there we'll meet,
                         my friend!

SCENE ELEVENTH

In Egypt. Daybreak. MEMNON'S STATUE *amid the sands.* PEER GYNT *enters on foot, and looks around him for a while.*

PEER GYNT Here I might fittingly start on my wanderings. –
    So now, for a change, I've become an Egyptian;
    But Egyptian on the basis of the Gyntish I.
    To Assyria next I will bend my steps.
    To begin right back at the world's creation
    Would lead to nought but bewilderment.
    I will go round about all the Bible history;
    Its secular traces I'll always be coming on;
    And to look, as the saying goes, into its seams,
    Lies entirely outside both my plan and my powers.

[*sits upon a stone*] Now I will rest me, and patiently wait
    Till the statue has sung its habitual dawn-song.
    When breakfast is over, I'll climb up the pyramid;
    If I've time, I'll look through its interior afterwards.
    Then I'll go round the head of the Red Sea by land;
    Perhaps I may hit on King Potiphar's grave. –
    Next I'll turn Asiatic. In Babylon I'll seek for
    The far-renowned harlots and hanging gardens –
    That's to say, the chief traces of civilisation.
    Then at one bound to the ramparts of Troy.
    From Troy there's a fareway by sea direct
    Across to the glorious ancient Athens –
    There on the spot will I, stone by stone,
    Survey the Pass that Leonidas guarded.
    I will get up the works of the better philosophers,
    Find the prison where Socrates suffered,
    A martyr – ; oh no, by-the-bye-there's a war there
                              at present – !
Well then, my Hellenism must even stand over.
[*looks at his watch*] It's really too bad, such an age as it takes
    For the sun to rise. I am pressed for time.
    Well then, from Troy – it was there I left off –
[*rises and listens*]
    What is that strange sort of murmur that's rushing – ?

Sunrise

MEMNON'S STATUE [*sings*]
    From the demigod's ashes there soar, youth-renewing,
        Birds ever singing.
        Zeus the Omniscient
        Shaped them contending.
        Owls of wisdom,
    My birds, where do they slumber?
    Thou must die if thou rede not
        The song's enigma!
PEER   How strange now – I really fancied there came
    From the statue a sound. Music, this, of the Past.
    I heard the stone – accents now rising, now sinking. –
    I will register it, for the learned to ponder.

[*notes in his pocket-book*]
>   'The statue did sing. I heard the sound plainly,
>   But didn't quite follow the text of the song.
>   The whole thing, of course, was hallucination. –
>   Nothing else of importance observed today.'

[*proceeds on his way*]

SCENE TWELFTH

Near the village of Gizeh. The great SPHINX *carved out of the rock. In the distance the spires and minarets of Cairo.* PEER GYNT *enters; he examines the Sphinx attentively, now through his eyeglass, now through his hollowed hand.*

PEER GYNT Now, where in the world have I met before
>   Something half forgotten that's like this hobgoblin?
>   For met it I have, in the north or the south.
>   Was it a person? And, if so, who?
>   That Memnon, it afterwards crossed my mind,
>   Was like the Old Man of the Dovrë, so called,
>   Just as he sat there, stiff and stark,
>   Planted on end on the stumps of pillars. –
>   But this most curious mongrel here,
>   This changeling, a lion and woman in one –
>   Does he come to me, too, from a fairy-tale,
>   Or from a remembrance of something real?
>   From a fairy-tale? Ho, I remember the fellow!
>   Why, of course it's the Boyg, that I smote on the skull –
>   That is, I dreamt it – I lay in fever. –
[*going closer*] The self-same eyes, and the self-same lips –
>   Not quite so lumpish; a little more cunning;
>   But the same, for the rest, in all essentials. –
>   Ay, so that's it, Boyg; so you're like a lion
>   When one sees you from behind and meets you in
>   the daytime!
>   Are you still good at riddling? Come, let us try.

Now we shall see if you answer as last time!
[*calls out towards the Sphinx*] Hei, Boyg, who are you?
A VOICE [*behind the Sphinx*]   Ach, Sphinx, *wer bist du?*
PEER   What! Echo answers in German! How strange!
THE VOICE *Wer bist du?*
PEER   It speaks it quite fluently too!
     That observation is new, and my own.
     [*notes in his book*] 'Echo in German. Dialect, Berlin.'

    BEGRIFFENFELDT *comes out from behind the Sphinx.*

BEGRIFFENFELDT A man!
PEER   Oh, then it was he that was chattering.
     [*notes again*] 'Arrived in the sequel at other results.'
BEGRIFFENFELDT [*with all sorts of restless antics*]
     Excuse me, *mein Herr* – ! *Eine Lebensfrage* – !
     What brings you to this place precisely today?
PEER   A visit. I'm greeting a friend of my youth.
BEGRIFFENFELDT What? The Sphinx – ?
PEER [*nods*]   Yes, I knew him in days gone by.
BEGRIFFENFELDT *Famos!* – And that after such a night!
     My temples are hammering as though they would burst!
     You know him, man! Answer! Say on! Can you tell
     What he is?
PEER   What he is? Yes, that's easy enough.
     He's himself.
BEGRIFFENFELDT [*with a bound*]
                         Ha, the riddle of life lightened forth
     In a flash to my vision! – It's certain he is
     Himself?
PEER   Yes, he says so, at any rate.
BEGRIFFENFELDT Himself! Revolution! thine hour is at hand!
     [*takes off his hat*] Your name, pray, *mein Herr*?
PEER   I was christened Peer Gynt.
BEGRIFFENFELDT [*in rapt admiration*]
     Peer Gynt! Allegoric! I might have foreseen it. –
     Peer Gynt? That must clearly imply: The Unknown –
     The Comer whose coming was foretold to me –
PEER   What, really? And now you are here to meet – ?
BEGRIFFENFELDT Peer Gynt! Profound! Enigmatic! Incisive!

Each word, as it were, an abysmal lesson!
What are you?

PEER [*modestly*]   I've always endeavoured to be
Myself. For the rest, here's my passport, you see.

BEGRIFFENFELDT Again that mysterious word at the bottom.
[*seizes him by the wrist*]
To Cairo! The Interpreters' Kaiser is found!

PEER   Kaiser?

BEGRIFFENFELDT Come on!

PEER   Am I really known – ?

BEGRIFFENFELDT [*dragging him away*]
The Interpreters' Kaiser – on the basis of Self!

SCENE THIRTEENTH

*In Cairo. A large courtyard, surrounded by high walls and build-
ings. Barred windows; iron cages.*
THREE KEEPERS *in the courtyard.* A FOURTH *comes in.*

THE NEWCOMER Schafmann, say, where's the director gone?

A KEEPER He drove out this morning some time before dawn.

THE FIRST I think something must have occurred to annoy him;
For last night –

ANOTHER   Hush, be quiet; he's there at the door!

BEGRIFFENFELDT *leads* PEER GYNT *in, locks the gate,
and puts the key in his pocket.*

PEER [*to himself*] Indeed an exceedingly gifted man;
Almost all that he says is beyond comprehension.
[*looks around*] So this is the Club of the Savants, eh?

BEGRIFFENFELDT Here you will find them, every man
                                        jack of them –
The group of Interpreters threescore and ten;
It's been lately increased by a hundred and sixty –
[*shouts to the Keepers*] Mikkel, Schlingelberg, Schafmann, Fuchs –
Into the cages with you at once!

THE KEEPERS We!

BEGRIFFENFELDT   Who else, pray? Get in, get in!
  When the world twirls around, we must twirl with it too.
  [*forces them into a cage*]
  He's arrived this morning, the mighty Peer –
  The rest you can guess – I need say no more.
  [*locks the cage door, and throws the key into a well*]

PEER   But, my dear Herr Doctor and Director, pray – ?

BEGRIFFENFELDT Neither one nor the other! I was before –
  Herr Peer, are you secret? I must ease my heart –

PEER [*with increasing uneasiness*] What is it?

BEGRIFFENFELDT   Promise you will not tremble.

PEER   I will do my best, but –

BEGRIFFENFELDT [*draws him into a corner, and whispers*]
                    The Absolute Reason
  Departed this life at eleven last night.

PEER   God help me – !

BEGRIFFENFELDT   Why, yes, it's extremely deplorable.
  And as I'm placed, you see, it is doubly unpleasant;
  For this institution has passed up to now
  For what's called a madhouse.

PEER   A madhouse, ha!

BEGRIFFENFELDT Not now, understand!

PEER [*softly, pale with fear*]   Now I see what the place is!
  And the man is mad – and there's none that knows it!
                            [*tries to steal away*]

BEGRIFFENFELDT [*following him*]
  However, I hope you don't misunderstand me?
  When I said he was dead, I was talking stuff.
  He's beside himself. Started clean out of his skin –
  Just like my compatriot Münchausen's fox.

PEER   Excuse me a moment –

BEGRIFFENFELDT [*holding him back*] I meant like an eel –
  It was not like a fox. A needle through his eye –
  And he writhed on the wall –

PEER   Where can rescue be found?

BEGRIFFENFELDT A snick round his neck, and whip! out
                                    of his skin!

PEER   He's raving! He's utterly out of his wits!

BEGRIFFENFELDT Now it's patent, and can't be dissimulated,
      That this from-himself-going must have for result
      A complete revolution by sea and land.
      The persons one hitherto reckoned as mad,
      You see, became normal last night at eleven,
      Accordant with Reason in its newest phase.
      And more, if the matter be rightly regarded,
      It's patent that, at the aforementioned hour,
      The sane folks, so called, began forthwith to rave.
PEER   You mentioned the hour, sir, my time is but scant –
BEGRIFFENFELDT Your time, did you say? There you jog
                                    my remembrance!

   [opens a door and calls out]
      Come forth all! The time that shall be is proclaimed!
      Reason is dead and gone; long live Peer Gynt!
PEER   Now, my dear good fellow – !

     The LUNATICS *come one by one, and at intervals,*
              into the courtyard.

BEGRIFFENFELDT   Good morning! Come forth,
      And hail the dawn of emancipation!
      Your Kaiser has come to you!
PEER   Kaiser?
BEGRIFFENFELDT   Of course!
PEER   But the honour's so great, so entirely excessive –
BEGRIFFENFELDT Oh, do not let any false modesty sway you
      At an hour such as this.
PEER   But at least give me time – !
      No, indeed, I'm not fit; I'm completely dumbfounded!
BEGRIFFENFELDT A man who has fathomed the Sphinx's
                                 meaning!
      A man who's himself!
PEER   Ay, but that's just the rub.
      It's true that in everything I am myself;
      But here the point is, if I follow your meaning,
      To be, so to phrase it, outside oneself.
BEGRIFFENFELDT Outside? No, there you are strangely mistaken!
      It's here, sir, that one is oneself with a vengeance;
      Oneself, and nothing whatever besides.

We go, full sail, as our very selves.
Each one shuts himself up in the barrel of self,
In the self-fermentation he dives to the bottom –
With the self-bung he seals it hermetically,
And seasons the staves in the well of self.
No one has tears for the other's woes;
No one has mind for the other's ideas.
We're our very selves, both in thought and tone,
Ourselves to the spring-board's uttermost verge –
And so, if a Kaiser's to fill the throne,
It is clear that you are the very man.

PEER   O would that the devil – !

BEGRIFFENFELDT   Come, don't be cast down;
Almost all things in nature are new at the first.
'Oneself' – come, here you shall see an example;
I'll choose you at random the first man that comes.
  [*to a gloomy figure*]
Good-day, Huhu! Well, my boy, wandering round
For ever with misery's impress upon you?

HUHU   Can I help it, when the people,
              Race by race, dies untranslated?
  [*to Peer Gynt*] You're a stranger; will you listen?

PEER [*bowing*] Oh, by all means!

HUHU   Lend your ear then. –
              Eastward far, like brow-borne garlands,
              Lie the Malabarish seaboards.
              Hollanders and Portugueses
              Compass all the land with culture.
              There, moreover, swarms are dwelling
              Of the pure-bred Malabaris.
              These have muddled up the language,
              They now lord it in the country. –
              But in long-departed ages
              There the orang-outang was ruler.
              He, the forest's lord and master,
              Freely fought and snarled in freedom.
              As the hand of nature shaped him,
              Just so grinned he, just so gaped he.
              He could shriek unreprehended;

He was ruler in his kingdom. –
Ah, but then the foreign yoke came,
Marred the forest-tongue primeval.
Twice two hundred years of darkness
Brooded o'er the race of monkeys;
And, you know, nights so protracted
Bring a people to a standstill. –
Mute are now the wood-notes primal;
Grunts and growls are heard no longer –
If we'd utter our ideas,
It must be by means of language.
What constraint on all and sundry!
Hollanders and Portugueses,
Half-caste race and Malabaris,
All alike must suffer by it. –
I have tried to fight the battle
Of our real, primal wood-speech –
Tried to bring to life its carcass –
Proved the people's right of shrieking –
Shrieked myself, and shown the need of
Shrieks in poems for the people. –
Scantly, though, my work is valued. –
Now I think you grasp my sorrow.
Thanks for lending me a hearing –
Have you counsel, let me hear it!

PEER [*softly*]   It is written: Best be howling
With the wolves that are about you.

[*aloud*]   Friend, if I remember rightly,
There are bushes in Morocco,
Where orang-outangs in plenty
Live with neither bard nor spokesman –
Their speech sounded Malabarish –
It was classical and pleasing.
Why don't you, like other worthies,
Emigrate to serve your country?

HUHU   Thanks for lending me a hearing –
I will do as you advise me.

[*with a large gesture*] East! thou hast disowned thy singer!
West! thou hast orang-outangs still!   [*goes*]

BEGRIFFENFELDT Well, was he himself? I should rather think so.
        He's filled with his own affairs, simply and solely.
        He's himself in all that comes out of him —
        Himself, just because he's beside himself.
        Come here! Now I'll show you another one,
        Who's no less, since last evening, accordant with Reason.
    [*to a Fellah, with a mummy on his back*]
        King Apis, how goes it, my mighty lord?
THE FELLAH [*wildly, to Peer Gynt*] Am I King Apis?
PEER [*getting behind the Doctor*]   I'm sorry to say
        I'm not quite at home in the situation;
        But I certainly gather, to judge by your tone —
THE FELLAH Now you too are lying.
BEGRIFFENFELDT   Your Highness should state
        How the whole matter stands.
THE FELLAH   Yes, I'll tell him my tale.
    [*turns to Peer Gynt*] Do you see whom I bear on my shoulders?
                His name was King Apis of old.
                Now he goes by the title of mummy,
                And withal he's completely dead.
                    All the pyramids yonder he builded,
                And hewed out the mighty Sphinx,
                And fought, as the Doctor puts it,
                With the Turks, both to *rechts* and *links*.
                    And therefore the whole of Egypt
                Exalted him as a god,
                And set up his image in temples,
                In the outward shape of a bull. —
                    But I am this very King Apis,
                I see that as clear as day;
                And if you don't understand it,
                You shall understand it soon.
                    King Apis, you see, was out hunting,
                And got off his horse awhile,
                And withdrew himself unattended
                To a part of my ancestor's land.
                    But the field that King Apis manured
                Has nourished me with its corn,
                And if further proofs are demanded,

Know, I have invisible horns.
Now, isn't it most accursed
That no one will own my might!
By birth I am Apis of Egypt,
But a fellah in other men's sight.
　　　Can you tell me what course to follow? –
Then counsel me honestly. –
The problem is how to make me
Resemble King Apis the Great.

PEER　　　　　Build pyramids then, your highness,
And carve out a greater Sphinx,
And fight, as the Doctor puts it,
With the Turks, both to *rechts* and *links*.

THE FELLAH　　Ay, that is all mighty fine talking!
A fellah! A hungry louse!
I, who scarcely can keep my hovel
Clear even of rats and mice.
　　　Quick, man – think of something better,
That'll make me both great and safe,
And further, exactly like to
King Apis that's on my back!

PEER　　　　　What if your highness hanged you,
And then, in the lap of earth,
'Twixt the coffin's natural frontiers,
Kept still and completely dead.

THE FELLAH　　I'll do it! My life for a halter!
To the gallows with hide and hair! –
At first there will be some difference,
But that time will smooth away.
　　　　　　　　　[*goes off and prepares to hang himself*]

BEGRIFFENFELDT There's a personality for you, Herr Peer –
　　A man of method –

PEER　　　　　　　　　Yes, yes; I see – ;
　　But he'll really hang himself! God grant us grace!
　　I'll be ill – I can scarcely command my thoughts!

BEGRIFFENFELDT A state of transition; it won't last long.

PEER　Transition? To what? With your leave – I must go –

BEGRIFFENFELDT [*holding him*] Are you crazy?

PEER　　　　　　　　　Not yet – . Crazy? Heaven forbid!

A commotion. THE MINISTER HUSSEIN *forces his
way through the crowd.*

HUSSEIN They tell me a Kaiser has come today.
   [*to Peer Gynt*] It is you?
PEER [*in desperation*]   Yes, that is a settled thing!
HUSSEIN Good. – Then no doubt there are notes to be
                           answered?
PEER [*tearing his hair*] Come on! Right you are, sir – the
                      madder the better!
HUSSEIN Will you do me the honour of taking a dip?
   [*bowing deeply*] I am a pen.
PEER [*bowing still deeper*]   Why then I am quite clearly
   A rubbishy piece of imperial parchment.
HUSSEIN My story, my lord, is concisely this:
   They take me for a sand-box, and I am a pen.
PEER   My story, Sir Pen, is, to put it briefly:
   I'm a blank sheet of paper that no one will write on.
HUSSEIN No man understands in the least what I'm good for;
   They all want to use me for scattering sand with!
PEER   I was in a woman's keeping a silver-clasped book –
   It's one and the same misprint to be either mad or sane!
HUSSEIN [*with high leap*] Just fancy, what an exhausting life:
   To be a pen and never taste the edge of a knife!
PEER   Just fancy, for a reindeer to leap from on high –
   To fall and fall – and never feel the ground beneath
                        your hoofs!
HUSSEIN A knife! I am blunt – quick, mend me and slit me!
   The world will go to ruin if they don't mend my
                     point for me!
PEER   A pity for the world which, like other self-made things,
   Was reckoned by the Lord to be so excellently good.
BEGRIFFENFELDT Here's a knife!
HUSSEIN [*seizing it*]   Ah, how I shall lick up the ink now!
   Oh, what rapture to cut oneself! [*cuts his throat*]
BEGRIFFENFELDT [*stepping aside*]   Pray do not sputter.
PEER [*in increasing terror*] Hold him!
HUSSEIN   Ay, hold me! That is the word!
   Hold! Hold the pen! On the desk with the paper – ! [*falls*]

I'm outworn. The postscript – remember it, pray:
He lived and he died as a fate-guided pen!

PEER [*dizzily*]

What shall I – ! What am I? Thou mighty – , hold fast!
I am all that thou wilt – I'm a Turk, I'm a sinner –
A hill–troll – but help – there was something that burst – !
[*shrieks*] I cannot just hit on thy name at the moment –
Oh, come to my aid, thou – all madmen's protector!
[*sinks down insensible*]

BEGRIFFENFELDT [*with a wreath of straw in his* hand, *gives a bound and sits astride of him*]

Ha! See him in the mire enthroned –
Beside himself – ! To crown him now!
[*presses the wreath on Peer Gynt's head, and shouts*]
Long life, long life to Self–hood's Kaiser!

SCHAFMANN [*in the cage*] *Es lebe hoch der grosse Peer!*

ACT FIFTH

SCENE FIRST

On board a ship on the North Sea, off the Norwegian coast. Sunset. Stormy weather.

PEER GYNT, *a vigorous old man, with grizzled hair and beard, is standing aft on the poop. He is dressed half sailor-fashion, with a pea-jacket and long boots. His clothing is rather the worse for wear; he himself is weather-beaten, and has a somewhat harder expression.* THE CAPTAIN *is standing beside the steersman at the wheel. The crew are forward.*

PEER GYNT [*leans with his arms on the bulwark, and gazes towards the land*] Look at Hallingskarv in his winter furs –
    He's ruffling it, old one, in the evening glow.
    The Jokel, his brother, stands behind him askew;
    He's got his green ice-mantle still on his back.
    The Flogefånn, now, she is mighty fine –
    Lying there like a maiden in spotless white.
    Don't you be madcaps, old boys that you are!
    Stand where you stand; you're but granite knobs.
THE CAPTAIN [*shouts forward*]
    Two hands to the wheel, and the lantern aloft!
PEER   It's blowing up stiff –
THE CAPTAIN   – for a gale tonight.
PEER   Can one see the Rondë Hills from the sea?
THE CAPTAIN No, how should you? They lie at the back of
                           the snow-fields.
PEER   Or Blåhö?
THE CAPTAIN   No; but from up in the rigging,
    You've a glimpse, in clear weather, of Galdhöpiggen.
PEER   Where does Hårteig lie?

THE CAPTAIN [*pointing*]   About over there.

PEER   I thought so.

THE CAPTAIN You know where you are, it appears.

PEER   When I left the country, I sailed by here;
   And the dregs, says the proverb, hang in to the last.
  [*spits, and gazes at the coast*]
   In there, where the scaurs and the clefts lie blue –
   Where the valleys, like trenches, gloom narrow and black,
   And underneath, skirting the open fiords –
   It's in places like these human beings abide.
  [*looks at the Captain*]
   They build far apart in this country.

THE CAPTAIN   Ay;
   Few are the dwellings and far between.

PEER   Shall we get in by day-break?

THE CAPTAIN   Thereabouts;
   If we don't have too dirty a night altogether.

PEER   It grows thick in the west.

THE CAPTAIN   It does so.

PEER   Stop a bit!
   You might put me in mind when we make up accounts –
   I'm inclined, as the phrase goes, to do a good turn
   To the crew –

THE CAPTAIN   I thank you.

PEER   It won't be much.
   I have dug for gold, and lost what I found –
   We are quite at loggerheads, Fate and I.
   You know what I've got in safe keeping on board –
   That's all I have left – the rest's gone to the devil.

THE CAPTAIN It's more than enough, though, to make
            you of weight
   Among people at home here.

PEER   I've no relations.
   There's no one awaiting the rich old curmudgeon. –
   Well; that saves you, at least, any scenes on the pier!

THE CAPTAIN Here comes the storm.

PEER   Well, remember then –
   If any of your crew are in real need,
   I won't look too closely after the money –

THE CAPTAIN That's kind. They are most of them ill enough off;
  They have all got their wives and their children at home.
  With their wages alone they can scarce make ends meet;
  But if they come home with some cash to the good,
  It will be a return not forgot in a hurry.

PEER What do you say? Have they wives and children?
  Are they married?

THE CAPTAIN   Married? Ay, every man of them.
  But the one that is worst off of all is the cook;
  Black famine is ever at home in his house.

PEER Married? They've folks that await them at home?
  Folks to be glad when they come? Eh?

THE CAPTAIN   Of course,
  In poor people's fashion.

PEER   And come they one evening,
  What then?

THE CAPTAIN Why, I dare say the goodwife will fetch
  Something good for a treat –

PEER   And a light in the sconce?

THE CAPTAIN Ay, ay, may be two; and a dram to their supper.

PEER And there they sit snug! There's a fire on the hearth!
  They've their children about them! The room's full
          of chatter;
  Not one hears another right out to an end,
  For the joy that is on them – !

THE CAPTAIN   It's likely enough.
  So it's really kind, as you promised just now,
  To help eke things out.

PEER [*thumping the bulwark*] I'll be damned if I do!
  Do you think I am mad? Would you have me fork out
  For the sake of a parcel of other folks' brats?
  I've slaved much too sorely in earning my cash!
  There's nobody waiting for old Peer Gynt.

THE CAPTAIN Well well; as you please then; your money's
          your own.

PEER Right! Mine it is, and no one else's.
  We'll reckon as soon as your anchor is down!
  Take my fare, in the cabin, from Panama here.
  Then brandy all round to the crew. Nothing more.

If I give a doit more, slap my jaw for me, Captain.

THE CAPTAIN I owe you a quittance, and not a thrashing –
    But excuse me, the wind's blowing up to a gale.
    [*He goes forward. It has fallen dark; lights are lit in the cabin.
    The sea increases. Fog and thick clouds*]

PEER   To have a whole bevy of youngsters at home –
    Still to dwell in their minds as a coming delight –
    To have others' thoughts follow you still on your
                                                    path! –
    There's never a soul gives a thought to me. –
    Lights in the sconces! I'll put out those lights.
    I will hit upon something! – I'll make them all drunk –
    Not one of the devils shall go sober ashore.
    They shall all come home drunk to their children
                                            and wives!
    They shall curse; bang the table till it rings again –
    They shall scare those that wait for them out of
                                            their wits!
    The goodwife shall scream and rush forth from
                                            the house –
    Clutch her children along! All their joy gone to ruin!
    [*The ship gives a heavy lurch; he staggersand keeps his balance
    with difficulty*]
    Why, that was a buffet and no mistake.
    The sea's hard at labour, as though it were paid for it –
    It's still itself here on the coasts of the north –
    A cross-sea, as wry and wrong-headed as ever –
    [*listens*]
    Why, what can those screams be?

THE LOOKOUT [*forward*]   A wreck a-lee!

THE CAPTAIN [*on the main deck, shouts*]
    Helm hard a-starboard! Bring her up to the wind!

THE MATE Are there men on the wreck?

THE LOOKOUT   I can just see three!

PEER   Quick! lower the stern boat –

THE CAPTAIN   She'd fill ere she floated. [*goes forward*]

PEER   Who can think of that now?
    [*to some of the crew*]   If you're men, to the rescue!
    What the devil, if you should get a bit of a ducking!

THE BOATSWAIN It's out of the question in such a sea.

PEER   They are screaming again! There's a lull in the wind. –
  Cook, will you risk it? Quick! I will pay –

THE COOK No, not if you offered me twenty pounds-sterling –

PEER   You hounds! You chicken-hearts! Can you forget
  These are men that have goodwives and children
            at home?
  There they're sitting and waiting –

THE BOATSWAIN   Well, patience is wholesome.

THE CAPTAIN Bear away from that sea!

THE MATE   There the wreck turned over!

PEER   All is silent of a sudden – !

THE BOATSWAIN Were they married, as you think,
  There are three new-baked widows even now in
            the world.

  [*The storm increases. Peer Gynt moves away aft*]

PEER   There is no faith left among men any more –
  No Christianity – well may they say it and write it –
  Their good deeds are few and their prayers are
            still fewer,
  And they pay no respect to the Powers above them. –
  In a storm like tonight's, he's a terror, the Lord is.
  These beasts should be careful, and think, what's
            the truth,
  That it's dangerous playing with elephants –
  And yet they must openly brave his displeasure!
  I am no whit to blame; for the sacrifice
  I can prove I stood ready, my money in hand.
  But how does it profit me? – What says the proverb?
  A conscience at ease is a pillow of down.
  Oh ay, that is all very well on dry land,
  But I'm blest if it matters a snuff on board ship,
  When a decent man's out on the seas with such riff-raff.
  At sea one never can be one's self;
  One must go with the others from deck to keel;
  If for boatswain and cook the hour of vengeance
            should strike,
  I shall no doubt be swept to the deuce with the rest –
  One's personal welfare is clean set aside –

One counts but as a sausage in slaughtering-time. –
My mistake is this: I have been too meek;
And I've had no thanks for it after all.
Were I younger, I think I would shift the saddle,
And try how it answered to lord it awhile.
There is time enough yet! They shall know in the parish
That Peer has come sailing aloft o'er the seas!
I'll get back the farmstead by fair means or foul –
I will build it anew; it shall shine like a palace.
But none shall be suffered to enter the hall!
They shall stand at the gateway, all twirling their caps –
They shall beg and beseech – that they freely may do;
But none gets so much as a farthing of mine.
If I've had to howl 'neath the lashes of fate,
Trust me to find folks I can lash in my turn –

THE STRANGE PASSENGER [*stands in the darkness at Peer* Gynt's
   side, and salutes him in friendly fashion]
               Good evening!

PEER   Good evening! What – ? Who are you?

THE PASSENGER Your fellow-passenger, at your service.

PEER   Indeed? I thought I was the only one.

THE PASSENGER A mistaken impression, which now is set right.

PEER   But it's singular that, for the first time tonight,
       I should see you –

THE PASSENGER I never come out in the day-time.

PEER   Perhaps you are ill? You're as white as a sheet –

THE PASSENGER No, thank you – my health is uncommonly
                                                    good.

PEER   What a raging storm!

THE PASSENGER   Ay, a blessed one, man!

PEER   A blessed one?

THE PASSENGER   Sea's running high as houses.
       Ah, one can feel one's mouth watering!
       Just think of the wrecks that tonight will be shattered –
       And think, too, what corpses will drive ashore!

PEER   Lord save us!

THE PASSENGER   Have ever you seen a man strangled,
       Or hanged – or drowned?

PEER   This is going too far – !

THE PASSENGER The corpses all laugh. But their laughter
                                                    is forced;
    And the most part are found to have bitten their
                                                    tongues.
PEER   Hold off from me – !
THE PASSENGER   Only one question pray!
    If we, for example, should strike on a rock,
    And sink in the darkness –
PEER   You think there is danger?
THE PASSENGER I really don't know what I ought to say.
    But suppose, now, I float and you go to the bottom –
PEER   Oh, rubbish –
THE PASSENGER   It's just a hypothesis.
    But when one is placed with one foot in the grave,
    One grows soft-hearted and open-handed –
PEER [puts his hand in his pocket] Ho, money!
THE PASSENGER   No, no; but perhaps you would kindly
    Make me a gift of your much-esteemed carcass – ?
PEER   This is too much!
THE PASSENGER   No more than your body, you know!
    To help my researches in science –
PEER   Begone!
THE PASSENGER But think, my dear sir – the advantage is yours!
    I'll have you laid open and brought to the light.
    What I specially seek is the centre of dreams –
    And with critical care I'll look into your seams –
PEER   Away with you!
THE PASSENGER   Why, my dear sir – a drowned corpse – !
PEER   Blasphemer! You're goading the rage of the storm!
    I call it too bad! Here it's raining and blowing,
    A terrible sea on, and all sorts of signs
    Of something that's likely to shorten our days –
    And you carry on so as to make it come quicker!
THE PASSENGER You're in no mood, I see, to negotiate further;
    But time, you know, brings with it many a change –
  [nods in a friendly fashion]
    We'll meet when you're sinking, if not before;
    Perhaps I may then find you more in the humour.
                    [goes into the cabin]

PEER   Unpleasant companions these scientists are!
            With their freethinking ways –
        [*to the Boatswain, who is passing*] Hark, a word with you, friend!
            That passenger? What crazy creature is he?
THE BOATSWAIN I know of no passenger here but yourself.
PEER   No others? This thing's getting worse and worse.
        [*to the Ship's Boy, who comes out of the cabin*]
            Who went down the companion just now?
THE BOY   The ship's dog, sir! [*passes on*]
THE LOOKOUT [*shouts*] Land close ahead!
PEER   Where's my box? Where's my trunk?
            All the baggage on deck!
THE BOATSWAIN   We have more to attend to!
PEER   It was nonsense, captain! 'Twas only my joke –
            As sure as I'm here I will help the cook –
THE CAPTAIN The jib's blown away!
THE MATE   And there went the foresail!
THE BOATSWAIN [*shrieks from forward*]
            Breakers under the bow!
THE CAPTAIN   She will go to shivers!
                            [*The ship strikes. Noise and confusion*]

SCENE SECOND

*Close under the land, among sunken rocks and surf. The ship
sinks. The jolly-boat, with two men in her, is seen for a moment
through the scud. A sea strikes her; she fills and upsets. A shriek is
heard; then all is silent for a while. Shortly afterwards the boat
appears floating bottom upwards.*

    PEER GYNT *comes to the surface near the boat.*

PEER   Help! Help! A boat! Help! I'll be drowned!
            Save me, oh Lord – as saith the text!
        [*clutches hold of the boat's keel*]
THE COOK [*comes up on the other side*]
            Oh, Lord God – for my children's sake,
            Have mercy! Let me reach the land!
        [*seizes hold of the keel*]

PEER   Let go!

THE COOK   Let go!

PEER   I'll strike!

THE COOK   So'll I!

PEER   I'll crush you down with kicks and blows!
       Let go your hold! She won't float two!

THE COOK I know it! Yield!

PEER   Yield you!

THE COOK   Oh yes!
   [*they fight; one of the Cook's hands is disabled; he clings on
   with the other*]

PEER   Off with that hand!

THE COOK   Oh, kind sir – spare!
       Think of my little ones at home!

PEER   I need my life far more than you,
       For I am lone and childless still.

THE COOK Let go! You've lived, and I am young!

PEER   Quick; haste you; sink – you drag us down.

THE COOK Have mercy! Yield in heaven's name!
       There's none to miss and mourn for you –
   [*his hand slips; he screams*]
       I'm drowning!

PEER [*seizing him*]   By this wisp of hair
       I'll hold you; say your Lord's Prayer, quick!

THE COOK I can't remember; all turns black –

PEER   Come, the essentials in a word – !

THE COOK Give us this day – !

PEER   Skip that part, Cook;
       You'll get all you need, safe enough.

THE COOK Give us this day –

PEER   The same old song!
       One sees you were a cook in life –
   [*the Cook slips from his grasp*]

THE COOK [*sinking*] Give us this day our –   [*disappears*]

PEER   Amen, lad!
       To the last gasp you were yourself. –
   [*draws himself up on to the bottom of the boat*]
       So long as there is life there's hope –

THE STRANGE PASSENGER [*catches hold of the boat*]
       Good morning!

PEER   Hoy!

THE PASSENGER   I heard you shout. –
 It's pleasant finding you again.
 Well? So my prophecy came true!

PEER Let go! Let go! 'twill scarce float one!

THE PASSENGER I'm striking out with my left leg.
 I'll float, if only with their tips
 My fingers rest upon this ledge.
 But apropos: your body –

PEER   Hush!

THE PASSENGER The rest, of course, is done for, clean –

PEER No more!

THE PASSENGER Exactly as you please. [*silence*]

PEER Well?

THE PASSENGER I am silent.

PEER   Satan's tricks! –
 What now?

THE PASSENGER I'm waiting.

PEER [*tearing his hair*]   I'll go mad! –
 What are you?

THE PASSENGER [*nods*] Friendly.

PEER   What else? Speak!

THE PASSENGER What think you? Do you know none other
 That's like me?

PEER   Do I know the devil – ?

THE PASSENGER [*in a low voice*] Is it his way to light a lantern
 For life's night-pilgrimage through fear?

PEER Ah, come! When once the thing's cleared up,
 You'd seem a messenger of light?

THE PASSENGER Friend – have you once in each half-year
 Felt all the earnestness of dread?

PEER Why, one's afraid when danger threatens –
 But all your words have double meanings.

THE PASSENGER Ay, have you gained but once in life
 The victory that is given in dread?

PEER [*looks at him*] Came you to ope for me a door,
 'Twas stupid not to come before.
 What sort of sense is there in choosing
 Your time when seas gape to devour one?

THE PASSENGER Were, then, the victory more likely
         Beside your hearth-stone, snug and quiet?
PEER   Perhaps not; but your talk befooled me.
         How could you fancy it awakening?
THE PASSENGER Where I come from, there smiles are prized
         As highly as pathetic style.
PEER   All has its time; what fits the taxman,
         So says the text, would damn the bishop.
THE PASSENGER The host whose dust inurned has slumbered
         Treads not on weekdays the *cothurnus*.
PEER   Avaunt thee, bugbear! Man, begone!
         I will not die! I must ashore!
THE PASSENGER Oh, as for that, be reassured –
         One dies not midmost of Act Five.   [*glides away*]
PEER   Ah, there he let it out at last –
         He was a sorry moralist.

SCENE THIRD

*Churchyard in a high-lying mountain parish. A funeral is
going on. By the grave, the* PRIEST *and a gathering of people.
The last verse of the psalm is being sung.* PEER GYNT *passes
by on the road.*

PEER [*at the gate*]
         Here's a countryman going the way of all flesh.
         God be thanked that it isn't me.
    [*enters the churchyard*]
THE PRIEST [*speaking beside the grave*]
             Now, when the soul has gone to meet its doom,
         And here the dust lies, like an empty pod –
         Now, my dear friends, we'll speak a word or two
         About this dead man's pilgrimage on earth.
             He was not wealthy, neither was he wise,
         His voice was weak, his bearing was unmanly,
         He spoke his mind abashed and faltering,

He scarce was master at his own fireside;
He sidled into church, as though appealing for leave,
Like other men, to take his place.

It was from Gudbrandsdale, you know, he came.
When here he settled he was but a lad –
And you remember how, to the very last,
He kept his right hand hidden in his pocket.

That right hand in the pocket was the feature
That chiefly stamped his image on the mind –
And therewithal his writhing, his abashed
Shrinking from notice wheresoe'er he went.

But, though he still pursued a path aloof,
And ever seemed a stranger in our midst,
You all know what he strove so hard to hide –
The hand he muffled had four fingers only. –

I well remember, many years ago,
One morning; there were sessions held at Lunde.
'Twas war-time, and the talk in every mouth
Turned on the country's sufferings and its fate.

I stood there watching. At the table sat
The Captain, 'twixt the bailiff and the sergeants;
Lad after lad was measured up and down,
Passed, and enrolled, and taken for a soldier.
The room was full, and from the green outside,
Where thronged the young folks, loud the laughter rang.

A name was called, and forth another stepped,
One pale as snow upon the glacier's edge.
They bade the youth advance; he reached the table;
We saw his right hand swaddled in a clout –
He gasped, he swallowed, battling after words –
But, though the Captain urged him, found no voice.
Ah yes, at last! Then with his cheek aflame,
His tongue now failing him, now stammering fast,
He mumbled something of a scythe that slipped
By chance, and shore his finger to the skin.

Straightway a silence fell upon the room.
Men bandied meaning glances; they made mouths;
They stoned the boy with looks of silent scorn.
He felt the hail-storm, but he saw it not.

Then up the Captain stood, the grey old man;
He spat, and pointed forth, and thundered 'Go!'
    And the lad went. On both sides men fell back,
Till through their midst he had to run the gauntlet.
He reached the door; from there he took to flight –
Up, up he went – through wood and over hillside,
Up through the stone-slips, rough, precipitous.
He had his home up there among the mountains. –
    It was some six months later he came here,
With mother, and betrothed, and little child.
He leased some ground upon the high hillside,
There where the waste lands trend away towards Lomb.
He married the first moment that he could;
He built a house; he broke the stubborn soil;
He throve, as many a cultivated patch
Bore witness, bravely clad in waving gold.
At church he kept his right hand in his pocket –
But sure I am at home his fingers nine
Toiled every bit as hard as others' ten. –
One spring the torrent washed it all away.
    Their lives were spared. Ruined and stripped of all,
He set to work to make another clearing;
And, ere the autumn, smoke again arose
From a new, better-sheltered, mountain farm-house.
Sheltered? From torrent – not from avalanche;
Two years, and all beneath the snow lay buried.
    But still the avalanche could not daunt his spirit.
He dug, and raked, and carted – cleared the ground –
And the next winter, ere the snow-blasts came,
A third time was his little homestead reared.
    Three sons he had, three bright and stirring boys;
They must to school, and school was far away –
And they must clamber where the hill-track failed,
By narrow ledges through the headlong scaur.
What did he do? The eldest had to manage
As best he might, and, where the path was worst,
His father cast a rope round him to stay him –
The others on his back and arms he bore.
    Thus he toiled, year by year, till they were men.

Now might he well have looked for some return.
In the New World, three prosperous gentlemen
Their school-going and their father have forgotten.

  He was short-sighted. Out beyond the circle
Of those most near to him he nothing saw.
To him seemed meaningless as cymbals' tinkling
Those words that to the heart should ring like steel.
His race, his fatherland, all things high and shining,
Stood ever, to his vision, veiled in mist.

  But he was humble, humble, was this man;
And since that sessions-day his doom oppressed him,
As surely as his cheeks were flushed with shame,
And his four fingers hidden in his pocket. –
Offender 'gainst his country's laws? Ay, true!
But there is one thing that the law outshineth
Sure as the snow-white tent of Glittertind
Has clouds, like higher rows of peaks, above it.
No patriot was he. Both for church and state
A fruitless tree. But there, on the upland ridge,
In the small circle where he saw his calling,
There he was great, because he was himself.
His inborn note rang true unto the end.
His days were as a lute with muted strings.
And therefore, peace be with thee, silent warrior,
That fought the peasant's little fight, and fell!

  It is not ours to search the heart and reins –
That is no task for dust, but for its ruler –
Yet dare I freely, firmly, speak my hope:
He scarce stands crippled now before his God!

[*The gathering disperses. Peer Gynt remains behind, alone.*]

PEER   Now that is what I call Christianity!
Nothing to seize on one's mind unpleasantly. –
And the topic – immovably being oneself –
That the pastor's homily turned upon –
Is full, in its essence, of edification.

[*looks down upon the grave*]

Was it he, I wonder, that hacked through his knuckle
That day I was out hewing logs in the forest?
Who knows? If I weren't standing here with my staff

By the side of the grave of this kinsman in spirit,
I could almost believe it was I that slept,
And heard in a vision my panegyric. –
It's a seemly and Christianlike custom indeed
This casting a so-called memorial glance
In charity over the life that is ended.
I shouldn't at all mind accepting my verdict
At the hands of this excellent parish priest.
Ah well, I dare say I have some time left
Ere the gravedigger comes to invite me to stay with him –
And as Scripture has it: What's best is best –
And: Enough for the day is the evil thereof –
And further: Discount not thy funeral. –
Ah, the church, after all, is the true consoler.
I've hitherto scarcely appreciated it –
But now I feel clearly how blessed it is
To be well assured upon sound authority:
Even as thou sowest thou shalt one day reap. –
One must be oneself; for oneself and one's own
One must do one's best, both in great and in small
                                        things.
If the luck goes against you, at least you've the honour
Of a life carried through in accordance with principle. –
Now homewards! Though narrow and steep the path,
Though Fate to the end may be never so biting –
Still old Peer Gynt will pursue his own way,
And remain what he is: poor, but virtuous ever.

                                        [goes out]

SCENE FOURTH

A hillside seamed by the dry bed of a torrent. A ruined mill-house
beside the stream. The ground is torn up, and the whole place
waste. Further up the hill, a large farm-house.
    An auction is going on in front of the farm-house. There is a
great gathering of people, who are drinking, with much noise.
PEER GYNT *is sitting on a rubbish-heap beside the mill.*

PEER   Forward and back, and it's just as far;
        Out and in, and it's just as strait. –
        Time wears away and the river gnaws on.
        Go roundabout, the Boyg said – and here one must.
A MAN DRESSED IN MOURNING.
        Now there is only rubbish left over.
    [*catches sight of Peer Gynt*] Are there strangers here too?
                                    God be with you, good friend!
PEER   Well met! You have lively times here today.
        Is't a christening junket or a wedding feast?
MAN IN MOURNING I'd rather call it a house–warming treat –
        The bride is laid in a wormy bed.
PEER   And the worms are squabbling for rags and clouts.
MAN IN MOURNING That's the end of the ditty; it's over
                                            and done.
PEER   All the ditties end just alike;
        And they're all old together; I knew 'em as a boy.
A LAD OF TWENTY [*with a casting-ladle*]
        Just look what a rare thing I've been buying!
        In this Peer Gynt cast his silver buttons.
ANOTHER Look at mine, though! The money-bag bought
                                        for a halfpenny.
A THIRD No more, eh? Twopence for the pedlar's pack!
PEER Peer Gynt? Who was he?
MAN IN MOURNING   All I know is this:
        He was kinsman to Death and to Aslak the Smith.
A MAN IN GREY You're forgetting me, man! Are you mad
                                        or drunk?

MAN IN MOURNING You forget that at Hegstad was a storehouse
                                                                    door.
MAN IN GREY Ay, true; but we know you were never dainty.
MAN IN MOURNING If only she doesn't give Death the slip –
MAN IN GREY Come, kinsman! A dram, for our kinship's sake!
MAN IN MOURNING To the deuce with your kinship! You're
                                    maundering in drink –
MAN IN GREY Oh, rubbish; blood's never so thin as all that;
        One cannot but feel one's akin to Peer Gynt.

                                        [goes off with him]

PEER [to himself] One meets with acquaintances.
A LAD [calls after the Man in Mourning]   Mother that's dead
        Will be after you, Aslak, if you wet your whistle.
PEER [rises] The agriculturists' saying seems scarce to hold here:
        The deeper one harrows the better it smells.
A LAD [with a bear's skin]
        Look, the cat of the Dovrë! Well, only his fell.
        It was he chased the trolls out on Christmas Eve.
ANOTHER [with a reindeer-skull]
        Here is the wonderful reindeer that bore,
        At Gendin, Peer Gynt over edge and scaur.
A THIRD [with a hammer, calls out to the Man in Mourning]
        Hei, Aslak, this sledge-hammer, say, do you know it?
        Was it this that you used when the devil clove the wall?
A FOURTH [empty-handed]
        Mads Moen, here's the invisible cloak
        Peer Gynt and Ingrid flew off through the air with.
PEER   Brandy here, boys! I feel I'm grown old –
        I must put up to auction my rubbish and lumber!
A LAD What have you to sell, then?
PEER   A palace I have –
        It lies in the Rondë; it's solidly built.
THE LAD A button is bid!
PEER   You must run to a dram.
        'Twere a sin and a shame to bid anything less.
ANOTHER He's a jolly old boy this!
    [the bystanders crowd round him]
PEER [shouts]   Grane, my steed;
        Who bids?
ONE OF THE CROWD Where's he running?

PEER   Why, far in the west!
      Near the sunset, my lads! Ah, that courser can fly
      As fast, ay, as fast as Peer Gynt could lie.

VOICES. What more have you got?

PEER   I've both rubbish and gold!
      I bought it with ruin; I'll sell it at a loss.

A LAD Put it up!

PEER   A dream of a silver-clasped book!
      That you can have for an old hook and eye.

THE LAD To the devil with dreams!

PEER   Here's my Kaiserdom!
      I throw it in the midst of you; scramble for it!

THE LAD Is the crown given in?

PEER   Of the loveliest straw.
      It will fit whoever first puts it on.
      Hei, there is more yet! An addled egg!
      A madman's grey hair! And the Prophet's beard!
      All these shall be his that will show on the hillside
      A post that has writ on it: Here lies your path!

THE BAILIFF [who has come up]
      You're carrying on, my good man, so that almost
      I think that your path will lead straight to the lock-up.

PEER [hat in hand]
      Quite likely. But, tell me, who was Peer Gynt?

THE BAILIFF Oh, nonsense –

PEER   Your pardon! Most humbly I beg – !

THE BAILIFF Oh, he's said to have been an abominable liar –

PEER A liar – ?

THE BAILIFF   Yes – all that was strong and great
      He made believe always that he had done it.
      But, excuse me, friend – I have other duties –   [goes

PEER   And where is he now, this remarkable man?

AN ELDERLY MAN He fared over seas to a foreign land;
      It went ill with him there, as one well might foresee –
      It's many a year now since he was hanged.

PEER   Hanged! Ay, ay! Why, I thought as much;
      Our lamented Peer Gynt was himself to the last. [bows]
      Goodbye – and best thanks for today's merry meeting.

    [goes a few steps, but stops again]

You joyous youngsters, you comely lasses –
Shall I pay my shot with a traveller's tale?
SEVERAL VOICES Do you know any?
PEER   Nothing more easy. –
    [*he comes nearer; a look of strangeness comes over him*]
        I was gold-digging once in San Francisco.
        There were mountebanks swarming all over the town.
        One with his toes could perform on the fiddle;
        Another could dance a Spanish halling on his knees;
        A third, I was told, kept on making verses
        While his brain-pan was having a hole bored right
                                                    through it.
        To the mountebank-meeting came also the devil –
        Thought he'd try his luck with the rest of them.
        His talent was this: in a manner convincing,
        He was able to grunt like a flesh-and-blood pig.
        He was not recognised, yet his manners attracted.
        The house was well filled; expectation ran high.
        He stepped forth in a cloak with an ample cape to it;
        Man muss sich drappiren, as the Germans say.
        But under the mantle – what none suspected –
        He'd managed to smuggle a real live pig.
        And now he opened the representation;
        The devil he pinched, and the pig gave voice.
        The whole thing purported to be a fantasia
        On the porcine existence, both free and in bonds;
        And all ended up with a slaughter-house squeal –
        Whereupon the performer bowed low and retired. –
        The critics discussed and appraised the affair;
        The tone of the whole was attacked and defended.
        Some fancied the vocal expression too thin,
        While some thought the death-shriek too carefully
                                                    studied;
        But all were agreed as to one thing: *qua* grunt,
        The performance was grossly exaggerated. –
        Now that, you see, came of the devil's stupidity
        In not taking the measure of his public first.
                            [*he bows and goes off. A puzzled
                                silence comes over the crowd*]

SCENE FIFTH

Whitsun Eve. − In the depths of the forest. To the back, in a
clearing, is a hut with a pair of reindeer horns over the porch-gable.
    PEER GYNT *is creeping among the undergrowth, gathering wild*
onions.

PEER   Well, this is one standpoint. Where is the next?
        One should try all things and choose the best.
        Well, I have done so − beginning from Caesar,
        And downwards as far as to Nebuchadnezzar.
        So I had, after all, to go through Bible history −
        The old boy's had to take to his mother again.
        After all it is written: Of the earth art thou come. −
        The main thing in life is to fill one's belly.
        Fill it with onions? That's not much good −
        I must take to cunning, and set out snares.
        There's water in the beck here; I shan't suffer thirst;
        And I count as the first 'mong the beasts after all.
        When my time comes to die − as most likely it will −
        I shall crawl in under a wind-fallen tree;
        Like the bear, I will heap up a leaf-mound above me,
        And I'll scratch in big print on the bark of the tree:
        Here rests Peer Gynt, that decent soul,
        Kaiser o'er all of the other beasts. −
        Kaiser? [*laughs inwardly*] Why, you old soothsayer-
                                              humbug!
        No Kaiser are you; you are nought but an onion.
        I'm going to peel you now, my good Peer!
        You won't escape either by begging or howling.
[*takes an onion and pulls off layer after layer*]
        There lies the outermost layer, all torn;
        That's the shipwrecked man on the jolly-boat's keel.
        Here's the passenger layer, scanty and thin −
        And yet in its taste there's a tang of Peer Gynt.
        Next underneath is the gold-digger ego;

The juice is all gone – if it ever had any.
This coarse-grained layer with the hardened skin
Is the peltry-hunter by Hudson's Bay.
The next one looks like a crown – oh, thanks!
We'll throw it away without more ado.
Here's the archaeologist, short but sturdy;
And here is the Prophet, juicy and fresh.
He stinks, as the Scripture has it, of lies,
Enough to bring the water to an honest man's eyes.
This layer that rolls itself softly together
Is the gentleman, living in ease and good cheer.
The next one seems sick. There are black streaks upon it –
Black symbolises both parsons and niggers.

[*pulls off several layers at once*]
What an enormous number of swathings!
Isn't the kernel soon coming to light?

[*pulls the whole onion to pieces*]
I'm blest if it is! To the innermost centre,
It's nothing but swathings – each smaller and smaller. –
Nature is witty!

[*throws the fragments away*] The devil take brooding!
If one goes about thinking, one's apt to stumble.
Well, I can at any rate laugh at that danger;
For here on all fours I am firmly planted.

[*scratches his head*] A queer enough business, the whole
                                                concern!
Life, as they say, plays with cards up its sleeve;
But when one snatches at them, they've disappeared,
And one grips something else – or else nothing at all.

[*he has come near to the hut; he catches sight of it and starts*]
This hut? On the heath – ! Ha!
                              [*rubs his eyes*] It seems exactly
As though I had known this same building before. –
The reindeer-horns jutting above the gable! –
A mermaid, shaped like a fish from the navel! –
Lies! there's no mermaid! But nails – and planks –
Bars too, to shut out hobgoblin thoughts! –

SOLVEIG [*singing in the hut*] Now all is ready for Whitsun Eve.
        Dearest boy of mine, far away,

        Comest thou soon?
      Is thy burden heavy,
        Take time, take time –
        I will await thee;
        I promised of old.

PEER [*rises, quiet and deadly pale*]
      One that's remembered – and one that's forgot.
      One that has squandered – and one that has saved. –
      Oh, earnest! – and never can the game be played o'er!
      Oh, dread! – here was my Kaiserdom!

                        [*hurries off along the wood path*]

SCENE SIXTH

Night. A heath, with fir-trees. A forest fire has been raging; charred tree-trunks are seen stretching for miles. White mists here and there clinging to the earth. PEER GYNT *comes running over the heath.*

PEER   Ashes, fog-scuds, dust wind-driven –
        Here's enough for building with!
        Stench and rottenness within it;
        All a whited sepulchre.
        Figments, dreams, and still-born knowledge
        Lay the pyramid's foundation;
        O'er them shall the work mount upwards,
        With its step on step of falsehood.
        Earnest shunned, repentance dreaded,
        Flaunt at the apex like a scutcheon,
        Fill the trump of judgment with their
        '*Petrus Gyntus Caesar fecit!*'

[*listens*] What is this, like children's weeping?
        Weeping, but half-way to song. –
        Thread-balls at my feet are rolling! –

[*kicking at them*] Off with you! You block my path!

THE THREAD-BALLS [*on the ground*]
        We are thoughts;
        Thou shouldst have thought us –

Feet to run on
Thou shouldst have given us!

PEER [*going round about*] I have given life to one –
'Twas a bungled, crook-legged thing!

THE THREAD-BALLS We should have soared up
Like clangorous voices –
And here we must trundle
As grey-yarn thread-balls.

PEER [*stumbling*] Thread-clue! You accursed scamp!
Would you trip your father's heels? [*flees*]

WITHERED LEAVES [*flying before the wind*]
We are a watchword;
Thou shouldst have proclaimed us!
See how thy dozing
Has woefully riddled us.
The worm has gnawed us
In every crevice;
We have never twined us
Like wreaths round fruitage.

PEER   Not in vain your birth, however –
Lie but still and serve as manure.

A SIGHING IN THE AIR We are songs;
Thou shouldst have sung us! –
A thousand times over
Hast thou cowed us and smothered us.
Down in thy heart's pit
We have lain and waited –
We were never called forth.
In thy gorge be poison!

PEER   Poison thee, thou foolish stave!
Had I time for verse and stuff? [*attempts a short cut*]

DEWDROPS [*dripping from the branches*]
We are tears
Unshed for ever.
Ice-spears, sharp-wounding,
We could have melted.
Now the barb rankles
In the shaggy bosom –
The wound is closed over;

	Our power is ended.
PEER	Thanks – I wept in Rondë-cloisters –
	None the less my tail-part smarted!
BROKEN STRAWS	We are deeds;
	Thou shouldst have achieved us!
	Doubt, the throttler,
	Has crippled and riven us.
	On the Day of Judgment
	We'll come a-flock,
	And tell the story –
	Then woe to you!
PEER	Rascal-tricks! How dare you debit
	What is negative against me? [*hastens away*]
ÅSE'S VOICE [*far away*]	Fie, what a post-boy!
	Hu, you've upset me!
	Snow's newly fallen here –
	Sadly it's smirched me. –
	You've driven me the wrong way.
	Peer, where's the castle?
	The Fiend has misled you
	With the switch from the cupboard!
PEER	Better haste away, poor fellow!
	With the devil's sins upon you,
	Soon you'll faint upon the hillside –
	Hard enough to bear one's own sins.

[*runs off*]

SCENE SEVENTH

Another part of the heath

PEER GYNT [*sings*] A sexton! A sexton! where are you, hounds?
A song from braying precentor-mouths;
Around your hat-brim a mourning band; –
My dead are many; I must follow their biers!

THE BUTTON-MOULDER, *with a box of tools, and a large casting-ladle, comes from a side-path.*

BUTTON-MOULDER Well met, old gaffer!

PEER Good evening, friend.

BUTTON-MOULDER The man's in a hurry. Why, where is
he going?

PEER To a grave-feast.

BUTTON-MOULDER Indeed? My sight's not very good –
Excuse me – your name doesn't chance to be Peer?

PEER Peer Gynt, as the saying is.

THE BUTTON-MOULDER That I call luck!
It's precisely Peer Gynt I am sent for tonight.

PEER You're sent for? What do you want?

BUTTON-MOULDER Why, see here;
I'm a button-moulder. You're to go into my ladle.

PEER And what to do there?

BUTTON-MOULDER To be melted up.

PEER To be melted?

BUTTON-MOULDER Here it is, empty and scoured.
Your grave is dug ready, your coffin bespoke.
The worms in your body will live at their ease –
But I have orders, without delay,
On Master's behalf to fetch in your soul.

PEER It can't be! Like this, without any warning – !

BUTTON-MOULDER It's an old tradition at burials and births
To appoint in secret the day of the feast,
With no warning at all to the guest of honour.

PEER Ay, ay, that's true. All my brain's awhirl.
You are – ?

BUTTON-MOULDER Why, I told you – a button-moulder.

PEER I see! A pet child has many nicknames.
So that's it, Peer; it is there you're to harbour!
But these, my good man, are most unfair proceedings!
I'm sure I deserve better treatment than this –
I'm not nearly so bad as perhaps you think –
I've done a good deal of good in the world –
At worst you may call me a sort of a bungler –
But certainly not an exceptional sinner.

BUTTON-MOULDER Why that is precisely the rub, my man;
You're no sinner at all in the higher sense;
That's why you're excused all the torture-pangs,

                    And land, like others, in the casting-ladle.
PEER   Give it what name you please – call it ladle or pool;
                    Spruce ale and swipes, they are both of them beer.
                    Avaunt from me, Satan!
BUTTON-MOULDER   You can't be so rude
                    As to take my foot for a horse's hoof?
PEER   On horse's hoof or on fox's claws –
                    Be off; and be careful what you're about!
BUTTON-MOULDER My friend, you're making a great mistake.
                    We're both in a hurry, and so, to save time,
                    I'll explain the reason of the whole affair.
                    You are, with your own lips you told me so,
                    No sinner on the so-called heroic scale –
                    Scarce middling even –
PEER   Ah, now you're beginning
                    To talk common sense
BUTTON-MOULDER   Just have patience a bit –
                    But to call you virtuous would be going too far. –
PEER   Well, you know I have never laid claim to that.
BUTTON-MOULDER You're nor one thing nor t'other then,
                                             only so-so.
                    A sinner of really grandiose style
                    Is nowadays not to be met on the highways.
                    It wants much more than merely to wallow in mire;
                    For both vigour and earnestness go to a sin.
PEER   Ay, it's very true, that remark of yours;
                    One has to lay on, like the old Berserkers.
BUTTON-MOULDER You, friend, on the other hand, took
                                             your sin lightly.
PEER   Only outwardly, friend, like a splash of mud.
BUTTON-MOULDER Ah, we'll soon be at one now. The
                                             sulphur pool
                    Is no place for you, who but plashed in the mire.
PEER   And in consequence, friend, I can go as I came?
BUTTON-MOULDER No, in consequence, friend, I must
                                             melt you up.
PEER   What tricks are these that you've hit upon
                    At home here, while I've been in foreign parts?
BUTTON-MOULDER The custom's as old as the Snake's creation;

It's designed to prevent loss of good material.
You've worked at the craft – you must know that often
A casting turns out, to speak plainly, mere dross;
The buttons, for instance, have sometimes no loop
                           to them.
    What did you do, then?

PEER   Flung the rubbish away.

BUTTON-MOULDER Ah, yes; Jon Gynt was well known
                             for a waster,
So long as he'd aught left in wallet or purse.
But Master, you see, he is thrifty, he is;
And that is why he's so well-to-do.
He flings nothing away as entirely worthless
That can be made use of as raw material.
Now, you were designed for a shining button
On the vest of the world; but your loop gave way;
So into the waste-box you needs must go,
And then, as they phrase it, be merged in the mass.

PEER   You're surely not meaning to melt me up,
    With Dick, Tom, and Harry, into something new?

BUTTON-MOULDER That's just what I do mean, and nothing else.
    We've done it already to plenty of folks.
    At Kongsberg they do just the same with money
    That's been current so long that its stamp's worn away.

PEER   But this is the wretchedest miserliness!
    My dear good friend, let me get off free –
    A loopless button, a worn out farthing –
    What is that to a man in your Master's position?

BUTTON-MOULDER Oh, so long as, and seeing, the spirit is in you,
    One always has value as so much metal.

PEER   No, I say! No! With both teeth and claws
    I'll fight against this! Sooner anything else!

BUTTON-MOULDER But what else? Come now, be reasonable.
    You know you're not airy enough for heaven –

PEER   I'm not hard to content; I don't aim so high –
    But I won't be deprived of one doit of my Self.
    Have me judged by the law in the old-fashioned way!
    For a certain time place me with Him of the Hoof –
    Say a hundred years, come the worst to the worst;

That, now, is a thing that one surely can bear;
For they say the torment is only moral,
So it can't be so pyramid-like after all.
It is, as 'tis written, a mere transition;
And as the fox said: One waits; there comes
An hour of deliverance; one lives in seclusion,
And hopes in the meantime for happier days. –
But this other notion – to have to be merged,
Like a mote, in the carcass of some outsider –
This casting-ladle business, this Gynt-cessation –
It stirs up my innermost soul in revolt!

BUTTON-MOULDER Bless me, my dear Peer, there is surely
                                               no need
To get so wrought up about trifles like this.
Yourself you never have been at all –
Then what does it matter, your dying right out?

PEER Have *I* not been – ? I could almost laugh!
Peer Gynt, then, has been something else, I suppose!
No, Button-moulder, you judge in the dark.
If you could but look into my very reins,
You'd find only Peer there, and Peer all through –
Nothing else in the world, no, nor anything more.

BUTTON-MOULDER It's impossible. Here I have got my orders.
Look, here it is written: Peer Gynt shalt thou summon.
He has set at defiance his life's design;
Clap him into the ladle with other spoilt goods.

PEER What nonsense! They must mean some other person.
Is it really Peer? It's not Rasmus, or Jon?

BUTTON-MOULDER It is many a day since I melted them.
So come quietly now, and don't waste my time.

PEER I'll be damned if I do! Ay, 'twould be a fine thing
If it turned out tomorrow someone else was meant.
You'd better take care what you're at, my good man!
Think of the onus you're taking upon you –

BUTTON-MOULDER I have it in writing –

PEER   At least give me time!

BUTTON-MOULDER What good would that do you?

PEER   I'll use it to prove
That I've been myself all the days of my life;

And that's the question that's in dispute.
BUTTON-MOULDER You'll prove it? And how?
PEER   Why, by vouchers and witnesses.
BUTTON-MOULDER I'm sadly afraid Master will not accept them.
PEER   Impossible! However, enough for the day – !
        My dear man, allow me a loan of myself;
        I'll be back again shortly. One is born only once,
        And one's self, as created, one fain would stick to.
        Come, are we agreed?
BUTTON-MOULDER   Very well then, so be it.
        But remember, we meet at the next cross-roads.

                                        [*Peer Gynt runs off*]

SCENE EIGHTH

A further point on the heath

PEER [*running hard*] Time is money, as the scripture says.
        If I only knew where the cross-roads are –
        They may be near and they may be far.
        The earth burns beneath me like red-hot iron.
        A witness! A witness! Oh, where shall I find one?
        It's almost unthinkable here in the forest.
        The world is a bungle! A wretched arrangement,
        When a right must be proved that's as patent as day!

    AN OLD MAN, *bent with age, with a staff in his hand and a bag
    on his back, is trudging in front of him.*

OLD MAN [*stops*] Dear, kind sir – a trifle to a houseless soul!
PEER   Excuse me; I've got no small change in my pocket –
OLD MAN Prince Peer! Oh, to think we should meet again – !
PEER   Who are you?
OLD MAN   You forget the Old Man in the Rondë?
PEER   Why, you're never – ?
OLD MAN   The King of the Dovrë, my boy!
PEER   The Dovrë-King? Really? The Dovrë-king? Speak!

OLD MAN Oh, I've come terribly down in the world – !

PEER   Ruined?

OLD MAN   Ay, plundered of every stiver.
        Here am I tramping it, starved as a wolf.

PEER   Hurrah! Such a witness doesn't grow on the trees!

OLD MAN My Lord Prince, too, has grizzled a bit since we met.

PEER   My dear father-in-law, the years gnaw and wear one. –
        Well, well, a truce to all private affairs –
        And pray, above all things, no family jars.
        I was then a sad madcap –

OLD MAN   Oh yes; oh yes –
        His Highness was young; and what won't one do then?
        But his Highness was wise in rejecting his bride;
        He saved himself thereby both worry and shame;
        For since then she's utterly gone to the bad –

PEER   Indeed!

OLD MAN   She has led a deplorable life;
        And, just think – she and Trond are now living together.

PEER   Which Trond?

OLD MAN   Of the Valfjeld.

PEER   It's he? Aha;
        It was he I cut out with the saeter-girls.

OLD MAN But my grandson has flourished – grown both
                                        stout and great,
        And has strapping children all over the country –

PEER   Now, my dear man, spare us this flow of words –
        I've something quite different troubling my mind. –
        I've got into rather a ticklish position,
        And am greatly in need of a witness or voucher –
        That's how you could help me best, father-in-law,
        And I'll find you a trifle to drink my health with.

OLD MAN You don't say so; can I be of use to his Highness?
        You'll give me a character, then, in return?

PEER   Most gladly. I'm somewhat hard pressed for cash,
        And must cut down expenses in every direction.
        Now hear what's the matter. No doubt you remember
        That night when I came to the Rondë a-wooing –

OLD MAN Why, of course, my Lord Prince!

PEER   Oh, no more of the Prince!

But no matter. You wanted, by sheer brute force,
To bias my sight, with a slit in the lens,
And to change me about from Peer Gynt to a troll.
What did I do then? I stood out against it –
Swore I would stand on no feet but my own;
Love, power, and glory at once I renounced,
And all for the sake of remaining myself.
Now this fact, you see, you must swear to in Court –

OLD MAN No, I'm blest if I can.

PEER   Why, what nonsense is this?

OLD MAN You surely don't want to compel me to lie?
You pulled on the troll-breeches, don't you remember,
And tasted the mead –

PEER   Ay, you lured me seductively –
But I flatly declined the decisive test,
And that is the thing you must judge your man by.
It's the end of the ditty that all depends on.

OLD MAN But it ended, Peer, just in the opposite way.

PEER What rubbish is this?

OLD MAN   When you left the Rondë,
You inscribed my motto upon your 'scutcheon.

PEER What motto?

OLD MAN   The potent and sundering word.

PEER The word?

OLD MAN   That which severs the whole race of men
From the troll-folk. Troll! To thyself be enough!

PEER [*falls back a step*] Enough!

OLD MAN   And with every nerve in your body,
You've being living up to it ever since.

PEER What, I? Peer Gynt?

OLD MAN [*weeps*]   It's ungrateful of you!
You've lived as a troll, but have still kept it secret.
The word I taught you has shown you the way
To swing yourself up as a man of substance –
And now you must needs come and turn up your nose
At me and the word you've to thank for it all.

PEER Enough! A hill-troll! An egoist!
This must be all rubbish; that's perfectly certain!

OLD MAN [*pulls out a bundle of old newspapers*]

I dare say you think that we've no newspapers?
Wait; here I'll show you in red and black,
How the Bloksberg Post eulogises you;
And the Heklefield Journal has done the same
Ever since the winter you left the country. –
Do you care to read them? You're welcome, Peer.
Here's an article, look you, signed 'Stallionhoof'.
And here too is one: 'On Troll-Nationalism'.
The writer points out and lays stress on the truth
That horns and a tail are of little importance,
So long as one has but a strip of the hide.
'Our enough,' he concludes, 'gives the hall-mark
                                                    of trolldom
To man,' – and proceeds to cite you as an instance.

PEER   A hill-troll? I?

OLD MAN   Yes, that's perfectly clear.

PEER   Might as well have stayed quietly where I was?
       Might have stopped in the Rondë in comfort and peace?
       Saved my trouble and toil and no end of shoe-leather?
       Peer Gynt – a troll? Why it's rubbish! It's stuff!
       Goodbye! There's a halfpenny to buy you tobacco.

OLD MAN   Nay, my good Prince Peer!

PEER   Let me go! You're mad,
       Or else doting. Off to the hospital with you!

OLD MAN   Oh, that is exactly what I'm in search of.
       But, as I told you, my grandson's offspring
       Have become overwhelmingly strong in the land,
       And they say that I only exist in books.
       The saw says: One's kin are unkindest of all;
       I've found to my cost that that saying is true.
       It's cruel to count as mere figment and fable –

PEER   My dear man, there are others who share the same fate.

OLD MAN   And ourselves we've no Mutual Aid Society,
       No alms-box or Penny Savings Bank –
       In the Rondë, of course, they'd be out of place.

PEER   No, that cursed: 'To thyself be enough' was the
                                                    word there!

OLD MAN   Oh, come now, the Prince can't complain of
                                                    the word.

And if he could manage by hook or by crook –
PEER   My man, you have got on the wrong scent entirely;
      I'm myself, as the saying goes, fairly cleaned out –
OLD MAN You surely can't mean it? His Highness a beggar?
PEER   Completely. His Highness's ego's in pawn.
      And it's all your fault, you accursed trolls!
      That's what comes of keeping bad company.
OLD MAN So there came my hope toppling down from its
                            perch again!
      Goodbye! I had best struggle on to the town –
PEER   What would you do there?
OLD MAN   I will go to the theatre.
      The papers are clamouring for national talents –
PEER   Good luck on your journey; and greet them from me.
      If I can but get free, I will go the same way.
      A farce I will write them, a mad and profound one;
      Its name shall be: '*Sic transit gloria mundi.*'
                    [*He runs off along the road; the
                      Old Man shouts after him*]

SCENE NINTH

At a cross-road

PEER GYNT. Now comes the pinch, Peer, as never before!
      This Dovrish Enough has passed judgment upon you.
      The vessel's a wreck; one must float with the spars.
      All else; only not to the spoilt-goods heap!
BUTTON-MOULDER [*at the cross-road*]
      Well now, Peer Gynt, have you found your voucher?
PEER   Have we reached the cross-road? Well, that's short work!
BUTTON-MOULDER I can see on your face, as it were on
                          a signboard,
      The gist of the paper before I've read it.
PEER   I got tired of the hunt – One might lose one's way –
BUTTON-MOULDER Yes; and what does it lead to, after all?

PEER   True enough; in the wood, and by night as well –
BUTTON-MOULDER There's an old man, though, trudging.
                                        Shall we call him here?
PEER   No let him go. He is drunk, my dear fellow!
BUTTON-MOULDER But perhaps he might –
PEER   Hush; no – let him be!
BUTTON-MOULDER Well, shall we begin then?
PEER   One question only:
       What is it, at bottom, this 'being oneself'?
BUTTON-MOULDER A singular question, most odd in the mouth
       Of a man who just now –
PEER   Come, a straightforward answer.
BUTTON-MOULDER To be oneself is: to slay oneself.
       But on you that answer is doubtless lost;
       And therefore we'll say: to stand forth everywhere
       With Master's intention displayed like a signboard.
PEER   But suppose a man never has come to know
       What Master meant with him?
BUTTON-MOULDER   He must divine it.
PEER   But how oft are divinings beside the mark –
       Then one's carried *ad undas* in middle career.
BUTTON-MOULDER That is certain, Peer Gynt; in default
                                        of divining
       The cloven-hoofed gentleman finds his best hook.
PEER   This matter's excessively complicated. –
       See here! I no longer plead being myself –
       It might not be easy to get it proven.
       That part of my case I must look on as lost.
       But just now, as I wandered alone o'er the heath,
       I felt my conscience-shoe pinching me;
       I said to myself: After all, you're a sinner –
BUTTON-MOULDER You seem bent on beginning all over again –
PEER   No, very far from it; a great one I mean;
       Not only in deeds, but in words and desires.
       I've lived a most damnable life abroad –
BUTTON-MOULDER Perhaps; I must ask you to show me
                                        the schedule!
PEER   Well well, give me time; I will find out a parson,
       Confess with all speed, and then bring you his voucher.

BUTTON-MOULDER Ay, if you can bring me that, then it is clear
   You may yet escape from the casting-ladle.
   But Peer, I'd my orders —
PEER   The paper is old;
   It dates no doubt from a long past period —
   At one time I lived with disgusting slackness,
   Went playing the prophet, and trusted in Fate.
   Well, may I try?
BUTTON-MOULDER   But — !
PEER   My dear fellow,
   I'm sure you can't have so much to do.
   Here, in this district, the air is so bracing,
   It adds an ell to the people's ages.
   Recollect what the Justedal parson wrote:
   'It's seldom that any one dies in this valley.'
BUTTON-MOULDER To the next cross-roads then; but not a
               step further.
PEER A priest I must catch, if it be with the tongs.

             [he starts running]

SCENE TENTH

*A heather-clad hillside with a path following the
windings of the ridge.*

PEER This may come in useful in many ways,
   Said Esben as he picked up a magpie's wing.
   Who could have thought one's account of sins
   Would come to one's aid on the last night of all?
   Well, whether or no, it's a ticklish business;
   A move from the frying-pan into the fire —
   But then there's a proverb of well-tried validity
   Which says that as long as there's life, there's hope.

 A LEAN PERSON, *in a priest's cassock, kilted-up high, and with a
birding net over his shoulder, comes hurrying along the ridge.*

PEER   Who goes there? A priest with a fowling-net!
        Hei, hop! I'm the spoilt child of fortune indeed!
        Good evening, Herr Pastor! the path is bad –
THE LEAN ONE Ah yes; but what wouldn't one do for a soul?
PEER   Aha! then there's someone bound heavenwards?
THE LEAN ONE   No;
        I hope he is taking a different road.
PEER   May I walk with Herr Pastor a bit of the way?
THE LEAN ONE With pleasure; I'm partial to company.
PEER   I should like to consult you –
THE LEAN ONE   *Heraus*! Go ahead!
PEER   You see here before you a good sort of man.
        The laws of the state I have strictly observed,
        Have made no acquaintance with fetters or bolts –
        But it happens at times that one misses one's footing
        And stumbles –
THE LEAN ONE   Ah yes; that occurs to the best of us.
PEER   Now these trifles you see –
THE LEAN ONE   Only trifles?
PEER   Yes; from sinning *en gros* I have ever refrained.
THE LEAN ONE Oh then, my dear fellow, pray leave
                                        me in peace –
        I'm not the person you seem to think me. –
        You look at my fingers? What see you in them?
PEER   A nail-system somewhat extremely developed.
THE LEAN ONE And now? You are casting a glance at my feet?
PEER [*pointing*] That's a natural hoof?
THE LEAN ONE   So I flatter myself.
PEER [*raises his hat*] I'd have taken my oath you were
                                        simply a parson;
        And I find I've the honour – well, best is best –
        When the hall door stands wide – shun the kitchen way;
        When the king's to be met with – avoid the lackey.
THE LEAN ONE Your hand! You appear to be free from
                                        prejudice.
        Say on then, my – friend; in what way can I serve you?
        Now you mustn't ask me for wealth or power;
        I couldn't supply them although I should hang for it.
        You can't think how slack the whole business is –

Transactions have dwindled most pitiably.
Nothing doing in souls; only now and again
A stray one –

PEER   The race has improved so remarkably?

THE LEAN ONE No, just the reverse; it's sunk shamefully low –
The majority end in a casting-ladle.

PEER   Ah yes – I have heard that ladle mentioned;
In fact, 'twas the cause of my coming to you.

THE LEAN ONE Speak out!

PEER   If it were not too much to ask,
I should like –

THE LEAN ONE   A harbour of refuge? eh?

PEER   You've guessed my petition before I have asked.
You tell me the business is going awry;
So I dare say you will not be over-particular.

THE LEAN ONE But, my dear –

PEER   My demands are in no way excessive.
I shouldn't insist on a salary;
But treatment as friendly as things will permit.

THE LEAN ONE A fire in your room?

PEER   Not too much fire – and chiefly
The power of departing in safety and peace –
The right, as the phrase goes, of freely withdrawing
Should an opening offer for happier days.

THE LEAN ONE My dear friend, I vow I'm sincerely distressed;
But you cannot imagine how many petitions
Of similar purport good people send in
When they're quitting the scene of their earthly activity.

PEER   But now that I think of my past career,
I feel I've an absolute claim to admission –

THE LEAN ONE 'Twas but trifles, you said –

PEER   In a certain sense –
But, now I remember, I've trafficked in slaves –

THE LEAN ONE There are men that have trafficked in wills
                                        and souls,
But who bungled it so that they failed to get in.

PEER   I've shipped Bramah-figures in plenty to China.

THE LEAN ONE Mere fustian again! Why, we laugh at
                                        such things.

There are people that ship off far gruesomer figures
In sermons, in art, and in literature –
Yet have to stay out in the cold –

PEER   Ah, but then,
Do you know – I once went and set up as prophet!

THE LEAN ONE In foreign parts? Humbug! Why, most
                                        people's *Sehen*
Ins Blaue ends in the casting-ladle.
If you've no more than that to rely upon,
With the best of goodwill, I can't possibly house you.

PEER   But hear this: in a shipwreck – I clung to a boat's keel –
And it's written: A drowning man grasps at a straw –
Furthermore it is written: You're nearest yourself –
So I half-way divested a cook of his life.

THE LEAN ONE It were all one to me if a kitchen-maid
You had half-way divested of something else.
What sort of stuff is this half-way jargon,
Saving your presence? Who, think you, would care
To throw away dearly-bought fuel in times
Like these on such spiritless rubbish as this?
There now, don't be enraged; 'twas your sins that
                                        I scoffed at;
And excuse my speaking my mind so bluntly. –
Come, my dearest friend, banish this stuff from your head,
And get used to the thought of the casting-ladle.
What would you gain if I lodged you and boarded you?
Consider; I know you're a sensible man.
Well, you'd keep your memory; that's so far true –
But the retrospect o'er recollection's domain
Would be, both for heart and for intellect,
What the Swedes call 'Mighty poor sport' indeed.
You have nothing either to howl or to smile about,
No cause for rejoicing nor yet for despair,
Nothing to make you feel hot or cold;
Only a sort of a something to fret over.

PEER   It is written: It's never so easy to know
Where the shoe is tight that one isn't wearing.

THE LEAN ONE Very true; I have – praise be to so-and-so! –
No occasion for more than a single odd shoe.

But it's lucky we happened to speak of shoes;
It reminds me that I must be hurrying on –
I'm after a roast that I hope will prove fat;
So I really mustn't stand gossiping here. –

PEER   And may one enquire, then, what sort of sin-diet
The man has been fattened on?

THE LEAN ONE   I understand
He has been himself both by night and by day,
And that, after all, is the principal point.

PEER   Himself? Then do such folks belong to your parish?

THE LEAN ONE That depends; the door, at least, stands ajar
                                        for them.
Remember, in two ways a man can be himself –
There's a right and wrong side to the jacket.
You know they have lately discovered in Paris
A way to take portraits by help of the sun.
One can either produce a straightforward picture,
Or else what is known as a negative one.
In the latter the lights and the shades are reversed,
And they're apt to seem ugly to commonplace eyes;
But for all that the likeness is latent in them,
And all you require is to bring it out.
If, then, a soul shall have pictured itself
In the course of its life by the negative method,
The plate is not therefore entirely cashiered –
But without more ado they consign it to me.
I take it in hand, then, for further treatment,
And by suitable methods effect its development.
I steam it, I dip it, I burn it, I scour it,
With sulphur and other ingredients like that,
Till the image appears which the plate was designed for –
That, namely, which people call positive.
But if one, like you, has smudged himself out,
Neither sulphur nor potash avails in the least.

PEER   I see; one must come to you black as a raven
To turn out a white ptarmigan? Pray what's the name
Inscribed 'neath the negative counterfeit
That you're now to transfer to the positive side?

THE LEAN ONE The name's Peter Gynt.

PEER   Peter Gynt! Indeed?
      Is Herr Gynt himself?
THE LEAN ONE   Yes, he vows he is.
PEER   Well, he's one to be trusted, that same Herr Peter.
THE LEAN ONE You know him, perhaps?
PEER   Oh yes, after a fashion –
      One knows all sorts of people.
THE LEAN ONE   I'm pressed for time;
      Where saw you him last?
PEER   It was down at the Cape.
THE LEAN ONE *Di Buona Speranza?*
PEER   Just so; but he sails
      Very shortly again, if I'm not mistaken.
THE LEAN ONE I must hurry off then without delay.
      I only hope I may catch him in time!
      That Cape of Good Hope – I could never abide it –
      It's ruined by missionaries from Stavanger.
                                   [*he rushes off southwards*]
PEER   The stupid hound! There he takes to his heels
      With his tongue lolling out. He'll be finely sold.
      It delights me to humbug an ass like that.
      He to give himself airs, and to lord it forsooth!
      He's a mighty lot, truly, to swagger about!
      He'll scarcely grow fat at his present trade –
      He'll soon drop from his perch with his whole apparatus. –
      Hm, I'm not over-safe in the saddle either;
[*a shooting star is seen; he nods after it*]
      I'm expelled, one may say, from self-owning nobility.
      Bear all hail from Peer Gynt, Brother Starry-Flash!
      To flash forth, to go out, and be naught at a gulp –
[*pulls himself together as though in terror, and goes deeper in
among the mists; stillness for awhile; then he cries*]
      Is there no one, no one in all the turmoil –
      In the void no one, no one in heaven – !
[*He comes forward again further down, throws his hat upon the
ground, and tears at his hair. By degrees a stillness comes over him*]
      So unspeakably poor, then, a soul can go back
      To nothingness, into the grey of the mist.
      Thou beautiful earth, be not angry with me

That I trampled thy grasses to no avail.
Thou beautiful sun, thou hast squandered away
Thy glory of light in an empty hut.
There was no one within it to hearten and warm –
The owner, they tell me, was never at home.
Beautiful sun and beautiful earth,
You were foolish to bear and give light to my mother.
The spirit is niggard and nature lavish;
And dearly one pays for one's birth with one's life. –
I will clamber up high, to the dizziest peak;
I will look once more on the rising sun,
Gaze till I'm tired o'er the promised land;
Then try to get snowdrifts piled up over me.
They can write above them: 'Here No One lies buried';
And afterwards – then – ! let things go as they can.

CHURCH-GOERS. [*singing on the forest path*]
       Oh, morning thrice blessed,
       When the tongues of God's kingdom
       Struck the earth like to flaming steel!
       From the earth to His dwelling
       Now the heirs' song ascendeth
       In the tongue of the kingdom of God.

PEER [*crouches as in terror*]
       Never look there! There all's desert and waste. –
       I fear I was dead long before I died.
       [*tries to slink in among the bushes,
       but comes upon the cross-roads*]

BUTTON-MOULDER Good morning, Peer Gynt! Where's
                         the list of your sins?

PEER Do you think that I haven't been whistling and shouting
    As hard as I could?

BUTTON-MOULDER   And met no one at all?

PEER Not a soul but a tramping photographer.

BUTTON-MOULDER Well, the respite is over.

PEER   Ay, everything's over.
    The owl smells the daylight. just list to the hooting!

BUTTON-MOULDER It's the matin-bell ringing –

PEER [*pointing*]   What's that shining yonder?

BUTTON-MOULDER Only light from a hut.

PEER   And that wailing sound – ?
BUTTON-MOULDER But a woman singing.
PEER   Ay, there – there I'll find
    The list of my sins –
BUTTON-MOULDER [*seizing him*] Set your house in order!
    [*they have come out of the underwood, and are standing*
    near the hut. Day is dawning]
PEER   Set my house in order? It's there! Away!
    Get you gone! Though your ladle were huge as a coffin,
    It were too small, I tell you, for me and my sins!
BUTTON-MOULDER Well, to the third cross-road, Peer; but then – !
                          [*turns aside and goes*]
PEER [*approaches the hut*] Forward and back, and it's just as far.
    Out and in, and it's just as strait.
  [*stops*] No! – like a wild, an unending lament,
    Is the thought: to come back, to go in, to go home.
  [*takes a few steps on, but stops again*]
    Roundabout, said the Boyg!
  [*hears singing in the hut*]   Ah, no; this time at least
    Right through, though the path may be never so strait!

He runs towards the hut; at the same moment SOLVEIG *appears in*
the doorway, dressed for church, with psalm-book wrapped in a
kerchief, and a staff in her hand. She stands there erect and mild.

PEER [*flings himself down on the threshold*]
    Hast thou doom for a sinner, then speak it forth!
SOLVEIG He is here! He is here! Oh, to God be the praise!
  [*stretches out her arms as though groping for him*]
PEER   Cry out all my sins and my trespasses!
SOLVEIG In nought hast thou sinned, oh my own only boy.
  [*gropes for him again, and finds him*]
BUTTON-MOULDER [*behind the house*]
    The sin-list, Peer Gynt?
PEER   Cry aloud my crime!
SOLVEIG [*sits down beside him*]
    Thou hast made all my life as a beautiful song.
    Blessed be thou that at last thou hast come!
    Blessed, thrice blessed our Whitsun-morn meeting!
PEER   Then I am lost!

SOLVEIG `   There is one that rules all things.
PEER [*laughs*] Lost! Unless thou canst answer riddles.
SOLVEIG Tell me them.
PEER   Tell them! Come on! To be sure!
    Canst thou tell where Peer Gynt has been since
                          we parted?
SOLVEIG Been?
PEER   With his destiny's seal on his brow;
    Been, as in God's thought he first sprang forth!
    Canst thou tell me? If not, I must get me home –
    Go down to the mist-shrouded regions.
SOLVEIG [*smiling*] Oh, that riddle is easy.
PEER   Then tell what thou knowest!
    Where was I, as myself, as the whole man, the true man?
    Where was I, with God's sigil upon my brow?
SOLVEIG In my faith, in my hope, and in my love.
PEER [*starts back*]
    What sayest thou – ? Peace! These are juggling words.
    Thou art mother thyself to the man that's there.
SOLVEIG Ay, that I am; but who is his father?
    Surely he that forgives at the mother's prayer.
PEER [*a light shines in his face; he cries*]
    My mother; my wife; oh, thou innocent woman! –
    In thy love – oh, there hide me, hide me!
  [*clings to her and hides his face in her lap.*]

              A long silence. The sun rises.

SOLVEIG [*sings softly*]
    Sleep thou, dearest boy of mine!
    I will cradle thee, I will watch thee –

      The boy has been sitting on his mother's lap.
    They two have been playing all the life-day long.

      The boy has been resting at his mother's breast
    All the life-day long. God's blessing on my joy!

      The boy has been lying close in to my heart
    All the life-day long. He is weary now.

      Sleep thou, dearest boy of mine!
    I will cradle thee, I will watch thee.

BUTTON-MOULDER'S VOICE [*behind the house*]
     We'll meet at the last cross-road again, Peer;
     And then we'll see whether – I say no more.
SOLVEIG [*sings louder in the full daylight*]
      I will cradle thee, I will watch thee;
     Sleep and dream thou, dear my boy!

THE END

A DOLL'S HOUSE

Characters

TORVALD HELMER

NORA, *his wife*

DOCTOR RANK

MRS LINDGREN*

NILS KROGSTAD

THE HELMERS' THREE CHILDREN

ANNA,† *their nurse*

A MAID–SERVANT [ELLEN]

A PORTER

The action passes in HELMER'S *house* [*a flat*]
in Christiania.

---

* In the original 'Fru Linde'.
† In the original 'Anne-Marie'.

ACT FIRST

A room, comfortably and tastefully, but not expensively, furnished. In the back, on the right, a door leads to the hall; on the left another door leads to HELMER'S *study. Between the two doors a pianoforte. In the middle of the left wall a door, and nearer the front a window. Near the window a round table with armchairs and a small sofa. In the right wall, somewhat to the back, a door, and against the same wall, farther forward, a porcelain stove; in front of it a couple of armchairs and a rocking-chair. Between the stove and the side-door a small table. Engravings on the walls. A whatnot with china and bric-à-brac. A small bookcase filled with handsomely bound books. Carpet. A fire in the stove. It is a winter day.*

A bell rings in the hall outside. Presently the outer door of the flat is heard to open. Then NORA *enters, humming gaily. She is in outdoor dress, and carries several parcels, which she lays on the right-hand table. She leaves the door into the hall open, and a* PORTER *is seen outside, carrying a Christmas-tree and a basket, which he gives to the maid-servant who has opened the door.*

NORA Hide the Christmas-tree carefully, Ellen; the children must on no account see it before this evening, when it's lighted up. [*to the Porter, taking out her purse*] How much?

PORTER Fifty öre.

NORA There is a crown. No, keep the change.

[*the Porter thanks her and goes.*]
[*Nora shuts the door. She continues smiling in quiet glee as she takes off her outdoor things. Taking from her pocket a bag of macaroons, she eats one or two. Then she goes on tiptoe to her husband's door and listens.*]

NORA Yes, he is at home. [*she begins humming again, crossing to the table on the right*]

HELMER [*in his room*]. Is that my lark twittering there?

NORA [*busy opening some of her parcels*]. Yes, it is.

HELMER Is it the squirrel frisking around?

NORA Yes!

HELMER When did the squirrel get home?

NORA Just this minute. [*hides the bag of macaroons in her pocket and wipes her mouth*] Come here, Torvald, and see what I've been buying.

HELMER Don't interrupt me.

[*a little later he opens the door and looks in, pen in hand*] Buying, did you say? What! All that? Has my little spendthrift been making the money fly again?

NORA Why, Torvald, surely we can afford to launch out a little now. It's the first Christmas we haven't had to pinch.

HELMER Come, come; we can't afford to squander money.

NORA Oh yes, Torvald, do let us squander a little, now – just the least little bit! You know you'll soon be earning heaps of money.

HELMER Yes, from New Year's Day. But there's a whole quarter before my first salary is due.

NORA Never mind; we can borrow in the meantime.

HELMER Nora! [*he goes up to her and takes her playfully by the ear*] Still my little featherbrain! Supposing I borrowed a thousand crowns today, and you made ducks and drakes of them during Christmas week, and then on New Year's Eve a tile blew off the roof and knocked my brains out –

NORA [*laying her hand on his mouth*]. Hush! How can you talk so horridly?

HELMER But supposing it were to happen – what then?

NORA If anything so dreadful happened, it would be all the same to me whether I was in debt or not.

HELMER But what about the creditors?

NORA They! Who cares for them? They're only strangers.

HELMER Nora, Nora! What a woman you are! But seriously, Nora, you know my principles on these points. No debts! No borrowing! Home life ceases to be free and beautiful as soon as it is founded on borrowing and debt. We two have held out bravely till now, and we are not going to give in at the last.

NORA [*going to the fireplace*]. Very well – as you please, Torvald.

HELMER [*following her*]. Come, come; my little lark mustn't droop her wings like that. What? Is my squirrel in the sulks? [*takes out his purse*] Nora, what do you think I have here?

NORA [*turning round quickly*]. Money!

HELMER There! [*gives her some notes*] Of course I know all sorts of things are wanted at Christmas.

NORA [*counting*]. Ten, twenty, thirty, forty. Oh, thank you, thank you, Torvald! This will go a long way.

HELMER I should hope so.

NORA Yes, indeed; a long way! But come here, and let me show you all I've been buying. And so cheap! Look, here's a new suit for Ivar, and a little sword. Here are a horse and a trumpet for Bob. And here are a doll and a cradle for Emmy. They're only common, but they're good enough for her to pull to pieces. And dress-stuffs and kerchiefs for the servants. I ought to have got something better for old Anna.

HELMER And what's in that other parcel?

NORA [*crying out*]. No, Torvald, you're not to see that until this evening!

HELMER Oh! Ah! But now tell me, you little spendthrift, have you thought of anything for yourself?

NORA For myself! Oh, I don't want anything.

HELMER Nonsense! Just tell me something sensible you would like to have.

NORA No, really I don't know of anything – well, listen, Torvald –

HELMER Well?

NORA [*playing with his coat-buttons, without looking him in the face*]. If you really want to give me something, you might, you know – you might –

HELMER Well? Out with it!

NORA [*quickly*]. You might give me money, Torvald. Only just what you think you can spare; then I can buy something with it later on.

HELMER But, Nora –

NORA Oh, please do, dear Torvald, please do! I should hang the money in lovely gilt paper on the Christmas-tree. Wouldn't that be fun?

HELMER What do they call the birds that are always making the money fly?

NORA Yes, I know – spendthrifts,* of course. But please do as I ask you, Torvald. Then I shall time to think what I want most. Isn't that very sensible, now?

Spillefugl, literally 'playbird', means a gambler.

HELMER [*smiling*]. Certainly; that is to say, if you really kept the money I gave you, and really spent it on something for yourself. But it all goes in housekeeping, and for all manner of useless things, and then I have to pay up again.

NORA But, Torvald –

HELMER Can you deny it, Nora dear? [*he puts his arm round her*] It's a sweet little lark, but it gets through a lot of money. No one would believe how much it costs a man to keep such a little bird as you.

NORA For shame! How can you say so? Why, I save as much as ever I can.

HELMER [*laughing*]. Very true – as much as you can – but that's precisely nothing.

NORA [*hums and smiles with covert glee*]. H'm! If you only knew, Torvald, what expenses we larks and squirrels have.

HELMER You're a strange little being! Just like your father – always on the lookout for all the money you can lay your hands on; but the moment you have it, it seems to slip through your fingers; you never know what becomes of it. Well, one must take you as you are. It's in the blood. Yes, Nora, that sort of thing is hereditary.

NORA I wish I had inherited many of papa's qualities.

HELMER And I don't wish you anything but just what you are – my own, sweet little song-bird. But I say – it strikes me you look so – so – what shall I call it? – so suspicious today –

NORA Do I?

HELMER You do, indeed. Look me full in the face.

NORA [*looking at him*]. Well?

HELMER [*threatening with his finger*]. Hasn't the little sweet-tooth been playing pranks today?

NORA No; how can you think such a thing!

HELMER Didn't she just look in at the confectioner's?

NORA No, Torvald; really –

HELMER Not to sip a little jelly?

NORA No, certainly not.

HELMER Hasn't she even nibbled a macaroon or two?

NORA No, Torvald, indeed, indeed!

HELMER Well, well, well; of course I'm only joking.

NORA [*goes to the table on the right*]. I shouldn't think of doing what you disapprove of.

HELMER No, I'm sure of that; and, besides, you've given me your word – [*going towards her*] Well, keep your little Christmas secrets to yourself, Nora darling. The Christmas-tree will bring them all to light, I dare say.

NORA Have you remembered to invite Doctor Rank?

HELMER No. But it's not necessary; he'll come as a matter of course. Besides. I shall ask him when he looks in today. I've ordered some capital wine. Nora, you can't think how I look forward to this evening.

NORA And I too. How the children will enjoy themselves, Torvald!

HELMER Ah, it's glorious to feel that one has an assured position and ample means. Isn't it delightful to think of?

NORA Oh, it's wonderful!

HELMER Do you remember last Christmas? For three whole weeks beforehand you shut yourself up every evening till long past midnight to make flowers for the Christmas-tree, and all sorts of other marvels that were to have astonished us. I was never so bored in my life.

NORA I didn't bore myself at all.

HELMER [*smiling*]. But it came to little enough in the end, Nora.

NORA Oh, are you going to tease me about that again? How could I help the cat getting in and pulling it all to pieces?

HELMER To be sure you couldn't, my poor little Nora. You did your best to give us all pleasure, and that's the main point. But, all the same, it's a good thing the hard times are over.

NORA Oh, isn't it wonderful?

HELMER Now I needn't sit here boring myself all alone; and you needn't tire your blessed eyes and your delicate little fingers –

NORA [*clapping her hands*]. No, I needn't, need I, Torvald? Oh, how wonderful it is to think of! [*takes his arm*] And now I'll tell you how I think we ought to manage, Torvald. As soon as Christmas is over – [*the hall-door bell rings*] Oh, there's a ring! [*arranging the room*] That's somebody come to call. How tiresome!

HELMER I'm 'not at home' to callers; remember that.

ELLEN [*in the doorway*]. A lady to see you, ma'am.

NORA Show her in.

ELLEN [*to Helmer*]. And the doctor has just come, sir.

HELMER Has he gone into my study?

ELLEN. Yes, sir.   [*Helmer goes into his study*]

Ellen ushers in MRS LINDEN, *in travelling costume, and goes out, closing the door*

MRS LINDEN [*embarrassed and hesitating*]. How do you do, Nora?

NORA [*doubtfully*]. How do you do?

MRS LINDEN I see you don't recognize me.

NORA No, I don't think – oh yes! – I believe – [*suddenly brightening*] What, Christina! Is it really you?

MRS LINDEN Yes; really I!

NORA Christina! And to think I didn't know you! But how could I – [*more softly*] How changed you are, Christina!

MRS LINDEN Yes, no doubt. In nine or ten years –

NORA Is it really so long since we met? Yes, so it is. Oh, the last eight years have been a happy time, I can tell you. And now you have come to town? All that long journey in mid-winter! How brave of you!

MRS LINDEN I arrived by this morning's steamer.

NORA To have a merry Christmas, of course. Oh, how delightful! Yes, we will have a merry Christmas. Do take your things off. Aren't you frozen? [*helping her*] There; now we'll sit cosily by the fire. No, you take the armchair; I shall sit in this rocking-chair. [*seizes her hands*] Yes, now I can see the dear old face again. It was only at the first glance – But you're a little paler, Christina – and perhaps a little thinner.

MRS LINDEN And much, much older, Nora.

NORA Yes, perhaps a little older – not much – ever so little. [*she suddenly checks herself; seriously*] Oh, what a thoughtless wretch I am! Here I sit chattering on, and – Dear, dear Christina, can you forgive me!

MRS LINDEN What do you mean, Nora?

NORA [*softly*]. Poor Christina! I forgot: you are a widow.

MRS LINDEN Yes; my husband died three years ago.

NORA I know, I know; I saw it in the papers. Oh, believe me, Christina, I did mean to write to you; but I kept putting it off, and something always came in the way.

MRS LINDEN I can quite understand that, Nora dear.

NORA No, Christina; it was horrid of me. Oh, you poor darling, how much you must have gone through! – And he left you nothing?

MRS LINDEN Nothing.

NORA And no children?

MRS LINDEN None.

NORA Nothing, nothing at all?

MRS LINDEN Not even a sorrow or a longing to dwell upon.

NORA [*looking at her incredulously*]. My dear Christina, how is that possible?

MRS LINDEN [*smiling sadly and stroking her hair*]. Oh, it happens so sometimes, Nora.

NORA So utterly alone! How dreadful that must be! I have three of the loveliest children. I can't show them to you just now; they're out with their nurse. But now you must tell me everything.

MRS LINDEN No, no; I want you to tell me –

NORA No, you must begin; I won't be egotistical today. Today I'll think only of you. Oh! but I must tell you one thing – perhaps you've heard of our great stroke of fortune?

MRS LINDEN No. What is it?

NORA Only think! my husband has been made manager of the Joint Stock Bank.

MRS LINDEN Your husband! Oh, how fortunate!

NORA Yes; isn't it? A lawyer's position is so uncertain, you see, especially when he won't touch any business that's the least bit – shady, as of course Torvald never would; and there I quite agree with him. Oh! you can imagine how glad we are. He is to enter on his new position at the New Year, and then he'll have a large salary, and percentages. In future we shall be able to live quite differently – just as we please, in fact. Oh, Christina, I feel so light-hearted and happy! It's delightful to have lots of money, and no need to worry about things, isn't it?

MRS LINDEN Yes; at any rate it must be delightful to have what you need.

NORA No, not only what you need, but heaps of money – heaps!

MRS LINDEN [*smiling*]. Nora, Nora, haven't you learnt reason yet? In our schooldays you were a shocking little spendthrift.

NORA [*quietly smiling*]. Yes; that's what Torvald says I am still. [*holding up her forefinger*] But 'Nora, Nora' is not so silly as you all think. Oh! I haven't had the chance to be much of a spendthrift. We have both had to work.

MRS LINDEN You too?

NORA Yes, light fancy work: crochet, and embroidery, and things of that sort; [*carelessly*] and other work too. You know, of course, that Torvald left the Government service when we were married. He had little chance of promotion, and of course he required to make more money. But in the first year after our marriage he overworked himself terribly. He had to undertake all sorts of extra work, you know, and to slave early and late. He couldn't stand it, and fell dangerously ill. Then the doctors declared he must go to the South.

MRS LINDEN You spent a whole year in Italy, didn't you?

NORA Yes, we did. It wasn't easy to manage, I can tell you. It was just after Ivar's birth. But of course we had to go. Oh, it was a wonderful, delicious journey! And it saved Torvald's life. But it cost a frightful lot of money, Christina.

MRS LINDEN So I should think.

NORA Twelve hundred dollars! Four thousand eight hundred crowns! Isn't that a lot of money?

MRS LINDEN How lucky you had the money to spend!

NORA We got it from father, you must know.

MRS LINDEN Ah, I see. He died just about that time, didn't he?

NORA Yes, Christina, just then. And only think! I couldn't go and nurse him! I was expecting little Ivar's birth daily; and then I had my poor sick Torvald to attend to. Dear, kind old father! I never saw him again, Christina. Oh! that's the hardest thing I have had to bear since my marriage.

MRS LINDEN I know how fond you were of him. But then you went to Italy?

NORA Yes; you see, we had the money, and the doctors said we must lose no time. We started a month later.

MRS LINDEN And your husband came back completely cured?

NORA Sound as a bell.

MRS LINDEN But – the doctor?

NORA What do you mean?

MRS LINDEN I thought as I came in your servant announced the doctor –

NORA Oh yes; Doctor Rank. But he doesn't come professionally. He is our best friend, and never lets a day pass without looking in. No, Torvald hasn't had an hour's illness since that time. And the children are so healthy and well, and so am I. [*jumps up and claps her hands*] Oh, Christina, Christina, what a wonderful thing it is to live and to be happy! – Oh, but it's really too horrid of me! Here am I talking about nothing but my own concerns. [*seats herself upon a footstool close to Christina, and lays her arms on her friend's lap*] Oh, don't be angry with me! Now tell me, is it really true that you didn't love your husband? What made you marry him, then?

MRS LINDEN My mother was still alive, you see, bedridden and helpless; and then I had my two younger brothers to think of. I didn't think it would be right for me to refuse him.

NORA Perhaps it wouldn't have been. I suppose he was rich then?

MRS LINDEN Very well off, I believe. But his business was uncertain. It fell to pieces at his death, and there was nothing left.

NORA And then – ?

MRS LINDEN Then I had to fight my way by keeping a shop, a little school, anything I could turn my hand to. The last three years have been one long struggle for me. But now it is over, Nora. My poor mother no longer needs me; she is at rest. And the boys are in business, and can look after themselves.

NORA How free your life must feel!

MRS LINDEN No, Nora; only inexpressibly empty. No one to live for! [*stands up restlessly*] That's why I could not bear to stay any longer in that out-of-the-way corner. Here it must be easier to find something to take one up – to occupy one's thoughts. If I could only get some settled employment – some office work.

NORA But, Christina, that's such drudgery, and you look worn-out already. It would be ever so much better for you to go to some watering-place and rest.

MRS LINDEN [*going to the window*]. I have no father to give me the money, Nora.

NORA [*rising*]. Oh, don't be vexed with me.

MRS LINDEN [*going to her*]. My dear Nora, don't you be vexed with me. The worst of a position like mine is that it makes one so bitter. You have no one to work for, yet you have to be always on the strain. You must live, and so you become selfish. When I heard of the happy change in your fortunes – can you believe it? – I was glad for my own sake more than for yours.

NORA How do you mean? Ah, I see! You think Torvald can perhaps do something for you?

MRS LINDEN Yes, I thought so.

NORA And so he shall, Christina. Just you leave it all to me. I shall lead up to it beautifully! – I shall think of some delightful plan to put him in a good humour! Oh, I should so love to help you.

MRS LINDEN How good of you, Nora, to stand by me so warmly! Doubly good in you, who know so little of the troubles and burdens of life.

NORA I? I know so little of – ?

MRS LINDEN [smiling]. Oh, well – a little fancy-work, and so forth. – You're a child, Nora.

NORA [tosses her head and paces the room]. Oh, come, you mustn't be so patronizing!

MRS LINDEN No?

NORA You're like the rest. You all think I'm fit for nothing really serious –

MRS LINDEN Well, well –

NORA You think I've had no troubles in this weary world.

MRS LINDEN My dear Nora, you've just told me all your troubles.

NORA Pooh – those trifles! [softly] I haven't told you the great thing.

MRS LINDEN The great thing? What do you mean?

NORA I know you look down upon me, Christina; but you have no right to. You are proud of having worked so hard and so long for your mother.

MRS LINDEN I am sure I don't look down upon anyone; but it's true I am both proud and glad when I remember that I was able to keep my mother's last days free from care.

NORA And you're proud to think of what you have done for your brothers, too.

MRS LINDEN Have I not the right to be?

NORA Yes, indeed. But now let me tell you, Christina – I, too, have something to be proud and glad of.

MRS LINDEN I don't doubt it. But what do you mean?

NORA Hush! Not so loud. Only think, if Torvald were to hear! He mustn't – not for worlds! No one must know about it Christina – no one but you.

MRS LINDEN Why, what can it be?

NORA Come over here. [*draws her down beside her on the sofa*] Yes, Christina – I, too, have something to be proud and glad of. I saved Torvald's life.

MRS LINDEN Saved his life? How?

NORA I told you about our going to Italy. Torvald would have died but for that.

MRS LINDEN Well – and your father gave you the money.

NORA [*smiling*]. Yes, so Torvald and everyone believes; but –

MRS LINDEN But – ?

NORA Papa didn't give us one penny. It was *I* that found the money.

MRS LINDEN You? All that money?

NORA Twelve hundred dollars. Four thousand eight hundred crowns. What do you say to that?

MRS LINDEN My dear Nora, how did you manage it? Did you win it in the lottery?

NORA [*contemptuously*]. In the lottery? Pooh! Anyone could have done that!

MRS LINDEN Then wherever did you get it from?

NORA [*hums and smiles mysteriously*]. H'm; tra-la-la-la!

MRS LINDEN Of course you couldn't borrow it.

NORA No? Why not?

MRS LINDEN Why, a wife can't borrow without her husband's consent.

NORA [*tossing her head*]. Oh! when the wife has some idea of business, and knows how to set about things –

MRS LINDEN But, Nora, I don't understand –

NORA Well, you needn't. I never said I borrowed the money. There are many ways I may have got it. [*throws herself back on the sofa*] I may have got it from some admirer. When one is so – attractive as I am –

MRS LINDEN You're too silly, Nora.

NORA Now I'm sure you're dying of curiosity, Christina –

MRS LINDEN Listen to me, Nora dear: haven't you been a little rash?

NORA [*sitting upright again*]. Is it rash to save one's husband's life?

MRS LINDEN I think it was rash of you, without his knowledge –

NORA But it would have been fatal for him to know! Can't you understand that? He wasn't even to suspect how ill he was.

The doctors came to me privately and told me his life was in danger – that nothing could save him but a winter in the South. Do you think I didn't try diplomacy first? I told him how I longed to have a trip abroad, like other young wives; I wept and prayed; I said he ought to think of my condition, and not to thwart me; and then I hinted that he could borrow the money. But then, Christina, he got almost angry. He said I was frivolous, and that it was his duty as a husband not to yield to my whims and fancies – so he called them. Very well, thought I, but saved you must be; and then I found the way to do it.

MRS LINDEN And did your husband never learn from your father that the money was not from him?

NORA No; never. Papa died at that very time. I meant to have told him all about it, and begged him to say nothing. But he was so ill – unhappily, it wasn't necessary.

MRS LINDEN And you have never confessed to your husband?

NORA Good heavens! What can you be thinking of? Tell him, when he has such a loathing of debt! And besides – how painful and humiliating it would be for Torvald, with his manly self-respect, to know that he owed anything to me! It would utterly upset the relation between us; our beautiful, happy home would never again be what it is.

MRS LINDEN Will you never tell him?

NORA [*thoughtfully, half-smiling*]. Yes, some time perhaps – many, many years hence, when I'm – not so pretty. You mustn't laugh at me! Of course I mean when Torvald is not so much in love with me as he is now; when it doesn't amuse him any longer to see me dancing about, and dressing up and acting. Then it might be well to have something in reserve. [*breaking off*] Nonsense! nonsense! That time will never come. Now, what do you say to my grand secret, Christina? Am I fit for nothing now? You may believe it has cost me a lot of anxiety. It has been no joke to meet my engagements punctually. You must know, Christina, that in business there are things called instalments, and quarterly interest, that are terribly hard to provide for. So I've had to pinch a little here and there, wherever I could. I couldn't save much out of the housekeeping, for of course Torvald had to live well. And I couldn't let the children go about badly dressed; all I got for them, I spent on them, the blessed darlings!

MRS LINDEN Poor Nora! So it had to come out of your own pocket-money?

NORA Yes, of course. After all, the whole thing was my doing. When Torvald gave me money for clothes, and so on, I never spent more than half of it; I always bought the simplest and cheapest things. It's a mercy that everything suits me so well – Torvald never had any suspicions. But it was often very hard, Christina dear. For it's nice to be beautifully dressed – now, isn't it?

MRS LINDEN Indeed it is.

NORA Well, and besides that, I made money in other ways. Last winter I was so lucky – I got a heap of copying to do. I shut myself up every evening, and wrote far into the night. Oh, sometimes I was so tired, so tired. And yet it was splendid to work in that way and earn money. I almost felt as if I was a man.

MRS LINDEN Then how much have you been able to pay off?

NORA Well, I can't precisely say. It's difficult to keep that sort of business clear. I only know that I've paid everything I could scrape together. Sometimes I really didn't know where to turn. [*smiles*] Then I used to sit here and pretend that a rich old gentleman was in love with me –

MRS LINDEN What! What gentleman?

NORA Oh, nobody! – that he was dead now, and that when his will was opened, there stood in large letters: 'Pay over at once everything of which I die possessed to that charming person, Mrs Nora Helmer.'

MRS LINDEN But, my dear Nora – what gentleman do you mean?

NORA Oh dear, can't you understand? There wasn't any old gentleman: it was only what I used to dream and dream when I was at my wits' end for money. But it doesn't matter now – the tiresome old creature may stay where he is for me. I care nothing for him or his will; for now my troubles are over. [*springing up*] Oh, Christina, how glorious it is to think of! Free from all anxiety! Free, quite free. To be able to play and romp about with the children; to have things tasteful and pretty in the house, exactly as Torvald likes it! And then the spring will soon be here, with the great blue sky. Perhaps then we shall have a little holiday. Perhaps I shall see the sea again. Oh, what a wonderful thing it is to live and to be happy!

[*the hall-door bell rings*]

MRS LINDEN [*rising*]. There's a ring. Perhaps I had better go.

NORA No; do stay. No one will come here. It's sure to be someone for Torvald.

ELLEN [*in the doorway*]. If you please, ma'am, there's a gentleman to speak to Mr Helmer.

NORA Who is the gentleman?

KROGSTAD [*in the doorway*]. It is I, Mrs Helmer.

MRS LINDEN [*starts, and turns away to the window*]

NORA [*goes a step towards him, anxiously, speaking low*]. You? What is it? What do you want with my husband?

KROGSTAD Bank business – in a way. I hold a small post in the Joint Stock Bank, and your husband is to be our new chief, I hear.

NORA Then it is – ?

KROGSTAD Only tiresome business, Mrs Helmer; nothing more.

NORA Then will you please go to his study?   [*Krogstad goes*] [*she bows indifferently while she closes the door into the hall. Then she goes to the stove and looks to the fire.*]

MRS LINDEN Nora – who was that man?

NORA A Mr Krogstad – a lawyer.

MRS LINDEN Then it was really he?

NORA Do you know him?

MRS LINDEN I used to know him – many years ago. He was in a lawyer's office in our town.

NORA Yes, so he was.

MRS LINDEN How he has changed!

NORA I believe his marriage was unhappy.

MRS LINDEN And he is a widower now?

NORA With a lot of children. There! Now it will burn up. [*she closes the stove, and pushes the rocking-chair a little aside*]

MRS LINDEN His business is not of the most creditable, they say?

NORA Isn't it? I dare say not. I don't know. But don't let us think of business – it's so tiresome.

DR RANK *comes out of Helmer's room*

RANK [*still in the doorway*]. No, no; I'm in your way. I shall go and have a chat with your wife. [*shuts the door and sees Mrs Linden*] Oh, I beg your pardon. I'm in the way here too.

NORA No, not in the least. [*introduces them*] Doctor Rank – Mrs Linden.

RANK Oh, indeed; I've often heard Mrs Linden's name. I think I passed you on the stairs as I came up.

MRS LINDEN Yes; I go so very slowly. Stairs try me so much.

RANK Ah – you are not very strong?

MRS LINDEN Only overworked.

RANK Nothing more? Then no doubt you've come to town to find rest in a round of dissipation?

MRS LINDEN I have come to look for employment.

RANK Is that an approved remedy for overwork?

MRS LINDEN One must live, Doctor Rank.

RANK Yes, that seems to be the general opinion.

NORA Come, Doctor Rank – you want to live yourself.

RANK To be sure I do. However wretched I may be, I want to drag on as long as possible. All my patients, too, have the same mania. And it's the same with people whose complaint is moral. At this very moment Helmer is talking to just such a moral incurable –

MRS LINDEN [*softly*]. Ah!

NORA Whom do you mean?

RANK Oh, a fellow named Krogstad, a man you know nothing about – corrupt to the very core of his character. But even he began by announcing, as a matter of vast importance, that he must live.

NORA Indeed? And what did he want with Torvald?

RANK I haven't an idea; I only gathered that it was some bank business.

NORA I didn't know that Krog– that this Mr Krogstad had anything to do with the Bank?

RANK Yes. He has got some sort of place there. [*to Mrs Linden*] I don't know whether, in your part of the country, you have people who go grubbing and sniffing around in search of moral rottenness – and then, when they have found a 'case', don't rest till they have got their man into some good position, where they can keep a watch upon him. Men with a clean bill of health they leave out in the cold.

MRS LINDEN Well, I suppose the – delicate characters require most care.

RANK [*shrugs his shoulders*]. There we have it! It's that notion that makes society a hospital.

NORA [*deep in her own thoughts, breaks into half-stifled laughter, and claps her hands*]

RANK Why do you laugh at that? Have you any idea what 'society' is?

NORA What do I care for your tiresome society? I was laughing at something else – something excessively amusing. Tell me, Doctor Rank, are all the employees at the Bank dependent on Torvald now?

RANK Is that what strikes you as excessively amusing?

NORA [*smiles and hums*]. Never mind, never mind! [*walks about the room*] Yes; it is funny to think that we – that Torvald has such power over so many people. [*takes the bag from her pocket*] Doctor Rank, will you have a macaroon?

RANK What! – macaroons! I thought they were contraband here?

NORA Yes; but Christina brought me these.

MRS LINDEN What! I –

NORA Oh, well! Don't be frightened. You couldn't possibly know that Torvald had forbidden them. The fact is, he's afraid of me spoiling my teeth. But, oh bother, just for once! – That's for you, Doctor Rank! [*puts a macaroon into his mouth*] And you too, Christina. And I'll have one while we're about it – only a tiny one, or at most two. [*walks about again*] Oh dear, I am happy! There's only one thing in the world I really want.

RANK Well, what's that?

NORA There's something I should so like to say – in Torvald' hearing.

RANK Then why don't you say it?

NORA Because I daren't, it's so ugly.

MRS LINDEN Ugly?

RANK In that case you'd better not. But to us you might – What i it you would so like to say in Helmer's hearing?

NORA I should so love to say, 'Damn it all!'

RANK Are you out of your mind?

MRS LINDEN Good gracious, Nora – !

RANK Say it – there he is!

NORA [*hides the macaroons*]. Hush – sh – sh.

HELMER *comes out of his room, hat in hand, with his*
overcoat on his arm

NORA [*going to him*]. Well, Torvald dear, have you got rid of him?

HELMER Yes; he has just gone.

NORA Let me introduce you – this is Christina, who has come to town –

HELMER Christina? Pardon me, I don't know –

NORA Mrs Linden, Torvald dear – Christina Linden.

HELMER [*to Mrs Linden*]. Indeed! A school friend of my wife's, no doubt?

MRS LINDEN Yes, we knew each other as girls.

NORA And only think! She has taken this long journey on purpose to speak to you.

HELMER To speak to me!

MRS LINDEN Well, not quite –

NORA You see, Christina is tremendously clever at office work, and she's so anxious to work under a first-rate man of business in order to learn still more –

HELMER [*to Mrs Linden*]. Very sensible indeed.

NORA And when she heard you were appointed manager – it was telegraphed, you know – she started off at once, and – Torvald dear, for my sake, you must do something for Christina. Now, can't you?

HELMER It's not impossible. I presume Mrs Linden is a widow?

MRS LINDEN Yes.

HELMER And you have already had some experience of business?

MRS LINDEN A good deal.

HELMER Well, then, it's very likely I may be able to find a place for you.

NORA [*clapping her hands*]. There now! There now!

HELMER You have come at a fortunate moment, Mrs Linden.

MRS LINDEN Oh, how can I thank you – ?

HELMER [*smiling*]. There is no occasion. [*puts on his overcoat*] But for the present you must excuse me –

RANK Wait; I am going with you. [*fetches his fur coat from the hall and warms it at the fire*]

NORA Don't be long, Torvald dear.

HELMER Only an hour; not more.

NORA Are you going too, Christina?

MRS LINDEN [*putting on her walking things*]. Yes; I must set about looking for lodgings.

HELMER Then perhaps we can go together?

NORA [*helping her*]. What a pity we haven't a spare room for you; but it's impossible –

MRS LINDEN I shouldn't think of troubling you. Goodbye, dear Nora, and thank you for all your kindness.

NORA Goodbye for the present. Of course you'll come back this evening. And you, too, Doctor Rank. What! If you're well enough? Of course you'll be well enough. Only wrap up warmly. [*they go out, talking, into the hall. Outside on the stairs are heard children's voices*] There they are! There they are!

She runs to the outer door and opens it. The Nurse, ANNA,
enters the hall with the children

Come in! Come in! [*stoops down and kisses the children*] Oh, my sweet darlings! Do you see them, Christina? Aren't they lovely?

RANK Don't let us stand here chattering in the draught.

HELMER Come, Mrs Linden; only mothers can stand such a temperature. [*Dr Rank, Helmer, and Mrs Linden go down the stairs* [*Anna enters the room with the children; Nora also, shutting the door.*

NORA How fresh and bright you look! And what red cheeks you've got! Like apples and roses. [*the children chatter to her during what follows*] Have you had great fun? That's splendid. Oh, really! You've been giving Emmy and Bob a ride on your sledge! – both at once, only think! Why, you're quite a man, Ivar. Oh, give her to me a little, Anna. My sweet little dolly! [*takes the smallest from the Nurse and dances with her*] Yes, yes; mother will dance with Bob too. What! Did you have a game of snowballs? Oh, I wish I'd been there. No leave them, Anna; I'll take their things off. Oh yes, let me do it; it's such fun. Go to the nursery; you look frozen. You'll find some hot coffee on the stove.

[*the Nurse goes into the room on the left*

NORA [*takes off the children's things and throws them down anywhere, while the children talk all together.*] Really! A big dog ran after you! But he didn't bite you? No; dogs don't bite dear little dolly children. Don't peep into those parcels, Ivar. What is it

Wouldn't you like to know? Take care – it'll bite! What? Shall
we have a game? What shall we play at? Hide-and-seek? Yes,
let's play hide-and-seek. Bob shall hide first. Am I to? Yes, let
me hide first. [*she and the children play, with laughter and shouting,
in the room and the adjacent one to the right. At last Nora hides under
the table; the children come rushing in, look for her, but cannot find
her, hear her half-choked laughter, rush to the table, lift up the cover
and see her. Loud shouts. She creeps out, as though to frighten them.
Fresh shouts.*]

*Meanwhile there has been a knock at the door leading into the hall.
No one has heard it. Now the door is half opened, and* KROGSTAD
appears. He waits a little; the game is renewed.

KROGSTAD I beg your pardon, Mrs Helmer –

NORA [*with a suppressed cry, turns round and half jumps up*]. Ah! What
do you want?

KROGSTAD Excuse me; the outer door was ajar – somebody must
have forgotten to shut it –

NORA [*standing up*]. My husband is not at home, Mr Krogstad.

KROGSTAD I know it.

NORA Then what do you want here?

KROGSTAD To say a few words to you.

NORA To me? [*to the children, softly*] Go in to Anna. What? No, the
strange man won't hurt mamma. When he's gone we'll go on
playing. [*she leads the children into the left-hand room, and shuts the
door behind them*]
[*uneasy, in suspense*] It is to me you wish to speak?

KROGSTAD Yes, to you.

NORA Today? But it's not the first yet –

KROGSTAD No, today is Christmas Eve. It will depend upon
yourself whether you have a merry Christmas.

NORA What do you want? I'm not ready today –

KROGSTAD Never mind that just now. I have come about another
matter. You have a minute to spare?

NORA Oh yes, I suppose so; although –

KROGSTAD Good. I was sitting in the restaurant opposite, and I saw
your husband go down the street –

NORA Well?

KROGSTAD – with a lady.

NORA What then?

KROGSTAD May I ask if the lady was a Mrs Linden?

NORA Yes.

KROGSTAD Who has just come to town?

NORA Yes. Today.

KROGSTAD I believe she is an intimate friend of yours?

NORA Certainly. But I don't understand –

KROGSTAD I used to know her too.

NORA I know you did.

KROGSTAD Ah! You know all about it. I thought as much. Now, frankly, is Mrs Linden to have a place in the Bank?

NORA How dare you catechize me in this way, Mr Krogstad – you a subordinate of my husband's? But since you ask, you shall know. Yes, Mrs Linden is to be employed. And it is I who recommended her, Mr Krogstad. Now you know.

KROGSTAD Then my guess was right.

NORA [*walking up and down*]. You see one has a wee bit of influence after all. It doesn't follow because one's only a woman – When people are in a subordinate position, Mr Krogstad, they ough really to be careful how they offend anybody who – h'm –

KROGSTAD – who has influence?

NORA Exactly.

KROGSTAD [*taking another tone*]. Mrs Helmer, will you have the kindness to employ your influence on my behalf?

NORA What? How do you mean?

KROGSTAD Will you be so good as to see that I retain my sub ordinate position in the Bank?

NORA What do you mean? Who wants to take it from you?

KROGSTAD Oh, you needn't pretend ignorance. I can very well understand that it cannot be pleasant for your friend to mee me; and I can also understand now for whose sake I am to b hounded out.

NORA But I assure you –

KROGSTAD Come, come now, once for all: there is time yet, and advise you to use your influence to prevent it.

NORA But, Mr Krogstad, I have no influence – absolutely none.

KROGSTAD None? I thought you said a moment ago –

NORA Of course not in that sense. I! How can you imagine that should have any influence over my husband?

KROGSTAD Oh, I know your husband from our college days. I don't think he is any more inflexible than other husbands.

NORA If you talk disrespectfully of my husband, I must request you to leave the house.

KROGSTAD You are bold, madam.

NORA I am afraid of you no longer. When New Year's Day is over, I shall soon be out of the whole business.

KROGSTAD [*controlling himself*]. Listen to me, Mrs Helmer. If need be, I shall fight as though for my life to keep my little place in the Bank.

NORA Yes, so it seems.

KROGSTAD It's not only for the salary; that is what I care least about. It's something else — Well, I had better make a clean breast of it. Of course you know, like everyone else, that some years ago I – got into trouble.

NORA I think I've heard something of the sort.

KROGSTAD The matter never came into court; but from that moment all paths were barred to me. Then I took up the business you know about. I had to turn my hand to something; and I don't think I've been one of the worst. But now I must get clear of it all. My sons are growing up; for their sake I must try to recover my character as well as I can. This place in the Bank was the first step; and now your husband wants to kick me off the ladder, back into the mire.

NORA But I assure you, Mr Krogstad, I haven't the least power to help you.

KROGSTAD That is because you have not the will; but I can compel you.

NORA You won't tell my husband that I owe you money?

KROGSTAD H'm; suppose I were to?

NORA It would be shameful of you. [*with tears in her voice*] The secret that is my joy and my pride – that he should learn it in such an ugly, coarse way – and from you. It would involve me in all sorts of unpleasantness –

KROGSTAD Only unpleasantness?

NORA [*hotly*]. But just do it. It's you that will come off worst, for then my husband will see what a bad man you are, and then you certainly won't keep your place.

KROGSTAD I asked whether it was only domestic unpleasantness you feared?

NORA If my husband gets to know about it, he will of course pay you off at once, and then we shall have nothing more to do with you.

KROGSTAD [*coming a pace nearer*]. Listen, Mrs Helmer; either your memory is defective, or you don't know much about business. I must make the position a little clearer to you.

NORA How so?

KROGSTAD When your husband was ill, you came to me to borrow twelve hundred dollars.

NORA I knew of nobody else.

KROGSTAD I promised to find you the money –

NORA And you did find it.

KROGSTAD I promised to find you the money, on certain conditions. You were so much taken up at the time about your husband's illness, and so eager to have the wherewithal for your journey, that you probably did not give much thought to the details. Allow me to remind you of them. I promised to find you the amount in exchange for a note of hand, which I drew up.

NORA Yes, and I signed it.

KROGSTAD Quite right. But then I added a few lines, making your father security for the debt. Your father was to sign this.

NORA Was to – ? He did sign it!

KROGSTAD I had left the date blank. That is to say, your father was himself to date his signature. Do you recollect that?

NORA Yes, I believe –

KROGSTAD Then I gave you the paper to send to your father, by post. Is not that so?

NORA Yes.

KROGSTAD And of course you did so at once; for within five or six days you brought me back the document with your father's signature; and I handed you the money.

NORA Well? Have I not made my payments punctually?

KROGSTAD Fairly – yes. But to return to the point: you were in great trouble at the time, Mrs Helmer.

NORA I was indeed!

KROGSTAD Your father was very ill, I believe?

NORA He was on his death-bed.

KROGSTAD And died soon after?

NORA Yes.

KROGSTAD Tell me, Mrs Helmer: do you happen to recollect the day of his death? The day of the month, I mean?

NORA Father died on the 29th of September.

KROGSTAD Quite correct. I have made inquiries. And here comes in the remarkable point – [*produces a paper*] – which I cannot explain.

NORA What remarkable point? I don't know –

KROGSTAD The remarkable point, madam, that your father signed this paper three days after his death!

NORA What! I don't understand –

KROGSTAD Your father died on the 29th of September. But look here: he has dated his signature October 2nd! Is not that remarkable, Mrs Helmer? [*Nora is silent*] Can you explain it? [*Nora continues silent*] It is noteworthy, too, that the words 'October 2nd' and the year are not in your father's handwriting, but in one which I believe I know. Well, this may be explained; your father may have forgotten to date his signature, and somebody may have added the date at random, before the fact of your father's death was known. There is nothing wrong in that. Everything depends on the signature. Of course it is genuine, Mrs Helmer? It was really your father himself who wrote his name here?

NORA [*after a short silence, throws her head back and looks defiantly at him*]. No, it was not. *I* wrote father's name.

KROGSTAD Ah! – Are you aware, madam, that that is a dangerous admission?

NORA How so? You will soon get your money.

KROGSTAD May I ask you one more question? Why did you not send the paper to your father?

NORA It was impossible. Father was ill. If I had asked him for his signature, I should have had to tell him why I wanted the money; but he was so ill I really could not tell him that my husband's life was in danger. It was impossible.

KROGSTAD Then it would have been better to have given up your tour.

NORA No, I couldn't do that; my husband's life depended on that journey. I couldn't give it up.

KROGSTAD And did it never occur to you that you were playing me false?

NORA That was nothing to me. I didn't care in the least about you. I couldn't endure you for all the cruel difficulties you made, although you knew how ill my husband was.

KROGSTAD Mrs Helmer, you evidently do not realize what you have been guilty of. But I can assure you it was nothing more and nothing worse that made me an outcast from society.

NORA You! You want me to believe that you did a brave thing to save your wife's life?

KROGSTAD The law takes no account of motives.

NORA Then it must be a very bad law.

KROGSTAD Bad or not, if I produce this document in court, you will be condemned according to law.

NORA I don't believe that. Do you mean to tell me that a daughter has no right to spare her dying father trouble and anxiety? – that a wife has no right to save her husband's life? I don't know much about the law, but I'm sure you'll find, somewhere or another, that that is allowed. And you don't know that – you, a lawyer! You must be a bad one, Mr Krogstad.

KROGSTAD Possibly. But business – such business as ours – I do understand. You believe that? Very well; now do as you please. But this I may tell you, that if I am flung into the gutter a second time, you shall keep me company. [bows and goes out through hall]

NORA [stands a while thinking, then tosses her head]. Oh, nonsense! He wants to frighten me. I'm not so foolish as that. [begins folding the children's clothes. Pauses] But – ? No, it's impossible! Why, I did it for love!

CHILDREN [at the door, left]. Mamma, the strange man has gone now.

NORA Yes, yes, I know. But don't tell anyone about the strange man. Do you hear? Not even papa!

CHILDREN No, mamma; and now will you play with us again?

NORA No, no; not now.

CHILDREN Oh, do, mamma; you know you promised.

NORA Yes, but I can't just now. Run to the nursery; I have so much to do. Run along, run along, and be good, my darlings. [she pushes them gently into the inner room, and closes the door behind them. Sits on the sofa, embroiders a few stitches, but soon pauses] No! [throws down the work, rises, goes to the hall door and calls out] Ellen, bring in the Christmas-tree! [goes to table, left, and opens the drawer; again pauses] No, it's quite impossible!

ELLEN [*with Christmas-tree*]. Where shall I stand it, ma'am?

NORA There, in the middle of the room.

ELLEN. Shall I bring in anything else?

NORA No, thank you, I have all I want.

[*Ellen, having put down the tree, goes out*]

NORA [*busy dressing the tree*]. There must be a candle here – and flowers there. – That horrible man! Nonsense, nonsense! there's nothing to be afraid of. The Christmas-tree shall be beautiful. I'll do everything to please you, Torvald; I'll sing and dance, and –

Enter HELMER *by the hall door, with a bundle of documents.*

NORA Oh! You're back already?

HELMER Yes. Has anybody been here?

NORA Here? No.

HELMER That's odd. I saw Krogstad come out of the house.

NORA Did you? Oh yes, by the bye, he was here for a minute.

HELMER Nora, I can see by your manner that he has been begging you to put in a good word for him.

NORA Yes.

HELMER And you were to do it as if of your own accord? You were to say nothing to me of his having been here. Didn't he suggest that too?

NORA Yes, Torvald; but –

HELMER Nora, Nora! And you could condescend to that! To speak to such a man, to make him a promise! And then to tell me an untruth about it!

NORA An untruth!

HELMER Didn't you say that nobody had been here? [*threatens with his finger*] My little bird must never do that again! A songbird must sing clear and true; no false notes. [*puts his arm round her*] That's so, isn't it? Yes, I was sure of it. [*lets her go*] And now we'll say no more about it. [*sits down before the fire*] Oh, how cosy and quiet it is here! [*glances into his documents*]

NORA [*busy with the tree, after a short silence*]. Torvald!

HELMER Yes.

NORA I'm looking forward so much to the Stenborgs' fancy ball the day after tomorrow.

HELMER And I'm on tenterhooks to see what surprise you have in store for me.

NORA Oh, it's too tiresome!

HELMER What is?

NORA I can't think of anything good. Everything seems so foolish and meaningless.

HELMER Has little Nora made that discovery?

NORA [*behind his chair, with her arms on the back*]. Are you very busy, Torvald?

HELMER Well —

NORA What papers are those?

HELMER Bank business.

NORA Already!

HELMER I have got the retiring manager to let me make some necessary changes in the staff and the organization. I can do this during Christmas week. I want to have everything straight by the New Year.

NORA Then that's why that poor Krogstad —

HELMER H'm.

NORA [*still leaning over the chair-back and slowly stroking his hair*]. If you hadn't been so very busy, I should have asked you a great, great favour, Torvald.

HELMER What can it be? Out with it.

NORA Nobody has such perfect taste as you; and I should so love to look well at the fancy ball. Torvald dear, couldn't you take me in hand, and settle what I'm to be, and arrange my costume for me?

HELMER Aha! So my wilful little woman is at a loss, and making signals of distress.

NORA Yes, please, Torvald. I can't get on without your help.

HELMER Well, well, I'll think it over, and we'll soon hit upon something.

NORA Oh, how good that is of you! [*goes to the tree again; pause* How well the red flowers show. — Tell me, was it anything so very dreadful this Krogstad got into trouble about?

HELMER Forgery, that's all. Don't you know what that means?

NORA Mayn't he have been driven to it by need?

HELMER Yes; or, like so many others, he may have done it in pure heedlessness. I am not so hard-hearted as to condemn a man absolutely for a single fault.

NORA No, surely not, Torvald!

HELMER Many a man can retrieve his character, if he owns his crime and takes the punishment.

NORA Punishment – ?

HELMER But Krogstad didn't do that. He evaded the law by means of tricks and subterfuges; and that is what has morally ruined him.

NORA Do you think that – ?

HELMER Just think how a man with a thing of that sort on his conscience must be always lying and canting and shamming. Think of the mask he must wear even towards those who stand nearest him – towards his own wife and children. The effect on the children – that's the most terrible part of it, Nora.

NORA Why?

HELMER Because in such an atmosphere of lies home life is poisoned and contaminated in every fibre. Every breath the children draw contains some germ of evil.

NORA [*closer behind him*]. Are you sure of that?

HELMER As a lawyer, my dear, I have seen it often enough. Nearly all cases of early corruption may be traced to lying mothers.

NORA Why – mothers?

HELMER It generally comes from the mother's side; but of course the father's influence may act in the same way. Every lawyer knows it too well. And here has this Krogstad been poisoning his own children for years past by a life of lies and hypocrisy – that is why I call him morally ruined. [*holds out both hands to her*] So my sweet little Nora must promise not to plead his cause. Shake hands upon it. Come, come, what's this? Give me your hand. That's right. Then it's a bargain. I assure you it would have been impossible for me to work with him. It gives me a positive sense of physical discomfort to come in contact with such people.

NORA [*draws her hand away, and moves to the other side of the Christmas-tree*] How warm it is here. And I have so much to do.

HELMER [*rises and gathers up his papers*]. Yes, and I must try to get some of these papers looked through before dinner. And I shall think over your costume too. Perhaps I may even find something to hang in gilt paper on the Christmas-tree. [*lays his hand on her head*] My precious little song-bird!

[*he goes into his room and shuts the door*]

NORA [*softly, after a pause*]. It can't be. It's impossible. It must be impossible!

ANNA [*at the door, left*]. The little ones are begging so prettily to come to mamma.

NORA No, no, no; don't let them come to me! Keep them with you, Anna.

ANNA Very well, ma'am.   [*shuts the door*]

NORA [*pale with terror*]. Corrupt my children! – Poison my home! [*short pause. She throws back her head*] It's not true! It can never, never be true!

ACT SECOND

The same room. In the corner, beside the piano, stands the Christmas-tree, stripped, and with the candles burnt out. Nora's outdoor things lie on the sofa.

NORA, *alone, is walking about restlessly. At last she stops by the sofa, and takes up her cloak.*

NORA [*dropping the cloak*]. There's somebody coming! [*goes to the hall door and listens*] Nobody; of course nobody will come today, Christmas Day; nor tomorrow either. But perhaps – [*opens the door and looks out*] – No, nothing in the letter-box; quite empty. [*comes forward*] Stuff and nonsense! Of course he won't really do anything. Such a thing couldn't happen. It's impossible! Why, I have three little children.

ANNA *enters from the left, with a large cardboard box*

ANNA I've found the box with the fancy dress at last.

NORA Thanks; put it down on the table.

ANNA [*does so*]. But I'm afraid it's very much out of order.

NORA Oh, I wish I could tear it into a hundred thousand pieces!

ANNA Oh no. It can easily be put to rights – just a little patience.

NORA I shall go and get Mrs Linden to help me.

ANNA Going out again? In such weather as this! You'll catch cold, ma'am, and be ill.

NORA Worse things might happen. – What are the children doing?

ANNA They're playing with their Christmas presents, poor little dears; but –

NORA Do they often ask for me?

ANNA You see, they've been so used to having their mamma with them.

NORA Yes; but, Anna, I can't have them so much with me in future.

ANNA Well, little children get used to anything.

NORA Do you think they do? Do you believe they would forget their mother if she went quite away?

ANNA Gracious me! Quite away?

NORA Tell me, Anna – I've so often wondered about it – how could you bring yourself to give your child up to strangers?

ANNA I had to when I came to nurse my little Miss Nora.

NORA But how could you make up your mind to it?

ANNA When I had the chance of such a good place? A poor girl who's been in trouble must take what comes. That wicked man did nothing for me.

NORA But your daughter must have forgotten you.

ANNA Oh no, ma'am, that she hasn't. She wrote to me both when she was confirmed and when she was married.

NORA [embracing her]. Dear old Anna – you were a good mother to me when I was little.

ANNA My poor little Nora had no mother but me.

NORA And if my little ones had nobody else, I'm sure you would – Nonsense, nonsense! [opens the box] Go in to the children. Now I must – You'll see how lovely I shall be tomorrow.

ANNA I'm sure there will be no one at the ball so lovely as my Miss Nora.   [she goes into the room on the left]

NORA [takes the costume out of the box, but soon throws it down again]. Oh, if I dared go out. If only nobody would come. If only nothing would happen here in the meantime. Rubbish; nobody is coming. Only not to think. What a delicious muff! Beautiful gloves, beautiful gloves! To forget – to forget! One, two, three, four, five, six – [with a scream] Ah, there they come.
[goes towards the door, then stands irresolute.]

MRS LINDEN enters from the hall, where she has taken off her things.

NORA Oh, it's you, Christina. There's nobody else there? I'm so glad you have come.

MRS LINDEN I hear you called at my lodgings.

NORA Yes, I was just passing. There's something you must help me with. Let us sit here on the sofa – so. Tomorrow evening there's to be a fancy ball at Consul Stenborg's overhead, and Torvald wants me to appear as a Neapolitan fisher-girl, and dance the tarantella; I learned it at Capri.

MRS LINDEN I see – quite a performance.

NORA Yes, Torvald wishes it. Look, this is the costume; Torvald had it made for me in Italy. But now it's all so torn, I don't know –

MRS LINDEN Oh, we shall soon set that to rights. It's only the trimming that has come loose here and there. Have you a needle and thread? Ah, here's the very thing.

NORA Oh, how kind of you.

MRS LINDEN [*sewing*]. So you're to be in costume tomorrow, Nora? I'll tell you what – I shall come in for a moment to see you in all your glory. But I've quite forgotten to thank you for the pleasant evening yesterday.

NORA [*rises and walks across the room*]. Oh, yesterday; it didn't seem so pleasant as usual. – You should have come to town a little sooner, Christina. – Torvald has certainly the art of making home bright and beautiful.

MRS LINDEN You too, I should think, or you wouldn't be your father's daughter. But tell me – is Doctor Rank always so depressed as he was last evening?

NORA No, yesterday it was particularly noticeable. You see, he suffers from a dreadful illness. He has spinal consumption, poor fellow. They say his father was a horrible man, so the son has been sickly from his childhood, you understand.

MRS LINDEN [*lets her sewing fall into her lap*]. Why, my darling Nora, how do you come to know such things?

NORA [*moving about the room*]. Oh, when one has three children, one sometimes has visits from women who are half – half doctors – and they talk of one thing and another.

MRS LINDEN [*goes on sewing; a short pause*]. Does Doctor Rank come here every day?

NORA Every day of his life. He has been Torvald's most intimate friend from boyhood, and he's a good friend of mine too. Doctor Rank is quite one of the family.

MRS LINDEN But tell me – is he quite sincere? I mean, isn't he rather given to flattering people?

NORA No, quite the contrary. Why should you think so?

MRS LINDEN When you introduced us yesterday he said he had often heard my name; but I noticed afterwards that your husband had no notion who I was. How could Doctor Rank – ?

NORA He was quite right, Christina. You see, Torvald loves me so indescribably, he wants to have me all to himself, as he says. When we were first married he was almost jealous if I even mentioned any of my old friends at home; so naturally I gave up doing it. But I often talk of the old times to Doctor Rank, for he likes to hear about them.

MRS LINDEN Listen to me, Nora! You are still a child in many ways. I am older than you, and have had more experience. I'll tell you something. You ought to get clear of all this with Doctor Rank.

NORA Get clear of what?

MRS LINDEN The whole affair, I should say. You were talking yesterday of a rich admirer who was to find you money –

NORA Yes, one who never existed, worse luck! What then?

MRS LINDEN Has Doctor Rank money?

NORA Yes, he has.

MRS LINDEN And nobody to provide for?

NORA Nobody. But – ?

MRS LINDEN And he comes here every day?

NORA Yes, I told you so.

MRS LINDEN I should have thought he would have had better taste.

NORA I don't understand you a bit.

MRS LINDEN Don't pretend, Nora. Do you suppose I can't guess who lent you the twelve hundred dollars?

NORA Are you out of your senses? How can you think such a thing? A friend who comes here every day! Why, the position would be unbearable!

MRS LINDEN Then it really is not he?

NORA No, I assure you. It never for a moment occurred to me – Besides, at that time he had nothing to lend; he came into his property afterwards.

MRS LINDEN Well, I believe that was lucky for you, Nora dear.

NORA No, really, it would never have struck me to ask Doctor Rank – And yet, I'm certain that if I did –

MRS LINDEN But of course you never would.

NORA Of course not. It's inconceivable that it should ever be necessary. But I'm quite sure that if I spoke to Doctor Rank –

MRS LINDEN Behind your husband's back?

NORA I must get clear of the other thing; that's behind his back too. I must get clear of that.

MRS LINDEN Yes, yes, I told you so yesterday; but –

NORA [*walking up and down*]. A man can manage these things much better than a woman.

MRS LINDEN One's own husband, yes.

NORA Nonsense. [*stands still*] When everything is paid, one gets back the paper.

MRS LINDEN Of course.

NORA And can tear it into a hundred thousand pieces, and burn it up, the nasty, filthy thing!

MRS LINDEN [*looks at her fixedly, lays down her work, and rises slowly*]. Nora, you are hiding something from me.

NORA Can you see it in my face?

MRS LINDEN Something has happened since yesterday morning. Nora, what is it?

NORA [*going towards her*]. Christina – ! [*listens*] Hush! There's Torvald coming home. Do you mind going into the nursery for the present? Torvald can't bear to see dressmaking going on. Get Anna to help you.

MRS LINDEN [*gathers some of the things together*]. Very well; but I shan't go away until you have told me all about it.

She goes out to the left, as HELMER *enters from the hall.*

NORA [*runs to meet him*]. Oh, how I've been longing for you to come, Torvald dear!

HELMER Was that the dressmaker – ?

NORA No, Christina. She's helping me with my costume. You'll see how nice I shall look.

HELMER Yes, wasn't that a happy thought of mine?

NORA Splendid! But isn't it good of me too, to have given in to you about the tarantella?

HELMER [*takes her under the chin*]. Good of you! To give in to your own husband? Well, well, you little madcap, I know you don't mean it. But I won't disturb you. I dare say you want to be 'trying on'.

NORA And you are going to work, I suppose?

HELMER Yes. [*shows her a bundle of papers*] Look here. I've just come from the Bank –   [*goes towards his room*]

NORA Torvald.

HELMER [*stopping*]. Yes?

NORA If your little squirrel were to beg you for something so prettily –

HELMER Well?

NORA Would you do it?

HELMER I must know first what it is.

NORA The squirrel would skip about and play all sorts of tricks if you would only be nice and kind.

HELMER Come, then, out with it.

NORA Your lark would twitter from morning till night –

HELMER Oh, that she does in any case.

NORA I'll be an elf and dance in the moonlight for you, Torvald.

HELMER Nora – you can't mean what you were hinting at this morning?

NORA [*coming nearer*]. Yes, Torvald, I beg and implore you!

HELMER Have you really the courage to begin that again?

NORA Yes, yes; for my sake, you must let Krogstad keep his place in the Bank.

HELMER My dear Nora, it's his place I intend for Mrs Linden.

NORA Yes, that's so good of you. But instead of Krogstad, you could dismiss some other clerk.

HELMER Why, this is incredible obstinacy! Because you have thoughtlessly promised to put in a word for him, I am to – !

NORA It's not that, Torvald. It's for your own sake. This man writes for the most scurrilous newspapers; you said so yourself. He can do you no end of harm. I'm so terribly afraid of him –

HELMER Ah, I understand; it's old recollections that are frightening you.

NORA What do you mean?

HELMER Of course you're thinking of your father.

NORA Yes – yes, of course. Only think of the shameful slanders wicked people used to write about father. I believe they would have got him dismissed if you hadn't been sent to look into the thing, and been kind to him, and helped him.

HELMER My little Nora, between your father and me there is all the difference in the world. Your father was not altogether unimpeachable. I am; and I hope to remain so.

NORA Oh, no one knows what wicked men may hit upon. We could live so quietly and happily now, in our cosy, peaceful home, you and I and the children, Torvald! That's why I beg and implore you –

HELMER And it is just by pleading his cause that you make it impossible for me to keep him. It's already known at the Bank that I intend to dismiss Krogstad. If it were now reported that the new manager let himself be turned round his wife's little finger –

NORA What then?

HELMER Oh, nothing, so long as a wilful woman can have her way – ! I am to make myself a laughing-stock to the whole staff, and set people saying that I am open to all sorts of outside influence? Take my word for it, I should soon feel the consequences. And besides – there is one thing that makes Krogstad impossible for me to work with –

NORA What thing?

HELMER I could perhaps have overlooked his moral failings at a pinch –

NORA Yes, couldn't you, Torvald?

HELMER And I hear he is good at his work. But the fact is, he was a college chum of mine – there was one of those rash friendships between us that one so often repents of later. I may as well confess it at once – he calls me by my Christian name;* and he is tactless enough to do it even when others are present. He delights in putting on airs of familiarity – Torvald here, Torvald there! I assure you it's most painful to me. He would make my position at the Bank perfectly unendurable.

NORA Torvald, surely you're not serious?

HELMER No? Why not?

NORA That's such a petty reason.

HELMER What! Petty! Do you consider me petty?

NORA No, on the contrary, Torvald dear; and that's just why –

HELMER Never mind; you call my motives petty; then I must be petty too. Petty! Very well! – Now we'll put an end to this, once for all. [goes to the door into the hall and calls] Ellen!

NORA What do you want?

HELMER [searching among his papers]. To settle the thing.

* In the original, 'we say "*Du*" to each other.'

ELLEN *enters*

Here, take this letter; give it to a messenger. See that he takes it at once. The address is on it. Here's the money.

ELLEN. Very well, sir.   [*goes with the letter*]

HELMER [*putting his papers together*]. There, Madam Obstinacy.

NORA [*breathless*]. Torvald – what was in the letter?

HELMER Krogstad's dismissal.

NORA Call it back again, Torvald! There's still time. Oh, Torvald, call it back again! For my sake, for your own, for the children's sake! Do you hear, Torvald? Do it! You don't know what that letter may bring upon us all.

HELMER Too late.

NORA Yes, too late.

HELMER My dear Nora, I forgive your anxiety, though it's anything but flattering to me. Why should you suppose that *I* would be afraid of a wretched scribbler's spite? But I forgive you all the same, for it's a proof of your great love for me. [*takes her in his arms*] That's as it should be, my own dear Nora. Let what will happen – when it comes to the pinch, I shall have strength and courage enough. You shall see: my shoulders are broad enough to bear the whole burden.

NORA [*terror-struck*]. What do you mean by that?

HELMER The whole burden, I say –

NORA [*with decision*]. That you shall never, never do!

HELMER Very well; then we'll share it, Nora, as man and wife. That is how it should be. [*petting her*] Are you satisfied now? Come, come, come, don't look like a scared dove. It's all nothing – foolish fancies. – Now you ought to play the tarantella through and practise with the tambourine. I shall sit in my inner room and shut both doors, so that I shall hear nothing. You can make as much noise as you please. [*turns round in doorway*] And when Rank comes, just tell him where I'm to be found.   [*he nods to her, and goes with his papers into his room, closing the door*]

NORA [*bewildered with terror, stands as though rooted to the ground, and whispers*]. He would do it. Yes, he would do it. He would do it, in spite of all the world. – No, never that, never, never! Anything rather than that! Oh, for some way of escape! What shall I do — ! [*hall bell rings*] Doctor Rank — ! Anything, anything, rather than — !

Nora draws her hands over her face, pulls herself together, goes to the door and opens it. RANK *stands outside hanging up his fur coat. During what follows it begins to grow dark.*

NORA Good afternoon, Doctor Rank. I knew you by your ring. But you mustn't go to Torvald now. I believe he's busy.

RANK And you? [*enters and closes the door*]

NORA Oh, you know very well, I have always time for you.

RANK Thank you. I shall avail myself of your kindness as long as I can.

NORA What do you mean? As long as you can?

RANK Yes. Does that frighten you?

NORA I think it's an odd expression. Do you expect anything to happen?

RANK Something I have long been prepared for; but I didn't think it would come so soon.

NORA [*catching at his arm*]. What have you discovered? Doctor Rank, you must tell me!

RANK [*sitting down by the stove*]. I am running down hill. There's no help for it.

NORA [*draws a long breath of relief*]. It's you — ?

RANK Who else should it be? — Why lie to one's self? I am the most wretched of all my patients, Mrs Helmer. In these last days I have been auditing my life-account — bankrupt! Perhaps before a month is over I shall lie rotting in the churchyard.

NORA Oh! What an ugly way to talk.

RANK The thing itself is so confoundedly ugly, you see. But the worst of it is, so many other ugly things have to be gone through first. There is only one last investigation to be made, and when that is over I shall know pretty certainly when the break-up will begin. There's one thing I want to say to you: Helmer's delicate nature shrinks so from all that is horrible: I will not have him in my sick-room —

NORA But, Doctor Rank —

RANK I won't have him, I say — not on any account! I shall lock my door against him. — As soon as I am quite certain of the worst, I shall send you my visiting-card with a black cross on it; and then you will know that the final horror has begun.

NORA Why, you're perfectly unreasonable today; and I did so want you to be in a really good humour.

RANK With death staring me in the face? – And to suffer thus for another's sin! Where's the justice of it? And in one way or another you can trace in every family some such inexorable retribution –

NORA [stopping her ears]. Nonsense, nonsense! Now cheer up!

RANK Well, after all, the whole thing's only worth laughing at. My poor innocent spine must do penance for my father's wild oats.

NORA [at table, left]. I suppose he was too fond of asparagus and Strasbourg pâte, wasn't he?

RANK Yes; and truffles.

NORA Yes, truffles, to be sure. And oysters, I believe?

RANK Yes, oysters; oysters, of course.

NORA And then all the port and champagne! It's sad that all these good things should attack the spine.

RANK Especially when the luckless spine attacked never had any good of them.

NORA Ah yes, that's the worst of it.

RANK [looks at her searchingly]. H'm –

NORA [a moment later]. Why did you smile?

RANK No; it was you that laughed.

NORA No; it was you that smiled, Doctor Rank.

RANK [standing up]. I see you're deeper than I thought.

NORA I'm in such a crazy mood today.

RANK So it seems.

NORA [with her hands on his shoulders]. Dear, dear Doctor Rank, death shall not take you away from Torvald and me.

RANK Oh, you'll easily get over the loss. The absent are soon forgotten.

NORA [looks at him anxiously]. Do you think so?

RANK People make fresh ties, and then –

NORA Who make fresh ties?

RANK You and Helmer will, when I am gone. You yourself are taking time by the forelock, it seems to me. What was that Mrs Linden doing here yesterday?

NORA Oh! – you're surely not jealous of poor Christina?

RANK Yes, I am. She will be my successor in this house. When I am out of the way, this woman will perhaps –

NORA Hush! Not so loud! She's in there.

RANK Today as well? You see!

NORA Only to put my costume in order – dear me, how unreasonable you are! [*sits on sofa*] Now do be good, Doctor Rank! Tomorrow you shall see how beautifully I shall dance; and then you may fancy that I'm doing it all to please you – and of course Torvald as well. [*takes various things out of box*] Doctor Rank, sit down here, and I'll show you something.

RANK [*sitting*]. What is it?

NORA Look here. Look!

RANK Silk stockings.

NORA Flesh-coloured. Aren't they lovely? It's so dark here now; but tomorrow – No, no, no; you must only look at the feet. Oh, well, I suppose you may look at the rest too.

RANK H'm –

NORA What are you looking so critical about? Do you think they won't fit me?

RANK I can't possibly give any competent opinion on that point.

NORA [*looking at him a moment*]. For shame! [*hits him lightly on the ear with the stockings*] Take that. [*rolls them up again*]

RANK And what other wonders am I to see?

NORA You shan't see any more; for you don't behave nicely. [*she hums a little, and searches among the things*]

RANK [*after a short silence*]. When I sit here gossiping with you, I can't imagine – I simply cannot conceive – what would have become of me if I had never entered this house.

NORA [*smiling*]. Yes, I think you do feel at home with us.

RANK [*more softly – looking straight before him*]. And now to have to leave it all –

NORA Nonsense. You shan't leave us.

RANK [*in the same tone*]. And not to be able to leave behind the slightest token of gratitude; scarcely even a passing regret – nothing but an empty place, that can be filled by the first comer.

NORA And if I were to ask you for – ? No –

RANK For what?

NORA For a great proof of your friendship.

RANK Yes – yes?

NORA I mean – for a very, very great service –

RANK Would you really, for once, make me so happy?

NORA Oh, you don't know what it is.

RANK Then tell me.

NORA No, I really can't, Doctor Rank. It's far, far too much – not only a service, but help and advice besides –

RANK So much the better. I can't think what you can mean. But go on. Don't you trust me?

NORA As I trust no one else. I know you are my best and truest friend. So I will tell you. Well then, Doctor Rank, there is something you must help me to prevent. You know how deeply, how wonderfully Torvald loves me; he wouldn't hesitate a moment to give his very life for my sake.

RANK [bending towards her]. Nora – do you think he is the only one who – ?

NORA [with a slight start]. Who – ?

RANK Who would gladly give his life for you?

NORA [sadly]. Oh!

RANK I have sworn that you shall know it before I – go. I shall never find a better opportunity. – Yes, Nora, now I have told you; and now you know that you can trust me as you can no one else.

NORA [standing up; simply and calmly]. Let me pass, please.

RANK [makes way for her, but remains sitting]. Nora –

NORA [in the doorway]. Ellen, bring the lamp. [crosses to the stove] Oh dear, Doctor Rank, that was too bad of you.

RANK [rising]. That I have loved you as deeply as – anyone else? Was that too bad of me?

NORA No, but that you should have told me so. It was so unnecessary –

RANK What do you mean? Did you know – ?

> ELLEN enters with the lamp; sets it on the table and
> goes out again.

RANK Nora – Mrs Helmer – I ask you, did you know?

NORA Oh, how can I tell what I knew or didn't know? I really can't say – How could you be so clumsy, Doctor Rank? It was all so nice!

RANK Well, at any rate, you know now that I am at your service, body and soul. And now, go on.

NORA [*looking at him*]. Go on – now?

RANK I beg you to tell me what you want.

NORA I can tell you nothing now.

RANK Yes, yes! You mustn't punish me in that way. Let me do for you whatever a man can.

NORA You can do nothing for me now. – Besides, I really want no help. You shall see it was only my fancy. Yes, it must be so. Of course! [*sits in the rocking-chair, looks at him and smiles*] You are a nice person, Doctor Rank! Aren't you ashamed of yourself, now that the lamp is on the table?

RANK No; not exactly. But perhaps I ought to go – for ever.

NORA No, indeed you mustn't. Of course you must come and go as you've always done. You know very well that Torvald can't do without you.

RANK Yes, but you?

NORA Oh, you know I always like to have you here.

RANK That is just what led me astray. You are a riddle to me. It has often seemed to me as if you liked being with me almost as much as being with Helmer.

NORA Yes; don't you see? There are people one loves, and others one likes to talk to.

RANK Yes – there's something in that.

NORA When I was a girl, of course I loved papa best. But it always delighted me to steal into the servants' room. In the first place, they never lectured me, and, in the second, it was such fun to hear them talk.

RANK Ah, I see; then it's their place I have taken?

NORA [*jumps up and hurries towards him*]. Oh, my dear Doctor Rank, I don't mean that. But you understand, with Torvald it's the same as with papa –

ELLEN *enters from the hall*

ELLEN. Please, ma'am – [*whispers to Nora, and gives her a card*]

NORA [*glancing at card*]. Ah! [*puts it in her pocket*]

RANK Anything wrong?

NORA No, no, not in the least. It's only – it's my new costume –

RANK Your costume? Why, it's there.

NORA Oh, that one, yes. But this is another that — I have ordered it — Torvald mustn't know —

RANK Aha! So that's the great secret.

NORA Yes, of course. Please go to him; he's in the inner room. Do keep him while I —

RANK Don't be alarmed; he shan't escape. [*goes into Helmer's room*]

NORA [*to Ellen*]. Is he waiting in the kitchen?

ELLEN. Yes, he came up the back stair —

NORA Didn't you tell him I was engaged?

ELLEN. Yes, but it was no use.

NORA He won't go away?

ELLEN. No, ma'am, not until he has spoken to you.

NORA Then let him come in; but quietly. And, Ellen — say nothing about it; it's a surprise for my husband.

ELLEN. Oh, yes, ma'am, I understand. [*she goes out*]

NORA It is coming! The dreadful thing is coming, after all. No, no, no, it can never be; it shall not!

She goes to Helmer's door and slips the bolt. Ellen opens the hall door for KROGSTAD, *and shuts it after him. He wears a travelling-coat, high boots, and a fur cap.*

NORA [*goes towards him*]. Speak softly; my husband is at home.

KROGSTAD All right. That's nothing to me.

NORA What do you want?

KROGSTAD A little information.

NORA Be quick, then. What is it?

KROGSTAD You know I have got my dismissal?

NORA I couldn't prevent it, Mr Krogstad. I fought for you to the last, but it was of no use.

KROGSTAD Does your husband care for you so little? He knows what I can bring upon you, and yet he dares —

NORA How could you think I should tell him?

KROGSTAD Well, as a matter of fact, I didn't think it. It wasn't like my friend Torvald Helmer to show so much courage —

NORA Mr Krogstad, be good enough to speak respectfully of my husband.

KROGSTAD Certainly, with all due respect. But since you are so anxious to keep the matter secret, I suppose you are a little clearer than yesterday as to what you have done.

NORA Clearer than you could ever make me.

KROGSTAD Yes, such a bad lawyer as I –

NORA What is it you want?

KROGSTAD Only to see how you are getting on, Mrs Helmer. I've been thinking about you all day. Even a mere money-lender, a gutter-journalist, a – in short, a creature like me – has a little bit of what people call feeling.

NORA Then show it; think of my little children.

KROGSTAD Did you and your husband think of mine? But enough of that. I only wanted to tell you that you needn't take this matter too seriously. I shall not lodge any information, for the present.

NORA No, surely not. I knew you wouldn't.

KROGSTAD The whole thing can be settled quite amicably. Nobody need know. It can remain among us three.

NORA My husband must never know.

KROGSTAD How can you prevent it? Can you pay off the balance?

NORA No, not at once.

KROGSTAD Or have you any means of raising the money in the next few days?

NORA None – that I will make use of.

KROGSTAD And if you had, it would not help you now. If you offered me ever so much money down, you should not get back your IOU.

NORA Tell me what you want to do with it.

KROGSTAD I only want to keep it – to have it in my possession. No outsider shall hear anything of it. So, if you have any desperate scheme in your head –

NORA What if I have?

KROGSTAD If you should think of leaving your husband and children –

NORA What if I do?

KROGSTAD Or if you should think of – something worse –

NORA How do you know that?

KROGSTAD Put all that out of your head.

NORA How did you know what I had in my mind?

KROGSTAD Most of us think of that at first. I thought of it, too; but I hadn't the courage –

NORA [tonelessly]. Nor I.

KROGSTAD [*relieved*]. No, one hasn't. You haven't the courage
either, have you?

NORA I haven't, I haven't.

KROGSTAD Besides, it would be very foolish. – Just one domestic
storm, and it's all over. I have a letter in my pocket for your
husband –

NORA Telling him everything?

KROGSTAD Sparing you as much as possible.

NORA [*quickly*]. He must never read that letter. Tear it up. I will
manage to get the money somehow –

KROGSTAD Pardon me, Mrs Helmer, but I believe I told you –

NORA Oh, I am not talking about the money I owe you. Tell me
how much you demand from my husband – I will get it.

KROGSTAD I demand no money from your husband.

NORA What do you demand then?

KROGSTAD I will tell you. I want to regain my footing in the
world. I want to rise; and your husband shall help me to do it.
For the last eighteen months my record has been spotless; I have
been in bitter need all the time; but I was content to fight my
way up, step by step. Now, I've been thrust down again, and I
will not be satisfied with merely being reinstated as a matter of
grace. I want to rise, I tell you. I must get into the Bank again,
in a higher position than before. Your husband shall create a
place on purpose for me –

NORA He will never do that!

KROGSTAD He will do it; I know him – he won't dare to show
fight! And when he and I are together there, you shall soon see!
Before a year is out I shall be the manager's right hand. It won't
be Torvald Helmer, but Nils Krogstad, that manages the Joint
Stock Bank.

NORA That shall never be.

KROGSTAD Perhaps you will – ?

NORA Now I have the courage for it.

KROGSTAD Oh, you don't frighten me! A sensitive, petted creature
like you –

NORA You shall see, you shall see!

KROGSTAD Under the ice, perhaps? Down into the cold, black
water? And next spring to come up again, ugly, hairless, un-
recognizable –

NORA You can't terrify me.

KROGSTAD Nor you me. People don't do that sort of thing, Mrs Helmer. And after all, what would be the use of it? I have your husband in my pocket all the same.

NORA Afterwards? When I am no longer – ?

KROGSTAD You forget, your reputation remains in my hands! [*Nora stands speechless and looks at him*] Well, now you are prepared. Do nothing foolish. As soon as Helmer has received my letter, I shall expect to hear from him. And remember that it is your husband himself who has forced me back again into such paths. That I will never forgive him. Goodbye, Mrs Helmer.

[*goes out through the hall.*]

NORA [*hurries to the door, opens it a little, and listens*] He's going. He's not putting the letter into the box. No, no, it would be impossible! [*opens the door farther and farther*] What's that? He's standing still; not going downstairs. Has he changed his mind? Is he – ? [*a letter falls into the box. Krogstad's footsteps are heard gradually receding down the stair. Nora utters a suppressed shriek, and rushes forward towards the sofa-table; pause*] In the letter-box! [*slips shrinkingly up to the hall door*] There it lies. – Torvald, Torvald – now we are lost!

MRS LINDEN *enters from the left with the costume*

MRS LINDEN There, I think it's all right now. Shall we just try it on?

NORA [*hoarsely and softly*]. Christina, come here.

MRS LINDEN [*throws down the dress on the sofa*]. What's the matter? You look quite distracted.

NORA Come here. Do you see that letter? There, see – through the glass of the letter-box.

MRS LINDEN Yes, yes, I see it.

NORA That letter is from Krogstad –

MRS LINDEN Nora – it was Krogstad who lent you the money?

NORA Yes; and now Torvald will know everything.

MRS LINDEN Believe me, Nora, it's the best thing for both of you.

NORA You don't know all yet. I have forged a name –

MRS LINDEN Good heavens!

NORA Now, listen to me, Christina; you shall bear me witness –

MRS LINDEN How 'witness'? What am I to – ?

NORA If I should go out of my mind – it might easily happen –

MRS LINDEN Nora!

NORA Or if anything else should happen to me – so that I couldn't be here – !

MRS LINDEN Nora, Nora, you're quite beside yourself!

NORA In case anyone wanted to take it all upon himself – the whole blame – you understand –

MRS LINDEN Yes, yes; but how can you think – ?

NORA You shall bear witness that it's not true, Christina. I'm not out of my mind at all; I know quite well what I'm saying; and I tell you nobody else knew anything about it; I did the whole thing, I myself. Remember that.

MRS LINDEN I shall remember. But I don't understand what you mean –

NORA Oh, how should you? It's the miracle coming to pass.

MRS LINDEN The miracle?

NORA Yes, the miracle. But it's so terrible, Christina; it mustn't happen for all the world.

MRS LINDEN I shall go straight to Krogstad and talk to him.

NORA Don't; he'll do you some harm.

MRS LINDEN Once he would have done anything for me.

NORA He?

MRS LINDEN Where does he live?

NORA Oh, how can I tell – ? Yes – [*feels in her pocket*] Here's his card. But the letter, the letter – !

HELMER [*knocking outside*]. Nora!

NORA [*shrieks in terror*]. Oh, what is it? What do you want?

HELMER Well, well, don't be frightened. We're not coming in; you've bolted the door. Are you trying on your dress?

NORA Yes, yes, I'm trying it on. It suits me so well, Torvald.

MRS LINDEN [*who has read the card*]. Why, he lives close by here.

NORA Yes, but it's no use now. We are lost. The letter is there in the box.

MRS LINDEN And your husband has the key?

NORA Always.

MRS LINDEN Krogstad must demand his letter back, unread. He must find some pretext –

NORA But this is the very time when Torvald generally –

MRS LINDEN Prevent him. Keep him occupied. I shall come back as quickly as I can.   [*she goes out hastily by the hall door*]

NORA [*opens Helmer's door and peeps in*]. Torvald!

HELMER Well, may one come into one's own room again at last? Come, Rank, we'll have a look – [*in the doorway*] But how's this?

NORA What, Torvald dear?

HELMER Rank led me to expect a grand transformation.

RANK [*in the doorway*]. So I understood. I suppose I was mistaken.

NORA No, no one shall see me in my glory till tomorrow evening.

HELMER Why, Nora dear, you look so tired. Have you been practising too hard?

NORA No, I haven't practised at all yet.

HELMER But you'll have to –

NORA Oh yes, I must, I must! But, Torvald, I can't get on at all without your help. I've forgotten everything.

HELMER Oh, we shall soon freshen it up again.

NORA Yes, do help me, Torvald. You must promise me – Oh, I'm so nervous about it. Before so many people – This evening you must give yourself up entirely to me. You mustn't do a stroke of work; you mustn't even touch a pen. Do promise, Torvald dear!

HELMER I promise. All this evening I shall be your slave. Little helpless thing – ! But, by the bye, I must just – [*going to hall door*]

NORA What do you want there?

HELMER Only to see if there are any letters.

NORA No, no, don't do that, Torvald.

HELMER Why not?

NORA Torvald, I beg you not to. There are none there.

HELMER Let me just see. [*is going*]

NORA [*at the piano, plays the first bars of the tarantella*]

HELMER [*at the door, stops*]. Aha!

NORA I can't dance tomorrow if I don't rehearse with you first.

HELMER [*going to her*]. Are you really so nervous, dear Nora?

NORA Yes, dreadfully! Let me rehearse at once. We have time before dinner. Oh, do sit down and play for me, Torvald dear; direct me and put me right, as you used to do.

HELMER With all the pleasure in life, since you wish it.

[*sits at the piano. Nora snatches the tambourine out of the box, and hurriedly drapes herself in a long parti-coloured shawl; then, with a bound, stands in the middle of the floor.*]

NORA Now play for me! Now I'll dance!

[*Helmer plays and Nora dances. Rank stands at the piano behind Helmer and looks on.*]

HELMER [*playing*]. Slower! Slower!

NORA Can't do it slower!

HELMER Not so violently, Nora.

NORA I must! I must!

HELMER [*stops*]. No, no, Nora – that will never do.

NORA [*laughs and swings her tambourine*]. Didn't I tell you so!

RANK Let me play for her.

HELMER [*rising*]. Yes, do – then I can direct her better.

[*Rank sits down to the piano and plays; Nora dances more and more wildly. Helmer stands by the stove and addresses frequent directions to her; she seems not to hear. Her hair breaks loose, and falls over her shoulders. She does not notice it, but goes on dancing.*]

MRS LINDEN *enters, and stands spellbound in the doorway.*

MRS LINDEN Ah – !

NORA [*dancing*]. We're having such fun here, Christina!

HELMER Why, Nora dear, you're dancing as if it were a matter of life and death.

NORA So it is.

HELMER Rank, stop! This is the merest madness. Stop, I say!

[*Rank stops playing, and Nora comes to a sudden standstill*]

HELMER [*going towards her*]. I couldn't have believed it. You've positively forgotten all I taught you.

NORA [*throws the tambourine away*]. You see for yourself.

HELMER You really do want teaching.

NORA Yes, you see how much I need it. You must practise with me up to the last moment. Will you promise me, Torvald?

HELMER Certainly, certainly.

NORA Neither today nor tomorrow must you think of anything but me. You mustn't open a single letter – mustn't look at the letter-box.

HELMER Ah, you're still afraid of that man –

NORA Oh yes, yes, I am.

HELMER Nora, I can see it in your face – there's a letter from him in the box.

NORA I don't know, I believe so. But you're not to read anything now; nothing ugly must come between us until all is over.

RANK [*softly, to Helmer*]. You mustn't contradict her.

HELMER [*putting his arm around her*]. The child shall have her own way. But tomorrow night, when the dance is over –

NORA Then you shall be free.

ELLEN *appears in the doorway, right.*

ELLEN. Dinner is on the table, ma'am.

NORA We'll have some champagne, Ellen.

ELLEN. Yes, ma'am.   [*goes out*]

HELMER Dear me! Quite a banquet.

NORA Yes, and we'll keep it up till morning. [*calling out*] And macaroons, Ellen – plenty – just this once.

HELMER [*seizing her hand*]. Come, come, don't let us have this wild excitement! Be my own little lark again.

NORA Oh yes, I will. But now go into the dining-room; and you too, Doctor Rank. Christina, you must help me to do up my hair.

RANK [*softly, as they go*]. There's nothing in the wind? Nothing – I mean – ?

HELMER Oh no, nothing of the kind. It's merely this babyish anxiety I was telling you about.   [*they go out to the right*]

NORA Well?

MRS LINDEN He's gone out of town.

NORA I saw it in your face.

MRS LINDEN He comes back tomorrow evening. I left a note for him.

NORA You shouldn't have done that. Things must take their course. After all, there's something glorious in waiting for the miracle.

MRS LINDEN What is it you're waiting for?

NORA Oh, you can't understand. Go to them in the dining-room; I shall come in a moment.

[*Mrs Linden goes into the dining-room. Nora stands for a moment as though collecting her thoughts; then looks at her watch.*]

NORA Five. Seven hours till midnight. Then twenty-four hours till the next midnight. Then the tarantella will be over. Twenty-four and seven? Thirty-one hours to live.

HELMER *appears at the door, right.*

HELMER What has become of my little lark?

NORA [*runs to him with open arms*]. Here she is!

ACT THIRD

The same room. The table, with the chairs around it, in the middle. A lighted lamp on the table. The door to the hall stands open. Dance music is heard from the floor above.

MRS LINDEN *sits by the table and absently turns the pages of a book. She tries to read, but seems unable to fix her attention; she frequently listens, and looks anxiously towards the hall door.*

MRS LINDEN [*looks at her watch*]. Not here yet; and the time is nearly up. If only he hasn't – [*listens again*] Ah, there he is. [*she goes into the hall and cautiously opens the outer door; soft footsteps are heard on the stairs; she whispers*] Come in; there is no one here.

KROGSTAD [*in the doorway*]. I found a note from you at my house. What does it mean?

MRS LINDEN I must speak to you.

KROGSTAD Indeed? And in this house?

MRS LINDEN I could not see you at my rooms. They have no separate entrance. Come in; we are quite alone. The servants are asleep, and the Helmers are at the ball upstairs.

KROGSTAD [*coming into the room*]. Ah! So the Helmers are dancing this evening? Really?

MRS LINDEN Yes. Why not?

KROGSTAD Quite right. Why not?

MRS LINDEN And now let us talk a little.

KROGSTAD Have we two anything to say to each other?

MRS LINDEN A great deal.

KROGSTAD I should not have thought so.

MRS LINDEN Because you have never really understood me.

KROGSTAD What was there to understand? The most natural thing in the world – a heartless woman throws a man over when a better match offers.

MRS LINDEN Do you really think me so heartless? Do you think I broke with you lightly?

KROGSTAD Did you not?

MRS LINDEN Do you really think so?

KROGSTAD If not, why did you write me that letter?

MRS LINDEN Was it not best? Since I had to break with you, was it not right that I should try to put an end to all that you felt for me?

KROGSTAD [*clenching his hands together*]. So that was it? And all this – for the sake of money!

MRS LINDEN You ought not to forget that I had a helpless mother and two little brothers. We could not wait for you, Nils, as your prospects then stood.

KROGSTAD Perhaps not; but you had no right to cast me off for the sake of others, whoever the others might be.

MRS LINDEN I don't know. I have often asked myself whether I had the right.

KROGSTAD [*more softly*]. When I had lost you, I seemed to have no firm ground left under my feet. Look at me now. I am a ship-wrecked man, clinging to a spar.

MRS LINDEN Rescue may be at hand.

KROGSTAD It was at hand; but then you came and stood in the way.

MRS LINDEN Without my knowledge, Nils. I did not know till today that it was you I was to replace in the Bank.

KROGSTAD Well, I take your word for it. But now that you do know, do you mean to give way?

MRS LINDEN No, for that would not help you in the least.

KROGSTAD Oh, help, help – ! I should do it whether or no.

MRS LINDEN I have learnt prudence. Life and bitter necessity have schooled me.

KROGSTAD And life has taught me not to trust fine speeches.

MRS LINDEN Then life has taught you a very sensible thing. But deeds you will trust?

KROGSTAD What do you mean?

MRS LINDEN You said you were a shipwrecked man, clinging to a spar.

KROGSTAD I have good reason to say so.

MRS LINDEN I too am shipwrecked, and clinging to a spar. I have no one to mourn for, no one to care for.

KROGSTAD You made your own choice.

MRS LINDEN No choice was left me.

KROGSTAD Well, what then?

MRS LINDEN Nils, how if we two shipwrecked people could join hands?

KROGSTAD What!

MRS LINDEN Two on a raft have a better chance than if each clings to a separate spar.

KROGSTAD Christina!

MRS LINDEN What do you think brought me to town?

KROGSTAD Had you any thought of me?

MRS LINDEN I must have work or I can't bear to live. All my life, as long as I can remember, I have worked; work has been my one great joy. Now I stand quite alone in the world, aimless and forlorn. There is no happiness in working for one's self. Nils, give me somebody and something to work for.

KROGSTAD I cannot believe in all this. It is simply a woman's romantic craving for self-sacrifice.

MRS LINDEN Have you ever found me romantic?

KROGSTAD Would you really – ? Tell me: do you know all my past?

MRS LINDEN Yes.

KROGSTAD And do you know what people say of me?

MRS LINDEN Did you not say just now that with me you could have been another man?

KROGSTAD I am sure of it.

MRS LINDEN Is it too late?

KROGSTAD Christina, do you know what you are doing? Yes, you do; I see it in your face. Have you the courage then – ?

MRS LINDEN I need someone to be a mother to, and your children need a mother. You need me, and I – I need you. Nils, I believe in your better self. With you I fear nothing.

KROGSTAD [seizing her hands]. Thank you – thank you, Christina. Now I shall make others see me as you do. – Ah, I forgot –

MRS LINDEN [listening]. Hush! The tarantella! Go! go!

KROGSTAD Why? What is it?

MRS LINDEN Don't you hear the dancing overhead? As soon as that is over they will be here.

KROGSTAD Oh yes, I shall go. Nothing will come of this, after all. Of course, you don't know the step I have taken against the Helmers.

MRS LINDEN Yes, Nils, I do know.

KROGSTAD And yet you have the courage to – ?

MRS LINDEN I know to what lengths despair can drive a man.

KROGSTAD Oh, if I could only undo it!

MRS LINDEN You could. Your letter is still in the box.

KROGSTAD Are you sure?

MRS LINDEN Yes; but –

KROGSTAD [*looking at her searchingly*]. Is that what it all means? You want to save your friend at any price. Say it out – is that your idea?

MRS LINDEN Nils, a woman who has once sold herself for the sake of others, does not do so again.

KROGSTAD I shall demand my letter back again.

MRS LINDEN No, no.

KROGSTAD Yes, of course. I shall wait till Helmer comes; I shall tell him to give it back to me – that it's only about my dismissal – that I don't want it read –

MRS LINDEN No, Nils, you must not recall the letter.

KROGSTAD But tell me, wasn't that just why you got me to come here?

MRS LINDEN Yes, in my first alarm. But a day has passed since then, and in that day I have seen incredible things in this house. Helmer must know everything; there must be an end to this unhappy secret. These two must come to a full understanding. They must have done with all these shifts and subterfuges.

KROGSTAD Very well, if you like to risk it. But one thing I can do, and at once –

MRS LINDEN [*listening*]. Make haste! Go, go! The dance is over; we're not safe another moment.

KROGSTAD I shall wait for you in the street.

MRS LINDEN Yes, do; you must see me home.

KROGSTAD I never was so happy in all my life!

[*Krogstad goes out by the outer door. The door between the room and the hall remains open.*]

MRS LINDEN [*arranging the room and getting her outdoor things together*]. What a change! What a change! To have someone to work for, to live for; a home to make happy! Well, it shall not be my fault if I fail. – I wish they would come. – [*listens*] Ah, here they are! I must get my things on. [*takes bonnet and cloak*]

Helmer's and Nora's voices are heard outside, a key is turned in the lock, and HELMER *drags* NORA *almost by force into the hall. She wears the Italian costume with a large black shawl over it. He is in evening dress, and wears a black domino, open.*

NORA [*struggling with him in the doorway*]. No, no, no! I won't go in! I want to go upstairs again; I don't want to leave so early!

HELMER But, my dearest girl – !

NORA Oh, please, please, Torvald, I beseech you – only one hour more!

HELMER Not one minute more, Nora dear; you know what we agreed. Come, come in; you're catching cold here. [*he leads her gently into the room in spite of her resistance*]

MRS LINDEN Good evening.

NORA Christina!

HELMER What, Mrs Linden! You here so late?

MRS LINDEN Yes, I ought to apologize. I did so want to see Nora in her costume.

NORA Have you been sitting here waiting for me?

MRS LINDEN Yes; unfortunately I came too late. You had gone upstairs already, and I felt I couldn't go away without seeing you

HELMER [*taking Nora's shawl off*]. Well then, just look at her! I assure you she's worth it. Isn't she lovely, Mrs Linden?

MRS LINDEN Yes, I must say –

HELMER Isn't she exquisite? Everyone said so. But she's dreadfully obstinate, dear little creature. What's to be done with her? Just think, I had almost to force her away.

NORA Oh, Torvald, you'll be sorry some day that you didn't let me stay, if only for one half-hour more.

HELMER There! You hear her, Mrs Linden? She dances her tarantella with wild applause, and well she deserved it, I must say – though there was, perhaps, a little too much nature in her rendering of the idea – more than was, strictly speaking, artistic. But never mind – the point is, she made a great success, a tremendous success. Was I to let her remain after that – to weaken the impression? Not if I know it. I took my sweet little Capri girl – my capricious little Capri girl, I might say – under my arm; a rapid turn round the room, a curtsey to all sides, and – as they say in novels – the lovely apparition vanished! An exit should always be effective, Mrs Linden; but I can't get Nora to see it. By Jove! it's warm here. [*throws his domino on a chair and opens the door to his room*] What! No light there? Oh, of course. Excuse me – [*goes in and lights candles*]

NORA [*whispers breathlessly*]. Well?

MRS LINDEN [*softly*]. I've spoken to him.

NORA And – ?

MRS LINDEN Nora – you must tell your husband everything –

NORA [*tonelessly*]. I knew it!

MRS LINDEN You have nothing to fear from Krogstad; but you must speak out.

NORA I shall not speak.

MRS LINDEN Then the letter will.

NORA Thank you, Christina. Now I know what I have to do. Hush – !

HELMER [*coming back*]. Well, Mrs Linden, have you admired her?

MRS LINDEN Yes; and now I must say good night.

HELMER What, already? Does this knitting belong to you?

MRS LINDEN [*takes it*]. Yes, thanks; I was nearly forgetting it.

HELMER Then you do knit?

MRS LINDEN Yes.

HELMER Do you know, you ought to embroider instead?

MRS LINDEN Indeed! Why?

HELMER Because it's so much prettier. Look now! You hold the embroidery in the left hand so, and then work the needle with the right hand, in a long, graceful curve – don't you?

MRS LINDEN Yes, I suppose so.

HELMER But knitting is always ugly. Just look – your arms close to your sides, and the needles going up and down – there's something Chinese about it. – They really gave us splendid champagne tonight.

MRS LINDEN Well, good night, Nora, and don't be obstinate any more.

HELMER Well said, Mrs Linden!

MRS LINDEN Good night, Mr Helmer.

HELMER [*accompanying her to the door*]. Good night, good night; I hope you'll get safely home. I should be glad to – but you have such a short way to go. Good night, good night.   [*she goes*]

HELMER [*shuts the door after her, and comes forward again*] At last we've
   got rid of her: she's a terrible bore.

NORA Aren't you very tired, Torvald?

HELMER No, not in the least.

NORA Nor sleepy?

HELMER Not a bit. I feel particularly lively. But you? You do look
   tired and sleepy.

NORA Yes, very tired. I shall soon sleep now.

HELMER There, you see. I was right after all not to let you stay
   longer.

NORA Oh, everything you do is right.

HELMER [*kissing her forehead*]. Now my lark is speaking like a
   reasonable being. Did you notice how jolly Rank was this
   evening?

NORA Indeed? Was he? I had no chance of speaking to him.

HELMER Nor I, much; but I haven't seen him in such good spirits
   for a long time. [*looks at Nora a little, then comes nearer her*] It's
   splendid to be back in our own home, to be quite alone
   together! – Oh, you enchanting creature!

NORA Don't look at me in that way, Torvald.

HELMER I am not to look at my dearest treasure? – at all the
   loveliness that is mine, mine only, wholly and entirely mine?

NORA [*goes to the other side of the table*]. You mustn't say these thing:
   to me this evening.

HELMER [*following*]. I see you have the tarantella still in your
   blood – and that makes you all the more enticing. Listen! the
   other people are going now. [*more softly*] Nora – soon the whole
   house will be still.

NORA Yes, I hope so.

HELMER Yes, don't you, Nora darling! When we are among
   strangers, do you know why I speak so little to you, and keep so
   far away, and only steal a glance at you now and then – do you
   know why I do it? Because I am fancying that we love each
   other in secret, that I am secretly betrothed to you, and that no
   one dreams that there is anything between us.

NORA Yes, yes, yes. I know all your thoughts are with me.

HELMER And then, when the time comes to go, and I put the
   shawl about your smooth, soft shoulders, and this glorious
   neck of yours, I imagine you are my bride, that our marriag

is just over, that I am bringing you for the first time to my home – that I am alone with you for the first time – quite alone with you, in your trembling loveliness! All this evening I have been longing for you, and you only. When I watched you swaying and whirling in the tarantella – my blood boiled – I could endure it no longer; and that's why I made you come home with me so early –

NORA Go now, Torvald! Go away from me. I won't have all this.

HELMER What do you mean? Ah, I see you're teasing me, little Nora! Won't – won't! Am I not your husband – ?

[a knock at the outer door]

NORA [starts]. Did you hear – ?

HELMER [going towards the hall]. Who's there?

RANK [outside]. It is I; may I come in for a moment?

HELMER [in a low tone, annoyed]. Oh! what can he want just now? [aloud] Wait a moment. [opens door] Come, it's nice of you to look in.

RANK I thought I heard your voice, and that put it into my head. [looks round] Ah, this dear old place! How cosy you two are here!

HELMER You seemed to find it pleasant enough upstairs, too.

RANK Exceedingly. Why not? Why shouldn't one take one's share of everything in this world? All one can, at least, and as long as one can. The wine was splendid –

HELMER Especially the champagne.

RANK Did you notice it? It's incredible the quantity I contrived to get down.

NORA Torvald drank plenty of champagne, too.

RANK Did he?

NORA Yes, and it always puts him in such spirits.

RANK Well, why shouldn't one have a jolly evening after a well-spent day?

HELMER Well-spent! Well, I haven't much to boast of in that respect.

RANK [slapping him on the shoulder]. But I have, don't you see?

NORA I suppose you have been engaged in a scientific investigation, Doctor Rank?

RANK Quite right.

HELMER Bless me! Little Nora talking about scientific investigations!

NORA Am I to congratulate you on the result?

RANK By all means.

NORA It was good, then?

RANK The best possible, both for doctor and patient – certainty.

NORA [*quickly and searchingly*]. Certainty?

RANK Absolute certainty. Wasn't I right to enjoy myself after that?

NORA Yes, quite right, Doctor Rank.

HELMER And so say I, provided you don't have to pay for it tomorrow.

RANK Well, in this life nothing is to be had for nothing.

NORA Doctor Rank – I'm sure you are very fond of masquerades?

RANK Yes, when there are plenty of amusing disguises –

NORA Tell me, what shall we two be at our next masquerade?

HELMER Little featherbrain! Thinking of your next already!

RANK We two? I'll tell you. You must go as a good fairy.

HELMER Ah, but what costume would indicate that?

RANK She has simply to wear her everyday dress.

HELMER Capital! But don't you know what you will be yourself?

RANK Yes, my dear friend, I am perfectly clear upon that point.

HELMER Well?

RANK At the next masquerade I shall be invisible.

HELMER What a comical idea!

RANK There's a big black hat – haven't you heard of the invisible hat? It comes down all over you, and then no one can see you.

HELMER [*with a suppressed smile*]. No, you're right there.

RANK But I'm quite forgetting what I came for. Helmer, give me a cigar – one of the dark Havanas.

HELMER With the greatest pleasure. [*hands cigar-case*]

RANK [*takes one and cuts the end off*]. Thank you.

NORA [*striking a wax match*]. Let me give you a light.

RANK A thousand thanks. [*she holds the match. He lights his cigar at it*] And now, Goodbye!

HELMER Goodbye, goodbye, my dear fellow.

NORA Sleep well, Doctor Rank.

RANK Thanks for the wish.

NORA Wish me the same.

RANK You? Very well, since you ask me – Sleep well. And thank for the light. [*he nods to them both and goes out*]

HELMER [*in an undertone*]. He's been drinking a good deal.

NORA [*absently*]. I dare say. [*Helmer takes his bunch of keys from his pocket and goes into the hall*] Torvald, what are you doing there?

HELMER I must empty the letter-box; it's quite full; there will be no room for the newspapers tomorrow morning.

NORA Are you going to work tonight?

HELMER You know very well I am not. – Why, how is this? Someone has been at the lock.

NORA The lock – ?

HELMER I'm sure of it. What does it mean? I can't think that the servants – ? Here's a broken hairpin. Nora, it's one of yours.

NORA [*quickly*]. It must have been the children –

HELMER Then you must break them of such tricks. – There! At last I've got it open. [*takes contents out and calls into the kitchen*] Ellen! – Ellen, just put the hall door lamp out.
[*he returns with letters in his hand, and shuts the inner door.*]

HELMER Just see how they've accumulated. [*turning them over*] Why, what's this?

NORA [*at the window*]. The letter! Oh no, no, Torvald!

HELMER Two visiting-cards – from Rank.

NORA From Doctor Rank?

HELMER [*looking at them*]. Doctor Rank. They were on the top. He must just have put them in.

NORA Is there anything on them?

HELMER There's a black cross over the name. Look at it. What an unpleasant idea! It looks just as if he were announcing his own death.

NORA So he is.

HELMER What! Do you know anything? Has he told you anything?

NORA Yes. These cards mean that he has taken his last leave of us. He is going to shut himself up and die.

HELMER Poor fellow! Of course I knew we couldn't hope to keep him long. But so soon – ! And to go and creep into his lair like a wounded animal –

NORA When we must go, it is best to go silently. Don't you think so, Torvald?

HELMER [*walking up and down*]. He had so grown into our lives, I can't realize that he is gone. He and his sufferings and his loneliness formed a sort of cloudy background to the sunshine of our happiness. – Well, perhaps it's best as it is – at any rate for him. [*stands still*] And perhaps for us too, Nora. Now we two are thrown entirely upon each other. [*takes her in his arms*] My darling wife! I feel as if I could never hold you close enough. Do you know, Nora, I often wish some danger might threaten you, that I might risk body and soul, and everything, everything, for your dear sake.

NORA [*tears herself from him, and says firmly*]. Now you shall read your letters, Torvald.

HELMER No, no; not tonight. I want to be with you, my sweet wife.

NORA With the thought of your dying friend – ?

HELMER You are right. This has shaken us both. Unloveliness has come between us – thoughts of death and decay. We must seek to cast them off. Till then – we will remain apart.

NORA [*her arms round his neck*]. Torvald! Good night! good night!

HELMER [*kissing her forehead*]. Good night, my little song-bird. Sleep well, Nora. Now I shall go and read my letters. [*he goes with the letters in his hand into his room and shuts the door*]

NORA [*with wild eyes, gropes about her, seizes Helmer's domino, throws it round her, and whispers quickly, hoarsely, and brokenly*]. Never to see him again. Never, never, never. [*throws her shawl over her head*] Never to see the children again. Never, never. – Oh, that black, icy water! Oh, that bottomless – ! If it were only over! Now he has it; he's reading it. Oh, no, no, no, not yet. Torvald, Goodbye – ! Goodbye, my little ones – !

She is rushing out by the hall; at the same moment HELMER *flings his door open, and stands there with an open letter in his hand.*

HELMER Nora!

NORA [*shrieks*]. Ah – !

HELMER What is this? Do you know what is in this letter?

NORA Yes, I know. Let me go! Let me pass!

HELMER [*holds her back*]. Where do you want to go?

NORA [*tries to break away from him*]. You shall not save me, Torvald.

HELMER [*falling back*]. True! Is what he writes true? No, no, it is impossible that this can be true.

NORA It is true. I have loved you beyond all else in the world.

HELMER Pshaw – no silly evasions!

NORA [*a step nearer him*]. Torvald – !

HELMER Wretched woman – what have you done!

NORA Let me go – you shall not save me! You shall not take my guilt upon yourself!

HELMER I don't want any melodramatic airs. [*locks the outer door*] Here you shall stay and give an account of yourself. Do you understand what you have done? Answer! Do you understand it?

NORA [*looks at him fixedly, and says with a stiffening expression*]. Yes; now I begin fully to understand it.

HELMER [*walking up and down*]. Oh! what an awful awakening! During all these eight years – she who was my pride and my joy – a hypocrite, a liar – worse, worse – a criminal. Oh, the unfathomable hideousness of it all! Ugh! Ugh!

NORA [*says nothing, and continues to look fixedly at him*]

HELMER I ought to have known how it would be. I ought to have foreseen it. All your father's want of principle – be silent! – all your father's want of principle you have inherited – no religion, no morality, no sense of duty. How I am punished for screening him! I did it for your sake; and you reward me like this.

NORA Yes – like this!

HELMER You have destroyed my whole happiness. You have ruined my future. Oh, it's frightful to think of! I am in the power of a scoundrel; he can do whatever he pleases with me, demand whatever he chooses; he can domineer over me as much as he likes, and I must submit. And all this disaster and ruin is brought upon me by an unprincipled woman!

NORA When I am out of the world you will be free.

HELMER Oh, no fine phrases. Your father, too, was always ready with them. What good would it do me, if you were 'out of the world', as you say? No good whatever! He can publish the story all the same; I might even be suspected of collusion. People will think I was at the bottom of it all and egged you on. And for all this I have you to thank – you whom I have done nothing but pet and spoil during our whole married life. Do you understand now what you have done to me?

NORA [*with cold calmness*]. Yes.

HELMER The thing is so incredible, I can't grasp it. But we must come to an understanding. Take that shawl off. Take it off, I say! I must try to pacify him in one way or another – the matter must be hushed up, cost what it may. – As for you and me, we must make no outward change in our way of life – no outward change, you understand. Of course, you will continue to live here. But the children cannot be left in your care. I dare not trust them to you. – Oh, to have to say this to one I have loved so tenderly – whom I still – ! But that must be a thing of the past. Henceforward there can be no question of happiness, but merely of saving the ruins, the shreds, the show – [*a ring; Helmer starts*] What's that? So late! Can it be the worst? Can he – ? Hide yourself, Nora; say you are ill.

NORA [*stands motionless. Helmer goes to the door and opens it*]

ELLEN [*half dressed, in the hall*]. Here is a letter for you, ma'am.

HELMER Give it to me. [*seizes the letter and shuts the door*] Yes, from him. You shall not have it. I shall read it.

NORA Read it!

HELMER [*by the lamp*]. I have hardly the courage to. We may both be lost, both you and I. Ah! I must know. [*hastily tears the letter open; reads a few lines, looks at an enclosure; with a cry of joy*] Nora!

NORA [*looks inquiringly at him*]

HELMER Nora! – Oh! I must read it again. – Yes, yes, it is so. I am saved! Nora, I am saved!

NORA And I?

HELMER You too, of course; we are both saved, both of us. Look here – he sends you back your promissory note. He writes that he regrets and apologizes, that a happy turn in his life – Oh, what matter what he writes. We are saved, Nora! No one can harm you. Oh, Nora, Nora – ; but first to get rid of this hateful thing. I'll just see – [*glances at the IOU*] No, I will not look at it; the whole thing shall be nothing but a dream to me. [*tears the IOU and both letters in pieces. Throws them into the fire and watches them burn*] There! it's gone! – He said that ever since Christmas Eve – Oh, Nora, they must have been three terrible days for you.

NORA I have fought a hard fight for the last three days.

HELMER And in your agony you saw no other outlet but – No; we won't think of that horror. We will only rejoice and repeat – it's over, all over! Don't you hear, Nora? You don't seem able to grasp it. Yes, it's over. What is this set look on your face? Oh my poor Nora, I understand; you cannot believe that I have forgiven you. But I have, Nora; I swear it. I have forgiven everything. I know that what you did was all for love of me.

NORA That is true.

HELMER You loved me as a wife should love her husband. It was only the means that, in your inexperience, you misjudged. But do you think I love you the less because you cannot do without guidance? No, no. Only lean on me; I will counsel you, and guide you. I should be no true man if this very womanly helplessness did not make you doubly dear in my eyes. You mustn't dwell upon the hard things I said in my first moment of terror, when the world seemed to be tumbling about my ears. I have forgiven you, Nora — I swear I have forgiven you.

NORA I thank you for your forgiveness. [goes out, to the right]

HELMER No, stay — ! [looking through the doorway] What are you going to do?

NORA [inside]. To take off my masquerade dress.

HELMER [in the doorway]. Yes, do, dear. Try to calm down, and recover your balance, my scared little song-bird. You may rest secure. I have broad wings to shield you. [walking up and down near the door] Oh, how lovely — how cosy our home is, Nora! Here you are safe; here I can shelter you like a hunted dove whom I have saved from the claws of the hawk. I shall soon bring your poor beating heart to rest; believe me, Nora, very soon. Tomorrow all this will seem quite different — everything will be as before. I shall not need to tell you again that I forgive you; you will feel for yourself that it is true. How could you think I could find it in my heart to drive you away, or even so much as to reproach you? Oh, you don't know a true man's heart, Nora. There is something indescribably sweet and soothing to a man in having forgiven his wife — honestly forgiven her, from the bottom of his heart. She becomes his property in a double sense. She is as though born again; she has become, so to speak, at once his wife and his child. That is what you shall henceforth be to me, my bewildered, helpless darling. Don't be troubled about anything, Nora; only open your heart to me, and I will be both will and conscience to you. [Nora enters in everyday dress] Why, what's this? Not gone to bed? You have changed your dress?

NORA Yes, Torvald; now I have changed my dress.

HELMER But why now, so late — ?

NORA I shall not sleep tonight.

HELMER But, Nora dear –

NORA [*looking at her watch*]. It's not so late yet. Sit down, Torvald; you and I have much to say to each other.

[*she sits at one side of the table*]

HELMER Nora – what does this mean? Your cold, set face –

NORA Sit down. It will take some time. I have much to talk over with you.

HELMER [*sits at the other side of the table*] You alarm me, Nora. I don't understand you.

NORA No, that is just it. You don't understand me; and I have never understood you – till tonight. No, don't interrupt. Only listen to what I say. – We must come to a final settlement, Torvald.

HELMER How do you mean?

NORA [*after a short silence*]. Does not one thing strike you as we sit here?

HELMER What should strike me?

NORA We have been married eight years. Does it not strike you that this is the first time we two, you and I, man and wife, have talked together seriously?

HELMER Seriously! What do you call seriously?

NORA During eight whole years, and more – ever since the day we first met – we have never exchanged one serious word about serious things.

HELMER Was I always to trouble you with the cares you could not help me to bear?

NORA I am not talking of cares. I say that we have never yet set ourselves seriously to get to the bottom of anything.

HELMER Why, my dearest Nora, what have you to do with serious things?

NORA There we have it! You have never understood me. – I have had great injustice done me, Torvald; first by father, and then by you.

HELMER What! By your father and me? – By us, who have loved you more than all the world?

NORA [*shaking her head*]. You have never loved me. You only thought it amusing to be in love with me.

HELMER Why, Nora, what a thing to say!

NORA Yes, it is so, Torvald. While I was at home with father, he used to tell me all his opinions, and I held the same opinions. I

I had others I said nothing about them, because he wouldn't have liked it. He used to call me his doll-child, and played with me as I played with my dolls. Then I came to live in your house –

HELMER What an expression to use about our marriage!

NORA [*undisturbed*]. I mean I passed from father's hands into yours. You arranged everything according to your taste; and I got the same tastes as you; or I pretended to – I don't know which – both ways, perhaps; sometimes one and sometimes the other. When I look back on it now, I seem to have been living here like a beggar, from hand to mouth. I lived by performing tricks for you, Torvald. But you would have it so. You and father have done me a great wrong. It is your fault that my life has come to nothing.

HELMER Why, Nora, how unreasonable and ungrateful you are! Have you not been happy here?

NORA No, never. I thought I was; but I never was.

HELMER Not – not happy!

NORA No; only merry. And you have always been so kind to me. But our house has been nothing but a playroom. Here I have been your doll-wife, just as at home I used to be papa's doll-child. And the children, in their turn, have been my dolls. I thought it fun when you played with me, just as the children did when I played with them. That has been our marriage, Torvald.

HELMER There is some truth in what you say, exaggerated and overstrained though it be. But henceforth it shall be different. Playtime is over; now comes the time for education.

NORA Whose education? Mine, or the children's?

HELMER Both, my dear Nora.

NORA Oh, Torvald, you are not the man to teach me to be a fit wife for you.

HELMER And you can say that?

NORA And I – how have I prepared myself to educate the children?

HELMER Nora!

NORA Did you not say yourself, a few minutes ago, you dared not trust them to me?

HELMER In the excitement of the moment! Why should you dwell upon that?

NORA No – you were perfectly right. That problem is beyond me. There is another to be solved first – I must try to educate myself. You are not the man to help me in that. I must set about it alone. And that is why I am leaving you.

HELMER [*jumping up*]. What – do you mean to say – ?

NORA I must stand quite alone if I am ever to know myself and my surroundings; so I cannot stay with you.

HELMER Nora! Nora!

NORA I am going at once. I dare say Christina will take me in for tonight –

HELMER You are mad! I shall not allow it! I forbid it!

NORA It is of no use your forbidding me anything now. I shall take with me what belongs to me. From you I will accept nothing, either now or afterwards.

HELMER What madness is this!

NORA Tomorrow I shall go home – I mean to what was my home. It will be easier for me to find some opening there.

HELMER Oh, in your blind inexperience –

NORA I must try to gain experience, Torvald.

HELMER To forsake your home, your husband, and your children! And you don't consider what the world will say!

NORA I can pay no heed to that. I only know that I must do it.

HELMER This is monstrous! Can you forsake your holiest duties in this way?

NORA What do you consider my holiest duties?

HELMER Do I need to tell you that? Your duties to your husband and your children.

NORA I have other duties equally sacred.

HELMER Impossible! What duties do you mean?

NORA My duties towards myself.

HELMER Before all else you are a wife and a mother.

NORA That I no longer believe. I believe that before all else I am a human being, just as much as you are – or at least that I should try to become one. I know that most people agree with you, Torvald, and that they say so in books. But henceforth I can't be satisfied with what most people say, and what is in books. I must think things out for myself, and try to get clear about them.

HELMER Are you not clear about your place in your own home?

Have you not an infallible guide in questions like these? Have you not religion?

NORA Oh, Torvald, I don't really know what religion is.

HELMER What do you mean?

NORA I know nothing but what Pastor Hansen told me when I was confirmed. He explained that religion was this and that. When I get away from all this and stand alone, I will look into that matter too. I will see whether what he taught me is right, or, at any rate, whether it is right for me.

HELMER Oh, this is unheard of! And from so young a woman! But if religion cannot keep you right, let me appeal to your conscience – for I suppose you have some moral feeling? Or, answer me: perhaps you have none?

NORA Well, Torvald, it's not easy to say. I really don't know – I am all at sea about these things. I only know that I think quite differently from you about them. I hear, too, that the laws are different from what I thought; but I can't believe that they can be right. It appears that a woman has no right to spare her dying father, or to save her husband's life! I don't believe that.

HELMER You talk like a child. You don't understand the society in which you live.

NORA No, I do not. But now I shall try to learn. I must make up my mind which is right – society or I.

HELMER Nora, you are ill; you are feverish; I almost think you are out of your senses.

NORA I have never felt so much clearness and certainty as tonight.

HELMER You are clear and certain enough to forsake husband and children?

NORA Yes, I am.

HELMER Then there is only one explanation possible.

NORA What is that?

HELMER You no longer love me.

NORA No; that is just it.

HELMER Nora! – Can you say so!

NORA Oh, I'm so sorry, Torvald; for you've always been so kind to me. But I can't help it. I do not love you any longer.

HELMER [mastering himself with difficulty]. Are you clear and certain on this point too?

NORA Yes, quite. That is why I will not stay here any longer.

HELMER And can you also make clear to me how I have forfeited
   your love?

NORA Yes, I can. It was this evening, when the miracle did not
   happen; for then I saw you were not the man I had imagined.

HELMER Explain yourself more clearly; I don't understand.

NORA I have waited so patiently all these eight years; for of course
   I saw clearly enough that miracles don't happen every day.
   When this crushing blow threatened me, I said to myself so
   confidently, 'Now comes the miracle!' When Krogstad's letter
   lay in the box, it never for a moment occurred to me that you
   would think of submitting to that man's conditions. I was
   convinced that you would say to him, 'Make it known to all the
   world'; and that then –

HELMER Well? When I had given my own wife's name up to
   disgrace and shame – ?

NORA Then I firmly believed that you would come forward, take
   everything upon yourself, and say, 'I am the guilty one.'

HELMER Nora – !

NORA You mean I would never have accepted such a sacrifice?
   No, certainly not. But what would my assertions have been
   worth in opposition to yours? – That was the miracle that I
   hoped for and dreaded. And it was to hinder that that I wanted
   to die.

HELMER I would gladly work for you day and night, Nora – bear
   sorrow and want for your sake. But no man sacrifices his
   honour, even for one he loves.

NORA Millions of women have done so.

HELMER Oh, you think and talk like a silly child.

NORA Very likely. But you neither think nor talk like the man
   I can share my life with. When your terror was over – not
   for what threatened me, but for yourself – when there was
   nothing more to fear – then it seemed to you as though
   nothing had happened. I was your lark again, your doll, just
   as before – whom you would take twice as much care of
   in future, because she was so weak and fragile. [*stands up*] Torvald – in that moment it burst upon me that I had been living
   here these eight years with a strange man, and had borne him
   three children. – Oh, I can't bear to think of it! I could tear
   myself to pieces!

HELMER [*sadly*]. I see it, I see it; an abyss has opened between us. –
But, Nora, can it never be filled up?

NORA As I now am, I am no wife for you.

HELMER I have strength to become another man.

NORA Perhaps – when your doll is taken away from you.

HELMER To part – to part from you! No, Nora, no; I can't grasp
the thought.

NORA [*going into the room on the right*]. The more reason for the
thing to happen. [*she comes back with outdoor things and a small
travelling-bag, which she places on a chair*]

HELMER Nora, Nora, not now! Wait till tomorrow.

NORA [*putting on cloak*]. I can't spend the night in a strange man's
house.

HELMER But can we not live here, as brother and sister – ?

NORA [*fastening her hat*]. You know very well that wouldn't last
long. [*puts on the shawl*] Goodbye, Torvald. No, I won't go to
the children. I know they are in better hands than mine. As I
now am, I can be nothing to them.

HELMER But some time, Nora – some time – ?

NORA How can I tell? I have no idea what will become of me.

HELMER But you are my wife, now and always!

NORA Listen, Torvald – when a wife leaves her husband's house, as
I am doing, I have heard that in the eyes of the law he is free
from all duties towards her. At any rate I release you from all
duties. You must not feel yourself bound, any more than I shall.
There must be perfect freedom on both sides. There, I give you
back your ring. Give me mine.

HELMER That too?

NORA That too.

HELMER Here it is.

NORA Very well. Now it is all over. I lay the keys here. The
servants know about everything in the house – better than I do.
Tomorrow, when I have started, Christina will come to pack
up the things I brought with me from home. I will have them
sent after me.

HELMER All over! all over! Nora, will you never think of me again?

NORA Oh, I shall often think of you, and the children, and this
house.

HELMER May I write to you, Nora?

NORA No – never. You must not.

HELMER But I must send you –

NORA Nothing, nothing.

HELMER I must help you if you need it.

NORA No, I say. I take nothing from strangers.

HELMER Nora – can I never be more than a stranger to you?

NORA [*taking her travelling-bag*]. Oh, Torvald, then the miracle of miracles would have to happen –

HELMER What is the miracle of miracles?

NORA Both of us would have to change so that – Oh, Torvald, I no longer believe in miracles.

HELMER But *I* will believe. Tell me! We must so change that – ?

NORA That communion between us shall be a marriage. Goodbye. [*she goes out by the hall door*]

HELMER [*sinks into a chair by the door with his face in his hands*]. Nora! Nora! [*he looks round and rises*] Empty. She is gone. [*a hope springs up in him*] Ah! The miracle of miracles – ?

[*from below is heard the reverberation of a heavy door closing*]

CURTAIN

HEDDA GABLER

Characters

GEORGE TESMAN[*]
HEDDA TESMAN, his wife
MISS JULIANA TESMAN, his aunt
MRS ELVSTED
JUDGE[†] BRACK
EILERT LÖVBORG
BERTA, servant at the Tesmans

The scene of the action is TESMAN'S *villa,*
in the west end of Christiania.

[*] Tesman, Christian whose name in the original is *Jörgen*, is described as *stipendiat i kulturhistorie* – that is to say, the holder of a scholarship for purposes of research into the History of Civilisation.
[†] In the original *Assessor*.

ACT FIRST

A spacious, handsome, and tastefully furnished drawing room, decorated in dark colours. In the back, a wide doorway with curtains drawn back, leading into a smaller room decorated in the same style as the drawing-room. In the right-hand wall of the front room, a folding door leading out to the hall. In the opposite wall, on the left, a glass door, also with curtains drawn back. Through the panes can be seen part of a verandah outside, and trees covered with autumn foliage. An oval table, with a cover on it, and surrounded by chairs, stands well forward. In front, by the wall on the right, a wide stove of dark porcelain, a high-backed armchair, a cushioned foot-rest, and two footstools. A settee, with a small round table in front of it, fills the upper right-hand corner. In front, on the left, a little way from the wall, a sofa. Further back than the glass door, a piano. On either side of the doorway at the back a whatnot with terra-cotta and majolica ornaments. — Against the back wall of the inner room a sofa, with a table, and one or two chairs. Over the sofa hangs the portrait of a handsome elderly man in a General's uniform. Over the table a hanging lamp, with an opal glass shade. — A number of bouquets are arranged about the drawing-room, in vases and glasses. Others lie upon the tables. The floors in both rooms are covered with thick carpets. — Morning light. The sun shines in through the glass door.

MISS JULIANA TESMAN, *with her bonnet on and carrying a parasol, comes in from the hall, followed by* BERTA, *who carries a bouquet wrapped in paper.* MISS TESMAN *is a comely and pleasant-looking lady of about sixty-five. She is nicely but simply dressed in a grey walking-costume.* BERTA *is a middle-aged woman of plain and rather countrified appearance.*

MISS TESMAN [*stops close to the door, listens, and says softly*] Upon my word, I don't believe they are stirring yet!

BERTA [*also softly*] I told you so, Miss. Remember how late the steamboat got in last night. And then, when they got home! — good Lord, what a lot the young mistress had to unpack before she could get to bed.

MISS TESMAN Well well – let them have their sleep out. But let us see that they get a good breath of the fresh morning air when they do appear. [*she goes to the glass door and throws it open*]

BERTA [*beside the table, at a loss what to do with the bouquet in her hand*] I declare there isn't a bit of room left. I think I'll put it down here, Miss. [*she places it on the piano*]

MISS TESMAN So you've got a new mistress now, my dear Berta. Heaven knows it was a wrench to me to part with you.

BERTA [*on the point of weeping*] And do you think it wasn't hard for me, too, Miss? After all the blessed years I've been with you and Miss Rina.

MISS TESMAN We must make the best of it, Berta. There was nothing else to be done. George can't do without you, you see – he absolutely can't. He has had you to look after him ever since he was a little boy.

BERTA Ah but, Miss Julia, I can't help thinking of Miss Rina lying helpless at home there, poor thing. And with only that new girl too! She'll never learn to take proper care of an invalid.

MISS TESMAN Oh, I shall manage to train her. And of course, you know, I shall take most of it upon myself. You needn't be uneasy about my poor sister, my dear Berta.

BERTA Well, but there's another thing, Miss. I'm so mortally afraid I shan't be able to suit the young mistress.

MISS TESMAN Oh well – just at first there may be one or two things –

BERTA Most like she'll be terrible grand in her ways.

MISS TESMAN Well, you can't wonder at that – General Gabler's daughter! Think of the sort of life she was accustomed to in her father's time. Don't you remember how we used to see her riding down the road along with the General? In that long black habit – and with feathers in her hat?

BERTA Yes, indeed – I remember well enough! – But, good Lord, I should never have dreamt in those days that she and Master George would make a match of it.

MISS TESMAN Nor I. – But by-the-bye, Berta – while I think of it: in future you mustn't say Master George. You must say Dr Tesman.

BERTA Yes, the young mistress spoke of that too – last night – the moment they set foot in the house. Is it true then, Miss?

MISS TESMAN Yes, indeed it is. Only think, Berta – some foreign
university has made him a doctor – while he has been abroad,
you understand. I hadn't heard a word about it, until he told me
himself upon the pier.

BERTA Well well, he's clever enough for anything, he is. But I
didn't think he'd have gone in for doctoring people.

MISS TESMAN No no, it's not that sort of doctor he is. [*nods
significantly*] But let me tell you, we may have to call him
something still grander before long.

BERTA You don't day so! What can that be, Miss?

MISS TESMAN [*smiling*] H'm – wouldn't you like to know! [*with
emotion*] Ah, dear dear – if my poor brother could only look up
from his grave now, and see what his little boy has grown into!
[*looks around*] But bless me, Berta – why have you done this?
Taken the chintz covers off all the furniture.

BERTA The mistress told me to. She can't abide covers on the
chairs, she says.

MISS TESMAN Are they going to make this their everyday sitting-
room then?

BERTA Yes, that's what I understood – from the mistress. Master
George – the doctor – he said nothing.

> GEORGE TESMAN *comes from the right into the inner room, hum-
> ming to himself, and carrying an unstrapped empty portmanteau.
> He is a middle-sized, young-looking man of thirty-three, rather
> stout, with a round, open, cheerful face, fair hair and beard. He
> wears spectacles, and is somewhat carelessly dressed in comfortable
> indoor clothes.*

MISS TESMAN Good morning, good morning, George.

TESMAN [*in the doorway between the rooms*] Aunt Julia! Dear Aunt
Julia! [*goes up to her and shakes hands warmly*] Come all this way –
so early! Eh?

MISS TESMAN Why, of course I had to come and see how you were
getting on.

TESMAN In spite of your having had no proper night's rest?

MISS TESMAN Oh, that makes no difference to me.

TESMAN Well, I suppose you got home all right from the pier? Eh?

MISS TESMAN Yes, quite safely, thank goodness. Judge Brack was
good enough to see me right to my door.

TESMAN We were so sorry we couldn't give you a seat in the carriage. But you saw what a pile of boxes Hedda had to bring with her.

MISS TESMAN Yes, she had certainly plenty of boxes.

BERTA [to Tesman] Shall I go in and see if there's anything I can do for the mistress?

TESMAN No thank you, Berta – you needn't. She said she would ring if she wanted anything.

BERTA [going towards the right] Very well.

TESMAN But look here – take this portmanteau with you.

BERTA [taking it] I'll put it in the attic.   [she goes out by the hall door]

TESMAN Fancy, Auntie – I had the whole of that portmanteau chock full of copies of the documents. You wouldn't believe how much I have picked up from all the archives I have been examining – curious old details that no one has had any idea of –

MISS TESMAN Yes, you don't seem to have wasted your time on your wedding trip, George.

TESMAN No, that I haven't. But do take off your bonnet, Auntie. Look here! Let me untie the strings – eh?

MISS TESMAN [while he does so] Well well – this is just as if you were still at home with us.

TESMAN [with the bonnet in his hand, looks at it from all sides] Why, what a gorgeous bonnet you've been investing in!

MISS TESMAN I bought it on Hedda's account.

TESMAN On Hedda's account? Eh?

MISS TESMAN Yes, so that Hedda needn't be ashamed of me if we happened to go out together.

TESMAN [patting her cheek] You always think of everything, Aunt Julia. [lays the bonnet on a chair beside the table] And now, look here – suppose we sit comfortably on the sofa and have a little chat, till Hedda comes.

[They seat themselves. She places her parasol in the corner of the sofa.]

MISS TESMAN [takes both his hands and looks at him] What a delight it is to have you again, as large as life, before my very eyes, George! My George – my poor brother's own boy!

TESMAN And it's a delight for me, too, to see you again, Aunt Julia! You, who have been father and mother in one to me.

MISS TESMAN Oh yes, I know you will always keep a place in your heart for your old aunts.

TESMAN And what about Aunt Rina? No improvement – eh?

MISS TESMAN Oh, no – we can scarcely look for any improvement in her case, poor thing. There she lies, helpless, as she has lain for all these years. But heaven grant I may not lose her yet awhile! For if I did, I don't know what I should make of my life, George – especially now that I haven't you to look after any more.

TESMAN [patting her back] There there there – !

MISS TESMAN [suddenly changing her tone] And to think that here are you a married man, George! – And that you should be the one to carry off Hedda Gabler – the beautiful Hedda Gabler! Only think of it – she, that was so beset with admirers!

TESMAN [hums a little and smiles complacently] Yes, I fancy I have several good friends about town who would like to stand in my shoes – eh?

MISS TESMAN And then this fine long wedding-tour you have had! More than five – nearly six months –

TESMAN Well, for me it has been a sort of tour of research as well. I have had to do so much grubbing among old records – and to read no end of books too, Auntie.

MISS TESMAN Oh yes, I suppose so. [more confidentially, and lowering her voice a little] But listen now, George – have you nothing – nothing special to tell me?

TESMAN As to our journey?

MISS TESMAN Yes.

TESMAN No, I don't know of anything except what I have told you in my letters. I had a doctor's degree conferred on me – but that I told you yesterday.

MISS TESMAN Yes, yes, you did. But what I mean is – haven't you any – any – expectations – ?

TESMAN Expectations?

MISS TESMAN Why you know, George – I'm your old auntie!

TESMAN Why, of course I have expectations.

MISS TESMAN Ah!

TESMAN I have every expectation of being a professor one of these days.

MISS TESMAN Oh yes, a professor –

TESMAN Indeed, I may say I am certain of it. But my dear Auntie – you know all about that already!

MISS TESMAN [*laughing to herself*] Yes, of course I do. You are quite right there. [*changing the subject*] But we were talking about your journey. It must have cost a great deal of money, George?

TESMAN Well, you see – my handsome travelling-scholarship went a good way.

MISS TESMAN But I can't understand how you can have made it go far enough for two.

TESMAN No, that's not easy to understand – eh?

MISS TESMAN And especially travelling with a lady – they tell me that makes it ever so much more expensive.

TESMAN Yes, of course – it makes it a little more expensive. But Hedda had to have this trip, Auntie! She really had to. Nothing else would have done.

MISS TESMAN No no, I suppose not. A wedding-tour seems to be quite indispensable nowadays. – But tell me now – have you gone thoroughly over the house yet?

TESMAN Yes, you may be sure I have. I have been afoot ever since daylight.

MISS TESMAN And what do you think of it all?

TESMAN I'm delighted! Quite delighted! Only I can't think what we are to do with the two empty rooms between this inner parlour and Hedda's bedroom.

MISS TESMAN [*laughing*] Oh my dear George, I dare say you may find some use for them – in the course of time.

TESMAN Why of course you are quite right, Aunt Julia! You mean as my library increases – eh?

MISS TESMAN Yes, quite so, my dear boy. It was your library I was thinking of.

TESMAN I am specially pleased on Hedda's account. Often and often, before we were engaged, she said that she would never care to live anywhere but in Secretary Falk's villa.*

MISS TESMAN Yes, it was lucky that this very house should come into the market, just after you had started.

TESMAN Yes, Aunt Julia, the luck was on our side, wasn't it – eh?

MISS TESMAN But the expense, my dear George! You will find it very expensive, all this.

TESMAN [*looks at her, a little cast down*] Yes, I suppose I shall, Aunt!

---

* In the original, *Statsrådinde Falks villa*, showing that it had belonged to the widow of a cabinet minister.

MISS TESMAN Oh, frightfully!

TESMAN How much do you think? In round numbers? – Eh?

MISS TESMAN Oh, I can't even guess until all the accounts come in.

TESMAN Well, fortunately, Judge Brack has secured the most favourable terms for me, so he said in a letter to Hedda.

MISS TESMAN Yes, don't be uneasy, my dear boy. – Besides, I have given security for the furniture and all the carpets.

TESMAN Security? You? My dear Aunt Julia – what sort of security could you give?

MISS TESMAN I have given a mortgage on our annuity.

TESMAN [*jumps up*] What! On your – and Aunt Rina's annuity!

MISS TESMAN Yes, I knew of no other plan, you see.

TESMAN [*placing himself before her*] Have you gone out of your senses, Auntie? Your annuity – it's all that you and Aunt Rina have to live upon.

MISS TESMAN Well well – don't get so excited about it. It's only a matter of form you know – Judge Brack assured me of that. It was he that was kind enough to arrange the whole affair for me. A mere matter of form, he said.

TESMAN Yes, that may be all very well. But nevertheless –

MISS TESMAN You will have your own salary to depend upon now. And, good heavens, even if we did have to pay up a little – ! To eke things out a bit at the start – ! Why, it would be nothing but a pleasure to us.

TESMAN Oh Auntie – will you never be tired of making sacrifices for me!

MISS TESMAN [*rises and lays her hand on his shoulders*] Have I any other happiness in this world except to smooth your way for you, my dear boy. You, who have had neither father nor mother to depend on. And now we have reached the goal, George! Things have looked black enough for us, sometimes; but, thank heaven, now you have nothing to fear.

TESMAN Yes, it is really marvellous how everything has turned out for the best.

MISS TESMAN And the people who opposed you – who wanted to bar the way for you – now you have them at your feet. They have fallen, George. Your most dangerous rival – his fall was the worst. And now he has to lie on the bed he has made for himself – poor misguided creature.

TESMAN Have you heard anything of Eilert? Since I went away, I mean.

MISS TESMAN Only that he is said to have published a new book.

TESMAN What! Eilert Lövborg! Recently – eh?

MISS TESMAN Yes, so they say. Heaven knows whether it can be worth anything! Ah, when your new book appears – that will be another story, George! What is it to be about?

TESMAN It will deal with the domestic industries of Brabant during the Middle Ages.

MISS TESMAN Fancy – to be able to write on such a subject as that!

TESMAN However, it may be some time before the book is ready. I have all these collections to arrange first, you see.

MISS TESMAN Yes, collecting and arranging – no one can beat you at that. There you are my poor brother's own son.

TESMAN I am looking forward eagerly to setting to work at it; especially now that I have my own delightful home to work in.

MISS TESMAN And, most of all, now that you have got the wife of your heart, my dear George.

TESMAN [*embracing her*] Oh yes, yes, Aunt Julia! Hedda – she is the best part of it all! I believe I hear her coming – eh?

HEDDA *enters from the left through the inner room. Her face and figure show refinement and distinction. Her complexion is pale and opaque. Her steel-grey eyes express a cold, unruffled repose. Her hair is of an agreeable brown, but not particularly abundant. She is dressed in a tasteful, somewhat loose-fitting morning gown.*

MISS TESMAN [*going to meet Hedda*] Good morning, my dear Hedda! Good morning, and a hearty welcome!

HEDDA [*holds out her hand*] Good morning, dear Miss Tesman! So early a call! That is kind of you.

MISS TESMAN [*with some embarrassment*] Well – has the bride slept well in her new home?

HEDDA Oh yes, thanks. Passably.

TESMAN [*laughing*] Passably! Come, that's good, Hedda! You were sleeping like a stone when I got up.

HEDDA Fortunately. Of course one has always to accustom one's self to new surroundings, Miss Tesman – little by little. [*looking towards the left*] Oh, there the servant has gone and opened the veranda door, and let in a whole flood of sunshine.

MISS TESMAN [*going towards the door*] Well, then we will shut it.

HEDDA No no, not that! Tesman, please draw the curtains. That will give a softer light.

TESMAN [*at the door*] All right – all right. – There now, Hedda, now you have both shade and fresh air.

HEDDA Yes, fresh air we certainly must have, with all these stacks of flowers. But – won't you sit down, Miss Tesman?

MISS TESMAN No, thank you. Now that I have seen that every-thing is all right here – thank heaven! – I must be getting home again. My sister is lying longing for me, poor thing.

TESMAN Give her my very best love, Auntie; and say I shall look in and see her later in the day.

MISS TESMAN Yes, yes, I'll be sure to tell her. But by-the-bye, George – [*feeling in her dress pocket*] – I had almost forgotten – I have something for you here.

TESMAN What is it, Auntie? Eh?

MISS TESMAN [*produces a flat parcel wrapped in newspaper and hands it to him*] Look here, my dear boy.

TESMAN [*opening the parcel*] Well, I declare! – Have you really saved them for me, Aunt Julia! Hedda! isn't this touching – eh?

HEDDA [*beside the whatnot on the right*] Well, what is it?

TESMAN My old morning-shoes! My slippers.

HEDDA Indeed. I remember you often spoke of them while we were abroad.

TESMAN Yes, I missed them terribly. [*goes up to her*] Now you shall see them, Hedda!

HEDDA [*going towards the stove*] Thanks, I really don't care about it.

TESMAN [*following her*] Only think – ill as she was, Aunt Rina embroidered these for me. Oh you can't think how many associations cling to them.

HEDDA [*at the table*] Scarcely for me.

MISS TESMAN Of course not for Hedda, George.

TESMAN Well, but now that she belongs to the family, I thought –

HEDDA [*interrupting*] We shall never get on with this servant, Tesman.

MISS TESMAN Not get on with Berta?

TESMAN Why, dear, what puts that in your head? Eh?

HEDDA [*pointing*] Look there! She has left her old bonnet lying about on a chair.

TESMAN [*in consternation, drops the slippers on the floor*] Why, Hedda –

HEDDA Just fancy, if anyone should come in and see it!

TESMAN But Hedda – that's Aunt Julia's bonnet.

HEDDA Is it?

MISS TESMAN [*taking up the bonnet*] Yes, indeed it's mine. And, what's more, it's not old, Madam Hedda.

HEDDA I really did not look closely at it, Miss Tesman.

MISS TESMAN [*trying on the bonnet*] Let me tell you it's the first time I have worn it – the very first time.

TESMAN And a very nice bonnet it is too – quite a beauty!

MISS TESMAN Oh, it's no such great things, George. [*looks around her*] My parasol – ? Ah, here. [*takes it*] For this is mine too – [*mutters*] not Berta's.

TESMAN A new bonnet and a new parasol! Only think, Hedda.

HEDDA Very handsome indeed.

TESMAN Yes, isn't it? Eh? But Auntie, take a good look at Hedda before you go! See how handsome she is!

MISS TESMAN Oh, my dear boy, there's nothing new in that. Hedda was always lovely. [*she nods and goes toward the right*]

TESMAN [*following*] Yes, but have you noticed what splendid condition she is in? How she has filled out on the journey?

HEDDA [*crossing the room*] Oh, do be quiet – !

MISS TESMAN [*who has stopped and turned*] Filled out?

TESMAN Of course you don't notice it so much now that she has that dress on. But I, who can see –

HEDDA [*at the glass door, impatiently*] Oh, you can't see anything.

TESMAN It must be the mountain air in the Tyrol –

HEDDA [*curtly, interrupting*] I am exactly as I was when I started.

TESMAN So you insist; but I'm quite certain you are not. Don't you agree with me, Auntie?

MISS TESMAN [*who has been gazing at her with folded hands*] Hedda is lovely – lovely – lovely. [*goes up to her, takes her head between both hands, draws it downwards, and kisses her hair*] God bless and preserve Hedda Tesman – for George's sake.

HEDDA [*gently freeing herself*] Oh – ! Let me go.

MISS TESMAN [*in quiet emotion*] I shall not let a day pass without coming to see you.

TESMAN No you won't, will you, Auntie? Eh?

MISS TESMAN Goodbye – goodbye!   [*She goes out by the hall door.*
                                         Tesman accompanies her.]

The door remains half open. Tesman can be heard repeating his message to Aunt Rina and his thanks for the slippers.

In the meantime, Hedda walks about the room, raising her arms and clenching her hands as if in desperation. Then she flings back the curtains from the glass door, and stands there looking out.

Presently, TESMAN *returns and closes the door behind him.*

TESMAN [*picks up the slippers from the floor*] What are you looking at, Hedda?

HEDDA [*once more calm and mistress of herself*] I am only looking at the leaves. They are so yellow — so withered.

TESMAN [*wraps up the slippers and lays them on the table*] Well, you see, we are well into September now.

HEDDA [*again restless*] Yes, to think of it! — already in — in September.

TESMAN Don't you think Aunt Julia's manner was strange, dear? Almost solemn? Can you imagine what was the matter with her? Eh?

HEDDA I scarcely know her, you see. Is she not often like that?

TESMAN No, not as she was today.

HEDDA [*leaving the glass door*] Do you think she was annoyed about the bonnet?

TESMAN Oh, scarcely at all. Perhaps a little, just at the moment —

HEDDA But what an idea, to pitch her bonnet about in the drawing-room! No one does that sort of thing.

TESMAN Well you may be sure Aunt Julia won't do it again.

HEDDA In any case, I shall manage to make my peace with her.

TESMAN Yes, my dear, good Hedda, if you only would.

HEDDA When you call this afternoon, you might invite her to spend the evening here.

TESMAN Yes, that I will. And there's one thing more you could do that would delight her heart.

HEDDA What is it?

TESMAN If you could only prevail on yourself to say *du** to her. For my sake, Hedda? Eh?

HEDDA No, no, Tesman — you really mustn't ask that of me. I have told you so already. I shall try to call her 'Aunt'; and you must be satisfied with that.

TESMAN Well well. Only I think now that you belong to the family, you —

* *Du* = 'thou': Tesman means 'If you could persuade yourself to *tutoyer* her.'

HEDDA H'm – I can't in the least see why –

[*she goes up towards the middle doorway*]

TESMAN [*after a pause*] Is there anything the matter with you, Hedda? Eh?

HEDDA I'm only looking at my old piano. It doesn't go at all well with all the other things.

TESMAN The first time I draw my salary, we'll see about exchanging it.

HEDDA No, no – no exchanging. I don't want to part with it. Suppose we put it there in the inner room, and then get another here in its place. When it's convenient, I mean.

TESMAN [*a little taken aback*] Yes – of course we could do that.

HEDDA [*takes up the bouquet from the piano*] These flowers were not here last night when we arrived.

TESMAN Aunt Julia must have brought them for you.

HEDDA [*examining the bouquet*] A visiting-card. [*takes it out and reads*] 'Shall return later in the day.' Can you guess whose card it is?

TESMAN No. Whose? Eh?

HEDDA The name is 'Mrs Elvsted'.

TESMAN Is it really? Sheriff Elvsted's wife? Miss Rysing that was.

HEDDA Exactly. The girl with the irritating hair, that she was always showing off. An old flame of yours I've been told.

TESMAN [*laughing*] Oh, that didn't last long; and it was before I met you, Hedda. But fancy her being in town!

HEDDA It's odd that she should call upon us. I have scarcely seen her since we left school.

TESMAN I haven't see her either for – heaven knows how long. I wonder how she can endure to live in such an out-of-the way hole – eh?

HEDDA [*after a moment's thought, says suddenly*] Tell me, Tesman – isn't it somewhere near there that he – that – Eilert Lövborg is living?

TESMAN Yes, he is somewhere in that part of the country.

BERTA *enters by the hall door.*

BERTA That lady, ma'am, that brought some flowers a little while ago, is here again. [*pointing*] The flowers you have in your hand, ma'am.

HEDDA Ah, is she? Well, please show her in.

Berta opens the door for MRS ELVSTED, *and goes out herself. – Mrs Elvsted is a woman of fragile figure, with pretty, soft features. Her eyes are light blue, large, round, and somewhat prominent, with a startled, inquiring expression. Her hair is remarkably light, almost flaxen, and unusually abundant and wavy. She is a couple of years younger than Hedd. She wears a dark visiting dress, tasteful, but not quite in the latest fashion.*

HEDDA [*receives her warmly*] How do you do, my dear Mrs Elvsted? It's delightful to see you again.

MRS ELVSTED [*nervously, struggling for self-control*] Yes, it's a very long time since we met.

TESMAN [*gives her his hand*] And we too – eh?

HEDDA Thanks for your lovely flowers –

MRS ELVSTED Oh, not at all – I would have come straight here yesterday afternoon; but I heard that you were away –

TESMAN Have you just come to town? Eh?

MRS ELVSTED I arrived yesterday, about midday. Oh, I was quite in despair when I heard that you were not at home.

HEDDA In despair! How so?

TESMAN Why, my dear Mrs Rysing – I mean Mrs Elvsted –

HEDDA I hope that you are not in any trouble?

MRS ELVSTED Yes, I am. And I don't know another living creature here that I can turn to.

HEDDA [*laying the bouquet on the table*] Come – let us sit here on the sofa –

MRS ELVSTED Oh, I am too restless to sit down.

HEDDA Oh no, you're not. Come here. [*she draws Mrs Elvsted down upon the sofa and sits at her side*]

TESMAN Well? What is it, Mrs Elvsted – ?

HEDDA Has anything particular happened to you at home?

MRS ELVSTED Yes – and no. Oh – I am so anxious you should not misunderstand me –

HEDDA Then your best plan is to tell us the whole story, Mrs Elvsted.

TESMAN I suppose that's what you have come for – eh?

MRS ELVSTED Yes, yes – of course it is. Well then, I must tell you – if you don't already know – that Eilert Lövborg is in town, too.

HEDDA Lövborg – !

TESMAN What! Has Eilert Lövborg come back? Fancy that, Hedda!

HEDDA Well well – I hear it.

MRS ELVSTED He has been here a week already. Just fancy – a whole week! In this terrible town, alone! With so many temptations on all sides.

HEDDA But, my dear Mrs Elvsted – how does he concern you so much?

MRS ELVSTED [*looks at her with a startled air, and says rapidly*] He was the children's tutor.

HEDDA Your children's?

MRS ELVSTED My husband's. I have none.

HEDDA Your step-children's, then?

MRS ELVSTED Yes.

TESMAN [*somewhat hesitatingly*] Then was he – I don't know how to express it – was he – regular enough in his habits to be fit for the post? Eh?

MRS ELVSTED For the last two years his conduct has been irreproachable.

TESMAN Has it indeed? Fancy that, Hedda!

HEDDA I hear it.

MRS ELVSTED Perfectly irreproachable, I assure you! In every respect. But all the same – now that I know he is here – in this great town – and with a large sum of money in his hands – I can't help being in mortal fear for him.

TESMAN Why did he not remain where he was? With you and your husband? Eh?

MRS ELVSTED After his book was published he was too restless and unsettled to remain with us.

TESMAN Yes, by-the-bye, Aunt Julia told me he had published a new book.

MRS ELVSTED Yes, a big book, dealing with the march of civilisation – in broad outline, as it were. It came out about a fortnight ago. And since it has sold so well, and been so much read – and made such a sensation –

TESMAN Has it indeed? It must be something he has had lying by since his better days.

MRS ELVSTED Long ago, you mean?

TESMAN Yes.

MRS ELVSTED No, he has written it all since he has been with us –
within the last year.

TESMAN Isn't that good news, Hedda? Think of that.

MRS ELVSTED Ah yes, if only it would last!

HEDDA Have you seen him here in town?

MRS ELVSTED No, not yet. I have had the greatest difficulty
in finding out his address. But this morning I discovered it
at last.

HEDDA [*looks searchingly at her*] Do you know, it seems to me a little
odd of your husband – h'm –

MRS ELVSTED [*starting nervously*] Of my husband! What?

HEDDA That he should send you to town on such an errand – that
he does not come himself and look after his friend.

MRS ELVSTED Oh no, no – my husband has no time. And besides,
I – I had some shopping to do.

HEDDA [*with a slight smile*] Ah, that is a different matter.

MRS ELVSTED [*rising quickly and uneasily*] And now I beg and implore you, Mr Tesman – receive Eilert Lövborg kindly if he
comes to you! And that he is sure to do. You see you were such
great friends in the old days. And then you are interested in the
same studies – the same branch of science – so far as I can
understand.

TESMAN We used to be at any rate.

MRS ELVSTED That is why I beg so earnestly that you – you too –
will keep a sharp eye upon him. Oh, you will promise me that,
Mr Tesman – won't you?

TESMAN With the greatest of pleasure, Mrs Rysing –

HEDDA Elvsted.

TESMAN I assure you I shall do all I possibly can for Eilert. You may
rely upon me.

MRS ELVSTED Oh, how very, very kind of you! [*presses his hands*]
Thanks, thanks, thanks! [*frightened*] You see, my husband is so
very fond of him!

HEDDA [*rising*] You ought to write to him, Tesman. Perhaps he
may not care to come to you of his own accord.

TESMAN Well, perhaps it would be the right thing to do, Hedda?
Eh?

HEDDA And the sooner the better. Why not at once?

MRS ELVSTED [*imploringly*] Oh, if you only would!

TESMAN I'll write this moment. Have you his address, Mrs – Mr
  Elvsted.

MRS ELVSTED Yes. [*takes a slip of paper from her pocket, and hands it t*
  him] Here it is.

TESMAN Good, good. Then I'll go in – [*looks about him*] By
  the-bye – my slippers? Oh, here. [*takes the packet and is abou*
  to go]

HEDDA Be sure you write him a cordial, friendly letter. And a goo
  long one too.

TESMAN Yes, I will.

MRS ELVSTED But please, please don't say a word to show that
  have suggested it.

TESMAN No, how could you think I would? Eh?

                    [*He goes out to the right, through the inner room*

HEDDA [*goes up to Mrs Elvsted, smiles, and says in a low voice*] There
  We have killed two birds with one stone.

MRS ELVSTED What do you mean?

HEDDA Could you not see that I wanted him to go?

MRS ELVSTED Yes, to write the letter –

HEDDA And that I might speak to you alone.

MRS ELVSTED [*confused*] About the same thing?

HEDDA Precisely.

MRS ELVSTED [*apprehensively*] But there is nothing more, Mr
  Tesman! Absolutely nothing!

HEDDA Oh yes, but there is. There is a great deal more – I can se
  that. Sit here – and we'll have a cosy, confidential chat.
  [*She forces Mrs Elvsted to sit in the easy-chair beside the stove, an*
  seats herself on one of the footstools.]

MRS ELVSTED [*anxiously, looking at her watch*] But, my dear Mr
  Tesman – I was really on the point of going.

HEDDA Oh, you can't be in such a hurry. – Well? Now tell m
  something about your life at home.

MRS ELVSTED Oh, that is just what I care least to speak about.

HEDDA But to me, dear – ? Why, weren't we schoolfellows?

MRS ELVSTED Yes, but you were in the class above me. Oh, hov
  dreadfully afraid of you I was then!

HEDDA Afraid of me?

MRS ELVSTED Yes, dreadfully. For when we met on the stairs yo
  used always to pull my hair.

HEDDA Did I, really?

MRS ELVSTED Yes, and once you said you would burn it off my head.

HEDDA Oh that was all nonsense, of course.

MRS ELVSTED Yes, but I was so silly in those days. – And since then, too – we have drifted so far – far apart from each other. Our circles have been so entirely different.

HEDDA Well then, we must try to drift together again. Now listen. At school we said *du** to each other; and we called each other by our Christian names –

MRS ELVSTED No, I am sure you must be mistaken.

HEDDA No, not at all! I can remember quite distinctly. So now we are going to renew our old friendship. [*draws the footstool closer to Mrs Elvsted*] There now! [*kisses her cheek*] You must say *du* to me and call me Hedda.

MRS ELVSTED [*presses and pats her hands*] Oh, how good and kind you are! I am not used to such kindness.

HEDDA There, there, there! And I shall say *du* to you, as in the old days, and call you my dear Thora.

MRS ELVSTED My name is Thea.

HEDDA Why, of course! I meant Thea. [*looks at her compassionately*] So you are not accustomed to goodness and kindness, Thea? Not in your own home?

MRS ELVSTED Oh, if I only had a home! But I haven't any; I have never had a home.

HEDDA [*looks at her for a moment*] I almost suspected as much.

MRS ELVSTED [*gazing helplessly before her*] Yes – yes – yes.

HEDDA I don't quite remember – was it not as housekeeper that you first went to Mr Elvsted's?

MRS ELVSTED I really went as governess. But his wife – his late wife – was an invalid, and rarely left her room. So I had to look after the housekeeping as well.

HEDDA And then – at last – you became mistress of the house.

MRS ELVSTED [*sadly*] Yes, I did.

HEDDA Let me see – about how long ago was that?

MRS ELVSTED My marriage?

HEDDA Yes.

MRS ELVSTED Five years ago.

HEDDA To be sure; it must be that.

see footnote, page 241.

MRS ELVSTED Oh those five years – ! Or at all events the last two or three of them! Oh, if you* could only imagine –

HEDDA [*giving her a little slap on the hand*] De? Fie, Thea!

MRS ELVSTED Yes, yes, I will try – Well, if – you could only imagine and understand –

HEDDA [*lightly*] Eilert Lövborg has been in your neighbourhood about three years, hasn't he?

MRS ELVSTED [*looks at here doubtfully*] Eilert Lövborg? Yes – he has.

HEDDA Had you known him before, in town here?

MRS ELVSTED Scarcely at all. I mean – I knew him by name of course.

HEDDA But you saw a good deal of him in the country?

MRS ELVSTED Yes, he came to us every day. You see, he gave the children lessons; for in the long run I couldn't manage it all myself.

HEDDA No, that's clear. And your husband – ? I suppose he is often away from home?

MRS ELVSTED Yes. Being sheriff, you know, he has to travel about a good deal in his district.

HEDDA [*leaning against the arm of the chair*] Thea – my poor, sweet Thea – now you must tell me everything – exactly as it stands.

MRS ELVSTED Well, then you must question me.

HEDDA What sort of a man is your husband, Thea? I mean – you know – in everyday life. Is he kind to you?

MRS ELVSTED [*evasively*] I am sure he means well in everything.

HEDDA I should think he must be altogether too old for you. There is at least twenty years' difference between you, is there not?

MRS ELVSTED [*irritably*] Yes, that is true, too. Everything about him is repellent to me! We have not a thought in common. We have no single point of sympathy – he and I.

HEDDA But is he not fond of you all the same? In his own way?

MRS ELVSTED Oh I really don't know. I think he regards me simply as a useful property. And then it doesn't cost much to keep me I am not expensive.

HEDDA That is stupid of you.

MRS ELVSTED [*shakes her head*] It cannot be otherwise – not with him. I don't think he really cares for anyone but himself – and perhaps a little for the children.

---

* Mrs Elvsted here uses the formal pronoun *De*, whereupon Hedda rebuke her. In her next speech Mrs Elvsted says *Du*.

HEDDA And for Eilert Lövborg, Thea?

MRS ELVSTED [*looking at her*] For Eilert Lövborg? What puts that into your head?

HEDDA Well, my dear – I should say, when he sends you after him all the way to town – [*smiling almost imperceptibly*] And besides, you said so yourself, to Tesman.

MRS ELVSTED [*with a little nervous twitch*] Did I? Yes, I suppose I did. [*vehemently, but not loudly*] No – I may just as well make a clean breast of it at once! For it must all come out in any case.

HEDDA Why, my dear Thea – ?

MRS ELVSTED Well, to make a long story short: My husband did not know that I was coming.

HEDDA What! Your husband didn't know it!

MRS ELVSTED No, of course not. For that matter, he was away from home himself – he was travelling. Oh, I could bear it no longer, Hedda! I couldn't indeed – so utterly alone as I should have been in future.

HEDDA Well? And then?

MRS ELVSTED So I put together some of my things – what I needed most – as quietly as possible. And then I left the house.

HEDDA Without a word?

MRS ELVSTED Yes – and took the train to town.

HEDDA Why, my dear, good Thea – to think of you daring to do it!

MRS ELVSTED [*rises and moves about the room*] What else could I possibly do?

HEDDA But what do you think your husband will say when you go home again?

MRS ELVSTED [*at the table, looks at her*] Back to him?

HEDDA Of course.

MRS ELVSTED I shall never go back to him again.

HEDDA [*rising and going towards her*] Then you have left your home – for good and all?

MRS ELVSTED Yes. There was nothing else to be done.

HEDDA But then – to take flight so openly.

MRS ELVSTED Oh, it's impossible to keep things of that sort secret.

HEDDA But what do you think people will say of you, Thea?

MRS ELVSTED They may say what they like, for aught *I* care. [*seats herself wearily and sadly on the sofa*] I have done nothing but what I had to do.

HEDDA [*after a short silence*] And what are your plans now? What do you think of doing.

MRS ELVSTED I don't know yet. I only know this, that I must live here, where Eilert Lövborg is – if I am to live at all.

HEDDA [*takes a chair from the table, seats herself beside her, and strokes her hands*] My dear Thea – how did this – this friendship – between you and Eilert Lövborg come about?

MRS ELVSTED Oh it grew up gradually. I gained a sort of influence over him.

HEDDA Indeed?

MRS ELVSTED He gave up his old habits. Not because I asked him to, for I never dared do that. But of course he saw how repulsive they were to me; and so he dropped them.

HEDDA [*concealing an involuntary smile of scorn*] Then you have re-claimed him – as the saying goes – my little Thea.

MRS ELVSTED So he says himself, at any rate. And he, on his side, has made a real human being of me – taught me to think, and to understand so many things.

HEDDA Did he give you lessons too, then?

MRS ELVSTED No, not exactly lessons. But he talked to me – talked about such an infinity of things. And then came the lovely, happy time when I began to share in his work – when he allowed me to help him!

HEDDA Oh he did, did he?

MRS ELVSTED Yes! He never wrote anything without my assistance.

HEDDA You were two good comrades, in fact?

MRS ELVSTED [*eagerly*] Comrades! Yes, fancy, Hedda – that is the very word he used! – Oh, I ought to feel perfectly happy; and yet I cannot; for I don't know how long it will last.

HEDDA Are you no surer of him than that?

MRS ELVSTED [*gloomily*] A woman's shadow stands between Eilert Lövborg and me.

HEDDA [*looks at her anxiously*] Who can that be?

MRS ELVSTED I don't know. Someone he knew in his – in his past. Someone he has never been able wholly to forget.

HEDDA What has he told you – about this?

MRS ELVSTED He has only once – quite vaguely – alluded to it.

HEDDA Well! And what did he say?

MRS ELVSTED He said that when they parted, she threatened to shoot him with a pistol.

HEDDA [*with cold composure*] Oh nonsense! No one does that sort of thing here.

MRS ELVSTED No. And that is why I think it must have been that red-haired singing-woman whom he once –

HEDDA Yes, very likely.

MRS ELVSTED For I remember they used to say of her that she carried loaded firearms.

HEDDA Oh – then of course it must have been she.

MRS ELVSTED [*wringing her hands*] And now just fancy, Hedda – I hear that this singing-woman – that she is in town again! Oh, I don't know what to do –

HEDDA [*glancing towards the inner room*] Hush! Here comes Tesman. [*rises and whispers*] Thea – all this must remain between you and me.

MRS ELVSTED [*springing up*] Oh yes – yes! For heaven's sake – !

GEORGE TESMAN, *with a letter in his hand, comes from the right through the inner room.*

TESMAN There now – the epistle is finished.

HEDDA That's right. And now Mrs Elvsted is just going. Wait a moment – I'll go with you to the garden gate.

TESMAN Do you think Berta could post the letter, Hedda dear?

HEDDA [*takes it*] I will tell her to.

BERTA *enters from the hall.*

BERTA Judge Brack wishes to know if Mrs Tesman will receive him.

HEDDA Yes, ask Judge Brack to come in. And look here – put this letter in the post.

BERTA [*taking the letter*] Yes, ma'am.

She opens the door for JUDGE BRACK *and goes out herself. Brack is a man of forty-five; thick-set, but well-built and elastic in his movements. His face is roundish with an aristocratic profile. His hair is short, still almost black, and carefully dressed. His eyebrows thick. His moustaches are also thick, with short-cut ends. He wears a well-cut walking-suit, a little too youthful for his age. He uses an eye-glass, which he now and then lets drop.*

BRACK [*with his hat in his hand, bowing*] May one venture to call so early in the day?

HEDDA Of course one may.

TESMAN [*presses his hand*] You are welcome at any time. [*introducing him*] Judge Brack – Miss Rysing –

HEDDA Oh – !

BRACK [*bowing*] Ah – delighted –

HEDDA [*looks at him and laughs*] It's nice to have a look at you by daylight, Judge!

BRACK So you find me – altered?

HEDDA A little younger, I think.

BRACK Thank you so much.

TESMAN But what do you think of Hedda – eh? Doesn't she look flourishing? She has actually –

HEDDA Oh, do leave me alone. You haven't thanked Judge Brack for all the trouble he has taken –

BRACK Oh, nonsense – it was a pleasure to me –

HEDDA Yes, you are a friend indeed. But here stands Thea all impatience to be off – so *au revoir* Judge. I shall be back again presently.   [*Mutual salutations. Mrs Elvsted and Hedda go out by the hall door.*]

BRACK Well – is your wife tolerably satisfied –

TESMAN Yes, we can't thank you sufficiently. Of course she talks of a little rearrangement here and there; and one or two things are still wanting. We shall have to buy some additional trifles.

BRACK Indeed!

TESMAN But we won't trouble you about these things. Hedda says she herself will look after what is wanting. – Shan't we sit down? Eh?

BRACK Thanks, for a moment. [*seats himself beside the table*] There is something I wanted to speak to you about, my dear Tesman.

TESMAN Indeed? Ah, I understand! [*seating himself*] I suppose it's the serious part of the frolic that is coming now. Eh?

BRACK Oh, the money question is not so very pressing; though, for that matter, I wish we had gone a little more economically to work.

TESMAN But that would never have done, you know! Think of Hedda, my dear fellow! You, who know her so well – ! I couldn't possibly ask her to put up with a shabby style of living!

BRACK No, no – that is just the difficulty.

TESMAN And then – fortunately – it can't be long before I receive my appointment.

BRACK Well, you see – such things are often apt to hang fire for a long time.

TESMAN Have you heard anything definite? Eh?

BRACK Nothing exactly definite – . [*interrupting himself*] But by-the-bye – I have one piece of news for you.

TESMAN Well?

BRACK Your old friend, Eilert Lövborg, has returned to town.

TESMAN I know that already.

BRACK Indeed! How did you learn it?

TESMAN From that lady who went out with Hedda.

BRACK Really? What was her name? I didn't quite catch it.

TESMAN Mrs Elvsted.

BRACK Aha – Sheriff Elvsted's wife? Of course – he has been living up in their regions.

TESMAN And fancy – I'm delighted to hear that he is quite a reformed character.

BRACK So they say.

TESMAN And then he has published a new book – eh?

BRACK Yes, indeed he has.

TESMAN And I hear it has made some sensation!

BRACK Quite an unusual sensation.

TESMAN Fancy – isn't that good news! A man of such extraordinary talents – I felt so grieved to think that he had gone irretrievably to ruin.

BRACK That was what everybody thought.

TESMAN But I cannot imagine what he will take to now! How in the world will he be able to make his living? Eh?

During the last words, HEDDA *has entered by the hall door.*

HEDDA [*to Brack, laughing with a touch of scorn*] Tesman is for ever worrying about how people are to make their living.

TESMAN Well you see, dear – we were talking about poor Eilert Lövborg.

HEDDA [*glancing at him rapidly*] Oh, indeed? [*sets herself in the armchair beside the stove and asks indifferently*] What is the matter with him?

TESMAN Well – no doubt he has run through all his property long ago; and he can scarcely write a new book every year – eh? So I really can't see what is to become of him.

BRACK Perhaps I can give you some information on that point.

TESMAN Indeed!

BRACK You must remember that his relations have a good deal of influence.

TESMAN Oh, his relations, unfortunately, have entirely washed their hands of him.

BRACK At one time they called him the hope of the family.

TESMAN At one time, yes! But he has put an end to all that.

HEDDA Who knows? [*with a slight smile*] I hear they have reclaimed him up at Sheriff Elvsted's –

BRACK And then this book that he has published –

TESMAN Well well, I hope to goodness they may find something for him to do. I have just written to him. I asked him to come and see us this evening, Hedda dear.

BRACK But my dear fellow, you are booked for my bachelor's party this evening. You promised on the pier last night.

HEDDA Had you forgotten, Tesman?

TESMAN Yes, I had utterly forgotten.

BRACK But it doesn't matter, for you may be sure he won't come.

TESMAN What makes you think that? Eh?

BRACK [*with a little hesitation, rising and resting his hands on the back of his chair*] My dear Tesman – and you too, Mrs Tesman – I think I ought not to keep you in the dark about something that – that –

TESMAN That concerns Eilert – ?

BRACK Both you and him.

TESMAN Well, my dear Judge, out with it.

BRACK You must be prepared to find your appointment deferred longer than you desired or expected.

TESMAN [*jumping up uneasily*] Is there some hitch about it? Eh?

BRACK The nomination may perhaps be made conditional on the result of a competition –

TESMAN Competition! Think of that, Hedda!

HEDDA [*leans further back in the chair*] Aha – aha!

TESMAN But who can my competitor be? Surely not – ?

BRACK Yes, precisely – Eilert Lövborg.

TESMAN [*clasping his hands*] No, no – it's quite impossible! Eh?

BRACK H'm — that is what it may come to, all the same.

TESMAN Well but, Judge Brack — it would show the most incredible lack of consideration for me. [*gesticulates with his arms*] For — just think — I'm a married man! We have married on the strength of these prospects, Hedda and I; and run deep into debt; and borrowed money from Aunt Julia too. Good heavens, they had as good as promised me the appointment. Eh?

BRACK Well, well, well — no doubt you will get it in the end; only after a contest.

HEDDA [*immovable in her armchair*] Fancy, Tesman, there will be a sort of sporting interest in that.

TESMAN Why, my dearest Hedda, how can you be so indifferent about it?

HEDDA [*as before*] I am not at all indifferent. I am most eager to see who wins.

BRACK In any case, Mrs Tesman, it is best that you should know how matters stand. I mean — before you set about the little purchases I hear you are threatening.

HEDDA This can make no difference.

BRACK Indeed! Then I have no more to say. Goodbye! [*to Tesman*] I shall look in on my way back from my afternoon walk, and take you home with me.

TESMAN Oh yes, yes — your news has quite upset me.

HEDDA [*reclining, holds out her hand*] Goodbye, Judge; and be sure you call in the afternoon.

BRACK Many thanks. Goodbye, goodbye!

TESMAN [*accompanying him to the door*] Goodbye my dear Judge! You must really excuse me —   [*Judge Brack goes out by the hall door*]

TESMAN [*crosses the room*] Oh Hedda — one should never rush into adventures. Eh?

HEDDA [*looks at him, smiling*] Do you do that?

TESMAN Yes, dear — there is no denying — it was adventurous to go and marry and set up house upon mere expectations.

HEDDA Perhaps you are right there.

TESMAN Well — at all events, we have our delightful home, Hedda! Fancy, the home we both dreamed of — the home we were in love with, I may almost say. Eh?

HEDDA [*rising slowly and wearily*] It was part of our compact that we were to go into society — to keep open house.

TESMAN Yes, if you only knew how I had been looking forward to
it! Fancy – to see you as hostess – in a select circle! Eh? Well,
well, well – for the present we shall have to get on without
society, Hedda – only to invite Aunt Julia now and then. – Oh,
I intended you to lead such an utterly different life, dear – !

HEDDA Of course I cannot have my man in livery just yet.

TESMAN Oh, no, unfortunately. It would be out of the question for
us to keep a footman, you know.

HEDDA And the saddle-horse I was to have had –

TESMAN [aghast] The saddle-horse!

HEDDA – I suppose I must not think of that now.

TESMAN Good heavens, no! – that's as clear as daylight!

HEDDA [goes up the room] Well, I shall have one thing at least to kill
time with in the meanwhile.

TESMAN [beaming] Oh thank heaven for that! What is it, Hedda.
Eh?

HEDDA [in the middle doorway, looks at him with covert scorn] My
pistols, George.

TESMAN [in alarm] Your pistols!

HEDDA [with cold eyes] General Gabler's pistols.

                    [she goes out through the inner room, to the left]

TESMAN [rushes up to the middle doorway and calls after her] No, for
heaven's sake, Hedda darling – don't touch those dangerous
things! For my sake Hedda! Eh?

ACT SECOND

The room at the Tesmans' as in the first Act, except that the piano has been removed, and an elegant little writing-table with the book-shelves put in its place. A smaller table stands near the sofa on the left. Most of the bouquets have been taken away. Mrs Elvsted's bouquet is upon the large table in front. − It is afternoon.

HEDDA, dressed to receive callers, is alone in the room. She stands by the open glass door, loading a revolver. The fellow to it lies in an open pistol-case on the writing-table.

HEDDA [*looks down the garden, and calls*] So you are here again, Judge!

BRACK [*is heard calling from a distance*] As you see, Mrs Tesman!

HEDDA [*raises the pistol and points*] Now I'll shoot you, Judge Brack!

BRACK [*calling unseen*] No, no, no! Don't stand aiming at me!

HEDDA This is what comes of sneaking in by the back way.
    [*She fires.*]

BRACK [*nearer*] Are you out of your senses − !

HEDDA Dear me − did I happen to hit you?

BRACK [*still outside*] I wish you would let these pranks alone!

HEDDA Come in then, Judge.

    JUDGE BRACK, *dressed as though for a men's party, enters by the glass door. He carries a light overcoat over his arm.*

BRACK What the deuce − haven't you tired of that sport, yet? What are you shooting at?

HEDDA Oh, I am only firing in the air.

BRACK [*gently takes the pistol out of her hand*] Allow me, madam! [*looks at it*] Ah − I know this pistol well! [*looks around*] Where is the case? Ah, here it is. [*lays the pistol in it, and shuts it*] Now we won't play at that game any more today.

HEDDA Then what in heaven's name would you have me do with myself?

BRACK Have you had no visitors?

HEDDA [*closing the glass door*] Not one. I suppose all our set are still out of town.

BRACK And is Tesman not at home either?

HEDDA [*at the writing-table, putting the pistol-case in a drawer which she shuts*] No. He rushed off to his aunt's directly after lunch; he didn't expect you so early.

BRACK H'm – how stupid of me not to have thought of that!

HEDDA [*turning her head to look at him*] Why stupid?

BRACK Because if I had thought of it I should have come a little – earlier.

HEDDA [*crossing the room*] Then you would have found no one to receive you; for I have been in my room changing my dress ever since lunch.

BRACK And is there no sort of little chink that we could hold a parley through?

HEDDA You have forgotten to arrange one.

BRACK That was another piece of stupidity.

HEDDA Well, we must just settle down here – and wait. Tesman is not likely to be back for some time yet.

BRACK Never mind; I shall not be impatient.

[*Hedda seats herself in the corner of the sofa. Brack lays his overcoat over the back of the nearest chair, and sits down, but keeps his hat in his hand. A short silence. They look at each other.*]

HEDDA Well?

BRACK [*in the same tone*] Well?

HEDDA I spoke first.

BRACK [*bending a little forward*] Come, let us have a cosy little chat, Mrs Hedda.

HEDDA [*leaning further back in the sofa*] Does it not seem like a whole eternity since our last talk? Of course I don't count those few words yesterday evening and this morning.

BRACK You mean since our last confidential talk? Our last *tête-à-tête*?

HEDDA Well yes – since you put it so.

BRACK Not a day passed but I have wished that you were home again.

HEDDA And I have done nothing but wish the same thing.

BRACK You? Really, Mrs Hedda? And I thought you had been enjoying your tour so much!

HEDDA Oh yes, you may be sure of that!

BRACK But Tesman's letters spoke of nothing but happiness.

HEDDA Oh, Tesman! You see, he thinks nothing is so delightful as grubbing in libraries and making copies of old parchments, or whatever you call them.

BRACK [*with a smile of malice*] Well, that is his vocation in life – or part of it at any rate.

HEDDA Yes, of course; and no doubt when it's your vocation – . But *I*! Oh, my dear Mr Brack, how mortally bored I have been.

BRACK [*sympathetically*] Do you really say so? In downright earnest?

HEDDA Yes, you can surely understand it – ! To go for six whole months without meeting a soul that knew anything of our circle, or could talk about things we were interested in.

BRACK Yes, yes – I too should feel that a deprivation.

HEDDA And then, what I found most intolerable of all –

BRACK Well?

HEDDA – was being everlastingly in the company of – one and the same person –

BRACK [*with a nod of assent*] Morning, noon, and night, yes – at all possible times and seasons.

HEDDA I said 'everlastingly'.

BRACK Just so. But I should have thought, with our excellent Tesman, one could –

HEDDA Tesman is – a specialist, my dear Judge.

BRACK Undeniable.

HEDDA And specialists are not at all amusing to travel with. Not in the long run at any rate.

BRACK Not even – the specialist one happens to love?

HEDDA Faugh – don't use that sickening word!

BRACK [*taken aback*] What do you say, Mrs Hedda?

HEDDA [*half laughing, half irritated*] You should just try it! To hear of nothing but the history of civilisation, morning, noon, and night –

BRACK Everlastingly.

HEDDA Yes yes yes! And then all this about the domestic industry of the middle ages – ! That's the most disgusting part of it!

BRACK [*looks searchingly at her*] But tell me – in that case, how am I to understand your – ? H'm –

HEDDA My accepting George Tesman, you mean?

BRACK Well, let us put it so.

HEDDA Good heavens, do you see anything so wonderful in that?

BRACK Yes and no – Mrs Hedda.

HEDDA I had positively danced myself tired, my dear Judge. My day was done – [*with a slight shudder*] Oh no – I won't say that; nor think it either!

BRACK You have assuredly no reason to.

HEDDA Oh, reasons – [*watching him closely*] And George Tesman – after all, you must admit that he is correctness itself.

BRACK His correctness and respectability are beyond all question.

HEDDA And I don't see anything absolutely ridiculous about him. – Do you?

BRACK Ridiculous? N–no – I shouldn't exactly say so –

HEDDA Well – and his powers of research, at all events, are untiring. – I see no reason why he should not one day come to the front, after all.

BRACK [*looks at her hesitatingly*] I thought that you, like everyone else, expected him to attain the highest distinction.

HEDDA [*with an expression of fatigue*] Yes, so I did. – And then, since he was bent, at all hazards, on being allowed to provide for me – I really don't know why I should not have accepted his offer?

BRACK No – if you look at it in that light –

HEDDA It was more than my other adorers were prepared to do for me, my dear Judge.

BRACK [*laughing*] Well, I can't answer for all the rest; but as for myself, you know quite well that I have always entertained a – a certain respect for the marriage tie – for marriage as an institution, Mrs Hedda.

HEDDA [*jestingly*] Oh, I assure you I have never cherished any hopes with respect to you.

BRACK All I require is a pleasant and intimate interior, where I can make myself useful in every way, and am free to come and go as – as a trusted friend –

HEDDA Of the master of the house, do you mean?

BRACK [*bowing*] Frankly – of the mistress first of all; but of course of the master too, in the second place. Such a triangular friendship – if I may call it so – is really a great convenience for all the parties, let me tell you.

HEDDA Yes, I have many a time longed for someone to make a
third on our travels. Oh – those railway-carriage *tête-à-têtes* – !

BRACK Fortunately your wedding journey is over now.

HEDDA [*shaking her head*] Not by a long – long way. I have only
arrived at a station on the line.

BRACK Well, then the passengers jump out and move about a little,
Mrs Hedda.

HEDDA I never jump out.

BRACK Really?

HEDDA No – because there is always someone standing by to –

BRACK [*laughing*] To look at your ankles, do you mean?

HEDDA Precisely.

BRACK Well but, dear me –

HEDDA [*with a gesture of repulsion*] I won't have it. I would rather
keep my seat where I happen to be – and continue the *tête-
à-tête*.

BRACK But suppose a third person were to jump in and join the
couple.

HEDDA Ah – that is quite another matter!

BRACK A trusted, sympathetic friend –

HEDDA – with a fund of conversation on all sorts of lively topics –

BRACK – and not the least bit of a specialist!

HEDDA [*with an audible sigh*] Yes, that would be a relief indeed.

BRACK [*hears the front door open, and glances in that direction*] The
triangle is completed.

HEDDA [*half aloud*] And on goes the train.

GEORGE TESMAN, *in a grey walking-suit, with a soft felt hat, enters
from the hall. He has a number of unbound books under his arm and
in his pockets.*

TESMAN [*goes up to the table beside the corner settee*] Ouf – what a load
for a warm day – all these books. [*lays them on the table*] I'm
positively perspiring, Hedda. Hallo – are you there already, my
dear Judge? Eh? Berta didn't tell me.

BRACK [*rising*] I came in through the garden.

HEDDA What books have you got there?

TESMAN [*stands looking them through*] Some new books on my
special subjects – quite indispensable to me.

HEDDA Your special subjects?

BRACK Yes, books on his special subjects, Mrs Tesman.

[*Brack and Hedda exchange a confidential smile*]

HEDDA Do you need still more books on your special subjects?

TESMAN Yes, my dear Hedda, one can never have too many of them. Of course one must keep up with all that is written and published.

HEDDA Yes, I suppose one must.

TESMAN [*searching among his books*] And look here – I have got hold of Eilert Lövborg's new book too. [*offering it to her*] Perhaps you would like to glance through it, Hedda? Eh?

HEDDA No, thank you. Or rather – afterwards perhaps.

TESMAN I looked into it a little on the way home.

BRACK Well, what do you think of it – as a specialist?

TESMAN I think it shows quite remarkable soundness of judgment. He never wrote like that before. [*putting the books together*] Now I shall take all these into my study. I'm longing to cut the leaves – ! And then I must change my clothes. [*to Brack*] I suppose we needn't start just yet? Eh?

BRACK Oh, dear no – there is not the slightest hurry.

TESMAN Well then, I will take my time. [*is going with his books, but stops in the doorway and turns*] By-the-bye, Hedda – Aunt Julia is not coming this evening.

HEDDA Not coming? Is it that affair of the bonnet that keeps her away?

TESMAN Oh, not at all. How could you think such a thing of Aunt Julia? Just fancy – ! The fact is, Aunt Rina is very ill.

HEDDA She always is.

TESMAN Yes, but today she is much worse than usual, poor dear.

HEDDA Oh, then it's only natural that her sister should remain with her. I must bear my disappointment.

TESMAN And you can't imagine, dear, how delighted Aunt Julia seemed to be – because you had come home looking so flourishing!

HEDDA [*half aloud, rising*] Oh, those everlasting Aunts!

TESMAN What?

HEDDA [*going to the glass door*] Nothing.

TESMAN Oh, all right.   [*he goes through the inner room, out to the right*

BRACK What bonnet were you talking about?

HEDDA Oh, it was a little episode with Miss Tesman this morning. She had laid down her bonnet on the chair there − [*looks at him and smiles*] − and I pretended to think it was the servant's.

BRACK [*shaking his head*] Now my dear Mrs Hedda, how could you do such a thing? To the excellent old lady, too!

HEDDA [*nervously crossing the room*] Well, you see − these impulses come over me all of a sudden; and I cannot resist them. [*throws herself down in the easy-chair by the stove*] Oh, I don't know how to explain it.

BRACK [*behind the easy-chair*] You are not really happy − that is at the bottom of it.

HEDDA [*looking straight before her*] I know of no reason why I should be − happy. Perhaps you can give me one?

BRACK Well − amongst other things, because you have got exactly the home you had set your heart on.

HEDDA [*looks up at him and laughs*] Do you too believe in that legend?

BRACK Is there nothing in it, then?

HEDDA Oh yes, there is something in it.

BRACK Well?

HEDDA There is this in it, that I made use of Tesman to see me home from evening parties last summer −

BRACK I, unfortunately, had to go quite a different way.

HEDDA That's true. I know you were going a different way last summer.

BRACK [*laughing*] Oh fie, Mrs Hedda! Well, then − you and Tesman − ?

HEDDA Well, we happened to pass here one evening; Tesman, poor fellow, was writhing in the agony of having to find conversation; so I took pity on the learned man −

BRACK [*smiles doubtfully*] You took pity? H'm −

HEDDA Yes, I really did. And so − to help him out of his torment − I happened to say, in pure thoughtlessness, that I should like to live in this villa.

BRACK No more than that?

HEDDA Not that evening.

BRACK But afterwards?

HEDDA Yes, my thoughtlessness had consequences, my dear Judge.

BRACK Unfortunately that too often happens, Mrs Hedda.

HEDDA Thanks! So you see it was this enthusiasm for Secretary Falk's villa that first constituted a bond of sympathy between George Tesman and me. From that came our engagement and our marriage, and our wedding journey, and all the rest of it. Well, well, my dear Judge – as you make your bed so you must lie, I could almost say.

BRACK This is exquisite! And you really cared not a rap about it all the time?

HEDDA No, heaven knows I didn't.

BRACK But now? Now that we have made it so homelike for you?

HEDDA Uh – the rooms all seem to smell of lavender and dried rose-leaves. – But perhaps it's Aunt Julia that has brought that scent with her.

BRACK [*laughing*] No, I think it must be a legacy from the late Mrs Secretary Falk.

HEDDA Yes, there is an odour of mortality about it. It reminds me of a bouquet – the day after the ball. [*clasps her hands behind her head, leans back in her chair and looks at him*] Oh, my dear Judge – you cannot imagine how horribly I shall bore myself here.

BRACK Why should not you, too, find some sort of vocation in life Mrs Hedda?

HEDDA A vocation – that should attract me?

BRACK If possible, of course.

HEDDA Heaven knows what sort of a vocation that could be. I often wonder whether – [*breaking off*] But that would never do either.

BRACK Who can tell? Let me hear what it is.

HEDDA Whether I might not get Tesman to go into politics, I mean.

BRACK [*laughing*] Tesman? No really now, political life is not the thing for him – not at all in his line.

HEDDA No, I dare say not. – But if I could get him into it all the same?

BRACK Why – what satisfaction could you find in that? If he is not fitted for that sort of thing, why should you want to drive him into it?

HEDDA Because I am bored, I tell you! [*after a pause*] So you think it quite out of the question that Tesman should ever get into the ministry?

BRACK H'm – you see, my dear Mrs Hedda – to get into the ministry, he would have to be a tolerably rich man.

HEDDA [*rising impatiently*] Yes, there we have it! It is this genteel poverty I have managed to drop into – ! [*crosses the room*] That is what makes life so pitiable! So utterly ludicrous! – For that's what it is.

BRACK Now *I* should say the fault lay elsewhere.

HEDDA Where, then?

BRACK You have never gone through any really stimulating experience.

HEDDA Anything serious, you mean?

BRACK Yes, you may call it so. But now you may perhaps have one in store.

HEDDA [*tossing her head*] Oh, you're thinking of the annoyances about this wretched professorship! But that must be Tesman's own affair. I assure you I shall not waste a thought upon it.

BRACK No, no, I dare say not. But suppose now that what people call – in elegant language – a solemn responsibility were to come upon you? [*smiling*] A new responsibility, Mrs Hedda?

HEDDA [*angrily*] Be quiet! Nothing of that sort will ever happen!

BRACK [*warily*] We will speak of this again a year hence – at the very outside.

HEDDA [*curtly*] I have no turn for anything of the sort, Judge Brack. No responsibilities for me!

BRACK Are you so unlike the generality of women as to have no turn for duties which – ?

HEDDA [*beside the glass door*] Oh, be quiet, I tell you! – I often think there is only one thing in the world I have any turn for.

BRACK [*drawing near to her*] And what is that, if I may ask?

HEDDA [*stands looking out*] Boring myself to death. Now you know it. [*turns, looks towards the inner room, and laughs*] Yes, as I thought! Here comes the Professor.

BRACK [*softly, in a tone of warning*] Come, come, come, Mrs Hedda!

GEORGE TESMAN, *dressed for the party, with his gloves and hat in his hand, enters from the right through the inner room.*

TESMAN Hedda, has no message come from Eilert Lövborg? Eh?

HEDDA No.

TESMAN Then you'll see he'll be here presently.

BRACK Do you really think he will come?

TESMAN Yes, I am almost sure of it. For what you were telling us this morning must have been a mere floating rumour.

BRACK You think so?

TESMAN At any rate, Aunt Julia said she did not believe for a moment that he would ever stand in my way again. Fancy that!

BRACK Well then, that's all right.

TESMAN [*placing his hat and gloves on a chair on the right*] Yes, but you must really let me wait for him as long as possible.

BRACK We have plenty of time yet. None of my guests will arrive before seven or half-past.

TESMAN Then meanwhile we can keep Hedda company, and see what happens. Eh?

HEDDA [*placing Brack's hat and overcoat upon the corner settee*] And at the worst Mr Lövborg can remain here with me.

BRACK [*offering to take his things*] Oh, allow me, Mrs Tesman! – What do you mean by 'at the worst'?

HEDDA If he won't go with you and Tesman.

TESMAN [*looks dubiously at her*] But, Hedda dear – do you think it would quite do for him to remain here with you? Eh? Remember, Aunt Julia can't come.

HEDDA No, but Mrs Elvsted is coming. We three can have a cup of tea together.

TESMAN Oh yes, that will be all right.

BRACK [*smiling*] And that would perhaps be the safest plan for him

HEDDA Why so?

BRACK Well, you know, Mrs Tesman, how you used to gird at my little bachelor parties. You declared they were adapted only for men of the strictest principles.

HEDDA But no doubt Mr Lövborg's principles are strict enough now. A converted sinner –

BERTA *appears at the hall door.*

BERTA There's a gentleman asking if you are at home, ma'am –

HEDDA Well, show him in.

TESMAN [*softly*] I'm sure it is he! Fancy that!

EILERT LÖVBORG *enters from the hall. He is slim and lean; of the same age as* TESMAN, *but looks older and somewhat worn-out. His hair and beard are of a blackish brown, his face long and pale, but with patches of colour on the cheeks. He is dressed in a well-cut black visiting suit, quite new. He has dark gloves and a silk hat. He stops near the door, and makes a rapid bow, seeming somewhat embarrassed.*

TESMAN [*goes up to him and shakes him warmly by the hand*] Well, my dear Eilert – so at last we meet again!

EILERT LÖVBORG [*speaks in a subdued voice*] Thanks for your letter, Tesman. [*approaching Hedda*] Will you too shake hands with me, Mrs Tesman?

HEDDA [*taking his hand*] I am glad to see you, Mr Lövborg. [*with a motion of her hand*] I don't know whether you two gentlemen – ?

LÖVBORG [*bowing slightly*] Judge Brack, I think.

BRACK [*doing likewise*] Oh yes – in the old days –

TESMAN [*to Lövborg, with his hands on his shoulders*] And now you must make yourself entirely at home, Eilert! Mustn't he, Hedda? – For I hear you are going to settle in town again? Eh?

LÖVBORG Yes, I am.

TESMAN Quite right, quite right. Let me tell you, I have got hold of your new book; but I haven't had time to read it yet.

LÖVBORG You may spare yourself the trouble.

TESMAN Why so?

LÖVBORG Because there is very little in it.

TESMAN Just fancy – how can you say so?

BRACK But it has been very much praised, I hear.

LÖVBORG That was what I wanted; so I put nothing into the book but what everyone would agree with.

BRACK Very wise of you.

TESMAN Well but, my dear Eilert – !

LÖVBORG For now I mean to win myself a position again – to make a fresh start.

TESMAN [*a little embarrassed*] Ah, that is what you wish to do? Eh?

LÖVBORG [*smiling, lays down his hat, and draws a packet wrapped in paper, from his coat pocket*] But when this one appears, George Tesman, you will have to read it. For this is the real book – the book I have put my true self into.

TESMAN Indeed? And what is it?

LÖVBORG It is the continuation.

TESMAN The continuation? Of what?

LÖVBORG Of the book.

TESMAN Of the new book?

LÖVBORG Of course.

TESMAN Why, my dear Eilert – does it not come down to our own days?

LÖVBORG Yes, it does; and this one deals with the future.

TESMAN With the future! But, good heavens, we know nothing of the future!

LÖVBORG No; but there is a thing or two to be said about it all the same. [*opens the packet*] Look here –

TESMAN Why, that's not your handwriting.

LÖVBORG I dictated it. [*turning over the pages*] It falls into two sections. The first deals with the civilising forces of the future. And here is the second – [*running through the pages towards the end*] – forecasting the probable line of development.

TESMAN How odd now! I should never have thought of writing anything of that sort.

HEDDA [*at the glass door, drumming on the pane*] H'm – I dare say not.

LÖVBORG [*replacing the manuscript in its paper and laying the packet on the table*] I brought it, thinking I might read you a little of it this evening.

TESMAN That was very good of you, Eilert. But this evening – [*looking back at Brack*] I don't see how we can manage it –

LÖVBORG Well then, some other time. There is no hurry.

BRACK I must tell you, Mr Lövborg – there is a little gathering at my house this evening – mainly in honour of Tesman, you know –

LÖVBORG [*looking for his hat*] Oh – then I won't detain you –

BRACK No, but listen – will you not do me the favour of joining us?

LÖVBORG [*curtly and decidedly*] No, I can't – thank you very much.

BRACK Oh, nonsense – do! We shall be quite a select little circle. And I assure you we shall have a 'lively time', as Mrs Hed – as Mrs Tesman says.

LÖVBORG I have no doubt of it. But nevertheless –

BRACK And then you might bring your manuscript with you, and read it to Tesman at my house. I could give you a room to yourselves.

TESMAN Yes, think of that, Eilert – why shouldn't you? Eh?

HEDDA [*interposing*] But, Tesman, if Mr Lövborg would really rather not! I am sure Mr Lövborg is much more inclined to remain here and have supper with me.

LÖVBORG [*looking at her*] With you, Mrs Tesman?

HEDDA And with Mrs Elvsted.

LÖVBORG Ah – [*lightly*] I saw her for a moment this morning.

HEDDA Did you? Well, she is coming this evening. So you see you are almost bound to remain, Mr Lövborg, or she will have no one to see her home.

LÖVBORG That's true. Many thanks, Mrs Tesman – in that case I will remain.

HEDDA Then I have one or two orders to give the servant –

She goes to the hall door and rings. BERTA *enters. Hedda talks to her in a whisper, and points towards the inner room. Berta nods and goes out again.*

TESMAN [*at the same time, to Lövborg*] Tell me, Eilert – is it this new subject – the future – that you are going to lecture about?

LÖVBORG Yes.

TESMAN They told me at the bookseller's that you are going to deliver a course of lectures this autumn.

LÖVBORG That is my intention. I hope you won't take it ill, Tesman.

TESMAN Oh no, not in the least! But – ?

LÖVBORG I can quite understand that it must be very disagreeable to you.

TESMAN [*cast down*] Oh, I can't expect you, out of consideration for me, to –

LÖVBORG But I shall wait till you have received your appointment.

TESMAN Will you wait? Yes but – yes but – are you not going to compete with me? Eh?

LÖVBORG No; it is only the moral victory I care for.

TESMAN Why, bless me – then Aunt Julia was right after all! Oh yes – I knew it! Hedda! Just fancy – Eilert Lövborg is not going to stand in our way!

HEDDA [*curtly*] Our way? Pray leave me out of the question.

[*She goes up towards the inner room, where Berta is placing a tray with decanters and glasses on the table. Hedda nods approval, and comes forward again. Berta goes out.*]

TESMAN [*at the same time*] And you, Judge Brack – what do you say to this? Eh?

BRACK Well, I say that a moral victory – h'm – may be all very fine –

TESMAN Yes, certainly. But all the same –

HEDDA [*looking at Tesman with a cold smile*] You stand there looking as if you were thunderstruck –

TESMAN Yes – so I am – I almost think –

BRACK Don't you see, Mrs Tesman, a thunderstorm has just passed over?

HEDDA [*pointing towards the room*] Will you not take a glass of cold punch, gentlemen?

BRACK [*looking at his watch*] A stirrup-cup? Yes, it wouldn't come amiss.

TESMAN A capital idea, Hedda! Just the thing! Now that the weight has been taken off my mind –

HEDDA Will you not join them, Mr Lövborg?

LÖVBORG [*with a gesture of refusal*] No, thank you. Nothing for me.

BRACK Why bless me – cold punch is surely not poison.

LÖVBORG Perhaps not for everyone.

HEDDA I will keep Mr Lövborg company in the meantime.

TESMAN Yes, yes, Hedda dear, do.

[*He and Brack go into the inner room, seat themselves, drink punch, smoke cigarettes, and carry on a lively conversation during what follows. Eilert Lövborg remains standing beside the stove. Hedda goes to the writing-table.*]

HEDDA [*raising her voice a little*] Do you care to look at some photographs, Mr Lövborg? You know Tesman and I made a tour in the Tyrol on our way home?

[*She takes up an album, and places it on the table beside the sofa, in the further corner of which she seats herself. Eilert Lövborg approaches, stops, and looks at her. Then he takes a chair and seats himself to her left.*]

HEDDA [*opening the album*] Do you see this range of mountains, Mr Lövborg? It's the Ortler group. Tesman has written the name underneath. Here it is: 'The Ortler group near Meran'.

LÖVBORG [*who has never taken his eyes off her, says softly and slowly*]
Hedda – Gabler!

HEDDA [*glancing hastily at him*] Ah! Hush!

LÖVBORG [*repeats softly*] Hedda Gabler!

HEDDA [*looking at the album*] That was my name in the old days –
when we two knew each other.

LÖVBORG And I must teach myself never to say Hedda Gabler
again – never, as long as I live.

HEDDA [*still turning over the pages*] Yes, you must. And I think you
ought to practise in time. The sooner the better, I should say.

LÖVBORG [*in a tone of indignation*] Hedda Gabler married? And
married to – George Tesman!

HEDDA Yes – so the world goes.

LÖVBORG Oh, Hedda, Hedda – how could you* throw yourself
away!

HEDDA [*looks sharply at him*] What? I can't allow this!

LÖVBORG What do you mean?

TESMAN *comes into the room and goes towards the sofa.*

HEDDA [*hears him coming and says in an indifferent tone*] And this is a
view from the Val d'Ampezzo, Mr Lövborg. Just look at these
peaks! [*looks affectionately up at Tesman*] What's the name of these
curious peaks, dear?

TESMAN Let me see. Oh, those are the Dolomites.

HEDDA Yes, that's it! – Those are the Dolomites, Mr Lövborg.

TESMAN Hedda, dear – I only wanted to ask whether I shouldn't
bring you a little punch after all? For yourself at any rate – eh?

HEDDA Yes, do, please; and perhaps a few biscuits.

TESMAN No cigarettes?

HEDDA No.

TESMAN Very well.

[*He goes into the inner room and out to the right. Brack sits in the inner
room, and keeps an eye from time to time on Hedda and Lövborg.*]

LÖVBORG [*softly, as before*] Answer me, Hedda – how could you go
and do this?

HEDDA [*apparently absorbed in the album*] If you continue to say *du* to
me I won't talk to you.

LÖVBORG May I not say *du* even when we are alone?

* He uses the familiar *Du*.

HEDDA No. You may think it; but you mustn't say it.

LÖVBORG Ah, I understand. It is an offence against George Tesman, whom you – love.

HEDDA [*glances at him and smiles*] Love? What an idea!

LÖVBORG You don't love him then!

HEDDA But I won't hear of any sort of unfaithfulness! Remember that.

LÖVBORG Hedda – answer me one thing –

HEDDA Hush!

TESMAN *enters with a small tray from the inner room.*

TESMAN Here you are! Isn't this tempting? [*he puts the tray on the table*]

HEDDA Why do you bring it yourself?*

TESMAN [*filling the glasses*] Because I think it's such fun to wait upon you, Hedda.

HEDDA But you have poured out two glasses. Mr Lövborg said he wouldn't have any –

TESMAN No, but Mrs Elvsted will soon be here, won't she?

HEDDA Yes; by-the-bye – Mrs Elvsted –

TESMAN Had you forgotten her? Eh?

HEDDA We were so absorbed in these photographs. [*shows him a picture*] Do you remember this little village?

TESMAN Oh, it's that one just below the Brenner Pass. It was there we passed the night –

HEDDA – and met that lively party of tourists.

TESMAN Yes, that was the place. Fancy – if we could only have had you with us, Eilert! Eh?

[*He returns to the inner room and sits beside Brack.*]

LÖVBORG Answer me one thing, Hedda –

HEDDA Well?

LÖVBORG Was there no love in your friendship for me either? Not a spark – not a tinge of love in it?

HEDDA I wonder if there was? To me it seems as though we were two good comrades – two thoroughly intimate friends. [*smilingly*] You especially were frankness itself.

LÖVBORG It was you that made me so.

HEDDA As I look back upon it all, I think there was really something beautiful, something fascinating – something daring –

* From this point onward Lövborg uses the formal *De.*

in – in that secret intimacy – that comradeship which no living creature so much as dreamed of.

LÖVBORG Yes, yes, Hedda! Was there not? – When I used to come to your father's in the afternoon – and the General sat over at the window reading his papers – with his back towards us –

HEDDA And we two on the corner sofa –

LÖVBORG Always with the same illustrated paper before us –

HEDDA For want of an album, yes.

LÖVBORG Yes, Hedda, and when I made my confessions to you – told you about myself, things that at that time no one else knew! There I would sit and tell you of my escapades – my days and nights of devilment. Oh, Hedda – what was the power in you that forced me to confess these things?

HEDDA Do you think it was any power in me?

LÖVBORG How else can I explain it? And all those – those round-about questions you used to put to me –

HEDDA Which you understood so particularly well –

LÖVBORG How could you sit and question me like that? Question me quite frankly –

HEDDA In roundabout terms, please observe.

LÖVBORG Yes, but frankly nevertheless. Cross-question me about – all that sort of thing?

HEDDA And how could you answer, Mr Lövborg?

LÖVBORG Yes, that is just what I can't understand – in looking back upon it. But tell me now, Hedda – was there not love at the bottom of our friendship? On your side, did you not feel as though you might purge my stains away – if I made you my confessor? Was it not so?

HEDDA No, not quite.

LÖVBORG What was your motive, then?

HEDDA Do think it quite incomprehensible that a young girl – when it can be done – without anyone knowing –

LÖVBORG Well?

HEDDA – should be glad to have a peep, now and then, into a world which – ?

LÖVBORG Which – ?

HEDDA – which she is forbidden to know anything about?

LÖVBORG So that was it?

HEDDA Partly. Partly – I almost think.

LÖVBORG Comradeship in the thirst for life. But why should not that, at any rate, have continued?

HEDDA The fault was yours.

LÖVBORG It was you that broke with me.

HEDDA Yes, when our friendship threatened to develop into something more serious. Shame upon you, Eilert Lövborg! How could you think of wronging your – your frank comrade.

LÖVBORG [*clenches his hands*] Oh, why did you not carry out your threat? Why did you not shoot me down?

HEDDA Because I have such a dread of scandal.

LÖVBORG Yes, Hedda, you are a coward at heart.

HEDDA A terrible coward. [*changing her tone*] But it was a lucky thing for you. And now you have found ample consolation at the Elvsteds'.

LÖVBORG I know what Thea has confided to you.

HEDDA And perhaps you have confided to her something about us?

LÖVBORG Not a word. She is too stupid to understand anything of that sort.

HEDDA Stupid?

LÖVBORG She is stupid about matters of that sort.

HEDDA And I am cowardly. [*bends over towards him, without looking him in the face, and says more softly*] But now I will confide something to you.

LÖVBORG [*eagerly*] Well?

HEDDA The fact that I dared not shoot you down –

LÖVBORG Yes!

HEDDA – that was not my arrant cowardice – that evening.

LÖVBORG [*looks at her a moment, understands, and whispers passionately*] Oh, Hedda! Hedda Gabler! Now I begin to see a hidden reason beneath our comradeship! You* and I – ! After all, then, it was your craving for life –

HEDDA [*softly, with a sharp glance*] Take care! Believe nothing of the sort!

[*Twilight has begun to fall. The hall door is opened from without by Berta*]

HEDDA [*closes the album with a bang and calls smilingly*] Ah, at last! My darling Thea – come along!

* In this speech he once more says *Du*. Hedda addresses him throughout as *De*.

MRS ELVSTED *enters from the hall. She is in evening dress.
The door is closed behind her.*

HEDDA [*on the sofa, stretches out her arms towards her*] My sweet Thea –
you can't think how I have been longing for you!
[*Mrs Elvsted, in passing, exchanges slight salutations with the gentlemen in the inner room, then goes up to the table and gives Hedda her
hand. Eilert Lövborg has risen. He and Mrs Elvsted greet each other
with a silent nod.*]

MRS ELVSTED Ought I to go in and talk to your husband for a
moment?

HEDDA Oh, not at all. Leave those two alone. They will soon be
going.

MRS ELVSTED Are they going out?

HEDDA Yes, to a supper-party.

MRS ELVSTED [*quickly, to Lövborg*] Not you?

LÖVBORG No.

HEDDA Mr Lövborg remains with us.

MRS ELVSTED [*takes a chair and is about to seat herself at his side*] Oh,
how nice it is here!

HEDDA No, thank you, my little Thea! Not there! You'll be good
enough to come over here to me. I will sit between you.

MRS ELVSTED Yes, just as you please.
[*She goes round the table and seats herself on the sofa on Hedda's right.
Lövborg re-seats himself on his chair.*]

LÖVBORG [*after a short pause, to Hedda*] Is not she lovely to look
at?

HEDDA [*lightly stroking her hair*] Only to look at!

LÖVBORG Yes. For we two – she and I – we are two real comrades.
We have absolute faith in each other; so we can sit and talk with
perfect frankness –

HEDDA Not round about, Mr Lövborg?

LÖVBORG Well –

MRS ELVSTED [*softly clinging close to Hedda*] Oh, how happy I am,
Hedda! For only think, he says I have inspired him too.

HEDDA [*looks at her with a smile*] Ah! Does he say that, dear?

LÖVBORG And then she is so brave, Mrs Tesman!

MRS ELVSTED Good heavens – am I brave?

LÖVBORG Exceedingly – where your comrade is concerned.

HEDDA Ah, yes – courage! If one only had that!

LÖVBORG What then? What do you mean?

HEDDA Then life would perhaps be liveable, after all. [*with a sudden change of tone*] But now, my dearest Thea, you really must have a glass of cold punch.

MRS ELVSTED No, thanks – I never take anything of that kind.

HEDDA Well then, you, Mr Lövborg.

LÖVBORG Nor I, thank you.

MRS ELVSTED No, he doesn't either.

HEDDA [*looks fixedly at him*] But if I say you shall?

LÖVBORG It would be of no use.

HEDDA [*laughing*] Then I, poor creature, have no sort of power over you?

LÖVBORG Not in that respect.

HEDDA But seriously, I think you ought to – for your own sake.

MRS ELVSTED Why, Hedda – !

LÖVBORG How so?

HEDDA Or rather on account of other people.

LÖVBORG Indeed?

HEDDA Otherwise people might be apt to suspect that – in your heart of hearts – you did not feel quite secure – quite confident in yourself.

MRS ELVSTED [*softly*] Oh please, Hedda – !

LÖVBORG People may suspect what they like – for the present.

MRS ELVSTED [*joyfully*] Yes, let them!

HEDDA I saw it plainly in Judge Brack's face a moment ago.

LÖVBORG What did you see?

HEDDA His contemptuous smile, when you dared not go with them into the inner room.

LÖVBORG Dared not? Of course I preferred to stop here and talk to you.

MRS ELVSTED What could be more natural, Hedda?

HEDDA But the Judge could not guess that. And I say, too, the way he smiled and glanced at Tesman when you dared not accept his invitation to this wretched little supper-party of his.

LÖVBORG Dared not! Do you say I dared not?

HEDDA I don't say so. But that was how Judge Brack understood it.

LÖVBORG Well, let him.

HEDDA Then you are not going with them?

LÖVBORG I will stay here with you and Thea.

MRS ELVSTED Yes, Hedda – how can you doubt that?

HEDDA [*smiles and nods approvingly to Lövborg*] Firm as a rock!
   Faithful to your principles, now and for ever! Ah, that is how a
   man should be! [*turns to Mrs Elvsted and caresses her*] Well now,
   what did I tell you, when you came to us this morning in such
   a state of distraction –

LÖVBORG [*surprised*] Distraction!

MRS ELVSTED [*terrified*] Hedda – oh Hedda – !

HEDDA You can see for yourself! You haven't the slightest reason
   to be in such mortal terror – [*interrupting herself*] There! Now we
   can all three enjoy ourselves!

LÖVBORG [*who has given a start*] Ah – what is all this, Mrs Tesman?

MRS ELVSTED Oh my God, Hedda! What are you saying? What are
   you doing?

HEDDA Don't get excited! That horrid Judge Brack is sitting
   watching you.

LÖVBORG So she was in mortal terror! On my account!

MRS ELVSTED [*softly and piteously*] Oh, Hedda – now you have
   ruined everything!

LÖVBORG [*looks fixedly at her for a moment. His face is distorted*] So that
   was my comrade's frank confidence in me?

MRS ELVSTED [*imploringly*] Oh, my dearest friend – only let me tell
   you –

LÖVBORG [*takes one of the glasses of punch, raises it to his lips, and says
   in a low, husky voice*] Your health, Thea! [*he empties the glass, puts
   it down, and takes the second*]

MRS ELVSTED [*softly*] Oh, Hedda, Hedda – how could you do this?

HEDDA I do it? I? Are you crazy?

LÖVBORG Here's to your health too, Mrs Tesman. Thanks for the
   truth. Hurrah for the truth! [*he empties the glass and is about to re-
   fill it.*]

HEDDA [*lays her hand on his arm*] Come, come – no more for the
   present. Remember you are going out to supper.

MRS ELVSTED No, no, no!

HEDDA Hush! They are sitting watching you.

LÖVBORG [*putting down the glass*] Now, Thea – tell me the truth –

MRS ELVSTED Yes.

LÖVBORG Did your husband know that you had come after me?

MRS ELVSTED [*wringing her hands*] Oh, Hedda – do you hear what he is asking?

LÖVBORG Was it arranged between you and him that you were to come to town and look after me? Perhaps it was the Sheriff himself that urged you to come? Aha, my dear – no doubt he wanted my help in his office! Or was it at the card-table that he missed me?

MRS ELVSTED [*softly, in agony*] Oh, Lövborg, Lövborg – !

LÖVBORG [*seizes a glass and is on the point of filling it*] Here's a glass for the old Sheriff too!

HEDDA [*preventing him*] No more just now. Remember, you have to read your manuscript to Tesman.

LÖVBORG [*calmly, putting down the glass*] It was stupid of me all this. Thea – to take it in this way, I mean. Don't be angry with me, my dear, dear comrade. You shall see – both you and the others – that if I was fallen once – now I have risen again! Thanks to you, Thea.

MRS ELVSTED [*radiant with joy*] Oh, heaven be praised – !

BRACK *has in the meantime looked at his watch. He and* TESMAN *rise and come into the drawing-room.*

BRACK [*takes his hat and overcoat*] Well, Mrs Tesman, our time has come.

HEDDA I suppose it has.

LÖVBORG [*rising*] Mine too, Judge Brack.

MRS ELVSTED [*softly and imploringly*] Oh, Lövborg, don't do it!

HEDDA [*pinching her arm*] They can hear you!

MRS ELVSTED [*with a suppressed shriek*] Ow!

LÖVBORG [*to Brack*] You were good enough to invite me.

Judge Brack. Well, are you coming after all?

LÖVBORG Yes, many thanks.

BRACK I'm delighted –

LÖVBORG [*to Tesman, putting the parcel of MS. in his pocket*] I should like to show you one or two things before I send it to the printers.

TESMAN Fancy – that will be delightful. But, Hedda dear, how is Mrs Elvsted to get home? Eh?

HEDDA Oh, that can be managed somehow.

LÖVBORG [*looking towards the ladies*] Mrs Elvsted? Of course, I'll come again and fetch her. [*approaching*] At ten or thereabouts, Mrs Tesman? Will that do?

HEDDA Certainly. That will do capitally.

TESMAN Well, then, that's all right. But you must not expect me so early, Hedda.

HEDDA Oh, you may stop as long – as long as ever you please.

MRS ELVSTED [*trying to conceal her anxiety*] Well then, Mr Lövborg – I shall remain here until you come.

LÖVBORG [*with his hat in his hand*] Pray do, Mrs Elvsted.

BRACK And now off goes the excursion train, gentlemen! I hope we shall have a lively time, as a certain fair lady puts it.

HEDDA Ah, if only the fair lady could be present unseen – !

BRACK Why unseen?

HEDDA In order to hear a little of your liveliness at first hand, Judge Brack.

BRACK [*laughing*] I should not advise the fair lady to try it.

TESMAN [*also laughing*] Come, you're a nice one, Hedda! Fancy that!

BRACK Well, goodbye, goodbye, ladies.

LÖVBORG [*bowing*] About ten o'clock, then,

> [*Brack, Lövborg, and Tesman go out by the hall door.*]

At the same time, BERTA *enters from the inner room with a lighted lamp, which she places on the drawing-room table; she goes out by the way she came.*

MRS ELVSTED [*who has risen and is wandering restlessly about the room*] Hedda – Hedda – what will come of all this?

HEDDA At ten o'clock – he will be here. I can see him already – with vine-leaves in his hair – flushed and fearless –

MRS ELVSTED Oh, I hope he may.

HEDDA And then, you see – then he will have regained control over himself. Then he will be a free man for all his days.

MRS ELVSTED Oh God! – if he would only come as you see him now!

HEDDA He will come as I see him – so, and not otherwise! [*rises and approaches* THEA] You may doubt him as long as you please; *I* believe in him. And now we will try –

MRS ELVSTED You have some hidden motive in this, Hedda!

HEDDA Yes, I have. I want for once in my life to have power to mould a human destiny.

MRS ELVSTED Have you not the power?

HEDDA I have not – and have never had it.

MRS ELVSTED Not your husband's?

HEDDA Do you think that is worth the trouble? Oh, if you could only understand how poor I am. And fate has made you so rich! [*clasps her passionately in her arms*] I think I must burn your hair off after all.

MRS ELVSTED Let me go! Let me go! I am afraid of you, Hedda!

BERTA [*in the middle doorway*] Tea is laid in the dining-room, ma'am.

HEDDA Very well. We are coming

MRS ELVSTED No, no, no! I would rather go home alone! At once!

HEDDA Nonsense! First you shall have a cup of tea, you little stupid. And then – at ten o'clock – Eilert Lövborg will be here – with vine-leaves in his hair.

> [*She drags Mrs Elvsted almost by force to the middle doorway*

ACT THIRD

The room at the Tesmans'. The curtains are drawn over the middle doorway, and also over the glass door. The lamp, half turned down, and with a shade over it, is burning on the table. In the stove, the door of which stands open, there has been a fire, which is now nearly burnt out.

MRS ELVSTED, *wrapped in a large shawl, and with her feet upon a footrest, sits close to the stove, sunk back in the armchair.* HEDDA, *fully dressed, lies sleeping upon the sofa, with a sofa-blanket over her.*

MRS ELVSTED [*after a pause, suddenly sits up in her chair, and listens eagerly. Then she sinks back again wearily, moaning to herself*] Not yet! – Oh God – oh God – not yet!

BERTA *slips cautiously in by the hall door. She has a letter in her hand.*

MRS ELVSTED [*turns and whispers eagerly*] Well – has anyone come?
BERTA [*softly*] Yes, a girl has just brought this letter.
MRS ELVSTED [*quickly, holding out her hand*] A letter! Give it to me!
BERTA No, it's for Dr Tesman, ma'am.
MRS ELVSTED Oh, indeed.
BERTA It was Miss Tesman's servant that brought it. I'll lay it here on the table.
MRS ELVSTED Yes, do.
BERTA [*laying down the letter*] I think I had better put out the lamp. It's smoking.
MRS ELVSTED Yes, put it out. It must soon be daylight now.
BERTA [*putting out the lamp*] It is daylight already, ma'am.
MRS ELVSTED Yes, broad day! And no one come back yet – !
BERTA Lord bless you, ma'am – I guessed how it would be.
MRS ELVSTED You guessed?
BERTA Yes, when I saw that a certain person had come back to town – and that he went off with them. For we've heard enough about that gentleman before now.

MRS ELVSTED Don't speak so loud. You will waken Mrs Tesman.

BERTA [*looks towards the sofa and sighs*] No, no – let her sleep, poor thing. Shan't I put some wood on the fire?

MRS ELVSTED Thanks, not for me.

BERTA Oh, very well.   [*she goes softly out by the hall door*]

HEDDA [*is wakened by the shutting of the door, and looks up*] What's that – ?

MRS ELVSTED It was only the servant.

HEDDA [*looking about her*] Oh, we're here – ! Yes, now I remember. [*sits erect upon the sofa, stretches herself, and rubs her eyes*] What o'clock is it, Thea?

MRS ELVSTED [*looks at her watch*] It's past seven.

HEDDA When did Tesman come home?

MRS ELVSTED He has not come.

HEDDA Not come home yet?

MRS ELVSTED [*rising*] No one has come.

HEDDA Think of our watching and waiting here till four in the morning –

MRS ELVSTED [*wringing her hands*] And how I watched and waited for him!

HEDDA [*yawns, and says with her hand before her mouth*] Well well – we might have spared ourselves the trouble.

MRS ELVSTED Did you get a little sleep?

HEDDA Oh yes; I believe I have slept pretty well. Have you not?

MRS ELVSTED Not for a moment. I couldn't, Hedda! – not to save my life.

HEDDA [*rises and goes towards her*] There there there! There's nothing to be so alarmed about. I understand quite well what has happened.

MRS ELVSTED Well, what do you think? Won't you tell me?

HEDDA Why, of course it has been a very late affair at Judge Brack's –

MRS ELVSTED Yes, yes – that is clear enough. But all the same –

HEDDA And then, you see, Tesman hasn't cared to come home and ring us up in the middle of the night. [*laughing*] Perhaps he wasn't inclined to show himself either – immediately after a jollification.

MRS ELVSTED But in that case – where can he have gone?

HEDDA Of course he has gone to his aunts' and slept there. They have his old room ready for him.

MRS ELVSTED No, he can't be with them, for a letter has just come for him from Miss Tesman. There it lies.

HEDDA Indeed? [*looks at the address*] Why yes, it's addressed in Aunt Julia's hand. Well then, he has remained at Judge Brack's. And as for Eilert Lövborg – he is sitting, with vine leaves in his hair, reading his manuscript.

MRS ELVSTED Oh, Hedda, you are just saying things you don't believe a bit.

HEDDA You really are a little blockhead, Thea.

MRS ELVSTED Oh yes, I suppose I am.

HEDDA And how mortally tired you look.

MRS ELVSTED Yes, I am mortally tired.

HEDDA Well then, you must do as I tell you. You must go into my room and lie down for a little while.

MRS ELVSTED Oh no, no – I shouldn't be able to sleep.

HEDDA I am sure you would.

MRS ELVSTED Well, but you husband is certain to come soon now; and then I want to know at once –

HEDDA I shall take care to let you know when he comes.

MRS ELVSTED Do you promise me, Hedda?

HEDDA Yes, rely upon me. Just you go in and have a sleep in the meantime.

MRS ELVSTED Thanks; then I'll try.   [*she goes off to the inner room*]

Hedda goes up to the glass door and draws back the curtains. The broad daylight streams into the room. Then she takes a little hand-glass from the writing-table, looks at herself in it, and arranges her hair. Next she goes to the hall door and presses the bell-button. BERTA *presently appears at the hall door.*

BERTA Did you want anything, ma'am?

HEDDA Yes; you must put some more wood in the stove. I am shivering.

BERTA Bless me – I'll make up the fire at once. [*she rakes the embers together and lays a piece of wood upon them; then stops and listens*] That was a ring at the front door, ma'am.

HEDDA Then go to the door. I will look after the fire.

BERTA It'll soon burn up.   [*she goes out by the hall door*]
[*Hedda kneels on the foot-rest and lays some more pieces of wood in the stove.*]

After a short pause, GEORGE TESMAN *enters from the hall. He steals on tiptoe towards the middle doorway and is about to slip through the curtains.*

HEDDA [*at the stove, without looking up*] Good morning.

TESMAN [*turns*] Hedda! [*approaching her*] Good heavens – are you up so early? Eh?

HEDDA Yes, I am up very early this morning.

TESMAN And I never doubted you were still sound asleep! Fancy that, Hedda!

HEDDA Don't speak so loud. Mrs Elvsted is resting in my room.

TESMAN Has Mrs Elvsted been here all night?

HEDDA Yes, since no one came to fetch her.

TESMAN Ah, to be sure.

HEDDA [*closes the door of the stove and rises*] Well, did you enjoy yourselves at Judge Brack's?

TESMAN Have you been anxious about me? Eh?

HEDDA No, I should never think of being anxious. But I asked if you had enjoyed yourself.

TESMAN Oh yes – for once in a way. Especially the beginning of the evening; for then Eilert read me part of his book. We arrived more than an hour too early – fancy that! And Brack had all sorts of arrangements to make – so Eilert read to me.

HEDDA [*seating herself by the table on the right*] Well? Tell me then –

TESMAN [*sitting on a footstool near the stove*] Oh, Hedda, you can't conceive what a book that is going to be! I believe it is one of the most remarkable things that have ever been written. Fancy that!

HEDDA Yes yes; I don't care about that –

TESMAN I must make a confession to you, Hedda. When he had finished reading – a horrid feeling came over me.

HEDDA A horrid feeling?

TESMAN I felt jealous of Eilert for having had it in him to write such a book. Only think, Hedda!

HEDDA Yes, yes, I am thinking!

TESMAN And then how pitiful to think that he – with all his gifts – should be irreclaimable, after all.

HEDDA I suppose you mean that he has more courage than the rest?

TESMAN No, not at all – I mean that he is incapable of taking his pleasure in moderation.

HEDDA And what came of it all – in the end?

TESMAN Well, to tell the truth, I think it might best be described as an orgy, Hedda.

HEDDA Had he vine-leaves in his hair?

TESMAN Vine-leaves? No, I saw nothing of the sort. But he made a long, rambling speech in honour of the woman who had inspired him in his work – that was the phrase he used.

HEDDA Did he name her?

TESMAN No, he didn't; but I can't help thinking he meant Mrs Elvsted. You may be sure he did.

HEDDA Well – where did you part from him?

TESMAN On the way to town. We broke up – the last of us at any rate – all together; and Brack came with us to get a breath of fresh air. And then, you see, we agreed to take Eilert home; for he had had far more than was good for him.

HEDDA I dare say.

TESMAN But now comes the strange part of it, Hedda; or, I should rather say, the melancholy part of it. I declare I am almost ashamed – on Eilert's account – to tell you –

HEDDA Oh, go on – !

TESMAN Well, as we were getting near town, you see, I happened to drop a little behind the others. Only for a minute or two – fancy that!

HEDDA Yes yes yes, but – ?

TESMAN And then, as I hurried after them – what do you think I found by the wayside? Eh?

HEDDA Oh, how should I know!

TESMAN You mustn't speak of it to a soul, Hedda! Do you hear! Promise me, for Eilert's sake. [draws a parcel, wrapped in paper, from his coat pocket] Fancy, dear – I found this.

HEDDA Is not that the parcel he had with him yesterday?

TESMAN Yes, it is the whole of his precious, irreplaceable manuscript! And he had gone and lost it, and knew nothing about it. Only fancy, Hedda! So deplorably –

HEDDA But why did you not give him back the parcel at once?

TESMAN I didn't dare to – in the state he was then in –

HEDDA Did you not tell any of the others that you had found it?

TESMAN Oh, far from it! You can surely understand that, for Eilert's sake, I wouldn't do that.

HEDDA So no one knows that Eilert Lövborg's manuscript is in your possession?

TESMAN No. And no one must know it.

HEDDA Then what did you say to him afterwards?

TESMAN I didn't talk to him again at all; for when we got in among the streets, he and two or three of the others gave us the slip and disappeared. Fancy that!

HEDDA Indeed! They must have taken him home then.

TESMAN Yes, so it would appear. And Brack, too, left us.

HEDDA And what have you been doing with yourself since?

TESMAN Well, I and some of the others went home with one of the party, a jolly fellow, and took our morning coffee with him; or perhaps I should rather call it our night coffee – eh? But now, when I have rested a little, and given Eilert, poor fellow, time to have his sleep out, I must take this back to him.

HEDDA [holds out her hand for the packet] No – don't give it to him! Not in such a hurry, I mean. Let me read it first.

TESMAN No, my dearest Hedda, I mustn't, I really mustn't.

HEDDA You must not?

TESMAN No – for you can imagine what a state of despair he will be in when he wakens and misses the manuscript. He has no copy of it, you must know! He told me so.

HEDDA [looking searchingly at him] Can such a thing not be reproduced? Written over again?

TESMAN No, I don't think that would be possible. For the inspiration, you see –

HEDDA Yes, yes – I suppose it depends on that – [lightly] But, by-the-bye – here is a letter for you.

TESMAN Fancy – !

HEDDA [handing it to him] It came early this morning.

TESMAN It's from Aunt Julia! What can it be? [he lays the packet on the other footstool, opens the letter, runs his eye through it, and jumps up] Oh, Hedda – she says that poor Aunt Rina is dying!

HEDDA Well, we were prepared for that.

TESMAN And that if I want to see her again, I must make haste. I'll run in to them at once.

HEDDA [suppressing a smile] Will you run?

TESMAN Oh, my dearest Hedda – if you could only make up your mind to come with me! Just think!

HEDDA [*rises and says wearily, repelling the idea*] No, no don't ask me. I will not look upon sickness and death. I loathe all sorts of ugliness.

TESMAN Well, well, then – ! [*bustling around*] My hat – ? My over-coat – ? Oh, in the hall – I do hope I mayn't come too late, Hedda! Eh?

HEDDA Oh, if you run –

BERTA *appears at the hall door.*

BERTA Judge Brack is at the door, and wishes to know if he may come in.

TESMAN At this time! No, I can't possibly see him.

HEDDA But I can. [*to Berta*] Ask Judge Brack to come in.

[Berta goes out]

HEDDA [*quickly, whispering*] The parcel, Tesman! [*she snatches it up from the stool*]

TESMAN Yes, give it to me!

HEDDA No, no, I will keep it till you come back.

[*She goes to the writing-table and places it in the bookcase. Tesman stands in a flurry of haste, and cannot get his gloves on.*]

JUDGE BRACK *enters from the hall.*

HEDDA [*nodding to him*] You are an early bird, I must say.

BRACK Yes, don't you think so! [*to Tesman*] Are you on the move, too?

TESMAN Yes, I must rush off to my aunts'. Fancy – the invalid one is lying at death's door, poor creature.

BRACK Dear me, is she indeed? Then on no account let me detain you. At such a critical moment –

TESMAN Yes, I must really rush – Goodbye! Goodbye!

[He hastens out by the hall door.]

HEDDA [*approaching*] You seem to have made a particularly lively night of it at your rooms, Judge Brack.

BRACK I assure you I have not had my clothes off, Mrs Hedda.

HEDDA Not you, either?

BRACK No, as you may see. But what has Tesman been telling you of the night's adventures?

HEDDA Oh, some tiresome story. Only that they went and had coffee somewhere or other.

BRACK I have heard about that coffee-party already. Eilert Lövborg
was not with them, I fancy?

HEDDA No, they had taken him home before that.

BRACK Tesman too?

HEDDA No, but some of the others, he said.

BRACK [*smiling*] George Tesman is really an ingenuous creature,
Mrs Hedda.

HEDDA Yes, heaven knows he is. Then is there something behind
all this?

BRACK Yes, perhaps there may be.

HEDDA Well then, sit down, my dear Judge, and tell your story in
comfort. [*She seats herself to the left of the table. Brack sits near her,
at the long side of the table.*]

HEDDA Now then?

BRACK I had special reasons for keeping track of my guests – last
night.

HEDDA Of Eilert Lövborg among the rest, perhaps?

BRACK Frankly, yes.

HEDDA Now you make me really curious –

BRACK Do you know where he and one or two of the others
finished the night, Mrs Hedda?

HEDDA If it is not quite unmentionable, tell me.

BRACK Oh no, it's not at all unmentionable. Well, they put in an
appearance at a particularly animated *soirée*.

HEDDA Of the lively kind?

BRACK Of the very liveliest –

HEDDA Tell me more of this, Judge Brack –

BRACK Lövborg, as well as the others, had been invited in advance.
I knew all about it. But he had declined the invitation; for now,
as you know, he has become a new man.

HEDDA Up at the Elvsteds', yes. But he went after all, then?

BRACK Well, you see, Mrs Hedda – unhappily the spirit moved
him at my rooms last evening –

HEDDA Yes, I hear he found inspiration.

BRACK Pretty violent inspiration. Well, I fancy that altered his
purpose; for we menfolk are unfortunately not always so firm in
our principles as we ought to be.

HEDDA Oh, I am sure you are an exception, Judge Brack. But as to
Lövborg – ?

BRACK To make a long story short – he landed at last in Mademoiselle Diana's rooms.

HEDDA Mademoiselle Diana's?

BRACK It was Mademoiselle Diana that was giving the *soirée*, to a
select circle of her admirers and her lady friends.

HEDDA Is she a red-haired woman?

BRACK Precisely.

HEDDA A sort of a – singer?

BRACK Oh yes – in her leisure moments. And moreover a mighty
huntress – of men – Mrs Hedda. You have no doubt heard of
her. Eilert Lövborg was one of her most enthusiastic protectors –
in the days of his glory.

HEDDA And how did all this end?

BRACK Far from amicably, it appears. After a most tender meeting,
they seem to have come to blows –

HEDDA Lövborg and she?

BRACK Yes. He accused her or her friends of having robbed him.
He declared that his pocket-book had disappeared – and other
things as well. In short, he seems to have made a furious
disturbance.

HEDDA And what came of it all?

BRACK It came to a general scrimmage, in which the ladies as
well as the gentlemen took part. Fortunately the police at last
appeared on the scene.

HEDDA The police too?

BRACK Yes. I fancy it will prove a costly frolic for Eilert Lövborg,
crazy being that he is.

HEDDA How so?

BRACK He seems to have made a violent resistance – to have hit
one of the constables on the head and torn the coat off his back.
So they had to march him off to the police-station with the rest.

HEDDA How have you learnt all this?

BRACK From the police themselves.

HEDDA [*gazing straight before her*] So that is what happened. Then he
had no vine-leaves in his hair.

BRACK Vine-leaves, Mrs Hedda?

HEDDA [*changing her tone*] But tell me now, Judge – what is your
real reason for tracking out Eilert Lövborg's movements so
carefully?

BRACK In the first place, it could not be entirely indifferent to me if it should appear in the police-court that he came straight from my house.

HEDDA Will the matter come into court then?

BRACK Of course. However, I should scarcely have troubled so much about that. But I thought that, as a friend of the family, it was my duty to supply you and Tesman with a full account of his nocturnal exploits.

HEDDA Why so, Judge Brack?

BRACK Why, because I have a shrewd suspicion that he intends to use you as a sort of blind.

HEDDA Oh, how can you think such a thing!

BRACK Good heavens, Mrs Hedda – we have eyes in our head. Mark my words! This Mrs Elvsted will be in no hurry to leave town again.

HEDDA Well, even if there should be anything between them, I suppose there are plenty of other places where they could meet.

BRACK Not a single home. Henceforth, as before, every respectable house will be closed against Eilert Lövborg.

HEDDA And so ought mine to be, you mean?

BRACK Yes. I confess it would be more than painful to me if this personage were to be made free of your house. How superfluous, how intrusive, he would be, if he were to force his way into –

HEDDA – into the triangle?

BRACK Precisely. It would simply mean that I should find myself homeless.

HEDDA [looks at him with a smile] So you want to be the one cock in the basket – that is your aim.

BRACK [nods slowly and lowers his voice] Yes, that is my aim. And for that I will fight – with every weapon I can command.

HEDDA [her smile vanishing] I see you are a dangerous person – when it comes to the point.

BRACK Do you think so?

HEDDA I am beginning to think so. And I am exceedingly glad to think – that you have no sort of hold over me.

BRACK [laughing equivocally] Well well, Mrs Hedda – perhaps you are right there. If I had, who knows what I might be capable of?

HEDDA Come come now, Judge Brack! That sounds almost like a threat.

BRACK [*rising*] Oh, not at all! The triangle, you know, ought, if possible, to be spontaneously constructed.

HEDDA There I agree with you.

BRACK Well, now I have said all I had to say; and I had better be getting back to town. Goodbye, Mrs Hedda. [*he goes towards the glass door*]

HEDDA [*rising*] Are you going through the garden?

BRACK Yes, it's a short cut for me.

HEDDA And then it is a back way, too.

BRACK Quite so. I have no objection to back ways. They may be piquant enough at times.

HEDDA When there is ball practice going on, you mean?

BRACK [*in the doorway, laughing to her*] Oh, people don't shoot their tame poultry, I fancy.

HEDDA [*also laughing*] Oh no, when there is only one cock in the basket –   [*They exchange laughing nods of farewell. He goes. She closes the door behind him.*]

[*Hedda, who has become quite serious, stands for a moment looking out. Presently she goes and peeps through the curtain over the middle doorway. Then she goes to the writing-table, takes Lövborg's packet out of the bookcase, and is on the point of looking through its contents. Berta is heard speaking loudly in the hall. Hedda turns and listens. Then she hastily locks up the packet in the drawer, and lays the key on the inkstand.*]

  EILERT LÖVBORG, *with his greatcoat on and his hat in his hand, tears open the hall door. He looks somewhat confused and irritated.*

Lövborg. [*looking towards the hall*] and I tell you I must and will come in! There! [*he closes the door, turns, sees Hedda, at once regains his self-control, and bows.*]

HEDDA [*at the writing-table*] Well, Mr Lövborg, this is rather a late hour to call for Thea.

LÖVBORG You mean rather an early hour to call on you. Pray pardon me.

HEDDA How do you know that she is still here?

LÖVBORG They told me at her lodgings that she had been out all night.

HEDDA [*going to the oval table*] Did you notice anything about the people of the house when they said that?

LÖVBORG [*looks inquiringly at her*] Notice anything about them?

HEDDA I mean, did they seem to think it odd?

LÖVBORG [*suddenly understanding*] Oh yes, of course! I am dragging her down with me! However, I didn't notice anything. – I suppose Tesman is not up yet.

HEDDA No – I think not –

LÖVBORG When did he come home?

HEDDA Very late.

LÖVBORG Did he tell you anything?

HEDDA Yes, I gathered that you had had an exceedingly jolly evening at Judge Brack's.

LÖVBORG Nothing more?

HEDDA I don't think so. However, I was so dreadfully sleepy –

MRS ELVSTED *enters through the curtains of the middle doorway.*

MRS ELVSTED [*going towards him*] Ah, Lövborg! At last – !

LÖVBORG Yes, at last. And too late!

MRS ELVSTED [*looks anxiously at him*] What is too late?

LÖVBORG Everything is too late now. It is all over with me.

MRS ELVSTED Oh no, no – don't say that!

LÖVBORG You will say the same when you hear –

MRS ELVSTED I won't hear anything!

HEDDA Perhaps you would prefer to talk to her alone? If so, I will leave you.

LÖVBORG No, stay – you too. I beg you to stay.

MRS ELVSTED Yes, but I won't hear anything, I tell you.

LÖVBORG It is not last night's adventures that I want to talk about

MRS ELVSTED What is it then – ?

LÖVBORG I want to say that now our ways must part.

MRS ELVSTED Part!

HEDDA [*involuntarily*] I knew it!

LÖVBORG You can be of no more service to me, Thea.

MRS ELVSTED How can you stand there and say that! No more service to you! Am I not to help you now, as before? Are we not to go on working together?

LÖVBORG Henceforward I shall do no work.

MRS ELVSTED [*despairingly*] Then what am I to do with my life?

LÖVBORG You must try to live your life as if you had never known me.

MRS ELVSTED But you know I cannot do that!

LÖVBORG Try if you cannot, Thea. You must go home again –

MRS ELVSTED [*in vehement protest*] Never in this world! Where you are, there will I be also! I will not let myself be driven away like this! I will remain here! I will be with you when the book appears.

HEDDA [*half aloud, in suspense*] Ah yes – the book!

LÖVBORG [*looks at her*] My book and Thea's; for that is what it is.

MRS ELVSTED Yes, I feel that it is. And that is why I have a right to be with you when it appears! I will see with my own eyes how respect and honour pour in upon you afresh. And the happiness – the happiness – oh, I must share it with you!

LÖVBORG Thea – our book will never appear.

HEDDA Ah!

MRS ELVSTED Never appear!

LÖVBORG Can never appear.

MRS ELVSTED [*in agonised foreboding*] Lövborg – what have you done with the manuscript?

HEDDA [*looks anxiously at him*] Yes, the manuscript – ?

MRS ELVSTED Where is it?

LÖVBORG The manuscript – well then – I have torn the manuscript into a thousand pieces.

MRS ELVSTED [*shrieks*] Oh no, no – !

HEDDA [*involuntarily*] But that's not –

LÖVBORG [*looks at her*] Not true, you think?

HEDDA [*collecting herself*] Oh well, of course – since you say so. But it sounded so improbable –

LÖVBORG It is true, all the same.

MRS ELVSTED [*wringing her hands*] Oh God – oh God, Hedda – torn his own work to pieces!

LÖVBORG I have torn my own life to pieces. So why should I not tear my life-work too – ?

MRS ELVSTED And you did this last night?

LÖVBORG Yes, I tell you! Tore it into a thousand pieces – and scattered them on the fiord – far out. There there is cool sea-water at any rate – let them drift upon it – drift with the current and the wind. And then presently they will sink – deeper and deeper – as I shall, Thea.

MRS ELVSTED Do you know, Lövborg, that what you have done
with the book – I shall think of it to my dying day as though
you had killed a little child.

LÖVBORG Yes, you are right. It is a sort of child-murder.

MRS ELVSTED How could you, then – ! Did not the child belong
to me too?

HEDDA [*almost inaudibly*] Ah, the child –

MRS ELVSTED [*breathing heavily*] It is all over then. Well well, now I
will go, Hedda.

HEDDA But you are not going away from town?

MRS ELVSTED Oh, I don't know what I shall do. I see nothing but
darkness before me.   [*she goes out by the hall door*]

HEDDA [*stands waiting for a moment*] So you are not going to see her
home, Mr Lövborg?

LÖVBORG I? Through the streets? Would you have people see her
walking with me?

HEDDA Of course I don't know what else may have happened last
night. But is it so utterly irretrievable?

LÖVBORG It will not end with last night – I know that perfectly
well. And the thing is that now I have no taste for that sort of
life either. I won't begin it anew. She has broken my courage
and my power of braving life out.

HEDDA [*looking straight before her*] So that pretty little fool has had
her fingers in a man's destiny. [*looks at him*] But all the same,
how could you treat her so heartlessly.

LÖVBORG Oh, don't say that I was heartless!

HEDDA To go and destroy what has filled her whole soul for
months and years! You do not call that heartless!

LÖVBORG To you I can tell the truth, Hedda.

HEDDA The truth?

LÖVBORG First promise me – give me your word – that what I now
confide in you Thea shall never know.

HEDDA I give you my word.

LÖVBORG Good. Then let me tell you that what I said just now was
untrue.

HEDDA About the manuscript?

LÖVBORG Yes. I have not torn it to pieces – nor thrown it into the
fiord.

HEDDA No, no – . But – where is it then?

LÖVBORG I have destroyed it none the less – utterly destroyed it,
Hedda!

HEDDA I don't understand.

LÖVBORG Thea said that what I had done seemed to her like a
child-murder.

HEDDA Yes, so she said.

LÖVBORG But to kill his child – that is not the worst thing a father
can do to it.

HEDDA Not the worst?

LÖVBORG Suppose now, Hedda, that a man – in the small hours
of the morning – came home to his child's mother after a
night of riot and debauchery, and said: 'Listen – I have been
here and there – in this place and in that. And I have taken
our child with me – to this place and to that. And I have
lost the child – utterly lost it. The devil knows into what
hands it may have fallen – who may have had their clutches
on it.'

HEDDA Well – but when all is said and done, you know – this was
only a book –

LÖVBORG Thea's pure soul was in that book.

HEDDA Yes, so I understand.

LÖVBORG And you can understand, too, that for her and me
together no future is possible.

HEDDA What path do you mean to take then?

LÖVBORG None. I will only try to make an end of it all – the
sooner the better.

HEDDA [a step nearer him] Eilert Lövborg – listen to me. – Will you
not try to – to do it beautifully?

LÖVBORG Beautifully? [smiling] With vine-leaves in my hair, as you
used to dream in the old days – ?

HEDDA No, no. I have lost my faith in the vine-leaves. But
beautifully nevertheless! For once in a way! – Goodbye! You
must go now – and do not come here any more.

LÖVBORG Goodbye, Mrs Tesman. And give George Tesman my
love. [he is on the point of going]

HEDDA No, wait! I must give you a memento to take with you.
[She goes to the writing-table and opens the drawer and the pistol-case;
then returns to Lövborg with one of the pistols.]

LÖVBORG [looks at her] This? Is this the memento?

HEDDA [*nodding slowly*] Do you recognise it? It was aimed at you once.

LÖVBORG You should have used it then.

HEDDA Take it — and do you use it now.

LÖVBORG [*puts the pistol in his breast pocket*] Thanks!

HEDDA And beautifully, Eilert Lövborg. Promise me that!

LÖVBORG Goodbye, Hedda Gabler.   [*he goes out by the hall door*] [*Hedda listens for a moment at the door. Then she goes up to the writing-table, takes out the packet of manuscript, peeps under the cover, draws a few of the sheets half out, and looks at them. Next she goes over and seats herself in the armchair beside the stove, with the packet in her lap. Presently she opens the stove door, and then the packet.*]

Hedda. [*throws one of the quires into the fire and whispers to herself*] Now I am burning your child, Thea! — Burning it, curly-locks! [*throwing one or two more quires into the stove*] Your child and Eilert Lövborg's. [*throws the rest in*] I am burning — I am burning your child.

ACT FOURTH

*The same rooms at the Tesmans'. It is evening. The drawing-room is in
darkness. The back room is light by the hanging lamp over the table. The
curtains over the glass door are drawn close.*

    HEDDA, *dressed in black, walks to and fro in the dark room. Then she
goes into the back room and disappears for a moment to the left. She is
heard to strike a few chords on the piano. Presently she comes in sight
again, and returns to the drawing-room.*

    BERTA *enters from the right, through the inner room, with a lighted
lamp, which she places on the table in front of the corner settee in the
drawing-room. Her eyes are red with weeping, and she has black ribbons
in her cap. She goes quietly and circumspectly out to the right. Hedda
goes up to the glass door, lifts the curtain a little aside, and looks out into
the darkness.*

    Shortly afterwards, MISS TESMAN, *in mourning, with a bonnet and veil
on, comes in from the hall. Hedda goes towards her and holds out her hand.*

MISS TESMAN Yes, Hedda, here I am, in mourning and forlorn; for
    now my poor sister has at last found peace.

HEDDA I have heard the news already, as you see. Tesman sent me
    a card.

MISS TESMAN Yes, he promised me he would. But nevertheless I
    thought that to Hedda – here in the house of life – I ought
    myself to bring the tidings of death.

HEDDA That was very kind of you.

MISS TESMAN Ah, Rina ought not to have left us just now. This is
    not the time for Hedda's house to be a house of mourning.

HEDDA [*changing the subject*] She died quite peacefully, did she not,
    Miss Tesman?

MISS TESMAN Oh, her end was so calm, so beautiful. And then she
    had the unspeakable happiness of seeing George once more –
    and bidding him goodbye. – Has he not come home yet?

HEDDA No. He wrote that he might be detained. But won't you sit down?

MISS TESMAN No thank you, my dear, dear Hedda. I should like to, but I have so much to do. I must prepare my dear one for her rest as well as I can. She shall go to her grave looking her best.

HEDDA Can I not help you in any way?

MISS TESMAN Oh, you must not think of it! Hedda Tesman must have no hand in such mournful work. Nor let her thoughts dwell on it either — not at this time.

HEDDA One is not always mistress of one's thoughts —

MISS TESMAN [*continuing*] Ah yes, it is the way of the world. At home we shall be sewing a shroud; and here there will soon be sewing too, I suppose — but of another sort, thank God!

GEORGE TESMAN *enters by the hall door.*

HEDDA. Ah, you have come at last!

TESMAN You here, Aunt Julia? With Hedda? Fancy that!

MISS TESMAN I was just going, my dear boy. Well, have you done all you promised?

TESMAN No; I'm really afraid I have forgotten half of it. I must come to you again tomorrow. To-day my brain is all in a whirl. I can't keep my thoughts together.

MISS TESMAN Why, my dear George, you mustn't take it in this way.

TESMAN Mustn't — ? How do you mean?

MISS TESMAN Even in your sorrow you must rejoice, as I do — rejoice that she is at rest.

TESMAN Oh yes, yes — you are thinking of Aunt Rina.

HEDDA You will feel lonely now, Miss Tesman.

MISS TESMAN Just at first, yes. But that will not last very long, I hope. I dare say I shall soon find an occupant for Rina's little room.

TESMAN Indeed? Who do you think will take it? Eh?

MISS TESMAN Oh, there's always some poor invalid or other in want of nursing, unfortunately.

HEDDA Would you really take such a burden upon you again?

MISS TESMAN A burden! Heaven forgive you, child — it has been no burden to me.

HEDDA But suppose you had a total stranger on your hands —

MISS TESMAN Oh, one soon makes friends with sick folk; and it's such an absolute necessity for me to have someone to live for. Well, heaven be praised, there may soon be something in this house, too, to keep an old aunt busy.

HEDDA Oh, don't trouble about anything here.

TESMAN Yes, just fancy what a nice time we three might have together, if – ?

HEDDA If – ?

TESMAN [*uneasily*] Oh nothing. It will all come right. Let us hope so – eh?

MISS TESMAN Well well, I dare say you two want to talk to each other. [*smiling*] And perhaps Hedda may have something to tell you too, George. Goodbye! I must go home to Rina. [*turning at the door*] How strange it is to think that now Rina is with me and with my poor brother as well!

TESMAN Yes, fancy that, Aunt Julia! Eh?

[*Miss Tesman goes out by the hall door.*]

HEDDA [*follows Tesman coldly and searchingly with her eyes*] I almost believe your Aunt Rina's death affects you more than it does your Aunt Julia.

TESMAN Oh, it's not that alone. It's Eilert I am so terribly uneasy about.

HEDDA [*quickly*] Is there anything new about him?

TESMAN I looked in at his rooms this afternoon, intending to tell him the manuscript was in safe keeping.

HEDDA Well, did you find him?

TESMAN No. He wasn't at home. But afterwards I met Mrs Elvsted, and she told me that he had been here early this morning.

HEDDA Yes, directly after you had gone.

TESMAN And he said that he had torn his manuscript to pieces – eh?

HEDDA Yes, so he declared.

TESMAN Why, good heavens, he must have been completely out of his mind! And I suppose you thought it best not to give it back to him, Hedda?

HEDDA No, he did not get it.

TESMAN But of course you told him that we had it?

HEDDA No. [*quickly*] Did you tell Mrs Elvsted?

TESMAN No; I thought I had better not. But you ought to have told him. Fancy, if, in desperation, he should go and do himself some injury! Let me have the manuscript, Hedda! I will take it to him at once. Where is it?

HEDDA [*cold and immovable, leaning on the armchair*] I have not got it.

TESMAN Have not got it? What in the world do you mean?

HEDDA I have burnt it – every line of it.

TESMAN [*with a violent movement of terror*] Burnt! Burnt Eilert's manuscript!

HEDDA Don't scream so. The servant might hear you.

TESMAN Burnt! Why, good God – ! No, no, no! It's impossible!

HEDDA It is so, nevertheless.

TESMAN Do you know what you have done, Hedda? It's unlawful appropriation of lost property. Fancy that! Just ask Judge Brack, and he'll tell you what it is.

HEDDA I advise you not to speak of it – either to Judge Brack or to anyone else.

TESMAN But how could you do anything so unheard-of? What put it into your head? What possessed you? Answer me that – eh?

HEDDA [*suppressing an almost imperceptible smile*] I did it for your sake, George.

TESMAN For my sake!

HEDDA This morning, when you told me about what he had read to you –

TESMAN Yes yes – what then?

HEDDA You acknowledged that you envied him his work.

TESMAN Oh, of course I didn't mean that literally.

HEDDA No matter – I could not bear the idea that anyone should throw you into the shade.

TESMAN [*in an outburst of mingled doubt and joy*] Hedda! Oh, is this true? But – but – I never knew you show your love like that before. Fancy that!

HEDDA Well, I may as well tell you that – just at this time – [*impatiently breaking off*] No, no; you can ask Aunt Julia. She will tell you, fast enough.

TESMAN Oh, I almost think I understand you, Hedda! [*clasps his hands together*] Great heavens! do you really mean it! Eh?

HEDDA Don't shout so. The servant might hear.

TESMAN [*laughing in irrepressible glee*] The servant! Why, how absurd you are, Hedda. It's only my old Berta! Why, I'll tell Berta myself.

HEDDA [*clenching her hands together in desperation*] Oh, it is killing me – it is killing me, all this!

TESMAN What is, Hedda? Eh?

HEDDA [*coldly, controlling herself*] All this – absurdity – George.

TESMAN Absurdity! Do you see anything absurd in my being overjoyed at the news! But after all – perhaps I had better not say anything to Berta.

HEDDA Oh – why not that too?

TESMAN No, no, not yet! But I must certainly tell Aunt Julia. And then that you have begun to call me George too! Fancy that! Oh, Aunt Julia will be so happy – so happy!

HEDDA When she hears that I have burnt Eilert Lövborg's manuscript – for your sake?

TESMAN No; by-the-bye – that affair of the manuscript – of course nobody must know about that. But that you love me so much, Hedda – Aunt Julia must really share my joy in that! I wonder, now, whether this sort of thing is usual in young wives? Eh?

HEDDA I think you had better ask Aunt Julia that question too.

TESMAN I will indeed, some time or other. [*looks uneasy and downcast again*] And yet the manuscript – the manuscript! Good God! it is terrible to think what will become of poor Eilert now.

MRS ELVSTED, *dressed as in the first Act, with hat and cloak, enters by the hall door.*

MRS ELVSTED [*greets them hurriedly, and says in evident agitation*] Oh, dear Hedda, forgive my coming again.

HEDDA What is the matter with you, Thea?

TESMAN Something about Eilert Lövborg again – eh?

MRS ELVSTED Yes! I am dreadfully afraid some misfortune has happened to him.

HEDDA [*seizes her arm*] Ah – do you think so?

TESMAN Why, good Lord – what makes you think that, Mrs Elvsted?

MRS ELVSTED I heard them talking of him at my boarding-house – just as I came in. Oh, the most incredible rumours are afloat about him today.

TESMAN Yes, fancy, so I heard too! And I can bear witness that he went straight home to bed last night. Fancy that!

HEDDA Well, what did they say at the boarding-house?

MRS ELVSTED Oh, I couldn't make out anything clearly. Either they knew nothing definite, or else − . They stopped talking when they saw me; and I did not dare to ask.

TESMAN [*moving about uneasily*] We must hope − we must hope that you misunderstood them, Mrs Elvsted.

MRS ELVSTED No, no; I am sure it was of him they were talking. And I heard something about the hospital or −

TESMAN The hospital?

HEDDA No − surely that cannot be!

MRS ELVSTED Oh, I was in such mortal terror! I went to his lodgings and asked for him there.

HEDDA You could make up your mind to that, Thea!

MRS ELVSTED What else could I do? I really could bear the suspense no longer.

TESMAN But you didn't find him either − eh?

MRS ELVSTED No. And the people knew nothing about him. He hadn't been home since yesterday afternoon, they said.

TESMAN Yesterday! Fancy, how could they say that?

MRS ELVSTED Oh, I am sure something terrible must have happened to him.

TESMAN Hedda dear − how would it be if I were to go and make inquiries − ?

HEDDA No, no − don't you mix yourself up in this affair.

JUDGE BRACK, *with his hat in his hand, enters by the hall door, which Berta opens, and closes behind him. He looks grave and bows in silence.*

TESMAN Oh, is that you, my dear Judge? Eh?

BRACK Yes. It was imperative I should see you this evening.

TESMAN I can see you have heard the news about Aunt Rina?

BRACK Yes, that among other things.

TESMAN Isn't it sad − eh?

BRACK Well, my dear Tesman, that depends on how you look at it.

TESMAN [*looks doubtfully at him*] Has anything else happened?

BRACK Yes.

HEDDA [*in suspense*] Anything sad, Judge Brack?

BRACK That, too, depends on how you look at it, Mrs Tesman.

MRS ELVSTED [*unable to restrain her anxiety*] Oh! it is something about Eilert Lövborg!

BRACK [*with a glance at her*] What makes you think that, Madam? Perhaps you have already heard something – ?

MRS ELVSTED [*in confusion*] No, nothing at all, but –

TESMAN Oh, for heaven's sake, tell us!

BRACK [*shrugging his shoulders*] Well, I regret to say Eilert Lövborg has been taken to the hospital. He is lying at the point of death.

MRS ELVSTED [*shrieks*] Oh God! oh God – !

TESMAN To the hospital! And at the point of death!

HEDDA [*involuntarily*] So soon then –

MRS ELVSTED [*wailing*] And we parted in anger, Hedda!

HEDDA [*whispers*] Thea – Thea – be careful!

MRS ELVSTED [*not heeding her*] I must go to him! I must see him alive!

BRACK It is useless, Madam. No one will be admitted.

MRS ELVSTED Oh, at least tell me what has happened to him? What is it?

TESMAN You don't mean to say that he has himself – Eh?

HEDDA Yes, I am sure he has.

BRACK [*keeping his eyes fixed upon her*] Unfortunately you have guessed quite correctly, Mrs Tesman.

MRS ELVSTED Oh, how horrible!

TESMAN Himself, then! Fancy that!

HEDDA Shot himself!

BRACK Rightly guessed again, Mrs Tesman.

MRS ELVSTED [*with an effort at self-control*] When did it happen, Mr Brack?

BRACK This afternoon – between three and four.

TESMAN But, good Lord, where did he do it? Eh?

BRACK [*with some hesitation*] Where? Well – I suppose at his lodgings.

MRS ELVSTED No, that cannot be; for I was there between six and seven.

BRACK Well then, somewhere else. I don't know exactly. I only know that he was found – . He had shot himself – in the breast.

MRS ELVSTED Oh, how terrible! That he should die like that!

HEDDA [*to Brack*] Was it in the breast?

BRACK Yes – as I told you.

HEDDA Not in the temple?

BRACK In the breast, Mrs Tesman.

HEDDA Well, well – the breast is a good place, too.

BRACK How do you mean, Mrs Tesman?

HEDDA [*evasively*] Oh, nothing – nothing.

TESMAN And the wound is dangerous, you say – eh?

BRACK Absolutely mortal. The end has probably come by this time.

MRS ELVSTED Yes, yes, I feel it. The end! The end! Oh, Hedda – !

TESMAN But tell me, how have you learnt all this?

BRACK [*curtly*] Through one of the police. A man I had some business with.

HEDDA [*in a clear voice*] At last a deed worth doing!

TESMAN [*terrified*] Good heavens, Hedda! what are you saying?

HEDDA I say there is beauty in this.

BRACK H'm, Mrs Tesman –

MRS ELVSTED Oh, Hedda, how can you talk of beauty in such an act!

HEDDA Eilert Lövborg has himself made up his account with life. He has had the courage to do – the one right thing.

MRS ELVSTED No, you must never think that was how it happened! It must have been in delirium that he did it.

TESMAN In despair!

HEDDA That he did not. I am certain of that.

MRS ELVSTED Yes, yes! In delirium! Just as when he tore up our manuscript.

BRACK [*starting*] The manuscript? Has he torn that up?

MRS ELVSTED Yes, last night.

TESMAN [*whispers softly*] Oh, Hedda, we shall never get over this.

BRACK H'm, very extraordinary.

TESMAN [*moving about the room*] To think of Eilert going out of the world in this way! And not leaving behind him the book that would have immortalised his name –

MRS ELVSTED Oh, if only it could be put together again!

TESMAN Yes, if it only could! I don't know what I would not give –

MRS ELVSTED Perhaps it can, Mr Tesman.

TESMAN What do you mean?

MRS ELVSTED [*searches in the pocket of her dress*] Look here. I have kept all the loose notes he used to dictate from.

HEDDA [*a step forward*] Ah – !

TESMAN You have kept them, Mrs Elvsted! Eh?

MRS ELVSTED Yes, I have them here. I put them in my pocket when I left home. Here they still are —

TESMAN Oh, do let me see them!

MRS ELVSTED [*hands him a bundle of papers*] But they are in such disorder — all mixed up.

TESMAN Fancy, if we could make something out of them, after all! Perhaps if we two put our heads together —

MRS ELVSTED Oh yes, at least let us try —

TESMAN We will manage it! We must! I will dedicate my life to this task.

HEDDA You, George? Your life?

TESMAN Yes, or rather all the time I can spare. My own collections must wait in the meantime. Hedda — you understand, eh? I owe this to Eilert's memory.

HEDDA Perhaps.

TESMAN And so, my dear Mrs Elvsted, we will give our whole minds to it. There is no use in brooding over what can't be undone — eh? We must try to control our grief as much as possible, and —

MRS ELVSTED Yes, yes, Mr Tesman, I will do the best I can.

TESMAN Well then, come here. I can't rest until we have looked through the notes. Where shall we sit? Here? No, in there, in the back room. Excuse me, my dear Judge. Come with me, Mrs Elvsted.

MRS ELVSTED Oh, if only it were possible!

[*Tesman and Mrs Elvsted go into the back room. She takes off her hat and cloak. They both sit at the table under the hanging lamp, and are soon deep in an eager examination of the papers. Hedda crosses to the stove and sits in the armchair. Presently* BRACK *goes up to her.*]

HEDDA [*in a low voice*] Oh, what a sense of freedom it gives one, this act of Eilert Lövborg's.

BRACK Freedom, Mrs Hedda? Well, of course, it is a release for him —

HEDDA I mean for me. It gives me a sense of freedom to know that a deed of deliberate courage is still possible in this world — a deed of spontaneous beauty.

BRACK [*smiling*] H'm — my dear Mrs Hedda —

HEDDA Oh, I know what you are going to say. For you are a kind of specialist too, like — you know!

BRACK [*looking hard at her*] Eilert Lövborg was more to you than perhaps you are willing to admit to yourself. Am I wrong?

HEDDA I don't answer such questions. I only know that Eilert Lövborg has had the courage to live his life after his own fashion. And then – the last great act, with its beauty! Ah! that he should have the will and the strength to turn away from the banquet of life – so early.

BRACK I am sorry, Mrs Hedda – but I fear I must dispel an amiable illusion.

HEDDA Illusion?

BRACK Which could not have lasted long in any case.

HEDDA What do you mean?

BRACK Eilert Lövborg did not shoot himself – voluntarily.

HEDDA Not voluntarily?

BRACK No. The thing did not happen exactly as I told it.

HEDDA [*in suspense*] Have you concealed something? What is it?

BRACK For poor Mrs Elvsted's sake I idealised the facts a little.

HEDDA What are the facts?

BRACK First, that he is already dead.

HEDDA At the hospital?

BRACK Yes – without regaining consciousness.

HEDDA What more have you concealed?

BRACK This – the event did not happen at his lodgings.

HEDDA Oh, that can make no difference.

BRACK Perhaps it may. For I must tell you – Eilert Lövborg was found shot in – in Mademoiselle Diana's boudoir.

HEDDA [*makes a motion as if to rise, but sinks back again*] That is impossible, Judge Brack! He cannot have been there again today.

BRACK He was there this afternoon. He went there, he said, to demand the return of something which they had taken from him. Talked wildly about a lost child –

HEDDA Ah – so that is why –

BRACK I thought probably he meant his manuscript; but now I hear he destroyed that himself. So I suppose it must have been his pocket-book.

HEDDA Yes, no doubt. And there – there he was found?

BRACK Yes, there. With a pistol in his breast-pocket, discharged. The ball had lodged in a vital part.

HEDDA In the breast – yes?

BRACK No – in the bowels.

HEDDA [*looks up at him with an expression of loathing*] That too! Oh, what curse is it that makes everything I touch turn ludicrous and mean?

BRACK There is one point more, Mrs Hedda – another disagreeable feature in the affair.

HEDDA And what is that?

BRACK The pistol he carried –

HEDDA [*breathless*] Well? What of it?

BRACK He must have stolen it.

HEDDA [*leaps up*] Stolen it! That is not true! He did not steal it!

BRACK No other explanation is possible. He must have stolen it – Hush!

TESMAN *and* MRS ELVSTED *have risen from the table in the back-room, and come into the drawing-room.*

TESMAN [*with the papers in both his hands*] Hedda, dear, it is almost impossible to see under that lamp. Think of that!

HEDDA Yes, I am thinking.

TESMAN Would you mind our sitting at your writing-table – eh?

HEDDA If you like. [*quickly*] No, wait! Let me clear it first!

TESMAN Oh, you needn't trouble, Hedda. There is plenty of room.

HEDDA No no, let me clear it, I say! I will take these things in and put them on the piano. There!
[*She has drawn out an object, covered with sheet music, from under the bookcase, places several other pieces of music upon it, and carries the whole into the inner room, to the left. Tesman lays the scraps of paper on the writing-table, and moves the lamp there from the corner table. He and Mrs Elvsted sit down and proceed with their work. Hedda returns.*]

HEDDA [*behind Mrs Elvsted's chair, gently ruffling her hair*] Well, my sweet Thea – how goes it with Eilert Lövborg's monument?

MRS ELVSTED [*looks dispiritedly up at her*] Oh, it will be terribly hard to put in order.

TESMAN We must manage it. I am determined. And arranging other people's papers is just the work for me.

[*Hedda goes over to the stove, and seats herself on one of the footstools. Brack stands over her, leaning on the armchair.*]

HEDDA [*whispers*] What did you say about the pistol?

BRACK [*softly*] That he must have stolen it.

HEDDA Why stolen it?

BRACK Because every other explanation ought to be impossible, Mrs Hedda.

HEDDA Indeed?

BRACK [*glances at her*] Of course Eilert Lövborg was here this morning. Was he not?

HEDDA Yes.

BRACK Were you alone with him?

HEDDA Part of the time.

BRACK Did you not leave the room whilst he was here?

HEDDA No.

BRACK Try to recollect. Were you not out of the room a moment?

HEDDA Yes, perhaps just a moment – out in the hall.

BRACK And where was your pistol-case during that time?

HEDDA I had it locked up in –

BRACK Well, Mrs Hedda?

HEDDA The case stood there on the writing-table.

BRACK Have you looked since, to see whether both the pistols are there?

HEDDA No.

BRACK Well, you need not. I saw the pistol found in Lövborg's pocket, and I knew it at once as the one I had seen yesterday – and before, too.

HEDDA Have you it with you?

BRACK No; the police have it.

HEDDA What will the police do with it?

BRACK Search till they find the owner.

HEDDA Do you think they will succeed?

BRACK [*bends over her and whispers*] No, Hedda Gabler – not so long as I say nothing.

HEDDA [*looks frightened at him*] And if you do not say nothing – what then?

BRACK [*shrugs his shoulders*] There is always the possibility that the pistol was stolen.

HEDDA [*firmly*] Death rather than that.

BRACK [*smiling*] People say such things – but they don't do them.

HEDDA [*without replying*] And supposing the pistol was not stolen, and the owner is discovered? What then?

BRACK Well, Hedda – then comes the scandal!

HEDDA The scandal!

BRACK Yes, the scandal – of which you are so mortally afraid. You will, of course, be brought before the court – both you and Mademoiselle Diana. She will have to explain how the thing happened – whether it was an accidental shot or murder. Did the pistol go off as he was trying to take it out of his pocket, to threaten her with? Or did she tear the pistol out of his hand, shoot him, and push it back into his pocket? That would be quite like her; for she is an able-bodied young person, this same Mademoiselle Diana.

HEDDA But *I* have nothing to do with all this repulsive business.

BRACK No. But you will have to answer the question: Why did you give Eilert the pistol? And what conclusions will people draw from the fact that you did give it to him?

HEDDA [*lets her head sink*] That is true. I did not think of that.

BRACK Well, fortunately, there is no danger, so long as I say nothing.

HEDDA [*looks up at him*] So I am in your power, Judge Brack. You have me at your beck and call, from this time forward.

BRACK [*whispers softly*] Dearest Hedda – believe me – I shall not abuse my advantage.

HEDDA I am in your power none the less. Subject to your will and your demands. A slave, a slave then! [*rises impetuously*] No, I cannot endure the thought of that! Never!

BRACK [*looks half-mockingly at her*] People generally get used to the inevitable.

HEDDA [*returns his look*] Yes, perhaps.

[*She crosses to the writing-table. Suppressing an involuntary smile, she imitates Tesman's intonations*]

Well? Are you getting on, George? Eh?

TESMAN Heaven knows, dear. In any case it will be the work of months.

HEDDA [*as before*] Fancy that! [*passes her hands softly through Mrs Elvsted's hair*] Doesn't it seem strange to you, Thea? Here are you sitting with Tesman – just as you used to sit with Eilert Lövborg?

MRS ELVSTED Ah, if I could only inspire your husband in the same way!

HEDDA Oh, that will come too – in time.

TESMAN Yes, do you know, Hedda – I really think I begin to feel something of the sort. But won't you go and sit with Brack again?

HEDDA Is there nothing I can do to help you two?

TESMAN No, nothing in the world. [*turning his head*] I trust to you to keep Hedda company, my dear Brack.

BRACK [*with a glance at Hedda*] With the very greatest of pleasure.

HEDDA Thanks. But I am tired this evening. I will go in and lie down a little on the sofa.

TESMAN Yes, do dear – eh?

[*Hedda goes into the back room and draws the curtains. A short pause. Suddenly she is heard playing a wild dance on the piano.*]

MRS ELVSTED [*starts from her chair*] Oh – what is that?

TESMAN [*runs to the doorway*] Why, my dearest Hedda – don't play dance-music tonight! Just think of Aunt Rina! And of Eilert too!

HEDDA [*puts her head out between the curtains*] And of Aunt Julia. And of all the rest of them. – After this, I will be quiet. [*closes the curtains again*]

TESMAN [*at the writing-table*] It's not good for her to see us at this distressing work. I'll tell you what, Mrs Elvsted – you shall take the empty room at Aunt Julia's, and then I will come over in the evenings, and we can sit and work there – eh?

HEDDA [*in the inner room*] I hear what you are saying, Tesman. But how am I to get through the evenings out here?

TESMAN [*turning over the papers*] Oh, I dare say Judge Brack will be so kind as to look in now and then, even though I am out.

BRACK [*in the armchair, calls out gaily*] Every blessed evening, with all the pleasure in life, Mrs Tesman! We shall get on capitally together, we two!

HEDDA [*speaking loud and clear*] Yes, don't you flatter yourself we will, Judge Brack? Now that you are the one cock in the basket –

[*a shot is heard within*]

[*Tesman, Mrs Elvsted, and Brack leap to their feet*]

TESMAN Oh, now she is playing with those pistols again.

He throws back the curtains and runs in, followed by Mrs Elvsted.
Hedda lies stretched on the sofa, lifeless. Confusion and cries.
BERTA *enters in alarm from the right.*

TESMAN [*shrieks to Brack*] Shot herself! Shot herself in the temple!
Fancy that!

BRACK [*half-fainting in the armchair*] Good God! – people don't do
such things.

THE MASTER BUILDER

Characters

HALVARD SOLNESS, *Master Builder*

ALINE SOLNESS, *his wife*

DOCTOR HERDAL, *physician*

KNUT BROVIK, *formerly an architect, now in Solness's employment*

RAGNAR BROVIK, *his son, draughtsman*

KAIA FOSLI, *his niece, book-keeper*

MISS HILDA WANGEL

Some Ladies

A Crowd in the street

The action passes in and about SOLNESS'S *house*

ACT FIRST

A plainly-furnished work-room in the house of HALVARD SOLNESS *Folding doors on the left lead out to the hall. On the right is the door leading to the inner rooms of the house. At the back is an open door into the draughtsmen's office. In front, on the left, a desk with books, papers and writing materials. Further back than the folding door, a stove. In the right-hand corner, a sofa, a table, and one or two chairs. On the table a water-bottle and glass. A smaller table, with a rocking-chair and armchair, in front on the right. Lighted lamps, with shades, on the table in the draughtsmen's office, on the table in the corner, and on the desk.*

In the draughtsmen's office sit KNUT BROVIK *and his son* RAGNAR, *occupied with plans and calculations. At the desk in the outer office stands* KAIA FOSLI, *writing in the ledger. Knut Brovik is a spare old man with white hair and beard. He wears a rather threadbare but well-brushed black coat, with spectacles, and a somewhat discoloured white neckcloth. Ragnar Brovik is a well-dressed, light-haired man in his thirties, with a slight stoop. Kaia Fosli is a slightly built girl, a little over twenty, carefully dressed, and delicate-looking. She has a green shade over her eyes. – All three go on working for some time in silence.*

KNUT BROVIK [*rises suddenly, as if in distress, from the table; breathes heavily and laboriously as he comes forward into the doorway*] No, I can't bear it much longer!

KAIA [*going up to him*] You are feeling very ill this evening, are you not, Uncle?

BROVIK Oh, I seem to get worse every day.

RAGNAR [*has risen and advances*] You ought to go home, father. Try to get a little sleep –

BROVIK [*impatiently*] Go to bed, I suppose? Would you have me stifled outright?

KAIA Then take a little walk.

RAGNAR Yes, do. I will come with you.

BROVIK [*with warmth*] I will not go till he comes! I am determined to have it out this evening with – [*in a tone of suppressed bitterness*] – with him – with the chief.

KAIA [*anxiously*] Oh no, uncle, – do wait awhile before doing that!

RAGNAR Yes, better wait, father!

BROVIK [*draws in breath laboriously*] Ha – ha – ! I haven't much time for waiting.

KAIA [*listening*] Hush! I hear him on the stairs.

[*all three go back to their work. A short silence.*]

HALVARD SOLNESS *comes in through the hall door. He is a man no longer young, but healthy and vigorous, with close-cut curly hair, dark moustache and dark thick eyebrows. He wears a greyish-green buttoned jacket with an upstanding collar and broad lapels. On his head he wears a soft grey felt hat, and he has one or two light portfolios under his arm.*

SOLNESS [*near the door, points towards the draughtsmen's office, and asks in a whisper*] Are they gone?

KAIA [*softly, shaking her head*] No. [*she takes the shade off her eyes. Solness crosses the room, throws his hat on a chair, places the portfolios on the table by the sofa, and approaches the desk again. Kaia goes on writing without intermission, but seems nervous and uneasy.*]

SOLNESS [*aloud*] What is that you are entering, Miss Fosli?

KAIA [*starts*] Oh, it is only something that –

SOLNESS Let me look at it, Miss Fosli. [*bends over her, pretends to be looking into the ledger, and whispers*] Kaia!

KAIA [*softly, still writing*] Well?

SOLNESS Why do you always take that shade off when I come?

KAIA [*as before*] I look so ugly with it on.

SOLNESS [*smiling*] Then you don't like to look ugly, Kaia?

KAIA [*half glancing up at him*] Not for all the world. Not in your eyes.

SOLNESS [*strokes her hair gently*] Poor, poor little Kaia –

KAIA [*bending her head*] Hush – they can hear you!

SOLNESS [*strolls across the room to the right, turns and pauses at the door of the draughtsmen's office.*] Has anyone been here for me?

RAGNAR [*rising*] Yes, the young couple who want a villa built, out at Lövstrand.

SOLNESS [*growling*] Oh, those two! They must wait. I am not quite clear about the plans yet.

RAGNAR [*advancing, with some hesitation*] They were very anxious to have the drawings at once.

SOLNESS [*as before*] Yes, of course – so they all are.

BROVIK [*looks up*] They say they are longing so to get into a house of their own.

SOLNESS Yes, yes – we know all that! And so they are content to take whatever is offered them. They get a – a roof over their heads – an address – but nothing to call a home. No thank you! In that case, let them apply to somebody else. Tell them that, the next time they call.

BROVIK [*pushes his glasses up on to his forehead and looks in astonishment at him*] To somebody else? Are you prepared to give up the commission?

SOLNESS [*impatiently*] Yes, yes, yes, devil take it! If that is to be the way of it – . Rather that, than build away at random. [*vehemently*] Besides, I know very little about these people as yet.

BROVIK The people are safe enough. Ragnar knows them. He is a friend of the family.

SOLNESS Oh, safe – safe enough! That is not at all what I mean. Good lord – don't you understand me either? [*angrily*] I won't have anything to do with these strangers. They may apply to whom they please, so far as I am concerned.

BROVIK [*rising*] Do you really mean that?

SOLNESS [*sulkily*] Yes I do. – For once in a way. [*he comes forward*]

Brovik exchanges a glance with Ragnar, who makes a warning gesture. Then BROVIK *comes into the front room.*

BROVIK May I have a few words with you?

SOLNESS Certainly.

BROVIK [*to Kaia*] Just go in there for moment, Kaia.

KAIA [*Uneasily*] Oh, but uncle –

BROVIK Do as I say, child. And shut the door after you.
[*Kaia goes reluctantly into the draughtsmen's office, glances anxiously and imploringly at Solness, and shuts the door.*]

BROVIK [*lowering his voice a little*] I don't want the poor children to know how I am.

SOLNESS Yes, you have been looking very poorly of late.

BROVIK It will soon be all over with me. My strength is ebbing – from day to day.

SOLNESS Won't you sit down?

BROVIK Thanks – may I?

SOLNESS [*placing the armchair more conveniently*] Here – take this chair. – And now?

BROVIK [*has seated himself with difficulty*] Well, you see, it's about Ragnar. That is what weighs most upon me. What is to become of him?

SOLNESS Of course your son will stay with me as long as ever he likes.

BROVIK But that is just what he does not like. He feels that he cannot stay here any longer.

SOLNESS Why, I should say he was very well off here. But if he wants more money, I should not mind –

BROVIK No, no! It is not that. [*impatiently*] But sooner or later he, too, must have a chance of doing something on his own account.

SOLNESS [*without looking at him*] Do you think that Ragnar has quite talent enough to stand alone?

BROVIK No, that is just the heartbreaking part of it – I have begun to have my doubts about the boy. For you have never said so much as – as one encouraging word about him. And yet I cannot but think there must be something in him – he can't be without talent.

SOLNESS Well, but he has learnt nothing – nothing thoroughly, I mean. Except, of course, to draw.

BROVIK [*looks at him with covert hatred, and says hoarsely*] You had learned little enough of the business when you were in my employment. But that did not prevent you from setting to work – [*breathing with difficulty*] – and pushing your way up and taking the wind out of my sails – mine, and so many other people's.

SOLNESS Yes, you see – circumstances favoured me.

BROVIK You are right there. Everything favoured you. But then how can you have the heart to let me go to my grave – without having seen what Ragnar is fit for? And of course I am anxious to see them married, too – before I go.

SOLNESS [*sharply*] Is it she who wishes it?

BROVIK Not Kaia so much as Ragnar – he talks about it every day [*appealingly*] You must help him to get some independen work now! I must see something that the lad has done. Do you hear?

SOLNESS [*peevishly*] Hang it, man, you can't expect me to drag commissions down from the moon for him!

BROVIK He has the chance of a capital commission at this very moment. A big bit of work.

SOLNESS [*Uneasily, startled*] Has he?

BROVIK If you would give your consent.

SOLNESS What sort of work do you mean?

BROVIK [*with some hesitation*] He can have the building of that villa out at Lövstrand.

SOLNESS That! Why I am going to build that myself.

BROVIK Oh, you don't much care about doing it.

SOLNESS [*flaring up*] Don't care! Who dares to say that?

BROVIK You said so yourself just now.

SOLNESS Oh, never mind what I say. – Would they give Ragnar the building of that villa?

BROVIK Yes. You see, he knows the family. And then – just for the fun of the thing – he has made drawings and estimates and so forth –

SOLNESS Are they pleased with the drawings? The people who will have to live in the house?

BROVIK Yes. If you would only look through them and approve of them –

SOLNESS Then they would let Ragnar build their home for them?

BROVIK They were immensely pleased with his idea. They thought it exceedingly original, they said.

SOLNESS Oho! Original! Not the old-fashioned stuff that *I* am in the habit of turning out!

BROVIK It seemed to them different.

SOLNESS [*with suppressed irritation*] So it was to see Ragnar that they came here – whilst I was out!

BROVIK They came to call upon you – and at the same time to ask whether you would mind retiring –

SOLNESS [*angrily*] Retire? I?

BROVIK In case you thought that Ragnar's drawings –

SOLNESS I! Retire in favour of your son!

BROVIK Retire from the agreement, they meant.

SOLNESS Oh, it comes to the same thing. [*laughs angrily*] So that is it, is it? Halvard Solness is to see about retiring now! To make room for younger men! For the very youngest, perhaps! He must make room! Room! Room!

BROVIK Why, good heavens! there is surely room for more than one single man –

SOLNESS Oh, there's not so very much room to spare either. But, be that as it may – I will never retire! I will never give way to anybody! Never of my own free will. Never in this world will I do that!

BROVIK [*rises with difficulty*] Then I am to pass out of life without any certainty? Without a gleam of happiness? Without any faith or trust in Ragnar? Without having seen a single piece of work of his doing? Is that to be the way of it?

SOLNESS [*turns half aside, and mutters*] H'm – don't ask more just now.

BROVIK I must have an answer to this one question. Am I to pass out of life in such utter poverty?

SOLNESS [*seems to struggle with himself; finally he says, in a low but firm voice*] You must pass out of life as best you can.

BROVIK Then be it so. [*he goes up the room*]

SOLNESS [*following him, half in desperation*] Don't you understand that I cannot help it? I am what I am, and I cannot change my nature!

BROVIK No; I suppose that you can't. [*reels and supports himself against the sofa-table*] May I have a glass of water?

SOLNESS By all means. [*fills a glass and hands it to him*]

BROVIK Thanks. [*drinks and puts the glass down again*]

SOLNESS [*goes up and opens the door of the draughtsmen's office*] Ragnar – you must come and take your father home.

RAGNAR *rises quickly. He and* KAIA *come into the work-room.*

RAGNAR What is the matter, father?

BROVIK Give me your arm. Now let us go.

RAGNAR Very well. You had better put your things on, too, Kaia.

SOLNESS Miss Fosli must stay – just for a moment. There is a letter I want written.

BROVIK [*looks at Solness*] Good night. Sleep well – if you can.

SOLNESS Good night.

[*Brovik and Ragnar go out by the hall-door.*]

[*Kaia goes to the desk. Solness stands with bent head, to the right, by the armchair.*]

KAIA [*dubiously*] Is there any letter?

SOLNESS [*curtly*] No, of course not. [*looks sternly at her*] Kaia!

KAIA [*anxiously, in a low voice*] Yes!

SOLNESS [*points imperatively to a spot on the floor*] Come here! At once!

KAIA [*hesitatingly*] Yes.

SOLNESS [*as before*] Nearer!

KAIA [*obeying*] What do you want with me?

SOLNESS [*looks at her for a while*] Is it you I have to thank for all this?

KAIA No, no, don't think that!

SOLNESS But confess now – you want to get married!

KAIA [*softly*] Ragnar and I have been engaged for four or five years, and so –

SOLNESS And so you think it time there were an end of it. Is not that so?

KAIA Ragnar and Uncle say I must. So I suppose I shall have to give in.

SOLNESS [*more gently*] Kaia, don't you really care a little bit for Ragnar, too?

KAIA I cared very much for Ragnar once – before I came here to you.

SOLNESS But you don't now? Not in the least?

KAIA [*passionately, clasping hands and holding them out towards him*] Oh, you know very well there is only one person I care for now! I shall never care for anyone else.

SOLNESS Yes, you say that. And yet you go away from me – leave me alone here with everything on my hands.

KAIA But could I not stay with you, even if Ragnar – ?

SOLNESS [*repudiating the idea*] No, no, that is quite impossible. If Ragnar leaves me and starts work on his own account, then of course he will need you himself.

KAIA [*wringing her hands*] Oh, I feel as if I could not be separated from you! It's quite, quite impossible!

SOLNESS Then be sure you get those foolish notions out of Ragnar's head. Marry him as much as you please – [*alters his tone*] I mean – don't let him throw up his good situation with me. For then I can keep you too, my dear Kaia.

KAIA Oh yes, how lovely that would be, if it could only be managed!

SOLNESS [*clasps her head with his two hands and whispers*] For I cannot get on without you, you see. I must have you with me every single day.

KAIA [*in nervous exaltation*] My God! My God!

SOLNESS [*kisses her hair*] Kaia – Kaia!

KAIA [*sinks down before him*] Oh, how good you are to me! How unspeakably good you are!

SOLNESS [*vehemently*] Get up! For goodness' sake get up! I think I hear someone. [*he helps her to rise. She staggers over to the desk.*]

> MRS SOLNESS *enters by the door on the right. She looks thin and wasted with grief, but shows traces of bygone beauty. Blonde ringlets. Dressed with good taste, wholly in black. Speaks somewhat slowly and in a plaintive voice.*

MRS SOLNESS [*in the doorway*] Halvard!

SOLNESS [*turns*] Oh, are you there, my dear – ?

MRS SOLNESS [*with a glance at Kaia*] I am afraid I am disturbing you.

SOLNESS Not in the least. Miss Fosli has only a short letter to write.

MRS SOLNESS Yes, so I see.

SOLNESS What do you want with me, Aline?

MRS SOLNESS I merely wanted to tell you that Dr Herdal is in the drawing-room. Won't you come and see him, Halvard?

SOLNESS [*looks suspiciously at her*]. H'm – is the doctor so very anxious to see me?

MRS SOLNESS Well, not exactly anxious. He really came to see me; but he would like to say how-do-you-do to you at the same time.

SOLNESS [*laughs to himself*] Yes, I dare say. Well, you must ask him to wait a little.

MRS SOLNESS Then you will come in presently?

SOLNESS Perhaps I will. Presently, presently, dear. In a little while.

MRS SOLNESS [*glancing again at Kaia*] Well now, don't forget, Halvard.
[*Withdraws and closes the door behind her.*]

KAIA [*softly*] Oh dear, oh dear – I am sure Mrs Solness thinks ill of me in some way!

SOLNESS Oh, not in the least. Not more than usual at any rate. But all the same, you had better go now, Kaia.

KAIA Yes, yes, now I must go.

SOLNESS [*severely*] And mind you get that matter settled for me. Do you hear?

KAIA Oh, if it only depended on me –

SOLNESS I will have it settled, I say! And tomorrow too – not a day later!

KAIA [*terrified*] If there's nothing else for it, I am quite willing to break off the engagement.

SOLNESS [*angrily*] Break it off. Are you mad? Would you think of breaking it off?

KAIA [*distracted*] Yes, if necessary. For I must – I must stay here with you! I can't leave you! That is utterly – utterly imposs-ible!

SOLNESS [*with a sudden outburst*] But deuce take it – how about Ragnar then! It's Ragnar that I –

KAIA [*looks at him with terrified eyes*] It is chiefly on Ragnar's account, that – that you – ?

SOLNESS [*collecting himself*] No, no, of course not! You don't understand me either. [*gently and softly*] Of course it is you I want to keep – you above everything, Kaia. But for that very reason, you must prevent Ragnar, too, from throwing up his situation. There, there – now go home.

KAIA Yes, yes – good night, then.

SOLNESS Good night. [*as she is going*] Oh, stop a moment! Are Ragnar's drawings in there?

KAIA I did not see him take them with him.

SOLNESS Then just go and find them for me. I might perhaps glance over them, after all.

KAIA [*happy*] Oh yes, please do!

SOLNESS For your sake, Kaia dear. Now, let me have them at once, please.

[*Kaia hurries into the draughtsmen's office, searches anxiously in the table-drawer, finds a portfolio and brings it with her.*]

KAIA Here are all the drawings.

SOLNESS Good. Put them down there on the table.

KAIA [*putting down the portfolio*] Good night, then. [*beseechingly*] And please, please think kindly of me.

SOLNESS Oh, that I always do. Good night, my dear little Kaia. [*glances to the right*] Go, go now!

MRS SOLNESS *and* DR HERDAL *enter by the door on the right. He is
a stoutish, elderly man, with a round, good-humoured face, clean-
shaven, with thin, light hair, and gold spectacles.*

MRS SOLNESS [*still in the doorway*] Halvard, I cannot keep the doctor
any longer.

SOLNESS Well then, come in here.

MRS SOLNESS [*to Kaia, who is turning down the desk-lamp*] Have you
finished the letter already, Miss Fosli?

KAIA [*in confusion*] The letter – ?

SOLNESS Yes, it was quite a short one.

MRS SOLNESS It must have been very short.

SOLNESS You may go now, Miss Fosli. And please come in good
time tomorrow morning.

KAIA I will be sure to. Good night, Mrs Solness.

[*she goes out by the hall door*]

MRS SOLNESS She must be quite an acquisition to you, Halvard,
this Miss Fosli.

SOLNESS Yes, indeed. She is useful in all sorts of ways.

MRS SOLNESS So it seems.

DR HERDAL Is she good at book-keeping too?

SOLNESS Well, of course she has had a good deal of practice
duringthese two years. And then she is so nice and willing to do
whatever one asks of her.

MRS SOLNESS Yes, that must be very delightful –

SOLNESS It is. Especially when one is not too much accustomed to
that sort of thing.

MRS SOLNESS [*in a tone of gentle remonstrance*] Can you say that,
Halvard?

SOLNESS Oh, no, no, my dear Aline; I beg your pardon.

MRS SOLNESS There's no occasion – Well then, Doctor, you will
come back later on, and havea cup of tea with us?

DR HERDAL I have only that one patient to see, and then I'll come
back.

MRS SOLNESS Thank you.   [*she goes out by the door on the right*]

SOLNESS Are you in a hurry, doctor?

DR HERDAL No, not at all.

SOLNESS May I have a little chat with you?

DR HERDAL With the greatest of pleasure.

SOLNESS Then let us sit down. [*he motions the doctor to take the rocking-chair, and sits down himself in the armchair. Looks searchingly at him*] Tell me – did you notice anything odd about Aline?

DR HERDAL Do you mean just now, when she was here?

SOLNESS Yes, in her manner to me. Did you notice anything?

DR HERDAL [*smiling*] Well, I admit – one couldn't well avoid noticing that your wife – h'm –

SOLNESS Well?

DR HERDAL – that your wife is not particularly fond of this Miss Fosli.

SOLNESS Is that all? I have noticed that myself.

DR HERDAL And I must say I am scarcely surprised at it.

SOLNESS At what?

DR HERDAL That she should not exactly approve of your seeing so much of another woman, all day and every day.

SOLNESS No, no, I suppose you are right there – and Aline too. But it's impossible to make any change.

DR HERDAL Could you not engage a clerk?

SOLNESS The first man that came to hand? No, thank you – that would never do for me.

DR HERDAL But now, if your wife – ? Suppose, with her delicate health, all this tries her too much?

SOLNESS Even then – I might almost say – it can make no difference. I must keep Kaia Fosli. No one else could fill her place.

DR HERDAL No one else?

SOLNESS [*curtly*] No, no one.

DR HERDAL [*drawing his chair closer*] Now listen to me, my dear Mr Solness. May I ask you a question, quite between ourselves?

SOLNESS By all means.

DR HERDAL Women, you see – in certain matters, they have a deucedly keen intuition –

SOLNESS They have, indeed. There is not the least doubt of that. But – ?

DR HERDAL Well, tell me now – if your wife can't endure this Kaia Fosli – ?

SOLNESS Well, what then?

DR HERDAL – may she not have just – just the least little bit of reason for this instinctive dislike?

SOLNESS [*looks at him and rises*] Oho!

DR HERDAL Now don't be offended – but hasn't she?

SOLNESS [*with curt decision*] No.

DR HERDAL No reason of any sort?

SOLNESS No other than her own suspicious nature.

DR HERDAL I know you have known a good many women in your time.

SOLNESS Yes, I have.

DR HERDAL And have been a good deal taken with some of them, too.

SOLNESS Oh yes, I don't deny it.

DR HERDAL But as regards Miss Fosli, then? There is nothing of that sort in this case?

SOLNESS No; nothing at all – on my side.

DR HERDAL But on her side?

SOLNESS I don't think you have any right to ask that question, doctor.

DR HERDAL Well, you know, we were discussing your wife's intuition.

SOLNESS So we were. And for that matter – [*lowers his voice*] – Aline's intuition, as you call it – in a certain sense, it has not been so far astray.

DR HERDAL Aha! there we have it!

SOLNESS [*sits down*] Doctor Herdal – I am going to tell you a strange story – if you care to listen to it.

DR HERDAL I like listening to strange stories.

SOLNESS Very well then. I dare say you recollect that I took Knut Brovik and his son into my employment – after the old man's business had gone to the dogs.

DR HERDAL Yes, so I have understood.

SOLNESS You see, they really are clever fellows, these two. Each of them has talent in his own way. But then the son took it into his head to get engaged; and the next thing, of course, was that he wanted to get married – and begin to build on his own account. That is the way with all these young people.

DR HERDAL [*laughing*] Yes, they have a bad habit of wanting to marry.

SOLNESS Just so. But of course that did not suit my plans; for I needed Ragnar myself – and the old man too. He is exceedingly good at calculating bearing strains and cubic contents – and all that sort of devilry, you know.

DR HERDAL Oh yes, no doubt that's indispensable.

SOLNESS Yes, it is. But Ragnar was absolutely bent on setting to work for himself. He would hear of nothing else.

DR HERDAL But he has stayed with you all the same.

SOLNESS Yes, I'll tell you how that came about. One day this girl, Kaia Fosli, came to see them on some errand or other. She had never been here before. And when I saw how utterly infatuated they were with each other, the thought occurred to me: if I cold only get her into the office here, then perhaps Ragnar too would stay where he is.

DR HERDAL That was not at all a bad idea.

SOLNESS Yes, but at the time I did not breathe a word of what was in my mind. I merely stood and looked at her – and kept on wishing intently that I could have her here. Then I talked to her a little, in a friendly way – about one thing and another. And then she went away.

DR HERDAL Well?

SOLNESS Well then, next day, pretty late in the evening, when old Brovik and Ragnar had gone home, she came here again, and behaved as if I had made an arrangement with her.

DR HERDAL An arrangement? What about?

SOLNESS About the very thing my mind had been fixed on. But I hadn't said one single word about it.

DR HERDAL That was most extraordinary.

SOLNESS Yes, was it not? And now she wanted to know what she was to do here – whether she could begin the very next morning, and so forth.

DR HERDAL Don't you think she did it in order to be with her sweetheart?

SOLNESS That was what occurred to me at first. But no, that was not it. She seemed to drift quite away from him – when once she had come here to me.

DR HERDAL She drifted over to you, then?

SOLNESS Yes, entirely. If I happen to look at her when her back is turned, I can tell that she feels it. She quivers and trembles the moment I come near her. What do you think of that?

DR HERDAL H'm – that's not very hard to explain.

SOLNESS Well, but what about the other thing? That she believed I had said to her what I had only wished and willed – silently – inwardly – to myself? What do you say to that? Can you explain that, Dr Herdal?

DR HERDAL No, I won't undertake to do that.

SOLNESS I felt sure you would not; and so I have never cared to talk about it till now. – But it's a cursed nuisance to me in the long run, you understand. Here have I got to go on day after day, pretending – . And it's a shame to treat her so, too, poor girl. [*vehemently*] But I cannot do anything else. For if she runs away from me – then Ragnar will be off too.

DR HERDAL And you have not told your wife the rights of the story?

SOLNESS No.

DR HERDAL Then why on earth don't you?

SOLNESS [*looks fixedly at him, and says in a low voice*] Because I seem to find a sort of – of salutary self-torture in allowing Aline to do me an injustice.

DR HERDAL [*shakes his head*] I don't in the least understand what you mean.

SOLNESS Well, you see – it is like paying off a little bit of a huge, immeasurable debt –

DR HERDAL To your wife?

SOLNESS Yes; and that always helps to relieve one's mind a little. One can breathe more freely for a while, you understand.

DR HERDAL No, goodness knows, I don't understand at all –

SOLNESS [*breaking off, rises again*] Well, well, well – then we won't talk any more about it. [*he saunters across the room, returns, and stops beside the table. Looks at the doctor with a sly smile*] I suppose you think you have drawn me out nicely now, doctor?

DR HERDAL [*with some irritation*] Drawn you out? Again I have not the faintest notion of what you mean, Mr Solness.

SOLNESS Oh come, out with it; I have seen it quite clearly, you know.

DR HERDAL What have you seen?

SOLNESS [*in a low voice, slowly*] That you have been quietly keeping an eye upon me.

DR HERDAL That *I* have! And why in all the world should I do that?

SOLNESS Because you think that I – [*passionately*] Well, devil take it – you think the same of me as Aline does.

DR HERDAL And what does she think about you?

SOLNESS [*having recovered his self-control*] She has begun to think that I am – that I am – ill.

DR HERDAL Ill! You! She has never hinted such a thing to me. Why, what can she think is the matter with you?

SOLNESS [*leans over the back of the chair and whispers*] Aline has made up her mind that I am mad. That is what she thinks.

DR HERDAL [*rising*] Why, my dear fellow – !

SOLNESS Yes, on my soul she does! I tell you it is so. And she has got you to think the same! Oh, I can assure you, doctor, I see it in your face as clearly as possible. You don't take me in so easily, I can tell you.

DR HERDAL [*looks at him in amazement*] Never, Mr Solness – never has such a thought entered my mind.

SOLNESS [*with an incredulous smile*] Really? Has it not?

DR HERDAL No, never! Nor your wife's mind either, I am convinced. I could almost swear to that.

SOLNESS Well, I wouldn't advise you to. For, in a certain sense, you see, perhaps – perhaps she is not so far wrong in thinking something of the kind.

DR HERDAL Come now, I really must say –

SOLNESS [*interrupting, with a sweep of his hand*] Well, well, my dear doctor – don't let us discuss this any further. We had better agree to differ. [*changes to a tone of quiet amusement*] But look here now, doctor – h'm –

DR HERDAL Well?

SOLNESS Since you don't believe that I am – ill – and crazy – and mad, and so forth –

DR HERDAL What then?

SOLNESS Then I dare say you fancy that I am an extremely happy man.

DR HERDAL Is that mere fancy?

SOLNESS [*laughs*] No, no – of course not! Heaven forbid! Only think – to be Solness the master builder! Halvard Solness! What could be more delightful?

DR HERDAL Yes, I must say it seems to me you have had the luck on your side to an astounding degree.

SOLNESS [*suppresses a gloomy smile*] So I have. I can't complain on that score.

DR HERDAL First of all that grim old robbers' castle was burnt down for you. And that was certainly a great piece of luck.

SOLNESS [*seriously*] It was the home of Aline's family. Remember that.

DR HERDAL Yes, it must have been a great grief to her.

SOLNESS She has not got over it to this day – not in all these twelve or thirteen years.

DR HERDAL But you – yourself – you rose upon the ruins. You began as a poor boy from a country village – and now you are at the head of your profession. Ah, yes, Mr Solness, you have undoubtedly had the luck on your side.

SOLNESS [*looking at him with embarrassment*] Yes, but that is just what makes me so horribly afraid.

DR HERDAL Afraid? Because you have the luck on your side!

SOLNESS It terrifies me – terrifies me every hour of the day. For sooner or later the luck must turn, you see.

DR HERDAL Oh nonsense! What should make the luck turn?

SOLNESS [*with firm assurance*] The younger generation!

DR HERDAL Pooh! The younger generation! You are not laid on the shelf yet, I should hope. Oh no – your position here is probably firmer now than it has ever been.

SOLNESS The luck will turn. I know it – I feel the day approaching. Someone or other will take it into his head to say: Give me a chance! And then all the rest will come clamouring after him, and shake their fists at me and shout: Make room – make room – ! Yes, just you see, doctor – presently the younger generation will come knocking at my door –

DR HERDAL [*laughing*] Well, and what if they do?

SOLNESS What if they do? Then there's an end of Halvard Solness. [*there is a knock at the door on the left.*]

SOLNESS [*starts*] What's that? Did you not hear something?

DR HERDAL Someone is knocking at the door.

SOLNESS [*loudly*] Come in.

HILDA WANGEL *enters by the hall door. She is of middle height, supple, and delicately built. Somewhat sunburnt. Dressed in a tourist costume, with skirt caught up for walking, a sailor's collar open at the throat, and a small sailor hat on her head. Knapsack on back, plaid in strap, and alpenstock.*

HILDA [*goes straight up to Solness, her eyes sparkling with happiness*] Good evening!

SOLNESS [*looks doubtfully at her*] Good evening –

HILDA [*laughs*] I almost believe you don't recognise me!

SOLNESS No – I must admit that – just for the moment –

DR HERDAL [*approaching*] But *I* recognise you, my dear young lady –

HILDA [*pleased*] Oh, is it you that –

DR HERDAL Of course it is. [*to Solness*] We met at one of the mountain stations this summer. [*to Hilda*] What became of the other ladies?

HILDA Oh, they went westward.

DR HERDAL They didn't much like all the fun we used to have in the evenings.

HILDA No, I believe they didn't.

DR HERDAL [*holds up his finger at her*] And I am afraid it can't be denied that you flirted a little with us.

HILDA Well, that was better fun than to sit there knitting stockings with all those old women.

DR HERDAL [*laughs*] There I entirely agree with you!

SOLNESS Have you come to town this evening?

HILDA Yes, I have just arrived.

DR HERDAL Quite alone, Miss Wangel?

HILDA Oh yes!

SOLNESS Wangel? Is your name Wangel?

HILDA [*looks in amused surprise at him*] Yes, of course it is.

SOLNESS Then you must be a daughter of the district doctor up at Lysanger?

HILDA [*as before*] Yes, who else's daughter should I be?

SOLNESS Oh, then I suppose we met up there, that summer when I was building a tower on the old church.

HILDA [*more seriously*] Yes, of course it was then we met.

SOLNESS Well, that is a long time ago.

HILDA [*looks hard at him*] It is exactly ten years.

SOLNESS You must have been a mere child then, I should think.

HILDA [*carelessly*] Well, I was twelve or thirteen.

DR HERDAL Is this the first time you have ever been up to town, Miss Wangel?

HILDA Yes, it is indeed.

SOLNESS And don't you know anyone here?

HILDA Nobody but you. And of course, your wife.

SOLNESS So you know her, too?

HILDA Only a little. We spent a few days together at the sanatorium.

SOLNESS Ah, up there?

HILDA She said I might come and pay her a visit if ever I came up to town. [*smiles*] Not that that was necessary.

SOLNESS Odd that she should never have mentioned it.

[*Hilda puts her stick down by the stove, takes off the knapsack and lays it and the plaid on the sofa. Dr Herdal offers to help her. Solness stands and gazes at her.*]

HILDA [*going towards him*] Well, now I must ask you to let me stay the night here.

SOLNESS I am sure there will be no difficulty about that.

HILDA For I have no other clothes than those I stand in, except a change of linen in my knapsack. And that has to go to the wash, for it's very dirty.

SOLNESS Oh yes, that can be managed. Now I'll just let my wife know —

DR HERDAL Meanwhile I will go and see my patient.

SOLNESS Yes, do; and come again later on.

DR HERDAL [*playfully, with a glance at Hilda*] Oh that I will, you may be very certain! [*laughs*] So your prediction has come true, Mr Solness!

SOLNESS How so?

DR HERDAL The younger generation did come knocking at your door.

SOLNESS [*cheerfully*] Yes, but in a very different way from what I meant.

DR HERDAL Very different, yes. That's undeniable.

[*He goes out by the hall-door.*]

SOLNESS [*opens the door on the right and speaks into the side room*] Aline! Will you come in here, please. Here is a friend of yours — Miss Wangel.

MRS SOLNESS [*appears in the doorway*] Who do you say it is? [*sees Hilda*]. Oh, is it you, Miss Wangel?

SOLNESS Miss Wangel has this moment arrived; and she would like to stay the night here.

MRS SOLNESS Here with us? Oh yes, certainly.

SOLNESS Till she can get her things a little in order, you know.

MRS SOLNESS I will do the best I can for you. It's no more than my duty. I suppose your trunk is coming on later?

HILDA I have no trunk.

MRS SOLNESS Well, it will be all right, I dare say. In the meantime, you must excuse my leaving you here with my husband, until I can get a room made a little more comfortable for you.

SOLNESS Can we not give her one of the nurseries? They are all ready as it is.

MRS SOLNESS Oh yes. There we have room and to spare. [to Hilda] Sit down now, and rest a little.   [she goes out to the right] [Hilda, with her hands behind her back, strolls about the room and looks at various objects. Solness stands in front, beside the table, also with his hands behind his back, and follows her with his eyes.]

HILDA [stops and looks at him] Have you several nurseries?

SOLNESS There are three nurseries in the house.

HILDA That's a lot. Then I suppose you have a great many children?

SOLNESS No. We have no child. But now you can be the child here, for the time being.

HILDA For tonight, yes. I shall not cry. I mean to sleep as sound as a stone.

SOLNESS Yes, you must be very tired, I should think.

HILDA Oh no! But all the same – it's so delicious to lie and dream.

SOLNESS Do you dream much of nights?

HILDA Oh yes! Almost always.

SOLNESS What do you dream about most?

HILDA I shan't tell you tonight. Another time perhaps.
   [She again strolls about the room, stops at the desk and turns over the books and papers a little.]

SOLNESS [approaching] Are you searching for anything?

HILDA No, I am merely looking at all these things. [turns] Perhaps I mustn't?

SOLNESS Oh, by all means.

HILDA Is it you that writes in this great ledger?

SOLNESS No, it's my book-keeper.

HILDA Is it a woman?

SOLNESS [smiles] Yes.

HILDA One you employ here, in your office?

SOLNESS Yes.

HILDA Is she married?

SOLNESS No, she is single.

HILDA Oh, indeed!

SOLNESS But I believe she is soon going to be married.

HILDA That's a good thing for her.

SOLNESS But not such a good thing for me. For then I shall have nobody to help me.

HILDA Can't you get hold of someone else who will do just as well?

SOLNESS Perhaps you would stay here and – and write in the ledger?

HILDA [*measures him with a glance*] Yes, I dare say! No, thank you – nothing of that sort for me.

[*She again strolls across the room, and sits down on the rocking-chair. Solness too goes to the table.*]

HILDA [*continuing*] For there must surely be plenty of other things to be done here. [*looks smilingly at him*] Don't you think so, too?

SOLNESS Of course. First of all, I suppose, you want to make a round of the shops, and get yourself up in the height of fashion.

HILDA [*amused*] No, I think I shall let that alone!

SOLNESS Indeed?

HILDA For you must know I have run through all my money.

SOLNESS [*laughs*] Neither trunk nor money, then?

HILDA Neither one nor the other. But never mind – it doesn't matter now.

SOLNESS Come now, I like you for that.

HILDA Only for that?

SOLNESS For that among other things. [*sits in the armchair*] Is your father alive still?

HILDA Yes, father's alive.

SOLNESS Perhaps you are thinking of studying here?

HILDA No, that hadn't occurred to me.

SOLNESS But I suppose you will be staying for some time?

HILDA That must depend upon circumstances.

[*She sits awhile rocking herself and looking at him, half seriously, half with a suppressed smile. Then she takes off her hat and puts it on the table in front of her.*]

HILDA Mr Solness!

SOLNESS Well?

HILDA Have you a very bad memory?

SOLNESS A bad memory? No, not that I am aware of.

HILDA Then have you nothing to say to me about what happened up there?

SOLNESS [*in momentary surprise*] Up at Lysanger? [*indifferently*] Why, it was nothing much to talk about it seems to me.

HILDA [*looks reproachfully at him*] How can you sit there and say such things?

SOLNESS Well, then, you talk to me about it.

HILDA When the tower was finished, we had grand doings in the town.

SOLNESS Yes, I shall not easily forget that day.

HILDA [*smiles*] Will you not? That comes well from you.

SOLNESS Comes well?

HILDA There was music in the churchyard – and many, many hundreds of people. We school-girls were dressed in white; and we all carried flags.

SOLNESS Ah yes, those flags – I can tell you I remember them!

HILDA Then you climbed right up the scaffolding, straight to the very top; and you had a great wreath with you; and you hung that wreath right away up on the weather-vane.

SOLNESS [*curtly interrupting*] I always did that in those days. It is an old custom.

HILDA It was so wonderfully thrilling to stand below and look up at you. Fancy, if he should fall over! He – the master builder himself!

SOLNESS [*as if to divert her from the subject*] Yes, yes, yes, that might very well have happened, too. For one of those white-frocked little devils – she went on in such a way, and screamed up at me so –

HILDA [*sparkling with pleasure*] 'Hurrah for Master Builder Solness!' Yes!

SOLNESS – and waved and flourished with her flag, so that I – so that it almost made me giddy to look at it.

HILDA [*in a lower voice, seriously*] That little devil – that was *I*.

SOLNESS [*fixes his eyes steadily upon her*] I am sure of that now. It must have been you.

HILDA [*lively again*] Oh, it was so gloriously thrilling! I could not have believed there was a builder in the whole world that could build such a tremendously high tower. And then, that you yourself should stand at the very top of it, as large as life! And that you should not be the least bit dizzy! It was that above everything that made one – made one dizzy to think of.

SOLNESS How could you be so certain that I was not?

HILDA [*scouting the idea*] No indeed! Oh no! I knew that instinctively. For if you had been, you could never have stood up there and sung.

SOLNESS [*looks at her in astonishment*] Sung? Did *I* sing?

HILDA Yes, I should think you did.

SOLNESS [*shakes his head*] I have never sung a note in my life.

HILDA Yes, indeed, you sang then. It sounded like harps in the air.

SOLNESS [*thoughtfully*] This is very strange – all this.

HILDA [*is silent awhile, looks at him and says in a low voice*] But then – it was after that – that the real thing happened.

SOLNESS The real thing?

HILDA [*sparking with vivacity*] Yes, I surely don't need to remind you of that?

SOLNESS Oh yes, do remind me a little of that, too.

HILDA Don't you remember that a great dinner was given in your honour at the Club?

SOLNESS Yes, to be sure. It must have been the same afternoon, for I left the place next morning.

HILDA And from the Club you were invited to come round to our house to supper.

SOLNESS Quite right, Miss Wangel. It is wonderful how all these trifles have impressed themselves on your mind.

HILDA Trifles! I like that! Perhaps it was a trifle, too, that I was alone in the room when you came in?

SOLNESS Were you alone?

HILDA [*without answering him*] You didn't call me a little devil then?

SOLNESS No, I suppose I did not.

HILDA You said I was lovely in my white dress, and that I looked like a little princess.

SOLNESS I have no doubt you did, Miss Wangel. – And besides – I was feeling so buoyant and free that day –

HILDA And then you said that when I grew up I should be your princess.

SOLNESS [*laughing a little*] Dear, dear – did I say that too?

HILDA Yes, you did. And when I asked how long I should have to wait, you said that you would come again in ten years – like a troll – and carry me off – to Spain or some such place. And you promised you would buy me a kingdom there.

SOLNESS [*as before*] Yes, after a good dinner one doesn't haggle about the halfpence. But did I really say all that?

HILDA [*laughs to herself*] Yes. And you told me, too, what the kingdom was to be called.

SOLNESS Well, what was it?

HILDA It was to be called the kingdom of Orangia,[1] you said.

SOLNESS Well, that was an appetising name.

HILDA No, I didn't like it a bit; for it seemed as though you wanted to make game of me.

SOLNESS I am sure that cannot have been my intention.

HILDA No, I should hope not – considering what you did next –

SOLNESS What in the world did I do next?

HILDA Well, that's the finishing touch, if you have forgotten that too. I should have thought no one could help remembering such a thing as that.

SOLNESS Yes, yes, just give me a hint, and then perhaps – Well?

HILDA [*looks fixedly at him*] You came and kissed me, Mr Solness.

SOLNESS [*open-mouthed*] I did!

HILDA Yes, indeed you did. You took me in both your arms, and bent my head back, and kissed me – many times.

SOLNESS Now really, my dear Miss Wangel – !

HILDA [*rises*] You surely cannot mean to deny it?

SOLNESS Yes, I do. I deny it altogether!

HILDA [*looks scornfully at him*] Oh, indeed!

[*She turns and goes slowly up to the stove, where she remains standing motionless, her face averted from him, her hands behind her back. Short pause.*]

SOLNESS [*goes cautiously up behind her*] Miss Wangel – !

HILDA [*is silent and does not move*]

SOLNESS Don't stand there like a statue. You must have dreamt all this. [*lays his hand on her arm*] Now just listen –

HILDA [*makes an impatient movement with her arm*]

SOLNESS [*as a thought flashes upon him*] Or – ! Wait a moment!
    There is something under all this, you may depend!

HILDA [*does not move*]

SOLNESS [*in a low voice, but with emphasis*] I must have thought all
    that. I must have wished it – have willed it – have longed to do
    it. And then – may not that be the explanation.

HILDA [*is still silent*]

SOLNESS [*impatiently*] Oh very well, deuce take it all – then I did do
    it, I suppose.

HILDA [*turns her head a little, but without looking at him*] Then you
    admit it now?

SOLNESS Yes – whatever you like.

HILDA You came and put your arms round me?

SOLNESS Oh yes!

HILDA And bent my head back?

SOLNESS Very far back.

HILDA And kissed me?

SOLNESS Yes, I did.

HILDA Many times?

SOLNESS As many as ever you like.

HILDA [*turns quickly toward him and has once more the sparkling
    expression of gladness in her eyes*] Well, you see, I got it out of
    you at last!

SOLNESS [*with a slight smile*] Yes – just think of my forgetting such a
    thing as that.

HILDA [*again a little sulky, retreats from him*] Oh, you have kissed so
    many people in your time, I suppose.

SOLNESS No, you mustn't think that of me.

[*Hilda seats herself in the armchair.*]

SOLNESS [*stands and leans against the rocking-chair. Looks observantly
    at her*] Miss Wangel!

HILDA Yes!

SOLNESS How was it now? What came of all this – between us
    two.

HILDA Why, nothing more came of it. You know that quite well.
    For then the other guests came in, and then – bah!

SOLNESS Quite so! The others came in. To think of my forgetting
    that too!

HILDA Oh, you haven't really forgotten anything: you are only a little ashamed of it all. I am sure one doesn't forget things of that kind.

SOLNESS No, one would suppose not.

HILDA [*lively again, looks at him*] Perhaps you have even forgotten what day it was?

SOLNESS What day – ?

HILDA Yes, on what day did you hang the wreath on the tower? Well? Tell me at once!

SOLNESS H'm – I confess I have forgotten the particular day. I only know it was ten years ago. Some time in autumn.

HILDA [*nods her head slowly several times*] It was ten years ago – on the 19th of September.

SOLNESS Yes, it must have been about that time. Fancy your remembering that too! [*stops*] But wait a moment – ! Yes – it's the 19th of September today.

HILDA Yes, it is; and the ten years are gone. And you didn't come – as you had promised me.

SOLNESS Promised you? Threatened, I suppose you mean?

HILDA I don't think there was any sort of threat in that.

SOLNESS Well then, a little bit of fun.

HILDA Was that all you wanted? To make fun of me?

SOLNESS Well, or to have a little joke with you. Upon my soul, I don't recollect. But it must have been something of that kind; for you were a mere child then.

HILDA Oh, perhaps I wasn't quite such a child either. Not such a mere chit as you imagine.

SOLNESS [*looks searchingly at her*] Did you really and seriously expect me to come again?

HILDA [*conceals a half-teasing smile*] Yes, indeed! I did expect that of you.

SOLNESS That I should come back to your home, and take you away with me?

HILDA Just like a troll – yes.

SOLNESS And make a princess of you?

HILDA That's what you promised.

SOLNESS And give you a kingdom as well?

HILDA [*looks up at the ceiling*] Why not? Of course it need not have been an actual, everyday sort of a kingdom.

SOLNESS But something else just as good?

HILDA Yes, at least as good. [*looks at him a moment*] I thought, if you could build the highest church-towers in the world, you could surely manage to raise a kingdom of one sort or another as well.

SOLNESS [*shakes his head*] I can't quite make you out, Miss Wangel.

HILDA Can you not? To me it seems all so simple.

SOLNESS No, I can't make up my mind whether you mean all you say, or are simply having a joke with me.

HILDA [*smiles*] Making fun of you, perhaps? I, too?

SOLNESS Yes, exactly. Making fun – of both of us. [*looks at her*] Is it long since you found out that I was married?

HILDA I have known it all along. Why do you ask me that?

SOLNESS [*lightly*] Oh, well, it just occurred to me. [*looks earnestly at her, and says in a low voice*] What have you come for?

HILDA I want my kingdom. The time is up.

SOLNESS [*laughs involuntarily*] What a girl you are!

HILDA [*gaily*] Out with my kingdom, Mr Solness! [*raps with her fingers*] The kingdom on the table!

SOLNESS [*pushing the rocking-chair nearer and sitting down*] Now seriously speaking – what have you come for? What do you really want to do here?

HILDA Oh, first of all, I want to go round and look at all the things that you have built.

SOLNESS That will give you plenty of exercise.

HILDA Yes, I know you have built a tremendous lot.

SOLNESS I have indeed – especially of late years.

HILDA Many church-towers among the rest? Immensely high ones?

SOLNESS No. I build no more church-towers now. Nor churches either.

HILDA What do you build then?

SOLNESS Homes for human beings.

HILDA [*reflectively*] Couldn't you build a little – a little bit of church-tower over these homes as well?

SOLNESS [*starting*] What do you mean by that?

HILDA I mean – something that points – points up into the free air. With the vane at a dizzy height.

SOLNESS [*pondering a little*] Strange that you should say that – for that is just what I am most anxious to do.

HILDA [*impatiently*] Why don't you do it, then?

SOLNESS [*shakes his head*] No, the people will not have it.

HILDA Fancy their not wanting it!

SOLNESS [*more lightly*] But now I am building a new home for myself – just opposite here.

HILDA For yourself?

SOLNESS Yes. It is almost finished. And on that there is a tower.

HILDA A high tower?

SOLNESS Yes.

HILDA Very high?

SOLNESS No doubt people will say it is too high – too high for a dwelling-house.

HILDA I'll go out to look at that tower first thing tomorrow morning.

SOLNESS [*sits resting his cheek on his hand, and gazes at her*] Tell me, Miss Wangel – what is your name? Your Christian name, I mean.

HILDA Why, Hilda, of course.

SOLNESS [*as before*] Hilda? Indeed?

HILDA Don't you remember that? You called me Hilda yourself – that day when you misbehaved.

SOLNESS Did I really.

HILDA But then you said 'little Hilda'; and I didn't like that.

SOLNESS Oh, you didn't like that, Miss Hilda?

HILDA No, not at such a time as that. But – 'Princess Hilda' – that will sound very well, I think.

SOLNESS Very well indeed. Princess Hilda of – of – what was to be the name of the kingdom?

HILDA Pooh! I won't have anything to do with that stupid kingdom. I have set my heart upon quite a different one!

SOLNESS [*has leaned back in the chair, still gazing at her*] Isn't it strange – ? The more I think of it now, the more it seems to me as though I had gone about all these years torturing myself with – h'm –

HILDA With what?

SOLNESS With the effort to recover something – some experience, which I seemed to have forgotten. But I never had the least inkling of what it could be.

HILDA You should have tied a knot in your pocket-handkerchief, Mr Solness.

SOLNESS In that case, I should simply have had to go racking my
   brains to discover what the knot could mean.

HILDA Oh yes, I suppose there are trolls of that kind in the world,
   too.

SOLNESS [*rises slowly*] What a good thing it is that you have come to
   me now.

HILDA [*looks deeply into his eyes*] Is it a good thing!

SOLNESS For I have been so lonely here. I have been gazing so
   helplessly at it all. [*in a lower voice*] I must tell you – I have begun
   to be afraid of the younger generation.

HILDA [*with a little snort of contempt*] Pooh – is the younger generation something to be afraid of?

SOLNESS It is indeed. And that is why I have locked and barred
   myself in. [*mysteriously*] I tell you the younger generation will
   one day come and thunder at my door! They will break in
   upon me!

HILDA Then I should say you ought to go out and open the door
   to the younger generation.

SOLNESS Open the door?

HILDA Yes. Let them come in to you on friendly terms, as it were.

SOLNESS No, no, no! The younger generation – it means retribution, you see. It comes, as if under a new banner, heralding the
   turn of fortune.

HILDA [*rises, looks at him, and says with a quivering twitch of her lips*]
   Can *I* be of any use to you, Mr Solness?

SOLNESS Yes, you can indeed! For you, too, come – under a new
   banner it seems to me. You marshalled against youth – !

   DR HERDAL *comes in by the hall-door.*

DR HERDAL What – you and Miss Wangel here still?

SOLNESS Yes. We have had no end of things to talk about.

HILDA Both old and new.

DR HERDAL Have you really?

HILDA Oh, it has been the greatest fun. For Mr Solness – he
   has such a miraculous memory. All the least little details he
   remembers instantly.

   MRS SOLNESS *enters by the door on the right.*

MRS SOLNESS Well, Miss Wangel, your room is quite ready for you
   now.

HILDA Oh, how kind you are to me!

SOLNESS [*to Mrs Solness*] The nursery?

MRS SOLNESS Yes, the middle one. But first let us go in to supper.

SOLNESS [*nods to Hilda*] Hilda shall sleep in the nursery, she shall.

MRS SOLNESS [*looks at him*] Hilda?

SOLNESS Yes, Miss Wangel's name is Hilda. I knew her when she was a child.

MRS SOLNESS Did you really, Halvard? Well, shall we go?

> [*she takes Dr Herdal's arm and goes out with him to the right.*]
> [*Hilda has meanwhile been collecting her travelling things.*]

HILDA [*softly and rapidly to Solness*] Is it true, what you said? Can I be of use to you?

SOLNESS [*takes the things from her*] You are the very being I have needed most.

HILDA [*looks at him with happy, wondering eyes and clasps her hands*] But then, great heavens – !

SOLNESS [*eagerly*] What – ?

HILDA Then I have my kingdom!

SOLNESS [*involuntarily*] Hilda – !

HILDA [*again with the quivering twitch of her lips*] Almost – I was going to say.

> [*She goes out to the right, Solness follows her.*]

ACT SECOND

A prettily furnished small drawing-room in SOLNESS'S *house. In the back,
a glass-door leading out to the verandah and garden. The right-hand corner
is cut off transversely by a large bay-window, in which are flower-stands.
The left-hand corner is similarly cut off by a transverse wall, in which is a
small door papered like the wall. On each side, an ordinary door. In front,
on the right, a console table with a large mirror over it. Well-filled stands of
plants and flowers. In front, on the left, a sofa with a table and chairs.
Further back, a bookcase. Well forward in the room, before the bay
window, a small table and some chairs.*

It is early in the day. SOLNESS *sits by the little table with* RAGNAR
BROVIK'S *portfolio open in front of him. He is turning the drawings over
and closely examining some of them.* MRS SOLNESS *moves about noise-
lessly with a small watering-pot, attending to her flowers. She is dressed in
black as before. Her hat, cloak and parasol lie on a chair near the mirror.
Unobserved by her,* SOLNESS *now and again follows her with his eyes.
Neither of them speaks.*

KAIA FOSLI *enters quietly by the door on the left.*

SOLNESS [*turns his head, and says in an off-hand tone of indifference*]
Well, is that you?

KAIA I merely wished to let you know that I have come.

SOLNESS Yes, yes, that's all right. Hasn't Ragnar come too?

KAIA No, not yet. He had to wait a little while to see the doctor.
But he is coming presently to hear –

SOLNESS How is the old man today?

KAIA Not well. He begs you to excuse him; he is obliged to keep
his bed today.

SOLNESS Why, of course; by all means let him rest. But now, get to
your work.

KAIA Yes. [*pauses at the door*] Do you wish to speak to Ragnar when
he comes?

SOLNESS No – I don't know that I have anything particular to say to him.

KAIA [*goes out again to the left*]

SOLNESS [*remains seated, turning over the drawings*]

MRS SOLNESS [*over beside the plants*] I wonder if he isn't going to die now, as well?

SOLNESS [*looks up at her*] As well as who?

MRS SOLNESS [*without answering*] Yes, yes – depend upon it, Halvard, old Brovik is going to die too. You'll see that he will.

SOLNESS My dear Aline, ought you not to go out for a little walk?

MRS SOLNESS Yes, I suppose I ought to.

[*she continues to attend the flowers*]

SOLNESS [*bending over the drawings*] Is she still asleep?

MRS SOLNESS [*looking at him*] Is it Miss Wangel you are sitting there thinking about?

SOLNESS [*indifferently*] I just happened to recollect her.

MRS SOLNESS Miss Wangle was up long ago.

SOLNESS Oh, was she?

MRS SOLNESS When I went in to see her, she was busy putting her things in order.

[*She goes in front of the mirror and slowly begins to put on her hat*]

SOLNESS [*after a short pause*] So we have found a use for one of our nurseries after all, Aline.

MRS SOLNESS Yes, we have.

SOLNESS That seems to me better than to have them all standing empty.

MRS SOLNESS That emptiness is dreadful; you are right there.

SOLNESS [*closes the portfolio, rises and approaches her*] You will find that we shall get on far better after this, Aline. Things will be more comfortable. Life will be easier – especially for you.

MRS SOLNESS [*looks at him*] After this?

SOLNESS Yes, believe me, Aline –

MRS SOLNESS Do you mean – because she has come here?

SOLNESS [*checking himself*] I mean, of course – when once we have moved into the new home.

MRS SOLNESS [*takes her cloak*] Ah, do you think so, Halvard? Will it be better then?

SOLNESS I can't think otherwise. And surely you think so too?

MRS SOLNESS I think nothing at all about the new house.

SOLNESS [*cast down*] It's hard for me to hear you say that; for you know it is mainly for your sake that I have built it.

[*he offers to help her on with her cloak*]

MRS SOLNESS [*evades him*] The fact is, you do far too much for my sake.

SOLNESS [*with a certain vehemence*] No, no, you really mustn't say that, Aline! I cannot bear to hear you say such things!

MRS SOLNESS Very well, then I won't say it, Halvard.

SOLNESS But I stick to what *I* said. You'll see that things will be easier for you in the new place.

MRS SOLNESS Oh, heavens – easier for me – !

SOLNESS [*eagerly*] Yes, indeed they will! You may be quite sure of that! For you see – there will be so very, very much there that will remind you of your own home –

MRS SOLNESS The home that used to be father's and mother's – and that was burnt to the ground –

SOLNESS [*in a low voice*] Yes, yes, my poor Aline. That was a terrible blow for you.

MRS SOLNESS [*breaking out in lamentation*] You may build as much as ever you like, Halvard – you can never build up again a real home for me!

SOLNESS [*crosses the room*] Well, in Heaven's name, let us talk no more about it then.

MRS SOLNESS We are not in the habit of talking about it. For you always put the thought away from you –

SOLNESS [*stops suddenly and looks at her*] Do I? And why should I do that? Put the thought away from me?

MRS SOLNESS Oh yes, Halvard, I understand you very well. You are so anxious to spare me – and to find excuses for me too – as much as ever you can.

SOLNESS [*with astonishment in his eyes*] You! Is it you – yourself, that you are talking about, Aline?

MRS SOLNESS Yes, who else should it be but myself?

SOLNESS [*involuntarily to himself*] That too!

MRS SOLNESS As for the old house, I wouldn't mind so much about that. When once misfortune was in the air – why –

SOLNESS Ah, you are right there. Misfortune will have its way – as the saying goes.

MRS SOLNESS But it's what came of the fire – the dreadful thing that followed – ! That is the thing! That, that, that!

SOLNESS [*vehemently*] Don't think about that, Aline!

MRS SOLNESS Ah, that is exactly what I cannot help thinking about. And now, at last, I must speak about it, too; for I don't seem to be able to bear it any longer. And then never to be able to forgive myself –

SOLNESS [*exclaiming*] Yourself – !

MRS SOLNESS Yes, for I had duties on both sides – both towards you and towards the little ones. I ought to have hardened myself – not to have let the horror take such hold upon me – nor the grief for the burning of my home. [*wrings her hands*] Oh, Halvard, if I had only had the strength!

SOLNESS [*softly, much moved, comes closer*] Aline – you must promise me never to think these thoughts any more. – Promise me that, dear!

MRS SOLNESS Oh, promise, promise! One can promise anything.

SOLNESS [*clenches his hands and crosses the room*] Oh, but this is hopeless, hopeless! Never a ray of sunlight! Not so much as a gleam of brightness to light up our home!

MRS SOLNESS This is no home, Halvard.

SOLNESS Oh no, you may well say that. [*gloomily*] And God knows whether you are not right in saying that it will be no better for us in the new house, either.

MRS SOLNESS It will never be any better. Just as empty – just as desolate – there as here.

SOLNESS [*vehemently*] Why in all the world have we built it then? Can you tell me that?

MRS SOLNESS No; you must answer that question for yourself.

SOLNESS [*glances suspiciously at her*] What do you mean by that, Aline?

MRS SOLNESS What do I mean?

SOLNESS Yes, in the devil's name! You said it so strangely – as if you had some hidden meaning in it.

MRS SOLNESS No, indeed, I assure you –

SOLNESS [*comes closer*] Oh, come now – I know what I know. I have both my eyes and my ears about me, Aline – you may depend upon that!

MRS SOLNESS Why, what are you talking about? What is it?

SOLNESS [*places himself in front of her*] Do you mean to say you don't find a kind of lurking, hidden meaning in the most innocent word I happen to say?

MRS SOLNESS *I* do you say? *I* do that?

SOLNESS [*laughs*] Ho-ho-ho! It's natural enough, Aline! When you have a sick man on your hands –

MRS SOLNESS [*anxiously*] Sick? Are you ill, Halvard?

SOLNESS [*violently*] A half-mad man then! A crazy man! Call me what you will.

MRS SOLNESS [*feels blindly for a chair and sits down*] Halvard – for God's sake –

SOLNESS But you are wrong, both you and the doctor. I am not in the state that you imagine.

[*he walks up and down the room. Mrs Solness follows him anxiously with her eyes. Finally he goes up to her.*]

SOLNESS [*calmly*] In reality there is nothing whatever the matter with me.

MRS SOLNESS No, there isn't, is there? But then what is it that troubles you so?

SOLNESS Why this, that I often feel ready to sink under this terrible burden of debt –

MRS SOLNESS Debt, do you say? But you owe no one anything, Halvard!

SOLNESS [*softly, with emotion*] I owe a boundless debt to you – to you – to you, Aline.

MRS SOLNESS [*rises slowly*] What is behind all this? You may just as well tell me at once.

SOLNESS But there is nothing behind it! I have never done you any wrong – not wittingly and willfully, at any rate. And yet – and yet it seems as though a crushing debt rested upon me and weighed me down.

MRS SOLNESS A debt to me?

SOLNESS Chiefly to you.

MRS SOLNESS Then you are – ill after all, Halvard.

SOLNESS [*gloomily*] I suppose I must be – or not far from it. [*looks towards the door to the right, which is opened at this moment*] Ah now it grows light.

HILDA WANGEL *comes in. She has made some alteration in her dress, and let down her skirt.*

HILDA Good morning, Mr Solness!

SOLNESS [*nods*] Slept well?

HILDA Quite deliciously! Like a child in a cradle. Oh – I lay and stretched myself like – like a princess!

SOLNESS [*smiles a little*] You were thoroughly comfortable then?

HILDA I should think so.

SOLNESS And no doubt you dreamed, too.

HILDA Yes, I did. But that was horrid.

SOLNESS Was it?

HILDA Yes, for I dreamed I was falling over a frightfully high, sheer precipice. Do you never have that kind of dream?

SOLNESS Oh yes – now and then –

HILDA It's tremendously thrilling – when you fall and fall –

SOLNESS It seems to make one's blood run cold.

HILDA Do you draw your legs up under you while you are falling?

SOLNESS Yes, as high as ever I can.

HILDA So do I.

MRS SOLNESS [*takes her parasol*] I must go into town now, Halvard. [*to Hilda*] And I'll try to get one or two things that you may require.

HILDA [*making a motion to throw her arms round her neck*] Oh, you dear, Mrs Solness! You are really much too kind to me! Frightfully kind –

MRS SOLNESS [*deprecatingly, freeing herself*] Oh, not at all. It's only my duty, so I am very glad to do it.

HILDA [*offended, pouts*] But really, I think I am quite fit to be seen in the streets – now that I've put my dress to rights. Or do you think I am not?

MRS SOLNESS To tell you the truth, I think people would stare at you a little.

HILDA [*contemptuously*] Pooh! Is that all? That only amuses me.

SOLNESS [*with suppressed ill-humour*] Yes, but people might take it into their heads that you were mad too, you see.

HILDA Mad? Are there so many mad people here in town, then?

SOLNESS [*points to his own forehead*] Here you see one at all events.

HILDA You – Mr Solness!

SOLNESS Have you not noticed that yet?

HILDA No, I certainly have not. [*reflects and laughs a little*] And yet – perhaps in one single thing.

SOLNESS Ah, do you hear that, Aline?

MRS SOLNESS What is that one single thing, Miss Wangel?

HILDA No, I won't say.

SOLNESS Oh yes, do!

HILDA No thank you – I am not so mad as that.

MRS SOLNESS When you and Miss Wangel are alone, I dare say she will tell you, Halvard.

SOLNESS Ah – you think she will?

MRS SOLNESS Oh yes, certainly. For you have known her so well in the past. Ever since she was a child – you tell me.

[*She goes out by the door on the left*]

HILDA [*after a little while*] Does your wife dislike me very much?

SOLNESS Did you think you noticed anything of the kind?

HILDA Did you notice it yourself?

SOLNESS [*evasively*] Aline has become exceedingly shy with strangers of late years.

HILDA Has she really?

SOLNESS But if only you could get to know her thoroughly – ! Ah, she is so good – so kind – so excellent a creature –

HILDA [*impatiently*] But if she is all that – what made her say that about her duty?

SOLNESS Her duty?

HILDA She said that she would go out and buy something for me, because it was her duty. Oh, I can't bear that ugly, horrid word!

SOLNESS Why not?

HILDA It sounds so cold and sharp, and stinging. Duty – duty – duty. Don't you think so, too? Doesn't it seem to sting you?

SOLNESS H'm – haven't thought much about it.

HILDA Yes, it does. And if she is so good – as you say she is – why should she talk in that way?

SOLNESS But, good Lord, what would you have had her say, then?

HILDA She might have said she would do it because she had taken a tremendous fancy to me. She might have said something like that – something really warm and cordial, you understand.

SOLNESS [*looks at her*] Is that how you would like to have it?

HILDA Yes, precisely. [*She wanders about the room, stops at the bookcase and looks at the books*] What a lot of books you have.

SOLNESS Yes, I have got together a good many.

HILDA Do you read them all, too?

SOLNESS I used to try to. Do you read much?

HILDA No, never! I have given it up. For it all seems so irrelevant.

SOLNESS That is just my feeling.

[*Hilda wanders about a little, stops at the small table, opens the portfolio and turns over the contents.*]

HILDA Are all these your drawings yours?

SOLNESS No, they are drawn by a young man whom I employ to help me.

HILDA Someone you have taught?

SOLNESS Oh yes, no doubt he has learnt something from me, too.

HILDA [*sits down*] Then I suppose he is very clever. [*looks at a drawing*] Isn't he?

SOLNESS Oh, he might be worse. For my purpose –

HILDA Oh yes – I'm sure he is frightfully clever.

SOLNESS Do you think you can see that in the drawings?

HILDA Pooh – these scrawlings! But if he has been learning from you –

SOLNESS Oh, so far as that goes – there are plenty of people here that have learnt from me, and have come to little enough for all that.

HILDA [*looks at him and shakes her head*] No, I can't for the life of me understand how you can be so stupid.

SOLNESS Stupid? Do you think I am so very stupid?

HILDA Yes, I do indeed. If you are content to go about here teaching all these people –

SOLNESS [*with a slight start*] Well, and why not?

HILDA [*rises, half serious, half laughing*] No indeed, Mr Solness! What can be the good of that? No one but you should be allowed to build. You should stand quite alone – do it all yourself. Now you know it.

SOLNESS [*involuntarily*] Hilda – !

HILDA Well!

SOLNESS How in the world did that come into your head?

HILDA Do you think I am so very far wrong then?

SOLNESS No, that's not what I mean. But now I'll tell you something.

HILDA Well?

SOLNESS I keep on – incessantly – in silence and alone – brooding on that very thought.

HILDA Yes, that seems to me perfectly natural.

SOLNESS [*looks somewhat searchingly at her*] Perhaps you have noticed it already?

HILDA No, indeed I haven't.

SOLNESS But just now – when you said you thought I was – off my balance? In one thing, you said –

HILDA Oh, I was thinking of something quite different.

SOLNESS What was it?

HILDA I am not going to tell you.

SOLNESS [*crosses the room*] Well, well – as you please. [*stops at the bow-window*] Come here, and I will show you something.

HILDA [*approaching*] What is it?

SOLNESS Do you see over here in the garden – ?

HILDA Yes?

SOLNESS [*points*] Right above the great quarry – ?

HILDA That new house, you mean?

SOLNESS The one that is being built, yes. Almost finished.

HILDA It seems to have a very high tower.

SOLNESS The scaffolding is still up.

HILDA Is that your new house?

SOLNESS Yes.

HILDA The house you are soon going to move into?

SOLNESS Yes.

HILDA [*looks at him*] Are there nurseries in that house, too?

SOLNESS Three, as there are here.

HILDA And no child.

SOLNESS And there never will be one.

HILDA [*with a half-smile*] Well, isn't it just as I said – ?

SOLNESS That – ?

HILDA That you are a little – a little mad after all.

SOLNESS Was that what you were thinking of?

HILDA Yes, of all the empty nurseries I slept in.

SOLNESS [*lowers his voice*] We have had children – Aline and I.

HILDA [*looks eagerly at him*] Have you – ?

SOLNESS Two little boys. They were of the same age.

HILDA Twins, then.

SOLNESS Yes, twins. It's eleven or twelve years ago now.

HILDA [*cautiously*] And so both of them – ? You have lost both the twins, then?

SOLNESS [*with quiet emotion*] We kept them only about three weeks. Or scarcely so much. [*bursts forth*] Oh, Hilda, I can't tell you what a good thing it is for me that you have come! For now at last I have someone to talk to!

HILDA Can you not talk to – her, too?

SOLNESS Not about this. Not as I want to talk and must talk. [*gloomily*] And not about so many other things, either.

HILDA [*in a subdued voice*] Was that all you meant when you said you need me?

SOLNESS That was mainly what I meant – at all events, yesterday. For today I am not so sure – [*breaking off*] Come here and let us sit down, Hilda. Sit there on the sofa – so that you can look into the garden. [*Hilda seats herself in the corner of the sofa. Solness brings a chair closer*] Should you like to hear about it?

HILDA Yes, I shall love to sit and listen to you.

SOLNESS [*sits down*] Then I will tell you all about it.

HILDA Now I can see both the garden and you, Mr Solness. So now, tell away! Begin!

SOLNESS [*points towards the bow-window*] Out there on the rising ground – where you see the new house –

HILDA Yes?

SOLNESS Aline and I lived there in the first years of our married life. There was an old house up there that had belonged to her mother; and we inherited it, and the whole of the great garden with it.

HILDA Was there a tower on that house, too?

SOLNESS No, nothing of the kind. From the outside it looked like a great, dark, ugly wooden box; but all the same, it was snug and comfortable enough inside.

HILDA Then did you pull down the ramshackle old place?

SOLNESS No, it was burnt down.

HILDA The whole of it?

SOLNESS Yes.

HILDA Was that a great misfortune for you?

SOLNESS That depends on how you look at it. As a builder, the fire was the making of me –

HILDA Well, but –

SOLNESS It was just after the birth of the two little boys –

HILDA The poor little twins, yes.

SOLNESS They came healthy and bonny into the world. And they were growing too – you could see the difference day to day.

HILDA Little children do grow quickly at first.

SOLNESS It was the prettiest sight in the world to see Aline lying with the two of them in her arms. – But then came the night of the fire –

HILDA [*excitedly*] What happened? Do tell me! Was anyone burnt?

SOLNESS No, not that. Every one got safe and sound out of the house –

HILDA Well, and what then – ?

SOLNESS The fright had shaken Aline terribly. The alarm – the escape – the breakneck hurry – and then the ice-cold night air – for they had to be carried out just as they lay – both she and the little ones.

HILDA Was it too much for them?

SOLNESS Oh no, they stood it well enough. But Aline fell into a fever, and it affected her milk. She would insist on nursing them herself; because it was her duty, she said. And both our little boys, they – [*clenching his hands*] – they – oh!

HILDA They did not get over that?

SOLNESS No, that they did not get over. That was how we lost them.

HILDA It must have been terribly hard for you.

SOLNESS Hard enough for me; but ten times harder for Aline. [*clenching his hands in suppressed fury*] Oh, that such things should be allowed to happen here in the world! [*shortly and firmly*] From the day I lost them, I had no heart for building churches.

HILDA Did you not like building the church-tower in our town?

SOLNESS I didn't like it. I know how free and happy I felt when that tower was finished.

HILDA *I* know that, too.

SOLNESS And now I shall never – never build anything of that sort again! Neither churches nor church-towers.

HILDA [*nods slowly*] Nothing but houses for people to live in.

SOLNESS Homes for human beings, Hilda.

HILDA But homes with high towers and pinnacles upon them.

SOLNESS If possible. [*adopts a lighter tone*] But, as I said before, the fire was the making of me – as a builder, I mean.

HILDA Why don't you call yourself an architect, like the others?

SOLNESS I have not been systematically enough taught for that. Most of what I know I have found out for myself.

HILDA But you succeeded all the same.

SOLNESS Yes, thanks to the fire. I laid out almost the whole of the garden in villa lots; and there I was able to build after my own heart. So I came to the front with a rush.

HILDA [looks keenly at him] You must surely be a very happy man, as matters stand with you.

SOLNESS [gloomily] Happy? Do you say that, too – like all the rest of them?

HILDA Yes, I should say you must be. If you could only cease thing about the two little children –

SOLNESS [slowly] The two little children – they are not so easy to forget, Hilda.

HILDA [somewhat uncertainly] Do you still feel their loss so much – after all these years?

SOLNESS [looks fixedly at her, without replying] A happy man you said –

HILDA Well, now, are you not happy – in other respects?

SOLNESS [continues to look at her] When I told you all this about the fire – h'm –

HILDA Well?

SOLNESS Was there not one special thought that you – that you seized upon?

HILDA [reflects in vain] No. What thought should that be?

SOLNESS [with subdued emphasis] It was simply and solely by that fire that I was enabled to build homes for human beings. Cosy, comfortable, bright homes, where father and mother and the whole troop of children can live in safety and gladness, feeling what a happy thing it is to be alive in the world – and most of all to belong to each other – in great things and in small.

HILDA [ardently] Well, and is it not a great happiness for you to be able to build such beautiful homes?

SOLNESS The price, Hilda! The terrible price I had to pay for the opportunity!

HILDA But can you never get over that?

SOLNESS No. That I might build homes for others, I had to forego – to forego for all time – the home that might have been my own. I mean a home for a troop of children – and for father and mother, too.

HILDA [*cautiously*] But need you have done that? For all time, you say?

SOLNESS [*nods slowly*] That was the price of this happiness that people talk about. [*breathes heavily*] This happiness – h'm – this happiness was not to be bought any cheaper, Hilda.

HILDA [*as before*] But may it not come right even yet?

SOLNESS Never in this world – never. That is another consequence of the fire – and of Aline's illness afterwards.

HILDA [*looks at him with an indefinable expression*] And yet you build all these nurseries.

SOLNESS [*seriously*] Have you never noticed, Hilda, how the impossible – how it seems to beckon and cry aloud to one?

HILDA [*reflecting*] The impossible? [*with animation*] Yes, indeed! Is that how you feel too?

SOLNESS Yes, I do.

HILDA Then there must be – a little of the troll in you too.

SOLNESS Why of the troll?

HILDA What would you call it, then?

SOLNESS [*rises*] Well, well, perhaps you are right. [*vehemently*] But how can I help turning into a troll, when this is how it always goes with me in everything – in everything!

HILDA How do you mean?

SOLNESS [*speaking low, with inward emotion*] Mark what I say to you, Hilda. All that I have succeeded in doing, building, creating – all the beauty, security, cheerful comfort – ay, and magnificence too – [*clenches his hands*] Oh, is it not terrible even to think of – ?

HILDA What is so terrible?

SOLNESS That all this I have to make up for, to pay for – not in money, but in human happiness. And not with my own happiness only, but with other people's too. Yes, yes, do you see that, Hilda? That is the price which my position as an artist has cost me – and others. And every single day I have to look on while the price is paid for me anew. Over again, and over again – and over again for ever!

HILDA [*rises and looks steadily at him*] Now I can see that you are thinking of – of her.

SOLNESS Yes, mainly of Aline. For Aline – she, too, had her
vocation in life, just as much as I had mine. [*his voice quivers*] But
her vocation has had to be stunted, and crushed, and shattered –
in order that mine might force its way to – to a sort of great
victory. For you must know that Aline – she, too, had a talent
for building.

HILDA She! For building?

SOLNESS [*shakes his head*] Not houses and towers, and spires – not
such things as I work away at –

HILDA Well, but what then?

SOLNESS [*softly, with emotion*] For building up the souls of little
children, Hilda. For building up children's souls in perfect
balance, and in noble and beautiful forms. For enabling them
to soar up into erect and full-grown human souls. That was
Aline's talent. And there it all lies now – unused and unusable
for ever – of no earthly service to anyone – just like the ruins
left by a fire.

HILDA Yes, but even if this were so – ?

SOLNESS It is so! It is so! I know it!

HILDA Well, but in any case it is not your fault.

SOLNESS [*fixes his eyes on her, and nods slowly*] Ah, that is the great,
the terrible question. That is the doubt that is gnawing me –
night and day.

HILDA That?

SOLNESS Yes. Suppose the fault was mine – in a certain sense.

HILDA Your fault! The fire!

SOLNESS All of it; the whole thing. And yet, perhaps – I may not
have had anything to do with it.

HILDA [*looks at him with a troubled expression*] Oh, Mr Solness – if
you can talk like that, I am afraid you must be – ill after all.

SOLNESS H'm – I don't think I shall ever be of quite sound mind
on that point.

RAGNAR BROVIK *cautiously opens the little door in the left-hand
corner. Hilda comes forward.*

RAGNAR [*when he sees Hilda*] Oh. I beg pardon, Mr Solness – [*he
makes a movement to withdraw*]

SOLNESS No, no, don't go. Let us get it over.

RAGNAR Oh, yes – if only we could.

SOLNESS I hear your father is no better?

RAGNAR Father is fast growing weaker – and therefore I beg and
implore you to write a few kind words for me on one of the
plans! Something for father to read before he –

SOLNESS [*vehemently*] I won't hear anything more about those
drawings of yours!

RAGNAR Have you looked at them?

SOLNESS Yes – I have.

RAGNAR And they are good for nothing? And *I* am good for
nothing, too?

SOLNESS [*evasively*] Stay here with me, Ragnar. You shall have
everything your own way. And then you can marry Kaia, and
live at your ease – and happily too, who knows? Only don'
think of building on your own account.

RAGNAR Well, well, then I must go home and tell father what you
say – I promised I would. – Is this what I am to tell father -
before he dies?

SOLNESS [*with a groan*] Oh tell him – tell him what you will, for me
Best to say nothing at all to him! [*with a sudden outburst*] I canno
do anything else, Ragnar!

RAGNAR May I have the drawings to take with me?

SOLNESS Yes, take them – take them by all means! They are lyin
there on the table.

RAGNAR [*goes to the table*] Thanks.

HILDA [*puts her hand on the portfolio*] No, no; leave them here.

SOLNESS Why?

HILDA Because I want to look at them, too.

SOLNESS But you have been – [*to Ragnar*] Well, leave them here
then.

RAGNAR Very well.

SOLNESS And go home at once to your father.

RAGNAR Yes, I suppose I must.

SOLNESS [*as if in desperation*] Ragnar – you must not ask me to d
what is beyond my power! Do you hear, Ragnar? You must no

RAGNAR No, no. I beg your pardon –

                    [*he bows, and goes out by the corner doo*
     [*Hilda goes over and sits down on a chair near the mirror*]

HILDA [*looks angrily at Solness*] That was a very ugly thing to do.

SOLNESS Do you think so, too?

HILDA Yes, it was horribly ugly – and hard and bad and cruel as well.

SOLNESS Oh, you don't understand my position.

HILDA No matter – . I say you ought not to be like that.

SOLNESS You said yourself, only just now, that no one but *I* ought to be allowed to build.

HILDA *I* may say such things – but you must not.

SOLNESS I most of all, surely, who have paid so dear for my position.

HILDA Oh yes – with what you call domestic comfort – and that sort of thing.

SOLNESS And with my peace of soul into the bargain.

HILDA [*rising*] Peace of soul! [*with feeling*] Yes, yes, you are right in that! Poor Mr Solness – you fancy that –

SOLNESS [*with a quiet, chuckling laugh*] Just sit down again, Hilda, and I'll tell you something funny.

HILDA [*sits down; with intent interest*] Well?

SOLNESS It sounds such a ludicrous little thing; for, you see, the whole story turns upon nothing but a crack in the chimney.

HILDA No more than that?

SOLNESS No, not to begin with.

[*He moves a chair nearer to Hilda and sits down*]

HILDA [*impatiently, taps on her knee*] Well, now for the crack in the chimney!

SOLNESS I had noticed the split in the flue long, long before the fire. Every time I went up into the attic, I looked to see if it was still there.

HILDA And it was?

SOLNESS Yes; for no one else knew about it.

HILDA And you said nothing?

SOLNESS Nothing.

HILDA And did not think of repairing the flue either?

SOLNESS Oh yes, I thought about it – but never got any further. Every time I intended to set to work, it seemed just as if a hand held me back. Not today, I thought – tomorrow; and nothing ever came of it.

HILDA But why did you keep putting it off like that?

SOLNESS Because I was revolving something in my mind. [*slowly, and in a low voice*] Through that little black crack in the chimney, I might, perhaps, force my way upwards – as a builder.

HILDA [*looking straight in front of her*] That must have been thrilling.

SOLNESS Almost irresistible – quite irresistible. For at that time it appeared to me a perfectly simple and straightforward matter. I would have had it happen in the winter-time – a little before midday. I was to be out driving Aline in the sleigh. The servants at home would have made huge fires in the stoves.

HILDA For, of course, it was to be bitterly cold that day?

SOLNESS Rather biting, yes – and they would want Aline to find it thoroughly snug and warm when she came home.

HILDA I suppose she is very chilly by nature?

SOLNESS She is. And as we drove home, we were to see the smoke.

HILDA Only the smoke?

SOLNESS The smoke first. But when we came up to the garden gate, the whole of the old timber-box was to be a rolling mass of flames. – That is how I wanted it to be, you see.

HILDA Oh, why, why could it not have happened so!

SOLNESS You may well say that, Hilda.

HILDA Well, but now listen, Mr Solness. Are you perfectly certain that the fire was caused by that little crack in the chimney!

SOLNESS No, on the contrary – I am perfectly certain that the crack in the chimney had nothing whatever to do with the fire.

HILDA What!

SOLNESS It has been clearly ascertained that the fire broke out in a clothes-cupboard – in a totally different part of the house.

HILDA Then what is all this nonsense you are talking about the crack in the chimney!

SOLNESS May I go on talking to you a little, Hilda?

HILDA Yes, if you'll only talk sensibly –

SOLNESS I will try to.

[*he moves his chair nearer*]

HILDA Out with it, then, Mr Solness.

SOLNESS [*confidentially*] Don't you agree with me, Hilda, that there exist special, chosen people who have been endowed with the power and faculty if desiring a thing, craving for a thing, willing a thing – so persistently and so – so inexorably – that at last it has to happen? Don't you believe that?

HILDA [*with an indefinable expression in her eyes*] If that is so, we shall see, one of these days, whether *I* am one of the chosen.

SOLNESS It is not one's self alone that can do such great things

Oh, no – the helpers and the servers – they must do their part too, if it is to be of any good. But they never come of themselves. One has to call upon them very persistently – inwardly, you understand.

HILDA What are these helpers and servers?

SOLNESS Oh, we can talk about that some other time. For the present, let us keep to this business of the fire.

HILDA Don't you think that fire would have happened all the same – even without your wishing for it?

SOLNESS If the house had been old Knut Brovik's, it would never have burnt down so conveniently for him. I am sure of that; for he does not know how to call for the helpers – no, nor for the servers, either. [*rises in unrest*] So you see, Hilda – it is my fault, after all, that the lives of the two little boys had to be sacrificed. And do you think it is not my fault, too, that Aline has never been the woman she should and might have been – and that she most longed to be?

HILDA Yes, but if it is all the work of these helpers and servers – ?

SOLNESS Who called for the helpers and servers? It was I! And they came and obeyed my will. [*in increasing excitement*] That is what people call having the luck on your side; but I must tell you what this sort of luck feels like! It feels like a great raw place here on my breast. And the helpers and servers keep on flaying pieces of skin off other people in order to close my sore! – But still the sore is not healed – never, never! Oh, if you knew how it can sometimes gnaw and burn!

HILDA [*looks attentively at him*] You are ill, Mr Solness. Very ill, I almost think.

SOLNESS Say mad; for that is what you mean.

HILDA No, I don't think there is much amiss with your intellect.

SOLNESS With what then? Out with it!

HILDA I wonder whether you were not sent into the world with a sickly conscience.

SOLNESS A sickly conscience? What devilry is that?

HILDA I mean that your conscience is feeble – too delicately built, as it were – hasn't strength to take a grip of things – to lift and bear what is heavy.

SOLNESS [*growls*] H'm! May I ask, then, what sort of a conscience one ought to have?

HILDA I should like your conscience to be – to be thoroughly robust.

SOLNESS Indeed? Robust, eh? Is your own conscience robust, may I ask?

HILDA Yes, I think it is. I have never noticed that it wasn't.

SOLNESS It has not been put very severely to the test, I should think.

HILDA [with a quivering of the lips] Oh, it was no such simple matter to leave father – I am so awfully fond of him.

SOLNESS Dear me! for a month or two –

HILDA I think I shall never go home again.

SOLNESS Never? Then why did you leave him?

HILDA [half-seriously, half-banteringly] Have you forgotten again that the ten years are up?

SOLNESS Oh nonsense. Was anything wrong at home? Eh?

HILDA [Quite seriously] It was this impulse within me that urged and goaded me to come – and lured and drew me on, as well.

SOLNESS [eagerly] There we have it! There we have it, Hilda! There is the troll in you too, as in me. For it's the troll in one, you see – it is that that calls to the powers outside us. And then you must give in – whether you will or no.

HILDA I almost think you are right, Mr Solness.

SOLNESS [walks about the room] Oh, there are devils innumerable abroad in the world, Hilda, that one never sees.

HILDA Devils, too?

SOLNESS [stops] Good devils and bad devils; light-haired devils and black-haired devils. If only you could always tell whether it is the light or dark ones that have got hold of you! [paces about] Ho-ho! Then it would be simple enough!

HILDA [follows him with her eyes] Or if one had a really vigorous, radiantly healthy conscience – so that one dared to do what one would.

SOLNESS [stops beside the console table] I believe, now, that most people are just as puny creatures as I am in that respect.

HILDA I shouldn't wonder.

SOLNESS [leaning against the table] In the sagas – have you read any of the old sagas?

HILDA Oh yes! When I used to read books, I –

SOLNESS In the sagas you read about vikings, who sailed to foreign lands, and plundered and burned and killed men –

HILDA And carried off women –

SOLNESS – and kept them in captivity –

HILDA – took them home in their ships –

SOLNESS – and behaved to them like – like the very worst of trolls.

HILDA [*looks straight before her, with a half-veiled look*] I think that must have been thrilling.

SOLNESS [*with a short, deep laugh*] To carry off women, eh?

HILDA To be carried off.

SOLNESS [*looks at her a moment*] Oh, indeed.

HILDA [*as if breaking the thread of the conversation*] But what made you speak of these vikings, Mr Solness?

SOLNESS Why, those fellows must have had robust consciences, if you like! When they got home again, they could eat and drink, and be as happy as children. And the women, too! They often would not leave them on any account. Can you understand that, Hilda?

HILDA Those women I can understand exceedingly well.

SOLNESS Oho! Perhaps you could do the same yourself?

HILDA Why not?

SOLNESS Live – of your own free will – with a ruffian like that?

HILDA If it was a ruffian I had come to love –

SOLNESS Could you come to love a man like that?

HILDA Good heavens, you know very well one can't choose whom one is going to love.

SOLNESS [*looks meditatively at her*] Oh no, I suppose it is the troll within one that's responsible for that.

HILDA [*half-laughing*] And all those blessed devils, that you know so well – both the light-haired and the dark-haired ones.

SOLNESS [*Quietly and warmly*] Then I hope with all my heart that the devils will choose carefully for you, Hilda.

HILDA For me they have chosen already – once and for all.

SOLNESS [*looks earnestly at her*] Hilda – you are like a wild bird of the woods.

HILDA Far from it. I don't hide myself away under the bushes.

SOLNESS No, no. There is rather something of the bird of prey in you.

HILDA That is nearer it – perhaps. [*very vehemently*] And why not a bird of prey? Why should not *I* go a-hunting – I, as well as the rest? Carry off the prey I want – if only I can get my claws into it, and do with it as I will.

SOLNESS Hilda – do you know what you are?

HILDA Yes, I suppose I am a strange sort of bird.

SOLNESS No. You are like a dawning day. When I look at you – I seem to be looking towards the sunrise.

HILDA Tell me, Mr Solness – are you certain that you have never called me to you? Inwardly, you know?

SOLNESS [*softly and slowly*] I almost think I must have.

HILDA What did you want with me?

SOLNESS You are the younger generation, Hilda.

HILDA [*smiles*] That younger generation that you are so afraid of?

SOLNESS [*nods slowly*] And which, in my heart, I yearn towards so deeply.

[*Hilda rises, goes to the little table, and fetches Ragnar Brovik's portfolio*

Hilda. [*holds out the portfolio to him*] We were talking of these drawings –

SOLNESS [*shortly, waving them away*] Put those things away! I have seen enough of them.

HILDA Yes, but you have to write your approval on them.

SOLNESS Write my approval on them? Never!

HILDA But the poor old man is lying at death's door! Can't you give him and his son this pleasure before they are parted? And perhaps he might get the commission to carry them out, too.

SOLNESS Yes, that is just what he would get. He has made sure of that – has my fine gentleman!

HILDA Then, good heavens – if that is so – can't you tell the least little bit of a lie for once in a way?

SOLNESS A lie? [*raging*] Hilda – take those devil's drawings out of my sight!

HILDA [*draws the portfolio a little nearer to herself*] Well, well, well don't bite me. – You talk of trolls – but I think you go on like a troll yourself. [*looks round*] Where do you keep your pen and ink?

SOLNESS There is nothing of the sort in here.

HILDA [*goes towards the door*] But in the office where that young lady is –

SOLNESS Stay where you are, Hilda! – I ought to tell a lie, you say. Oh yes, for the sake of his old father I might well do that – for in my time I have crushed him, trodden him under foot –

HILDA Him, too?

SOLNESS I needed room for myself. But this Ragnar – he must on no account be allowed to come to the front.

HILDA Poor fellow, there is surely no fear of that. If he has nothing in him –

SOLNESS [*comes closer, looks at her, and whispers*] If Ragnar Brovik gets his chance, he will strike me to the earth. Crush me – as I crushed his father.

HILDA Crush you? Has he the ability for that?

SOLNESS Yes, you may depend upon it he has the ability! He is the younger generation that stands ready to knock at my door – to make an end of Halvard Solness.

HILDA [*looks at him with quiet reproach*] And yet you would bar him out. Fie, Mr Solness!

SOLNESS The fight I have been fighting has cost heart's blood enough. – And I am afraid, too, that the helpers and servers will not obey me any longer.

HILDA Then you must go ahead without them. There is nothing else for it.

SOLNESS It is hopeless, Hilda. The luck is bound to turn. A little sooner or a little later. Retribution is inexorable.

HILDA [*in distress, putting her hands over her ears*] Don't talk like that! Do you want to kill me? To take from me what is more than my life?

SOLNESS And what is that?

HILDA The longing to see you great. To see you, with a wreath in your hand, high, high up upon a church-tower. [*calm again*] Come, out with your pencil now. You must have a pencil about you?

SOLNESS [*takes out his pocket-book*] I have one here.

HILDA [*lays the portfolio on the sofa-table*] Very well. Now let us two sit down here, Mr Solness.

SOLNESS [*seats himself at the table*]

HILDA [*stands behind him, leaning over the back of the chair*] And now we will write on the drawings. We must write very, very nicely and cordially – for this horrid Ruar – or whatever his name is.

SOLNESS [*writes a few words, turns his head and looks at her*] Tell me one thing, Hilda.

HILDA Yes!

SOLNESS If you have been waiting for me all these ten years –

HILDA What then?

SOLNESS Why have you never written to me? Then I could have answered you.

HILDA [*hastily*] No, no, no! That was just what I did not want.

SOLNESS Why not?

HILDA I was afraid the whole thing might fall to pieces. – But we were going to write on the drawings, Mr Solness.

SOLNESS So we were.

HILDA [*bends forward and looks over his shoulder while he writes*] Mind now, kindly and cordially! Oh how I hate – how I hate this Ruald –

SOLNESS [*writing*] Have you never really cared for anyone, Hilda?

HILDA For anyone else, I suppose you mean?

SOLNESS [*looks up at her*] For anyone else, yes. Have you never? In all these ten years? Never?

HILDA Oh yes, now and then. When I was perfectly furious with you for not coming.

SOLNESS Then you did take an interest in other people, too?

HILDA A little bit – for a week or so. Good heavens, Mr Solness, you surely know how such things come about.

SOLNESS Hilda – what is it you have come for?

HILDA Don't waste time talking. The poor old man might go and die in the meantime.

SOLNESS Answer me, Hilda. What do you want of me?

HILDA I want my kingdom.

SOLNESS H'm –

He gives a rapid glance toward the door on the left, and then goes on writing on the drawings. At the same moment MRS SOLNESS *enters.*

MRS SOLNESS Here are a few things I have got for you, Miss Wangel. The large parcels will be sent later on.

HILDA Oh, how very, very kind of you!

MRS SOLNESS Only my simple duty. Nothing more than that.

SOLNESS [*reading over what he has written*] Aline!

MRS SOLNESS Yes?

SOLNESS Did you notice whether the – the book-keeper was out there?

MRS SOLNESS Yes, of course, she was there.

SOLNESS [*puts the drawings in the portfolio*] H'm –

MRS SOLNESS She was standing at the desk, as she always is – when *I* go through the room.

SOLNESS [*rises*] Then I'll give this to her and tell her that –

HILDA [*takes the portfolio from him*] Oh, no, let me have the pleasure of doing that! [*goes to the door, but turns*] What is her name?

SOLNESS Her name is Miss Fosli.

HILDA Pooh, that sounds so cold! Her Christian name, I mean?

SOLNESS Kaia – I believe.

HILDA [*opens the door and calls out*] Kaia, come in here! Make haste! Mr Solness wants to speak to you.

KAIA FOSLI *appears at the door.*

KAIA [*looking at him in alarm*] Here I am – ?

HILDA [*handing her the portfolio*] See her, Kaia! You can take this home; Mr Solness has written on them now.

KAIA Oh, at last!

SOLNESS Give them to the old man as soon as you can.

KAIA I will go straight home with them.

SOLNESS Yes, do. Now Ragnar will have a chance of building for himself.

KAIA Oh, may he come and thank you for all – ?

SOLNESS [*harshly*] I won't have any thanks! Tell him that from me.

KAIA Yes, I will –

SOLNESS And tell him at the same time that henceforward I do not require his services – nor yours either.

KAIA [*softly and quiveringly*] Not mine either?

SOLNESS You will have other things to think of now, and to attend to; and that is a very good thing for you. Well, go home with the drawings now, Miss Fosli. At once! Do you hear?

KAIA [*as before*] Yes, Mr Solness.   [*she goes out*]

MRS SOLNESS Heavens! what deceitful eyes she has.

SOLNESS She? That poor little creature?

MRS SOLNESS Oh – I can see what I can see, Halvard. – Are you really dismissing them?

SOLNESS Yes.

MRS SOLNESS Her as well?

SOLNESS Was not that what you wished?

MRS SOLNESS But how can you get on without her – ? Oh well, no doubt you have someone else in reserve, Halvard.

HILDA [*playfully*] Well, *I* for one am not the person to stand at a desk.

SOLNESS Never mind, never mind – it will be all right, Aline. Now all you have to do is think about moving into our new home – as quickly as you can. This evening we will hang up the wreath – [*turns to Hilda*] What do you say to that, Miss Hilda?

HILDA [*looks at him with sparkling eyes*] It will be splendid to see you so high up once more.

SOLNESS Me!

MRS SOLNESS For Heaven's sake, Miss Wangel, don't imagine such a thing! My husband! – when he always gets so dizzy!

HILDA He get dizzy! No, I know quite well he does not!

MRS SOLNESS Oh yes, indeed he does.

HILDA But I have seen him with my own eyes right up at the top of a high church-tower!

MRS SOLNESS Yes, I hear people talk of that; but it is utterly impossible –

SOLNESS [*vehemently*] Impossible – impossible, yes! But there I stood all the same!

MRS SOLNESS O, how can you say so, Halvard? Why, you can't even bear to go out on the second-storey balcony here. You have always been like that.

SOLNESS You may perhaps see something different this evening.

MRS SOLNESS [*in alarm*] No, no, no! Please God I shall never see that. I will write at once to the doctor – and I am sure he won't let you do it.

SOLNESS Why, Aline – !

MRS SOLNESS Oh, you know you're ill, Halvard. This proves it! Oh God – Oh God!   [*she goes hastily out to the right*]

HILDA [*looks intently at him*] Is it so, or is it not?

SOLNESS That I turn dizzy?

HILDA That my master builder dares not – cannot – climb as high as he builds?

SOLNESS Is that the way you look at it?

HILDA Yes.

SOLNESS I believe there is scarcely a corner in me that is safe from you.

HILDA [*looks towards the bow-window*] Up there, then. Right up there –

SOLNESS [*approaches her*] You might have the topmost room in the tower, Hilda – there you might live like a princess.

HILDA [*indefinably, between earnest and jest*] Yes, that is what you promised me.

SOLNESS Did I really?

HILDA Fie, Mr Solness! You said I should be a princess, and that you would give me a kingdom. And then you went and – well!

SOLNESS [*cautiously*] Are you quite certain that this is not a dream – a fancy, that has fixed itself in your mind?

HILDA [*sharply*] Do you mean that you did not do it?

SOLNESS I scarcely know myself. [*more softly*] But now I know so much for certain, that I –

HILDA That you – ? Say it at once!

SOLNESS – that I ought to have done it.

HILDA [*exclaims with animation*] Don't tell me you can ever be dizzy!

SOLNESS This evening, then, we will hang up the wreath – Princess Hilda.

HILDA [*with a bitter curve of the lips*] Over your new home, yes.

SOLNESS Over the new house, which will never be a home for me.
                              [*he goes out through the garden door*]

HILDA [*looks straight in front of her with a far-away expression, and whispers to herself. The only words audible are*] – frightfully thrilling –

ACT THIRD

The large broad verandah of SOLNESS'S *dwelling-house. Part of the house, with outer door leading to the verandah, is seen to the left. A railing along the verandah to the right. At the back, from the end of the verandah, a flight of steps leads down to the garden below. Tall old trees in the garden spread their branches over the verandah and towards the house. Far to the right, in among the trees, a glimpse is caught of the lower part of the new villa, with scaffolding round so much as is seen of the tower. In the background the garden is bounded by an old wooden fence. Outside the fence, a street with low, tumble-down cottages.*

Evening sky with sun-lit clouds.

On the verandah, a garden bench stands along the wall of the house, and in front of the bench a long table. On the other side of the table, an armchair and some stools. All the furniture is of wicker-work.

MRS SOLNESS, *wrapped in a large white crepe shawl, sits resting in the armchair and gazes over to the right. Shortly after,* HILDA WANGEL *comes up the flight of steps from the garden. She is dressed as in the last act, and wears her hat. She has in her bodice a little nosegay of small common flowers.*

MRS SOLNESS [*turning her head a little*] Have you been round the garden, Miss Wangel?

HILDA Yes, I have been taking a look at it.

MRS SOLNESS And found some flowers too, I see.

HILDA Yes, indeed! There are such heaps of them in among the bushes.

MRS SOLNESS Are there, really? Still? You see I scarcely ever go there.

HILDA [*closer*] What! Don't you take a run down into the garden every day, then?

MRS SOLNESS [*with a faint smile*] I don't 'run' anywhere, nowadays.

HILDA Well, but do you not go down now and then to look at all the lovely things there?

MRS SOLNESS It has all become so strange to me. I am almost afraid
to see it again.

HILDA Your own garden!

MRS SOLNESS I don't feel that it is mine any longer.

HILDA What do you mean – ?

MRS SOLNESS No, no, it is not – not as it was in my mother's and
father's time. They have taken away so much – so much of the
garden, Miss Wangel. Fancy – they have parcelled it out – and
built houses for strangers – people that I don't know. And they
can sit and look in upon me from their windows.

HILDA [*with a bright expression*] Mrs Solness!

MRS SOLNESS Yes?

HILDA May I stay here with you a little?

MRS SOLNESS Yes, by all means, if you care to.

[*Hilda moves a stool close to the armchair and sits down*]

HILDA Ah – here one can sit and sun oneself like a cat.

MRS SOLNESS [*lays her hand softly on Hilda's neck*] It is nice of you to
be willing to sit with me. I thought you wanted to go in to my
husband.

HILDA What should I want with him?

MRS SOLNESS To help him, I thought.

HILDA No, thank you. And besides, he is not in. He is over there
with his workmen. But he looked so fierce that I did not dare to
talk to him.

MRS SOLNESS He is so kind and gentle in reality.

HILDA He!

MRS SOLNESS You do not really know him yet, Miss Wangel.

HILDA [*looks affectionately at her*] Are you pleased at the thought of
moving over to the new house?

MRS SOLNESS I ought to be pleased; for it is what Halvard wants –

HILDA Oh, not just on that account, surely?

MRS SOLNESS Yes, yes, Miss Wangel; for it is only my duty to
submit myself to him. But very often it is dreadfully difficult to
force one's mind to obedience.

HILDA Yes, that must be difficult indeed.

MRS SOLNESS I can tell you it is – when one has so many faults as I
have –

HILDA When one has gone through so much trouble as you have –

MRS SOLNESS How do you know about that?

HILDA Your husband told me.

MRS SOLNESS To me he very seldom mentions these things. — Yes, I can tell you I have gone through more than enough trouble in my life, Miss Wangel.

HILDA [*looks sympathetically at her and nods slowly*] Poor Mrs Solness. First of all there was the fire —

MRS SOLNESS [*with a sigh*] Yes, everything that was mine was burnt.

HILDA And then came what was worse.

MRS SOLNESS [*looking inquiringly at her*] Worse?

HILDA The worst of all.

MRS SOLNESS What do you mean?

HILDA [*softly*] You lost the two little boys.

MRS SOLNESS Oh, yes, the boys. But, you see, that was a thing apart. That was a dispensation of Providence; and in such things one can only bow in submission — yes, and be thankful, too.

HILDA Then you are so?

MRS SOLNESS Not always, I am sorry to say. I know well enough that it is my duty — but all the same I cannot.

HILDA No, no, I think that is only natural.

MRS SOLNESS And often and often I have to remind myself that it was a righteous punishment for me —

HILDA Why?

MRS SOLNESS Because I had not fortitude enough in misfortune.

HILDA But I don't see that —

MRS SOLNESS Oh, no, no, Miss Wangel — do not talk to me any more about the two little boys. We ought to feel nothing but joy in thinking of them; for they are so happy — so happy now. No, it is the small losses in life that cut one to the heart — the loss of all that other people look upon as almost nothing.

HILDA [*lays her arms on Mrs Solness's knees, and looks up at her affectionately*] Dear Mrs Solness — tell me what things you mean!

MRS SOLNESS As I say, only little things. All the old portraits were burnt on the walls. And all the old silk dresses were burnt, what had belonged to the family for generations and generations. And all mother's and grandmother's lace — that was burnt, too. And only think — the jewels, too! [*sadly*] And then all the dolls.

HILDA The dolls?

MRS SOLNESS [*choking with tears*] I had nine lovely dolls.

HILDA And they were burnt too?

MRS SOLNESS All of them. Oh, it was hard – so hard for me.

HILDA Had you put by all these dolls, then? Ever since you were little?

MRS SOLNESS I had not put them by. The dolls and I had gone on living together.

HILDA After you were grown up?

MRS SOLNESS Yes, long after that.

HILDA After you were married, too?

MRS SOLNESS Oh yes, indeed. So long as he did not see it – . But they were all burnt up, poor things. No one thought of saving them. Oh, it is so miserable to think of. You mustn't laugh at me, Miss Wangel.

HILDA I am not laughing in the least.

MRS SOLNESS For you see, in a certain sense, there was life in them, too. I carried them under my heart – like little unborn children.

DR HERDAL, *with his hat in his hand, comes out through the door, and observes Mrs Solness and Hilda.*

DR HERDAL Well, Mrs Solness, so you are sitting out here catching cold?

MRS SOLNESS I find it so pleasant and warm here today.

DR HERDAL Yes, yes. But is there anything going on here? I got a note from you.

MRS SOLNESS [*rises*] Yes, there is something I must talk to you about.

DR HERDAL Very well; then perhaps we better go in. [*to Hilda*] Still in your mountaineering dress, Miss Wangel?

HILDA [*gaily, rising*] Yes – in full uniform! But today I am not going climbing and breaking my neck. We two will stop quietly below and look on, doctor.

DR HERDAL What are we to look on at?

MRS SOLNESS [*softly, in alarm, to Hilda*] Hush, hush – for God's sake! He is coming! Try to get that idea out of his head. And let us be friends, Miss Wangel. Don't you think we can?

HILDA [*throws her arms impetuously round Mrs Solness's neck*] Oh, if we only could!

MRS SOLNESS [*gently disengages herself*] There, there, there! There he comes, doctor. Let me have a word with you.

DR HERDAL Is it about him?

MRS SOLNESS Yes, to be sure it's about him. Do come in.

[*She and the doctor enter the house*]

Next moment SOLNESS *comes up from the garden by the flight of steps. A serious look comes over Hilda's face.*

SOLNESS [*glances at the house-door, which is closed cautiously from within*] Have you noticed, Hilda, that as soon as I come, she goes?

HILDA I have noticed that as soon as you come, you make her go.

SOLNESS Perhaps so. But I cannot help it. [*looks observantly at her*] Are you cold, Hilda? I think you look cold.

HILDA I have just come up out of a tomb.

SOLNESS What do you mean by that?

HILDA That I have got chilled through and through, Mr Solness.

SOLNESS [*slowly*] I believe I understand –

HILDA What brings you up here just now?

SOLNESS I caught sight of you from over there.

HILDA But then you must have seen her too?

SOLNESS I knew she would go at once if I came.

HILDA Is it very painful for you that she should avoid you in this way?

SOLNESS In one sense, it's a relief as well.

HILDA Not to have her before your eyes?

SOLNESS Yes.

HILDA Not to be always seeing how heavily the loss of the little boys weighs upon her?

SOLNESS Yes. Chiefly that.

HILDA [*drifts across the verandah with her hands behind her back, stops at the railing and looks out over the garden*]

SOLNESS [*after a short pause*] Did you have a long talk with her?

HILDA [*stands motionless and does not answer*]

SOLNESS Had you a long talk, I asked?

HILDA [*is silent as before*]

SOLNESS What was she talking about, Hilda?

HILDA [*continues silent*]

SOLNESS Poor Aline! I suppose it was about the little boys.

HILDA [*a nervous shudder runs through her; then she nods hurriedly once or twice*]

SOLNESS She will never get over it – never in this world. [*approaches her*] Now you are standing there again like a statue; just as you stood last night.

HILDA [*turns and looks at him, with great serious eyes*] I am going away.

SOLNESS [*sharply*] Going away!

HILDA Yes.

SOLNESS But I won't allow you to!

HILDA What am I to do here now?

SOLNESS Simply to be here, Hilda!

HILDA [*measures him with a look*] Oh, thank you. You know it wouldn't end there.

SOLNESS [*heedlessly*] So much the better!

HILDA [*vehemently*] I cannot do any harm to one whom I know! I can't take away anything that belongs to her.

SOLNESS Who wants you to do that?

HILDA [*continuing*] A stranger, yes! for that is quite a different thing! A person I have never set eyes on. But one that I have come into close contact with – ! Oh no! Oh no! Ugh!

SOLNESS Yes, but I never proposed you should.

HILDA Oh, Mr Solness, you know quite well what the end of it would be. And that is why I am going away.

SOLNESS And what is to become of me when you are gone? What shall I have to live for then? – After that?

HILDA [*with the indefinable look in her eyes*] It is surely not so hard for you. You have your duties to her. Live for those duties.

SOLNESS Too late. These powers – these – these –

HILDA – devils –

SOLNESS Yes, these devils! And the troll within me as well – they have drawn all the life-blood out of her. [*laughs in desperation*] They did it for my happiness! Yes, yes! [*sadly*] And now she is dead – for my sake. And I am chained alive to a dead woman. [*in wild anguish*] I – I who cannot live without joy in life!
[*Hilda moves round the table and seats herself on the bench, with her elbows on the table, and her head supported by her hands.*]

HILDA [*sits and looks at him awhile*] What will you build next?

SOLNESS [*shakes his head*] I don't believe I shall build much more.

HILDA Not those cosy, happy homes for mother and father, and for the troop of children?

SOLNESS I wonder whether there will be any use for such homes in the coming time.

HILDA Poor Mr Solness! And you have gone all these ten years – and staked your whole life – on that alone.

SOLNESS Yes, you may well say so, Hilda.

HILDA [*with an outburst*] Oh, it all seems to me so foolish – so foolish!

SOLNESS All what?

HILDA Not to be able to grasp at your own happiness – at your own life! Merely because someone you know happens to stand in the way!

SOLNESS One whom you have no right to set aside.

HILDA I wonder whether one really has not the right! And yet, and yet – . Oh! if one could only sleep the whole thing away!

[*She lays her arms flat down on the table, rests the left side of her head on her hands, and shuts her eyes.*]

SOLNESS [*turns the armchair and sits down at the table*] Had you a cosy, happy home – up there with your father, Hilda?

HILDA [*without stirring, answers as if half asleep*] I had only a cage.

SOLNESS And you are determined not to go back to it?

HILDA [*as before*] The wild bird never wants to go back to the cage.

SOLNESS Rather range through the free air –

HILDA [*still as before*] The bird of prey loves to range –

SOLNESS [*lets his eyes rest on her*] If only one had the viking-spirit in life –

HILDA [*in her usual voice; opens her eyes but does not move*] And the other thing? Say what that was!

SOLNESS A robust conscience.

[*Hilda sits erect on the bench, with animation. Her eyes have once more the sparkling expression of gladness.*]

HILDA [*nods to him*] I know what you are going to build next!

SOLNESS Then you know more than I do, Hilda.

HILDA Yes, builders are such stupid people.

SOLNESS What is it to be then?

HILDA [*nods again*] The castle.

SOLNESS What castle?

HILDA My castle, of course.

SOLNESS Do you want a castle now?

HILDA Don't you owe me a kingdom, I should like to know?

SOLNESS You say I do.

HILDA Well – you admit you owe me this kingdom. And you can't have a kingdom without a royal castle, I should think.

SOLNESS [*more and more animated*] Yes, they usually go together.

HILDA Good! Then build it for me! This moment!

SOLNESS [*laughing*] Must you have that on the instant, too?

HILDA Yes, to be sure! For the ten years are up now, and I am not going to wait any longer. So – out with the castle, Mr Solness!

SOLNESS It's no light matter to owe you anything, Hilda.

HILDA You should have thought of that before. It is too late now. So – [*tapping the table*] – the castle on the table! It is my castle! I will have it at once!

SOLNESS [*more seriously, leans over towards her, with his arms on the table*] What sort of castle have you imagined, Hilda?

[*Her expression becomes more and more veiled. She seems gazing inwards at herself.*]

HILDA [*slowly*] My castle shall stand on a height – on a very great height – with a clear outlook on all sides, so that I can see far – far around.

SOLNESS And no doubt it is to have a high tower!

HILDA A tremendously high tower. And at the very top of the tower there shall be a balcony. And I will stand out upon it –

SOLNESS [*involuntarily clutches at his forehead*] How can you like to stand at such a dizzy height – ?

HILDA Yes, I will! Right up there will I stand and look down on the other people – on those that are building churches, and homes for mother and father and the troop of children. And you may come up and look on at it, too.

SOLNESS [*in a low tone*] Is the builder to be allowed to come up beside the princess?

HILDA If the builder will.

SOLNESS [*more softly*] Then I think the builder will come.

HILDA [*nods*] The builder – he will come.

SOLNESS But he will never be able to build any more. Poor builder!

HILDA [*animated*] Oh, yes, he will! We two will set to work together. And then we will build the loveliest – the very loveliest – thing in all the world.

SOLNESS [*intently*] Hilda – tell me what that is!

HILDA [*looks smilingly at him, shakes her head a little, pouts, and speaks as if to a child*] Builders – they are such very – very stupid people.

SOLNESS Yes, no doubt they are stupid. But now tell me what it is – the loveliest thing in the world – that we two are to build together?

HILDA [*is silent a little while, then says with an indefinable expression in her eyes*] Castles in the air.

SOLNESS Castles in the air?

HILDA [*nods*] Castles in the air, yes! Do you know what sort of thing a castle in the air is?

SOLNESS It is the loveliest thing in the world, you say.

HILDA [*rises with vehemence, and makes a gesture of repulsion with her hand*] Yes, to be sure it is! Castles in the air – they are so easy to build, too – [*looks scornfully at him*] – especially for the builders who have a – a dizzy conscience.

SOLNESS [*rises*] After this day we two will build together, Hilda.

HILDA [*with a half-dubious smile*] A real castle in the air?

SOLNESS Yes. One with a firm foundation under it.

RAGNAR BROVIK *comes out from the house. He is carrying a large green wreath with flowers and silk ribbons.*

HILDA [*with an outburst of pleasure*] The wreath! Oh, that will be glorious!

SOLNESS [*in surprise*] Have you brought the wreath, Ragnar?

RAGNAR I promised the foreman I would.

SOLNESS [*relieved*] Ah, then I suppose you father is better?

RAGNAR No.

SOLNESS Was he not cheered by what I wrote?

RAGNAR It came too late.

SOLNESS Too late!

RAGNAR When she came with it he was unconscious. He had had a stroke.

SOLNESS Why, then, you must go home to him! You must attend to your father!

RAGNAR He does not need me any more.

SOLNESS But surely you ought to be with him.

RAGNAR She is sitting by his bed.

SOLNESS [*rather uncertainly*] Kaia?

RAGNAR [*looking darkly at him*] Yes – Kaia.

SOLNESS Go home, Ragnar – both to him and to her. Give me the wreath.

RAGNAR [*suppresses a mocking smile*] You don't mean that you yourself – ?

SOLNESS I will take it down to them myself. [*takes the wreath from him*] And now you go home; we don't require you today.

RAGNAR I know you do not require me any more; but today I shall remain.

SOLNESS Well, remain then, since you are bent upon it.

HILDA [*at the railing*] Mr Solness, I will stand here and look on at you.

SOLNESS At me!

HILDA It will be fearfully thrilling.

SOLNESS [*in a low tone*] We will talk about that presently, Hilda.

[*He goes down the flight of steps with the wreath, and away through the garden*]

HILDA [*looks after him, then turns to Ragnar*] I think you might at least have thanked him

RAGNAR Thanked him? Ought I to have thanked him?

HILDA Yes, of course you ought!

RAGNAR I think it is rather you I ought to thank.

HILDA How can you say such a thing?

RAGNAR [*without answering her*] But I advise you to take care, Miss Wangel! For you don't know him rightly yet.

HILDA [*ardently*] Oh, no one knows him as I do!

RAGNAR [*laughs in exasperation*] Thank him, when he has held me down year after year! When he made father disbelieve in me – made me disbelieve in myself! And all merely that he might – !

HILDA [*as if divining something*] That he might – ? Tell me at once!

RAGNAR That he might keep her with him.

HILDA [*with a start towards him*] The girl at the desk.

RAGNAR Yes.

HILDA [*threateningly, clenching her hands*] That is not true! You are telling falsehoods about him!

RAGNAR I would not believe it either until today – when she said so herself.

HILDA [*as if beside herself*] What did she say? I will know! At once! at once!

RAGNAR She said that he had taken possession of her mind – her whole mind – centred all her thoughts upon himself alone. She says that she can never leave him – that she will remain here, where he is –

HILDA [*with flashing eyes*] She will not be allowed to!

RAGNAR [*as if feeling his way*] Who will not allow her?

HILDA [*rapidly*] He will not either!

RAGNAR Oh no – I understand the whole thing now. After this, she would merely be – in the way.

HILDA You understand nothing – since you can talk like that! No, *I* will tell you why he kept hold of her.

RAGNAR Well then, why?

HILDA In order to keep hold of you.

RAGNAR Has he told you so?

HILDA No, but it is so. It must be so! [*wildly*] I will – I will have it so!

RAGNAR And at the very moment when you came – he let her go.

HILDA It was you – you that he let go! What do you suppose he cares about strange women like her?

RAGNAR [*reflects*] Is it possible that all this time he has been afraid of me?

HILDA He afraid! I would not be so conceited if I were you.

RAGNAR Oh, he must have seen long ago that I had something in me, too. Besides – cowardly – that is just what he is, you see.

HILDA He! Oh yes, I am likely to believe that!

RAGNAR In a certain sense he is cowardly – he, the great master builder. He is not afraid of robbing others of their happiness – as he has done both for my father and me. But when it comes to climbing up a paltry bit of scaffolding – he will do anything rather than that.

HILDA Oh, you should just have seen him high, high up – at the dizzy height where I once saw him.

RAGNAR Did you see that?

HILDA Yes, indeed I did. How free and great he looked as he stood and fastened the wreath to the church vane!

RAGNAR I know that he ventured that, once in his life – one solitary time. It is a legend among us younger men. But no power on earth would induce him to do it again.

HILDA Today he will do it again!

RAGNAR [*scornfully*] Yes, I dare say!

HILDA We shall see it!

RAGNAR That neither you nor I will see.

HILDA [*with uncontrollable vehemence*] I will see it! I will and I must see it!

RAGNAR But he will not do it. He simply dare not do it. For you see he cannot get over this infirmity — master builder though he be.

MRS SOLNESS comes from the house on to the verandah.

MRS SOLNESS [*looks around*] Is he not here? Where has he gone to?

RAGNAR Mr Solness is down with the men.

HILDA He took the wreath with him.

MRS SOLNESS [*terrified*] Took the wreath with him! Oh God! Oh God! Brovik — you must go down to him! Get him to come back here!

RAGNAR Shall I say you want to speak to him, Mrs Solness?

MRS SOLNESS Oh yes, do! — No, no — don't say that *I* want anything! You can say that somebody is here, and that he must come at once.

RAGNAR Good. I will do so, Mrs Solness.

[*He goes down the flight of steps and away through the garden*]

MRS SOLNESS Oh, Miss Wangel, you can't think how anxious I feel about him.

HILDA Is there anything in this to be terribly frightened about?

MRS SOLNESS Oh yes; surely you can understand. Just think, if he were really to do it! If he should take it into his head to climb up the scaffolding!

HILDA [*eagerly*] Do you think he will?

MRS SOLNESS Oh, one can never tell what he might take into his head. I am afraid there is nothing he mightn't think of doing.

HILDA Aha! Perhaps you too think he is — well — ?

MRS SOLNESS Oh, I don't know what to think about him now. The doctor has been telling me all sorts of things; and putting it all together with several things I have heard him say —

DR HERDAL looks out, at the door.

DR HERDAL Is he not coming soon?

MRS SOLNESS Yes, I think so. I have sent for him at any rate.

DR HERDAL [*advancing*] I am afraid you will have to go in, my dear lady —

MRS SOLNESS Oh no! Oh no! I shall stay out here and wait for Halvard.

DR HERDAL But some ladies have just come to call on you –

MRS SOLNESS Good heavens, that too! And just at this moment!

DR HERDAL They say they positively must see the ceremony.

MRS SOLNESS Well, well, I suppose I must go to them after all. It is my duty.

HILDA Can't you ask the ladies to go away?

MRS SOLNESS No, that would never do. Now that they are here, it is my duty to see them. But do you stay out here in the meantime – and receive him when he comes.

DR HERDAL And try to occupy his attention as long as possible –

MRS SOLNESS Yes, do, dear Miss Wangel. Keep as firm hold of him as ever you can.

HILDA Would it not be best for you to do that?

MRS SOLNESS Yes; God knows that is my duty. But when one has duties in so many directions –

DR HERDAL [looks towards the garden] There he is coming.

MRS SOLNESS And I have to go in!

DR HERDAL [to Hilda] Don't say anything about my being here.

HILDA Oh no! I dare say I shall find something else to talk to Mr Solness about.

MRS SOLNESS And be sure you keep firm hold of him. I believe you can do it best.   [Mrs Solness and Dr Herdal go into the house]

Hilda remains standing on the verandah. SOLNESS *comes from the garden, up the flight of steps.*

SOLNESS Somebody wants me, I hear.

HILDA Yes; it is I, Mr Solness.

SOLNESS Oh, is it you, Hilda? I was afraid it might be Aline or the Doctor.

HILDA You are very easily frightened, it seems!

SOLNESS Do you think so?

HILDA Yes; people say that you are afraid to climb about – on the scaffoldings, you know.

SOLNESS Well, that is quite a special thing.

HILDA Then it is true that you are afraid to do it?

SOLNESS Yes, I am.

HILDA Afraid of falling down and killing yourself?

SOLNESS No, not of that.

HILDA Of what, then?

SOLNESS I am afraid of retribution, Hilda.

HILDA Of retribution? [*shakes her head*] I don't understand that.

SOLNESS Sit down, and I will tell you something.

HILDA Yes, do! At once!

[*She sits on a stool by the railing, and looks expectantly at him.*]

SOLNESS [*throws his hat on the table*] You know that I began by building churches.

HILDA [*nods*] I know that well.

SOLNESS For, you see, I came as a boy from a pious home in the country; and so it seemed to me that this church-building was the noblest task I could set myself.

HILDA Yes, yes.

SOLNESS And I venture to say that I built those poor little churches with such honest and warm and heartfelt devotion that – that –

HILDA That – ? Well?

SOLNESS Well, that I think that he ought to have been pleased with me.

HILDA He? What he?

SOLNESS He who was to have the churches, of course! He to whose honour and glory they were dedicated.

HILDA Oh, indeed! But are you certain, then, that – that he was not – pleased with you?

SOLNESS [*scornfully*] He pleased with me! How can you talk so, Hilda? He who gave the troll in me leave to lord it just as it pleased. He who bade them be at hand to serve me, both day and might – all these – all these –

HILDA Devils –

SOLNESS Yes, of both kinds. Oh no, he made me feel clearly enough that he was not pleased with me. [*mysteriously*] You see, that was really the reason why he made the old house burn down.

HILDA Was that why?

SOLNESS Yes, don't you understand? He wanted to give me the chance of becoming an accomplished master in my own sphere – so that I might build all the more glorious churches for him. At first I did not understand what he was driving at; but all of a sudden it flashed upon me.

HILDA When was that?

SOLNESS It was when I was building the church-tower up at Lysanger.

HILDA I thought so.

SOLNESS For you see, Hilda – up there, amidst those new surroundings, I used to go about musing and pondering within myself. Then I saw plainly why he had taken my little children from me. It was that I should have nothing else to attach myself to. No such thing as love and happiness, you understand. I was to be only a master builder – nothing else, and all my life long I was to go on building for him. [*laughs*] But I can tell you nothing came of that!

HILDA What did you do then?

SOLNESS First of all, I searched and tried my own heart –

HILDA And then?

SOLNESS Then I did the impossible – I, no less than he.

HILDA The impossible?

SOLNESS I had never before been able to climb up to a great, free height. But that day I did it.

HILDA [*leaping up*] Yes, yes, you did!

SOLNESS And when I stood there, high over everything, and was hanging the wreath over the vane, I said to him: Hear me now, thou Mighty One! From this day forward I will be a free builder – I too, in my sphere – just as thou in thine. I will never more build churches for thee – only homes for human beings.

HILDA [*with great sparkling eyes*] That was the song that I heard through the air!

SOLNESS But afterwards his turn came.

HILDA What do you mean by that?

SOLNESS [*looks despondently at her*] Building homes for human beings – is not worth a rap, Hilda.

HILDA Do you say that now?

SOLNESS Yes, for now I see it. Men have no use for these homes of theirs – to be happy in. And I should not have had any use for such a home, if I had had one. [*with a quiet, bitter laugh*] See, that is the upshot of the whole affair, however far back I look. Nothing really built; nor anything sacrificed for the chance of building. Nothing, nothing! the whole is nothing!

HILDA Then you will never build anything more?

SOLNESS [*with animation*] On the contrary, I am just going to begin!

HILDA What, then? What will you build? Tell me at once!

SOLNESS I believe there is only one possible dwelling-place for human happiness – and that is what I am going to build now.

HILDA [*looks fixedly at him*] Mr Solness – you mean our castles in the air.

SOLNESS The castles in the air – yes.

HILDA I am afraid you would turn dizzy before we got half-way up.

SOLNESS Not if I can mount hand in hand with you, Hilda.

HILDA [*with an expression of suppressed resentment*] Only with me? Will there be no others of the party?

SOLNESS Who else should there be?

HILDA Oh – that girl – that Kaia at the desk. Poor thing – don't you want to take her with you too?

SOLNESS Oho! Was it about her that Aline was talking to you?

HILDA Is it so – or is it not?

SOLNESS [*vehemently*] I will not answer such a question. You must believe in me, wholly and entirely!

HILDA All these ten years I have believed in you so utterly – so utterly.

SOLNESS You must go on believing in me!

HILDA Then let me see you stand free and high up!

SOLNESS [*sadly*] Oh Hilda – it is not every day that I can do that.

HILDA [*passionately*] I will have you do it! I will have it! [*imploringly*] Just once more, Mr Solness! Do the impossible once again!

SOLNESS [*stands and looks deep into her eyes*] If I try it, Hilda, I will stand up there and talk to him as I did that time before.

HILDA [*in rising excitement*] What will you say to him?

SOLNESS I will say to him: Hear me, Mighty Lord – thou may'st judge me as seems best to thee. But hereafter I will build nothing but the loveliest thing in the world –

HILDA [*carried away*] Yes – yes – yes!

SOLNESS – build it together with a princess, whom I love –

HILDA Yes, tell him that! Tell him that!

SOLNESS Yes. And then I will say to him: Now I shall go down and throw my arms round her and kiss her –

HILDA – many times! Say that!

SOLNESS – many, many times, I will say it!

HILDA And then – ?

SOLNESS Then I will wave my hat – and come down to the earth – and do as I said to him.

HILDA [*with outstretched arms*] Now I see you again as I did when there was song in the air!

SOLNESS [*looks at her with his head bowed*] How have you become what you are, Hilda?

HILDA How have you made me what I am?

SOLNESS [*shortly and firmly*] The princess shall have her castle.

HILDA [*jubilant, clapping her hands*] Oh, Mr Solness – ! My lovely, lovely castle. Our castle in the air!

SOLNESS On a firm foundation.

> *In the street a crowd of people has assembled, vaguely seen through the trees. Music of wind-instruments is heard far away behind the new house.*
>
> MRS SOLNESS, *with a fur collar round her neck,* DOCTOR HERDAL *with her white shawl on his arm, and some ladies, come out on the verandah.* RAGNAR BROVIK *comes at the same time up from the garden.*

MRS SOLNESS [*to Ragnar*] Are we to have music, too?

RAGNAR Yes. It's the band of the Mason's Union. [*to Solness*] The foreman asked me to tell you that he is ready now to go up with the wreath.

SOLNESS [*takes his hat*] Good. I will go down to him myself.

MRS SOLNESS [*anxiously*] What have you to do down there, Halvard?

SOLNESS [*curtly*] I must be down below with the men.

MRS SOLNESS Yes, down below – only down below.

SOLNESS That is where I always stand – on everyday occasions.

[*He goes down the flight of steps and away through the garden*]

MRS SOLNESS [*calls after him over the railing*] But do beg the man to be careful when he goes up! Promise me that, Halvard!

DR HERDAL [*to Mrs Solness*] Don't you see that I was right? He has given up all thought of that folly.

MRS SOLNESS Oh, what a relief! Twice workmen have fallen, and each time they were killed on the spot. [*turns to Hilda*] Thank you, Miss Wangel, for having kept such a firm hold upon him. I should never have been able to manage him.

DR HERDAL [*playfully*] Yes, yes, Miss Wangel, you know how to keep firm hold on a man, when you give your mind to it.

[*Mrs Solness and Dr Herdal go up to the ladies, who are standing nearer to the steps and looking over the garden. Hilda remains standing beside the railing in the foreground. Ragnar goes up to her.*]

RAGNAR [*with suppressed laughter, half whispering*] Miss Wangel – do you see all those young fellows down in the street?

HILDA Yes.

RAGNAR They are my fellow students, come to look at the master.

HILDA What do they want to look at him for?

RAGNAR They want to see how he daren't climb to the top of his own house.

HILDA Oh, that is what those boys want, is it?

RAGNAR [*spitefully and scornfully*] He has kept us down so long – now we are going to see him keep quietly down below himself.

HILDA You will not see that – not this time.

RAGNAR [*smiles*] Indeed! Then where shall we see him?

HILDA High – high up by the vane! That is where you will see him!

RAGNAR [*laughs*] Him! Oh yes, I dare say!

HILDA His will is to reach the top – so at the top you shall see him.

RAGNAR His will, yes; that I can easily believe. But he simply cannot do it. His head would swim round, long, long before he got half-way. He would have to crawl down again on his hands and knees.

DR HERDAL [*points across*] Look! There goes the foreman up the ladders.

MRS SOLNESS And of course he has the wreath to carry too. Oh, I do hope he will be careful!

RAGNAR [*stares incredulously and shouts*] Why, but it's –

HILDA [*breaking out in jubilation*] It is the master builder himself?

MRS SOLNESS [*screams with terror*] Yes, it is Halvard! Oh my great God – ! Halvard! Halvard!

DR HERDAL Hush! Don't shout to him!

MRS SOLNESS [*half beside herself*] I must go to him! I must get him to come down again!

DR HERDAL [*holds her*] Don't move, any of you! Not a sound!

HILDA [*immovable, follows Solness with her eyes*] He climbs and climbs. Higher and higher! Higher and higher! Look! Just look!

RAGNAR [*breathless*] He must turn now. He can't possibly help it.

HILDA He climbs and climbs. He will soon be at the top now.

MRS SOLNESS Oh, I shall die of terror. I cannot bear to see it.

DR HERDAL Then don't look up at him.

HILDA There he is standing on the topmost planks! Right at the top!

DR HERDAL Nobody must move! Do you dear?

HILDA [*exulting, with quiet intensity*] At last! At last! Now I see him great and free again!

RAGNAR [*almost voiceless*] But this is im—

HILDA So I have seen him all through these ten years. How secure he stands! Frightfully thrilling all the same. Look at him! Now he is hanging the wreath round the vane!

RAGNAR I feel as if I were looking at something utterly impossible

HILDA Yes, it is the impossible that he is doing now! [*with the indefinable expression in her eyes*] Can you see anyone else up there with him?

RAGNAR There is no one else.

HILDA Yes, there is one he is striving with.

RAGNAR You are mistaken.

HILDA Then do you hear no song in the air, either?

RAGNAR It must be the wind in the tree-tops.

HILDA *I* hear a song – a mighty song! [*shouts in wild jubilation and glee*] Look, look! Now he is waving his hat! He is waving it to us down here! Oh, wave, wave back to him! For now it is finished! [*Snatches the white shawl from the Doctor, waves it, and shouts up to Solness*] Hurrah for Master Builder Solness!

DR HERDAL Stop! Stop! For God's sake – !

[*The ladies on the verandah wave their pocket-handkerchiefs, and the shouts of 'Hurrah' are taken up in the street. Then they are suddenly silenced, and the crowd bursts out into a shriek of horror. A human body, with planks and fragments of wood, is vaguely perceived crashing down behind the trees.*]

MRS SOLNESS AND THE LADIES [*at the same time*]. He is falling! He is falling!

[*Mrs Solness totters, falls backwards, swooning, and is caught, amid cries and confusion, by the ladies.*]

The crowd in the street breaks down the fence and storms into the garden. At the same time DR HERDAL, *too, rushes down thither. A short pause.*

HILDA [*stares fixedly upwards and says, as if petrified*] My Master Builder.

RAGNAR [*supports himself, trembling, against the railing*] He must be dashed to pieces – killed on the spot.

ONE OF THE LADIES [*whilst Mrs Solness is carried into the house*]. Run down for the doctor –

RAGNAR I can't stir a root –

ANOTHER LADY. Then call to someone!

RAGNAR [*tries to call out*] How is it? Is he alive?

A VOICE [*below, in the garden*]. Mr Solness is dead!

OTHER VOICES [*nearer*]. The head is all crushed. – he fell right into the quarry.

HILDA [*turns to Ragnar, and says quietly*] I can't see him up there now.

RAGNAR This is terrible. So, after all, he could not do it.

HILDA [*as if in quiet spell-bound triumph*] But he mounted right to the top. And I heard harps in the air. [*waves her shawl in the air, and shrieks with wild intensity*] My – my Master Builder!